W9-BCS-122

By Ruth C. Lakeway
and Robert C. White, Jr.

Italian Art Song is a unique study of a long-neglected genre, *la lirica da camera,* which developed in the twentieth century. While the art song came late to Italy, nearly 200 known composers of this literature have been born since 1875, and well over 2,000 songs of this nature have been published since 1900.

From this rich repertory, Ruth C. Lakeway and Robert C. White analyze in detail more than 200 compositions for solo voice and piano. For each song they have provided the Italian text, with pronunciation markings, and a line-by-line, almost literal translation. In the commentary that follows, they take performers through the song, pointing out such interpretative considerations as tempo and dynamics and suggesting special techniques to bring out the emotional impact of the poetry.

The first chapter of the book traces the history of solo song in Italy, describing its beginnings around 1600, its decline after 1750, and its rebirth in the twentieth century, when it emerged free of its long domination by opera. Separate chapters devoted to the art songs of nine major composers—Alfano, Respighi, Pizzetti, Malipiero, Casella, Davico, Ghedini, Castelnuovo-Tedesco, and Petrassi—include their biographies and accounts of their interrelationships with other composers and contemporary movements, both artistic and political. The songs of nineteen other composers are translated and interpretively analyzed, and an appendix lists

(continued on back flap)

Italian Art Song

Italian Art Song

Ruth C. Lakeway and Robert C. White, Jr.

INDIANA UNIVERSITY PRESS · Bloomington and Indianapolis

Library of Congress Cataloging-in-Publication Data

Lakeway, Ruth C.
  Italian art song.

  Bibliography: p.
  Includes index.
1. Songs with piano—20th century—History and criticism.   2. Music—Italy—History and criticism.
I. White, Robert C. (Robert Charles), 1936–
II. Title.
ML2533.L25   1988   784.3'00945   87-46370
ISBN 0-253-33154-4
1 2 3 4 5   93 92 91 90 89

Contents

PREFACE

A sampling of vocal recital programs, professional or student, American or international, will generally include examples of German *Lieder,* French *mélodies,* and art songs from the singer's country of origin. Italy is most often *not* represented by song, but by operatic arias, extracted from larger works and transcribed for voice and piano from the original scoring. While their worth is unquestionable, these arias do not equate in form or intention with the classically defined art song. Yet, art song does exist in Italy in a large body of works known as *liriche da camera*—compositions for solo voice and piano that achieve a true synthesis of music and poetry while utilizing the piano for its unique contribution to the totality of expression. While the art song came late to Italy, nearly 200 known composers of *liriche da camera* have been born since 1875 and well over 2,000 songs have been published since 1900. We hope that in providing information on this great body of song literature we will encourage singers to explore and perform it, and that this book will ease their task in learning and appreciating it.

As background for the discussion of individual works, we include a survey of solo song in Italy from 1600 to the present, outlining its rise through the seventeenth century, its decline throughout the eighteenth, and its rebirth at the beginning of the twentieth, when it finally emerged as the *lirica da camera,* a true art-song form completely free from the long domination of opera. We have presented biographies and some description of the style of those composers we consider the major contributors to the *lirica da camera* form. This information will be of general interest to the performer as well as useful for program notes.

The greater part of the book provides translations of the poetry and suggestions for interpretation of over 200 selected *liriche da camera.* Before beginning the study, we catalogued over 1,500 songs. From that list several hundred were carefully examined for quality of text, musical setting, and general interest. For practical purposes several criteria for inclusion were established.

First, we confined our selection to compositions for solo voice and piano. Although many of the composers wrote prolifically for voice in combination with small instrumental groups, we felt that this medium was a subject for another study. We have included a very small number of songs that, though originally conceived for chamber ensemble, were transcribed by the composer for voice and piano. They were considered suitable only if the piano was used idiomatically; most transcriptions were rejected because they did not adequately convey the expression of the original compositions.

Second, we chose to work solely with the Italian language, even though many of the composers, reflecting the internationalism of the emerging twentieth century, were capable of and did set poetry in languages other than Italian. We also tried as often as possible to give preference to Italian poets.

Third, we selected those composers who are best known and represent the finest work within the art-song form—that is, equivalent to *Lied* and *mélodie*. We excluded the *composizioni da camera* of composers such as Donizetti, Bellini, and Verdi because they are too operatic in style or concept; the songs of Tosti, Denza, and others—the *canzoni napolitane*—which are a specialized form of sentimental ballad; and the songs of Donaudy, which are in the *stile antiche*. Likewise, folk-song arrangements were ruled out, but the use of a folk melody as an integral part of a sophisticated text setting, and folk poetry as a source of inspiration, were considered acceptable.

Finally, we excluded songs in which we felt the strict working out of a serialistic compositional system negated the primacy of the poetry, or in which the voice was used only for its timbre.

We expect some controversy over our choices and the relative importance of the composers we selected. In some cases an important composer did not write many songs, but each one was of first quality. In other cases one or two superb songs were written by a composer who never again matched that quality. The great composer Luigi Dallapiccola had to be excluded from this study because most of his songs were written for chamber ensemble with textures impossible to transcribe successfully for piano, and his few songs for voice and piano alone are settings of French and Spanish poetry.

In the final analysis we asked ourselves, "Would we like to sing this song or teach it to a student?" Accessibility was also considered in the selection process, but we did not exclude a superior song because it might be difficult to obtain.

With very few exceptions, the song texts in this volume are appearing for the first time with English translations. Each translation is original and is based on the Italian or transcribed text as it appears in the underlay and as it was set by the composer. As the work progressed and we fell under the spell of the incredibly beautiful Italian poetry, it became increasingly tempting to try to create beautiful English poetic equivalents. We avoided the temptation to smooth out the translations for what we felt to be the greater service of recognizable word order and specificity of image. Composers set specific words, and we translated them as accurately as we could, changing word orders or bending images only when the translations would have been meaningless without such alterations. These translations are meant primarily as an aid for the singer and the teacher; their use for program note material would require some rewriting into idiomatic English.

The reader will find inconsistencies in the spelling of certain words in the song texts. In the development of any language, some letters are dropped or changed through the years; and spelling is often determined by the period in which the poet lived. Many single consonants in early Italian have become doubled in contemporary Italian. In this book we have retained the spelling that appears in the underlying printed text of each song, except for obvious misprints.

Since we own a number of song copies with handwritten notes by the composers, a section on interpretation seemed essential to the completeness of this volume. Each song was examined for its structure, key relationships, texture, text settings, phrasing, and dynamics. Unusual scales and modalities are pointed out, along with timbre and articulation indications. In keeping with twentieth-century practice, the composers in this volume give very specific directions, usually written in contemporary Italian. Every such indication is translated in the notes on interpretation.

Many of the *liriche da camera* were published in sets, not always with any unique relationship between individual songs. For the notes on interpretation each set was examined for cyclical relationships, textual relationships, and contrasts in mood, tempo, and style—and recommendations have been made for programming the songs for performance. In many instances, considerable research was undertaken to clarify an obscure text reference in order to understand the musical setting in its proper context. Sometimes the history of the particular song is discussed. Then, using the combined total of our years as performers and teachers, we have made specific suggestions for breathing, phrasing, keyboard articulation, and balance to achieve the most effective performance of a work. We took advantage of our personal contact with the composers and/or with our teachers, who knew or worked with them. We expect our suggestions to be used only as aids to achieving a unique performance, but one which will remain close to the intentions of the composer and within the tradition of the art song.

Finally, we have provided publication information for the songs translated and discussed in this volume. We have listed a number of other songs we consider interesting and strongly recommend but could not analyze because of time and space limitations. An extensive bibliography of selected readings concludes the work.

No work of this scope can ever come close to being complete. New songs are being written and old songs discovered as we complete our writing. We are delighted with what we have been able to include, dismayed at what we had to leave out. At all times, however, we have maintained our major goal, that of attempting to encourage a widespread interest in the performance of a unique, worthwhile, and unfortunately neglected repertory—*la lirica da camera*—the Italian art song.

Ruth C. Lakeway   Saratoga Springs, New York

Robert C. White, Jr.   New York, New York

June 1987

ACKNOWLEDGMENTS

Grateful acknowledgment is made to Dr. Giùseppe Faustini, Professor of Italian, for his guidance in the English translations; to Dr. Pasquale G. Tatò, phonetition and phonologist, for his supervision of close and open vowels and use of syntactic doubling in the pronunciation of Italian and Italian dialects; to Sally Sanford for her expertise in Baroque vocal ornamentation; and to Annunciata Costa for her help and encouragement.

NOTE ON ITALIAN PRONUNCIATION

There are many excellent sources for the comprehensive study of Italian diction to which the singer may refer. Most of these admit, however, the need for dictionary reference to determine correct pronunciation in three major areas:

(1) The vowels e and o in accented syllables may be pronounced either open: [ɛ] and [ɔ], or close: [e] and [o].

(2) The consonant s may be pronounced either unvoiced: [s], or voiced [z].

(3) The consonants z and zz may be pronounced either unvoiced: [ts], or voiced: [dz].

In this book close e̲ and o̲ occurring in accented syllables and voiced s̲, z̲, and z̲z̲ are underlined in the Italian texts. In addition, syntactic doubling (when the initial consonant of the second of two adjoining words requires doubling in pronunciation) has been marked with a ligature (‿). The grave accent (ˋ) has been used throughout. Finally, the markings in regional poetry or texts in dialect follow the pronunciation in common use.

Italian Art Song

Introduction

A History of Italian Solo Song

Almost every significant reform in vocal music has been brought about because of a literary reaction against either the quality of the texts or the manner of using them. In the third decade of the sixteenth century the *frottola* was abruptly replaced by the madrigal, largely as a result of dissatisfaction with the carefree vulgarity of the frottola texts. Madrigal composers began choosing their texts very carefully from the better poets; Tasso and Petrarca, for example, were great favorites. As the century progressed, attempts were made to enhance the expression of the words by musical means. Gradually the number of voices increased, and the new polyphonic techniques developed. Imitation and text-painting were used in all voices throughout the texture of the composition, phrases became irregular, cadential endings were carefully concealed by overlapping voices, and intricate rhythmic patterns used in imitation created complex polyrhythmic effects. Progressive modulations, unprepared dissonances, sudden harmonic changes, and chromaticism created a tightly interwoven texture. In fact, the style became so complex that the words, ingeniously interpreted by musical means, often were no longer intelligible except to the performers themselves. Voices of protest rose again.

The Florentine Camerata and *stile rappresentativo*

In Florence, Vincenzo Galilei (c.1520–1591), a leading intellectual and father of the famous astronomer, voiced his concern in his *Dialogo della musica antica e della moderna.* He vigorously attacked the overly contrapuntal style and the extreme attempts at word-painting as being completely incapable of expressing the "conceptions of the mind." Influenced by the findings of his friend Girolomo Mei (1519–1594), a Roman scholar, Galilei urged a return to the text-setting ideals of the ancient Greeks, and the development of a new style of solo singing imitating the rhythms and inflections of impassioned and ordinary speech.

Under the patronage of Giovanni Bardi, Count of Vernio, and Jacopo Corsi, both wealthy noblemen, Galilei was able to present his ideas to an avant-garde group of literati, founded by Bardi, who were known as the Camerata, of which Galilei himself was a member. The group consisted of noblemen, writers, and musicians who met frequently to discuss new forms of the arts. Bardi made it possible for Galilei to develop the *stile rappresentativo,* as the new style was called, and it generated a considerable amount of excitement. It was not solo singing alone that precipitated this excitement.

Numerous songs for solo voice dating from the preceding centuries could be found. In fact, throughout the sixteenth century most of the polyphonic forms of vocal music in Italy and other countries had been published in two versions: one for several voices and the other for solo performance with lute or keyboard accompaniment. The Italian *frottola*, the Spanish *villancico*, the French *chanson*, the German polyphonic *Lied*, and the English madrigal, ayre, and lute song were all published in this manner, and many other songs were written expressly for performance by soloists. In all these earlier forms the emphasis was on the top melodic line. The other voices were written out and could be performed by instruments or by other voices, but the texture was basically polyphonic even when it was in chordal structure; and although the melody was in the top voice, all the voices were equal in importance.

The new monody, or *stile rappresentativo*, put the main emphasis on the bass line, the shape of which was largely determined by new feelings for harmonic progressions notated by figured bass. The melody, too, became more interesting as the chordal structure became more complex. Another distinguishing characteristic was the manner of performance. Whereas the older form required only a soloist and a keyboard player or lutenist (and often the singers accompanied themselves), the new style usually required three performers, since the bass was reinforced by a sustaining string or woodwind instrument. This method of performance allowed the melodic line, whether vocal or instrumental, to be heard unencumbered by accompanying voices; it became known as the *basso continuo* style.

In the last decades of the sixteenth century the "arousal of the affections" was considered the principal objective of poetry and music. It was to be accomplished once again by attempting to interpret the words by musical means: descending melodic intervals for expressions of grief, dotted rhythmic figures for words of agitation, and so forth. This was not unlike what the polyphonic madrigalists had tried to do, but with the text given to a single voice the words could be understood; and if the voice were accompanied, with the instruments providing chordal support rather than competition with the voice, the effect was quite different from the old style.

Giulio Caccini

Probably the most important member of the Camerata was Giulio Caccini (1545–1618), a noted singer and teacher of singing. By his own testimony Caccini began writing monodies in 1585. Although he was not an innovator of the style, he took an active part in its development. In 1602 he published *Le Nuove Musiche,* a set of twelve solo madrigals and ten arias, the earliest extant examples of Florentine monody. They were followed by another set of 29 airs and madrigals, published in 1614 with the title *Nuove Musiche e nuova maniera di scriverle.*

Although Caccini's songs are often spoken of together with *stile rappresentativo,* they are really not representative of the style that was destined to become the dramatic recitative of opera and oratorio. The *stile rappre-sentativo* was a recitative with very free rhythm based on the quantitative stress and syllabic accent of speech patterns. The flow of the melody closely followed the intonation, pitch levels, and phrase lengths of spoken language. Caccini's monodies, reflecting the innate Italian love for melody, are lyrical in character and follow the phrase lengths dictated by the form of the poem in a flowing cantilena style. His songs are designated "madrigal" and follow the free and through-composed form of that poetic genre. The number of lines, the number of syllables within a line, and the rhyming scheme may vary, but the last two lines usually have an equal number of syllables and are rhymed together. Caccini's arias are in strophic form and use the same number of lines and syllables, the same rhyming scheme, and the same bass line in all the verses, while the melody is usually varied in some way. The charm of any created art form lies not in how well the rules have been followed but in the manner that deviations are made without disrupting the initial form.

Caccini was consistent in the use of florid melismatic phrases at the approach to the final cadence. Florid ornamentation was used also to portray the character of specific words, such as *il sospirar* (the sigh), *te le gira* (turns them to you), *i vivi ardori* (the lively desires), and *il mio bel foco* (my beautiful fire), or words depicting anguish or joy. The word *moro* (I die) prompted a cessation of movement. Not wishing to leave the realization of the bass completely up to the performer, Caccini wrote fully figured basses that indicated the exact spacing of the chords.

Early Monodic Forms

Early monody usually took the form of the madrigal or the strophic aria. The madrigal began to decline about 1625, but other forms, such as the canzonet, remained popular. The bass line of the strophic aria was often a familiar melody, which was repeated for each verse, allowing for harmonic variation and an ornamented melody above. It was not considered good practice for a singer to repeat any ornament in the performance of an aria; constant variation was expected. At times, a composition was written in sections, alternating the more lyrical type of melody with the recitative style. Later these sections developed into individual movements and became the chamber cantata. Most of the monodies of Giacomo Carissimi (1605–1674) are typical of this type. His *Mesto in sen* could easily be considered a one-movement cantata. Another type, also used in the later cantata, may have developed from the Venetian *concertato* style. Violin parts were often added to play *ritornelli* at the beginning, between the verses, and at the end of the composition. The instruments were seldom used in combination with the voice, but rather as contrasting timbre and musical material. The result was a type of rondo, since the instrumental sections were usually identical on every appearance.

Some monodies were in the form of dialogues. They gave the composer the opportunity to depict character types by musical means; later they were absorbed into the larger dramatic form of opera. Dance rhythms and fast-moving bass lines, often with the same rhythm as the voice and with some imitation of the vocal line, were also popular; *Danza, danza fanciulla gentile* by Francesco Durante (1684–1755) is a good example. And a few very rapid patter songs can also be found, of which *Amore è bandito,* by Barbara Strozzi, adopted daughter of the poet Giulio Strozzi, is typical.

Influential Poets and Poetic Forms

Poetry in this period, too, was enjoying a freer form, which lent itself to monodic settings. The poet Giambattista Marino (1569–1625) achieved great fame in his lifetime. His poems, in free form, are superficial and insincere musings about sensual love, but their cleverness attracted the monodists, as did the poetry of Giambattista Guarini (1538–1612), whose *Pastor Fido* deals with the favorite topic of the love of Mertillo and Amarilli. Gabriello Chiabrera (1552–1638) wrote in imitation of Greek lyricists. Although his poems are elegant and artificial, they are charming for their melodious qualities and meter. Ottorino Rinuccini (1562–1621) was also a favorite poet and remains well known today as the librettist for Peri's *Daphne.*

Texts of older poets also retained popularity during this time. The *rime* of Francesco Petrarca (1304–1374) included *sonetti, canzoni, sestine, ballate,* and *madrigali*—love was a favorite subject. Pietro Bembo (1470–1547) patterned his poems after Petrarca and Giovanni Boccaccio (1313–1375). Torquato Tasso (1544–1595) usually wrote in *ottave rime,* which lent itself to monodies with repeated basses. His most famous work, *Gerusalemme Liberata,* has inspired the settings of many composers. His love poems were sincere and often very moving, inviting musical expression in line with Galilei's "conceptions of the mind." A return to these poets will be seen in the songs of the twentieth-century composers.

The Importance of Ducal Patronage

Some musicologists feel that the solo songs of the early seventeenth century reached a far greater public than opera did since they were written by singers and amateurs as well as by established composers, but they did not flourish much in areas that lacked the patronage of a ducal court.

The three main centers of monodic composition were Florence, Rome, and Venice; but the courts at Turin, Modena, Parma, Piacenza, and Ferrara were also important. The most experimental monodies were written at the Florentine center, but even with their radical departure from tradition, they were the first to fall out of favor. At Rome, tradition still held out for conservatism, although church organists, priests, and monks wrote monodies and applied the continuo style to sacred music. Venice got a later start.

Monodies did not appear there much before 1620, although the first collection had been published in 1611 by Marc Antonio Negri. The Venetian aria took on a more serious development in which the main emphasis was on the beauty of an extended melodic line with less thought about following the form of the poem or the rhythm of the words. This *arioso* style, used by Claudio Monteverdi (1567–1643), reflected the development of the aria as it gradually became different from the declamatory style of the recitative. Also, Monteverdi differed from some other composers in that he preferred to write out his vocal ornaments rather than leave them to the discretion of the singer.

Many monodies were not published as separate collections but were included in publications of other types of vocal composition—choral works or songs and arias for two or three voices. Some were published with accompaniments for clavicembalo or Spanish guitar.

New Developments in Text Treatment and Singing Technique

Eventually, composers began to divide a single text into different styles of recitative, arioso, and aria; and with the development of the aria a radical change took place in the treatment of the text. Words became less important for themselves. Phrases were often repeated, and long musical lines were sung with few syllabic changes. As the separation in style between the recitative and the aria widened, the technique of singing also developed in two directions. The recitative called for a *parlando* style, with short, crisp rhythms and accents corresponding to spoken dialogue; it was used for descriptions and to carry out the action of the drama. The aria was more suited to personal, introspective expression of emotion, and for this form the Italian composers created the graceful and smoothly flowing style known as *bel canto*. This style of singing was widely imitated and has influenced both vocal and instrumental music throughout the world to the present day.

With the *bel canto* technique came the development of the *da capo* aria. It was, at first, a simple ABA form, but it soon became a highly developed vehicle for the kind of vocal display that audiences were coming to expect and demand. There was a growing appreciation of the human voice as a solo instrument, perhaps as an inevitable result of Renaissance thought, which emphasized the importance of man as an individual. It also led to the recognition of the human body in art and to the pride of artists or composers, who now added their signatures to their artistic creations.

Along with the appreciation of vocal soloists came the increasing demand for professional singers. Competition ran high, and numerous manuals were written by voice teachers on ways of developing vocal techniques and of applying vocal ornaments to a melody. Caccini, for example, stated in his foreword to *Le Nuove Musiche* that he was putting forth that which he had learned from Scipione del Palla. Caccini also wrote detailed instructions for the execution of various vocal ornamentations, or *gorgia*. They were seldom written out in the songs, but were expected to be added at specified places in the vocal line, as dictated by the text, and executed according to the ability of the singer.

All teachers of singing considered correct intonation one of the first aims of voice instruction, with clear articulation of the words a very close second. In fact, many teachers listed these two goals in reverse order. All seemed to agree with Caccini that open vowels were more sonorous than close vowels, and, as such, they were advocated for all ornaments. In the most usual instructional method, singers first learned to produce sustained tones in the middle voice and then expanded the range by gradually adding tones to either end. These basic tones, called *accenti,* were then used as roots for diminutions or divisions (short melodic patterns consisting of turns, *cambiatas,* etc.). Everything was sung slowly using a medium tone without force. Volume had no importance, as it was never necessary to sing in a large auditorium or over a large orchestra. The exercises were mostly diatonic. Larger intervals were added gradually. After students learned to produce a tone of good quality on an evenly sustained pitch they were next taught the *esclamazio,* for use on long notes. It consisted of two types: a slow, smooth *crescendo* and *decrescendo* (*languida*), and the reverse (*viva*). The *esclamazio* was intended to express specific passions. Later, however, singers employed it on every long note regardless of the meaning of the text, and the technique became known, as it is today, as *messa di voce.*

The study of ornamentation is vast and controversial, part of the problem being the changes that have taken place in the terminology. A *trillo* did not mean the same thing to singers of the eighteenth century that it meant to Caccini. He used the term to mean the repetition of a note while gradually increasing the subdivision of the rhythmic impulses, made by a "beating in the throat" without aspiration of the breath. Later the term was applied to the rapid alternation of two notes, the present-day trill, which Caccini called *gruppo* and the Germans called *tremolo.* The latter term is now used in instrumental music to indicate either a rapidly reiterated note or a rapidly alternated interval. Monteverdi called this effect *stile concitato.* Today, in vocal music *tremolo* has come to mean excessive vibrato, and it is usually used in a derogatory way. It is easy to understand how confusion came about and still exists, even with all our modern research. However, no matter how complicated a passage became, it was important that the words still be understood. All the teachings warn against the overuse of ornaments, especially at cadences.

In the early part of the seventeenth century another branch of singing developed; it should be mentioned although it cannot be appreciated fully today since it no longer exists. This was the *castrato,* or artificial male soprano. Prepared and trained from young boyhood, the castrato was able to achieve a range, purity of tone, brilliance of technique, and endurance that can hardly be imagined today. The practice endured into the nineteenth century and was banned eventually for humanitarian reasons.

The important point to be brought out about the singing techniques of the seventeenth and eighteenth centuries, and even well into the nineteenth, is that it was all *legato.* Furthermore, the schools specifically established for the training of professional singers included instruction in poetry, literature, theory, and composing. Probably the reason that early Italian songs and arias are so vocally satisfying is that most of the composers were also singers.

After the death of Alessandro Scarlatti in 1725 there is little evidence of monodies or solo songs being written. Opera and oratorio had completed their circle of fire, and Italian solo song was to slumber for over 100 years.

The Nineteenth Century and *Il Risorgimento*

Practically every aspect of development in Italy has been greatly influenced by geography. The peninsula, surrounded by the Mediterranean on three sides and bordered by the Alps on the north, is also divided throughout by mountainous terrain. Strong individual characteristics of language and customs developed within the separated areas, which remained self-governed long after other European countries were well-established unities. The resulting spirit of fierce independence gave birth to the Renaissance, Italy's glorious contribution to European cultural and intellectual advancement, and this independence remains an Italian characteristic to the present day.

It was inevitable that strong families would dominate their own areas and at times accumulate tremendous power and wealth. Fortunately, most possessed a passion for culture as great as their love for political and economic supremacy. Thus, each principality became a cultural center for the development of philosophy, literature, and the arts. The growth of these centers reflected the individual tastes and desires of the ruling families; rivalry for superiority ran high, and no expense was thought too great to attract the finest minds and talents in order to dominate the intellectual and artistic worlds. In every artistic endeavor Italians reached the pinnacle of achievement, and Italian artists and musicians were sought after throughout all of Europe.

Military power was no less important, and Italy experienced almost constant warfare among the ruling houses and against invaders from all sides. Alliances strengthened certain areas that succeeded in organizing themselves into *ducati, ripubbliche, stati,* or *regni,* each self-governed. Even when these small dynasties were ruled by foreign forces, so strong was the Italian character that the culture could not be subjugated. Instead, the foreigners became Italianized. Even the strong movement of German Romanticism did not penetrate Italian literature and the arts. The most important influence of Romanticism in Italy was in politics. Patriotic heroism and idealism became the dominating theme of Italian thought in poetry and literature from about 1815 to 1870. This period of revolution and turbulent warfare is known as *Il Risorgimento,* an era of political struggle that finally ended in Italian independence from foreign domination. In the spring of 1871, Italy became unified under one government for the first time since the fall of the Roman Empire in the fifth century.

Italian Music in the Nineteenth Century

Artistic elements had to be of secondary importance during the critical period of *Il Risorgimento*. Opera, however, continued to dominate Italy's musical life; and Italian opera remained, as it had been since its inception, a dominating force throughout Europe. But only in Italy did opera obliterate all other forms of musical expression.

Solo song continued to exist and to be developed in countries outside of Italy. In Germany the accompanied solo *Lied* (or *Generalbass-lied*) developed steadily from the end of the sixteenth century until the first half of the eighteenth, when under the influence of the spreading Italian opera it almost gave way to the elaborate operatic aria form. After 1750, in the hands of such composers as Johann Adam Hiller (1728–1800), Johann Abraham Peter Schulz (1747–1800), Johann Friedrich Reichardt (1752–1814), and Karl Friedrich Zelter (1758–1832), the *Lied* took on a new lyrical development that continued through Haydn, Mozart, and Beethoven, finally to reach supreme heights in the nineteenth century. However, none of the beautiful songs of Schubert, Schumann, Brahms, and Wolf were heard in Italy. In the early years of *Lied* composition only one Italian name can be found, that of the brothers Gordigiani—Giovanni Battista (1795–1871) and Luigi (1806–1860). Better remembered than his brother, Luigi wrote about 300 songs, *canzonette,* and *romanze* and three volumes of *Canzoni popolari toscane.* His songs are characteristically Italian, many being in folk-song style. There may be hints of a relationship between these *canzoni* and the *Italian Lieder* of Hugo Wolf. In his own time Luigi was called *lo Schubert italiano.*

Most of the important opera composers of the nineteenth century also wrote a few *romanze da camera* (often listed in modern editions simply as *composizioni da camera*): Gioachino Antonio Rossini (1727–1868), Gaetano Donizetti (1797–1848), Vincenzo Bellini (1801–1835), and Giuseppe Verdi (1813–1901). These charming songs were written for the amateur singer with the sole purpose of providing vocal entertainment at *musicales* in private salons. There was little thought of creating an artistic composition in which the voice and the accompaniment are used equally to interpret the meaning of the words through the form of the poem. Instead, they are miniatures in operatic style with predominant vocal lines of flowing melodies with some cadenzas and embellishments. *Romanze da camera* or *liriche* were also written by a number of lesser composers, many of whom were teachers of singing—a possible indication that by the end of the nineteenth century the singers themselves were beginning to realize the need for a better quality of song literature.

Neapolitan Song

In addition to opera, the only vocal music that gained wide popularity in Italy during the nineteenth century was the "Neapolitan Song." These *canzoni napoletane* are generally not of the highest artistic quality. The texts are sentimental love poems designed to bring out every pathos that could tug at human heartstrings. A few of the composers who set them were endowed with a natural ability to write beautiful and appealing melodic lines. Probably the most memorable was Francesco Paolo Tosti (1846–1916), whose simple, flowing melodies depicted the sentiment of the words. He wrote hundreds of songs and reached a higher artistic level than most of the other composers of this type of *romanza da camera*. Many of his works were included in the concerts of the better-known opera stars of the period, and occasionally they occupy the same place today.

Among the many other composers known for their *canzoni napolitane* are: Vincenzo de Meglio (1825–1883), Luigi Denza (1846–922), Augusto Rotoli (1847–1904), Alberto Pestalozza (1851–1934), Alessandro Costa (1857–1953), Ruggiero Leoncavallo (1858–1919), Leopoldo Mugnone (1858–1941), Pier Adolfo Tirindelli (1858–1937), Vincenzo Di Chiara (1860–1937), Eduardo Di Capua (1865–1917), Enrico de Leva (1867–1955), Renato Brogi (1873–1924), Rodolfo Falvo (1873–1937), Enrico Cannio (1874–1949), and Giuseppe Capolongo (1877–1928). It is interesting to note that their dates of birth are all before the 1880s, the decade when most of the twentieth-century reformers were born.

Instrumental Music

Instrumental music, once so highly developed in Italy, declined in quality and quantity in inverse ratio to the increase in popularity of the *melodrama* (in English translation, "serious opera") demanded by the bourgeois public. Even the smallest town had at least one theater, and for more than 100 years *il teatro musicale* had dominated the musical life of every community. Instrumental accompaniments of opera were confined almost entirely to providing broken-chord harmonies under the melodic gymnastics of the singer. As the quality and difficulty of the accompaniments declined, so also did the performance level and technical proficiency of the instrumentalists. Verdi, for example, had many complaints when he attempted to find instrumentalists capable of playing his increasingly demanding scores. What independent instrumental music existed bore little trace of early Italian characteristics. Instead, it was modeled after the German Romantic style. Nearly every serious Italian musician went to Germany to study because of the low level of instrumental technical instruction in Italian conservatories, which existed almost exclusively for the training of singers. These musicians believed, of course, that by bringing the German symphonic tradition into Italy, Italian standards and goals would improve. But the German style was scorned by the opera-loving Italian public, caught up not only by popular appeal, but also by the publicity generated by Italian publishing houses, who were often deeply involved in all aspects of opera production. Not only instrumental music but also sacred music had fallen into deterioration. Opera, like a giant monster, had wrapped its tentacles around every other musical form and either extinguished it or made it into its own image.

Early Reformers

At the end of the nineteenth century several important composers tried to improve the state of Italian music. One of the first to be associated with this endeavor was Antonio Bazzini (1818–1897), a violinist who achieved success as a composer of string quartets and symphonies. As a concert artist he toured Italy, France, Germany, and Belgium, and he lived in France from 1852 to 1864. His only opera, *Turanda,* was premiered at La Scala but was not successful. He went to the Milan Conservatory in 1870 as a professor of composition and became its director in 1882. His works, while German in technique, were known for their Italian spontaneity and charm. They consisted of six string quartets, one string quintet, compositions for violin, and symphonic overtures. He also wrote non-operatic vocal music: two sacred cantatas, several settings of psalms, and songs—some of which were set to poems by Alice Barbi, a mezzo-soprano who had studied violin with him. Bazzini was a strong supporter of the several Società del Quartetto that were being founded in Italy, and he did a great deal to bring back Italy's love for instrumental music.

Of greater significance in the revival of symphonic and chamber music were the efforts made a few years later by Giovanni Sgambati (1841–1914), a pianist and conductor. He began to study piano at an early age and became famous for his playing and the classical character of his programs, which consisted of music by German and French composers. He studied with Franz Liszt in Rome and was the first to give orchestral concerts of the German masters. Sgambati gave the first performances in Rome of Beethoven's *Eroica* Symphony and his Piano Concerto in Eb major.

In 1869 Sgambati heard Wagner's music in Germany. In 1876, when Wagner visited Rome, the German embassy gave a concert in his honor that consisted entirely of Sgambati's compositions, including several of his songs. On Wagner's recommendation the German publishing house Schott published some music by Sgambati, and by 1881 he had become quite famous in Europe and America. In 1884 he was invited to represent Italy at the international concerts given in the Trocadéro in Paris. Two years later he became one of the five corresponding members of the French Institute. He concertized widely, conducting and playing many of his own compositions with much success. His *Requiem Mass,* first performed in London in 1896, was officially adopted in Italy for royal funerals.

Sgambati was also successful as a teacher, and in 1877 he helped found the Liceo Musicale in connection with the Accademia di Santa Cecilia in Rome. In 1881 he founded the Società del Quintetto, and from 1893 he was artistic director of the Società Filarmonica Romana. His contributions to classical music as teacher, composer, pianist, and conductor were gratefully recognized by the Italian government, from which he received many honors in his lifetime.

It is significant that Sgambati wrote no operas. He wrote more than 40 songs—in fact, his first two opus numbers consisted of two albums of songs. He also produced some transcriptions and composed music for piano, piano and violin, piano and orchestra, orchestra, chamber ensembles, and organ.

Giovanni Bolzoni (1841–1919) began to study music at the Parma Conservatory for a career as an orchestral violinist. He was able to promote orchestral and chamber music after he became director successively of the Istituto Musicale Morlacchi at Perugia, the Liceo Musicale of Piacenza, and the Liceo Musicale of Turin. In Turin he also conducted opera and concerts at the Teatro Regio, where his position as conductor had been recommended by Verdi. He composed both instrumental music and operas, but the latter were not successful. Although only one of his instrumental compositions, *Minuetto* for strings, remains in the repertory of orchestras today, Bolzoni is still remembered for his high ideals in instrumental music and for the outstanding quality of his teaching.

Luigi Mancinelli (1848–1921) was born in Orvieto and began studying violoncello in Florence at the age of twelve. He became first cellist in the orchestra of the Teatro della Pergola in that city. In 1874 he moved to Rome to play at the Teatro Apollo. It was there that he was given his first opportunity to conduct, when the orchestra was unexpectedly left without a conductor. He soon received other appointments as conductor and as director of music festivals. In 1881 he became the principal of the Liceo Musicale in Bologna, conductor of the Teatro Comunale, and *maestro di cappella* of San Petronio. During the five years that Mancinelli was in Bologna he composed two masses and many other sacred pieces, organized a symphony and quartet society, and was the first to acquaint the Bolognese with vocal and instrumental music by foreign composers. Although his own most important compositions were operas, he must be counted among those who promoted better musical standards in Italy during the late nineteenth and early twentieth centuries.

Antonio Scontrino (1850–1922) was the son of a Sicilian carpenter who played violin and guitar and used his talent to construct violins, guitars, cellos, double basses, and pianofortes. At the age of seven Antonio was playing in a family orchestra, on a cello his father had reconstructed into a small double bass with only three strings. Scontrino entered the Palermo Conservatory in 1861, and in 1870 he began touring as a concert double bassist.

Two years later he received financial aid from his home town of Trapani, Sicily, to study in Munich. In 1874 he went to England to play in the orchestra of the operatic impresario and producer James Henry Mapleson (1830–1901). He returned to Italy, and after teaching privately in Milan for several years, he accepted a professorship in 1891 to teach counterpoint and composition at the Palermo Conservatory. The next year he won a professorship at the Reale Istituto Musicale of Florence. Besides five operas, Scontrino composed orchestral music, string quartets, and many compositions for instruments and piano. He also wrote about 50 songs and other vocal chamber music.

Giuseppe Martucci was born in Capua in 1856 and died in Naples in 1909. He heads the list of important pioneers in the struggle of instrumental music against the supremacy of opera. He received his first music instruction from his father, a trombone player and bandmaster. When Giuseppe was four years old the family moved to Pozzuoli, near Naples, and at eight he played his first piano recital. In 1867 he won a competition at the Conservatorio di San Pietro a Maiella in Naples. His first compositions were published in 1871, and he left school to pursue a career as a concert pianist and chamber musician. He returned to Naples in 1880 to teach piano at the Conservatory. There, as conductor, he began his campaign to develop orchestral music in Italy. He presented concerts of music by Mozart, Beethoven, Mendelssohn, Schumann, and Brahms. Later, in 1886, he became director of the Liceo Musicale G. B. Martini in Bologna, where two years later he presented the first performance in Italy of Wagner's *Tristan und Isolde*. In Bologna his programs were greatly varied, with music of old masters and new. He worked constantly to improve Italy's cultural life. In 1902 he returned to Naples as director of the Conservatory and remained there until his death in 1909.

Martucci's compositions reflected his love of nineteenth-century German music, but they retained a personal style and Italian characteristics. Nearly all of his prolific writing was instrumental—orchestral, chamber, or solo works— but among his vocal music was an oratorio, *Samuel;* a *Messe di Gloria;* and numerous songs. The songs included the cycle *Pagine sparse* (Op. 68), *Due sogni* (Op. 68a), *Due Romanze* (Op. 72), and *Canzoni dei recordi* for contralto, baritone, and pianoforte. These songs were also orchestrated and are valued today as an example of the high cultural and artistic level achieved by Martucci as early as 1886; they were favorably received in other countries as contributions to the development of song writing.

Marco Enrico Bossi was born in 1861. His father, an organist, enrolled him at the age of ten in the Liceo Musicale in Bologna, where he studied for two years. He went on to the Milan Conservatory to study organ and composition until he was twenty years old. The next ten years were spent as organist and *maestro di capella* at the Como Cathedral. From 1891 to 1895 Bossi taught theory and organ at the Naples Conservatory. After that he became director of the Liceo Benedetto Marcello in Venice. In 1902 he returned to Bologna, and for ten years he was director of the Liceo Musicale. In 1916 he became the director of the Accademia di Santa Cecilia in Rome. His earliest compositions were in the field of opera, but most of his works were symphonic, chamber, or piano and organ compositions. He also wrote songs and a number of vocal works, including many sacred choral compositions. Bossi died at sea while returning from a concert tour in the United States on February 20, 1925. His compositions were important beginnings in the return to Italian non-operatic music.

Another important contributor to Italian instrumental music was Leone Sinigaglia (1868–1944). He studied composition with Bolzoni at the Liceo Musicale "G. Verdi" at Turin from 1889 to 1894. For the next five years Sinigaglia was in Vienna, where he knew Brahms and Goldmark. He studied orchestration with Dvořák and became very interested in folk music. Most of his compositions are instrumental chamber music, but Sinigaglia also wrote many songs and collected six books of *Vecchie canzoni popolari del Pie-monte,* which he freely transcribed.

Finally, Dom Lorenzo Perosi (1872–1956) is remembered for doing more than any other composer to improve the decadent state of sacred music. His father was director of music in the Cathedral at Tortona, and Perosi dedicated his life to the priesthood and the elevation of church music. After studying at the Milan Conservatory and with F. X. Ratisbon, he became *maestro de cappella* at Imola, and in 1894 he went to St. Marks in Venice. He was ordained a priest in 1896 and in 1898 was appointed musical director of the Sistine Chapel in Rome. The importance of this position enabled him to have even greater influence on Italian church music.

Perosi composed all forms of sacred music: oratorios, cantatas, masses, a requiem, psalms, a *Te Deum,* and many compositions for organ. He completed four out of a series of ten symphonies, each to be named after a different Italian city. In 1905 Pope Pius X made Perosi "Perpetual Master of the Pontifical Chapel." A mental breakdown, suffered first in 1917, interfered with his work from then until his death, but he is still remembered for the high level to which he was able to bring Italian sacred music. His compositions combined an old style with contemporary orchestration. He was not an innovator, but his music achieved great success, and his work toward the betterment of church music remains unparalleled.

Ferruccio Busoni

Perhaps the musician most concerned about the decadent state of music in Italy at the end of the nineteenth century was Ferruccio Benvenuto Busoni, an Italian who lived almost his entire life outside the country. He was born in Empoli, Tuscany, in 1866. His father, a clarinet player, was Italian; his mother, a pianist, was German. Busoni grew up in an environment conducive to producing a musician of outstanding quality. However, his life was spent divided in allegiance between the two countries of his parents' heritage, and he experienced many difficulties because of that.

Busoni's mother was an exceptionally well educated woman and an excellent musician, eminently qualified to give Busoni his early training. His first public recital took place in Vienna at the age of nine. At fifteen he toured Italy as a concert pianist and was made a member of the Philharmonic Academy of Bologna. (Mozart was the youngest member, at the age of fourteen.) Many of Busoni's vocal compositions were written during these early years. Sixteen of his 21 songs were written by the time he was sixteen years of age. Many of them were published within a year of their composition. Busoni's two choral works with orchestra were written in 1882. *Il Sabato del villaggio,* a cantata for soli, chorus, and orchestra on the poem by Leopardi, was performed at Bologna in 1882 and was dedicated to Luigi Mancinelli, who was then the principal of the Liceo Musicale and the conductor of the Teatro Comunale.

In 1886 Busoni went to Leipzig to study composition, and in 1889 he accepted a teaching position at the Conservatory at Helsingfors. There he met Gerda Sjöstrand, whom he married the next year. Also in 1890 he won the Rubinstein prize for composition and went to Moscow to teach at the Conservatory for a year. He concertized in America from 1891 to 1894 and taught for a time at the New England Conservatory in Boston. He then returned to Germany to make his home in Berlin. After playing in Italy in 1895 he wrote of his disappointment with the Italian orchestras and conductors. He complained that it would take considerable work to bring Italy up to the musical level that Germany had achieved many years earlier. The few Italian composers for whom Busoni felt any respect were writing in the German style, while in Germany his own music was frequently criticized because of its Italianate qualities. His Piano Concerto, Op. 39, was even criticized for its Italian title and names of the movements. Most of the musical directions in Busoni's music are in Italian rather than in German. In Italy, however, partly because of the German influence in his music and partly because he had lived away from his native country for so long, Busoni was considered a foreigner.

His longing for Italy was insistent, and in 1913 Busoni accepted the directorship of the Liceo Rossini (now officially called Liceo G. B. Martini) at Bologna. For many years this school of music had specialized in the training of operatic singers, especially women. Bologna itself had long enjoyed an academic atmosphere; it had been the first city to perform Wagner's music and had been chosen by Verdi for the first performance of his Requiem in 1874. The Liceo had reached its highest level under the directorship of Giuseppe Martucci, from 1886 to 1909.

Busoni realized that while bringing German conductors to Italy and presenting orchestral concerts of classical German music might raise musical standards and awareness, it could also kill the possibility for the development of characteristic Italian music. A strong factor in his decision to go to Bologna was his determination to write an opera that would be truly Italian. He hoped that living in Italy would be a source of inspiration for this work. He had great plans for the advancement of music, but much of his time was taken up with administrative duties, and he was constantly frustrated by the Italian complacency. Frequent strikes and a new socialist municipal administration made it impossible for him to continue. Busoni could not understand Italy's rejection of him, nor could he give up the idea that he had a duty to fulfil as a leader of Italian music. He felt that his mission to the whole art of music would be accomplished by way of Italian music.

Conditions were improving, however; concerts by violinists, cellists, harpists, organists, and pianists were gaining in popularity. Busoni, himself, after a successful concert in Rome in 1916, saw some hope in the younger musicians gathering around him. It was in Paris that he met Alfredo Casella for the first time, and in 1921 Busoni dedicated to him *Romanza and Scherzo* for pianoforte, Op. 54. Although Busoni could not accept Casella fully as a personal friend, he respected his ability as a pianist and appreciated his intellect and internationalism. And, he could sympathize only too well with Casella's own thwarted ambitions for Italian music. Later, when Casella founded the National Music Society for the defense of new Italian music, Busoni shared the triple honorary presidency with Toscanini and Bossi.

Early compositions by Busoni were Romantic in style, but his love for the classicists and his intellectual approach to musical form soon caused him to dislike music based on literary programs, and he sought to free music from literary influence. He began to develop new musical forms combined with classical principles. His forms were built through thematic development, but they were more abstract, freer, and more mobile than those of the classical period; yet they retained the classical spirit of lightness and clarity. Busoni forecast future tendencies in his treatment of orchestral instruments; he used instruments in solo effects and for tonal color. He felt that music should be valued for its own sake and should not be confined to performance by any specific medium. He experimented with different arrangements of whole and half steps and envisioned new means of musical expression. He also established a new school of piano playing emphasizing expressive interpretation rather than virtuosity—this was also to be a major change in vocal music in the twentieth century.

The circumstances of Busoni's life reflect the conditions of his times. With the decadent state of music schools in Italy, there was no alternative to his going to Austria and Germany to study. His directorship of the Liceo Rossini in Bologna lasted only until 1915. He spent the next five years in Zurich and returned to Berlin in 1920.

Even though Busoni made his home away from Italy for most of his life, he was always intensely conscious of his Italian nationality, which he always maintained. He tried to express through his music a liberation of the human spirit unbound by past conventions. The same liberation would be sought later, especially by Pizzetti and by Dallapiccola, each in his own way.

Busoni died in Berlin in 1924. His last work was his fourth opera, *Doktor Faust,* the final scene of which was finished by his student Phillip Jarnach. As he did for his other operas, Busoni wrote his own libretto. It is extremely complex and filled with mysticism and symbolism; perhaps the key to Busoni's own complex personality may be found in this last expression of himself.

The New Italian Music

It is significant that Busoni felt it necessary either to write or to adapt the librettos for his operas, for this approach was a common characteristic of the twentieth-century composers born in the next generation. The text once again became an important factor in shaping the form of the music, in developing the vocal line, and in determining the harmonic structure. The type of music thus created cannot be separated from the word, and for this reason it cannot easily be translated into other languages. Faithful interpretation of the text through the music was the prime reason for major changes during the twentieth century, just as it had influenced the development of Florentine monody. Syllabic treatment of the vocal line replaced the *fioratura* of the late *bel canto* era, and the curve of the vocal line was determined by the inflection of the spoken phrase. Accents and dramatic expression were emphasized by harmonic devices or by wider melodic skips. The accompaniment began to be just as important as the vocal line. Occasionally the vocal line was of secondary importance or was used as an obbligato to the instrumental melody.

In their hope to develop a distinctive Italian style, the new generation of Italian composers strongly rejected the German influence adopted by their nineteenth-century predecessors. But because a strong Italian style had not yet developed, the German influence was at first replaced by French and Russian characteristics. Thus, in the music of the early twentieth century new paths of modality and contrasts of color can be traced directly to French Impressionism and Russian orchestral techniques and modality. At the same time, counteraction to these foreign influences resulted in a return to the Baroque techniques of imitative counterpoint, linear melodies, and early forms.

New inspiration was found in the Italian countryside and in the sincerity and warmth of the country folk and their regional music. Lullabies became popular. Much of the music can be described as simple but full of instinctive emotion. It never sounds as though it were derived by mechanical means, but seems to develop from natural, physical sources in a predestined order of beauty and form rather than from superimposed disciplines.

The lyrical quality of the Italian language predisposes Italian melodies to follow lyrical curved lines. The immobile recitative style of French Impressionism could not be adapted to Italian vocal music. The German *Sprech-stimme* was in even greater opposition to the natural curve and diatonic flow of the Italian language and the Italian desire to express human emotion. Even the composers who embraced the twelve-tone system did so with an entirely Italian approach.

The new awareness of the importance of the text, with careful attention directed to the emotional impact of each word, brought about a change in the choice of texts for all vocal works. Besides those written by the composers themselves, texts were chosen from the ancient Greeks, the Bible, the medieval vulgate poets, great historical epochs, and oriental sources, as well as from the contemporary writers. The subjects ranged from purely fanciful creations to deeper intellectual content. Poetry about love was no longer the only desired topic.

The music had to follow the dictates of the poem. It was imperative that the accents of the words be set as they occur when spoken and not be stretched out to conform to a prescribed musical form. For this reason free verse was often preferred, since the music did not have to observe a poetic rhythm or include poetry's often monotonous repetition. The song could grow naturally and spontaneously, and the form could be allowed to evolve from the meaning of the poem. The closest fusion of words and music was reached when the composer and the poet were one and the same person. Besides expressing the specific words of the text, music now conveyed the highest human and philosophical meanings of life.

Orchestral forms that were not bound to tradition also evolved, and even opera began to be conceived as an orchestral form. Busoni, for example, considered the form of an opera as important as the form of a symphony. Orchestral instruments began to be used with voice, either in addition to the piano or instead of it. Accompaniments were no longer mere harmonic support for the vocal line, but were composed in combination with it. The voice was treated much as if it were an instrument, and the Italianate flow of the melody was transmitted to the accompanying instruments. In effect, the Baroque vocal chamber style was combined with contemporary form and harmonic techniques.

An Awakened Interest in Music History

About the time that German music was beginning to penetrate Italy's opera-dominated musical life, there arose an interest in the history of music. Until then Italy had been shockingly uninterested even in her own political and social history, much less that of other countries. With the unification of Italy in 1871, state education created a demand for textbooks and history books. None existed. Italians also became aware that the histories written by Germans extolled the accomplishments of their own countrymen and claimed many Italian innovations as their own. For this reason the few Italian history books written immediately after the Risorgimento were as chauvinistic as those of the Germans. It was not until 1914, with Arnaldo Bonaventura's account, that an authentic history of music in Italian could be written without prejudice.

With the strengthening of national consciousness and the interest in Italy's musical past came a genuine awakening of interest in the music itself. Compositions of Palestrina, Monteverdi, Caldara, Scarlatti, Corelli, Frescobaldi, and other composers of the seventeenth and eighteenth centuries began to be published and to be performed frequently on recital programs.

The Futurists

Early in the twentieth century, a new movement arose, started by a small group of Italian painters, sculptors, and writers who called themselves the Futurists. The writer Filippo Tommaso Marinetti (1876–1944) is given credit for founding it. Although the *Futurist Manifesto* was written in Italy, it first appeared in French, on February 20, 1909, in the Paris newspaper *Le Figaro.* Historically, it is important as the first indication of the bold, rebellious, youthful spirit appearing in Italy. According to Alfredo Casella, who was in Paris at the time, it was the only Italian artistic movement between 1870 and 1914 that received worldwide attention and had universal influence.

Besides Marinetti, the group included the sculptor Umberto Boccioni and the painters Carlo Carrà, Gino Severini, Giacomo Balla, and Luigi Russolo. Russolo is the author of another famous manifesto, *The Art of Noises,* which he wrote after hearing a performance in the Costanzi Theater in Rome of *Musica Futurista* by Balilla Pratella, a composition inspired by Marinetti's *Manifesto.* Russolo's article was sent to Pratella on March 11, 1913 in the form of a letter. It shows parallels between the evolution of musical dissonance and the growing multiplicity of machines, which Russolo believed were responsible for the increasing demand for more and more violent acoustic emotions.

A resumé by Pratella of the evolution of music from 1910 to 1917 lists eleven proclamations for the progress of Futurism in music. It recommends that young composers leave the conservatories and compose for themselves in their own way, not for the public and the masses in order to make money. Pratella attacks the "ignorant" critics and asks composers to found their own independent *rivista musicale.* He tells composers they should destroy the prejudice against new music and the preference for the past. Music must be new, not just a reconstruction of the past. The dominance of singers should be ended. The singers in an *opera d'arte* should have no more importance than the instruments of the orchestra. Free verse written by the composer must be substituted for set librettos. Composers must fight against the *romanze* of the type written by Tosti and Costa. The public must be turned against exhuming old works and toward advancing everything that is original and revolutionary.

Fascism and the Arts

Shortly after the First World War a new political movement reflected the social unrest and the national dissatisfaction with the settlement of the war for Italy. In 1922, Mussolini took over the government with his Fascist followers and proclaimed himself dictator. Italy soon became a totalitarian military state, and Mussolini did not hesitate to use militia and secret police against all opposition. The Fascists violently opposed Communism and Socialism. Unlike Communism, Fascism favored state organization in which each class had its distinct place and function. Despite its many abuses, this regime cultivated and promoted the arts, although not without political overtones. In Fascism the individual is responsible to the future of society as a whole. In the same way, contemporary composers had to make their art of value to their followers. Besides encouraging creative artists and composers, the new Fascist government sponsored the writing and publishing of textbooks and histories that would call attention to the old supremacy of Italy, not only in opera and song, but in every field of composition.

Gabriele d'Annunzio and the New Music Corporation

Probably one of the greatest friends of contemporary Italian musicians was the writer and flamboyant personality Gabriele d'Annunzio (1863–1938). His prose and poetry have been set to music by a great many twentieth-century composers. He was in France in 1909, when Ravel, Fauré, and Debussy formed the Independent Musical Society in opposition to the National Music Society, headed by Saint Saëns. The first president was Gabriel Fauré, and Alfredo Casella was one of the founders and served as general secretary from 1911 until 1914. D'Annunzio, who became a member in 1910, was enthusiastic about the Society's work in presenting contemporary compositions, and he kept up his subscription even after he returned to Italy. When Casella returned to Italy in 1923, after his French sojourn of seventeen years, he found that of all his old friends only Gian Francesco Malipiero had remained in touch with him and shared his views about the standards of musical culture in Italy. They decided to start an organization to attract the younger generation of musicians to current European musical thought. When d'Annunzio learned of their plan to start an organization to popularize contemporary music, he was at once an enthusiastic supporter and eager to participate in the project. It was to be called the New Music Corporation, and its first financial backing, $1,000, was given by Mrs. Elizabeth Sprague Coolidge. With other donations by Italian friends and the continued support of Mrs. Coolidge, the organization was able to arrange a series of events dedicated to contemporary music. Over 25 chamber works of the contemporary Italian school were written at Mrs. Coolidge's invitation by Respighi, Pizzetti, Alfano, Malipiero, Castelnuovo-Tedesco, and Casella.

The New Music Corporation functioned for five years and sponsored about 70 concerts, many of them featuring the first performances in Italy of music by contemporary European composers. Through these efforts Schoenberg's *Pierrot Lunaire* was given a tour of eight performances. This work incited violent public reaction in every city except Rome, and it was to have a great influence on Italy's younger composers.

Shortly before the founding of the New Music Corporation in Italy, a more important, world musical organization was being formed—the International Society for Contemporary Music. Guido M. Gatti and Alfredo Casella were asked to organize an Italian section of this society. At the first I.S.C.M. Festival, in Salzburg in August 1923, Italy was represented by some songs by Malipiero and a work by Castelnuovo-Tedesco. The New Music Corporation later became the Italian section of I.S.C.M., and in September 1930 a Festival of Contemporary Music was held in Venice. In 1933 another important Italian Festival was begun, the Maggio Musicale at Florence. In the summer of the same year, the Chigi Musical Academy was founded in Siena. Some composers, Respighi among them, did not always wish to have their music performed under the auspices of particular organizations or festivals, while others were frustrated when their works were not chosen, but the cause of contemporary Italian music went forward.

La generazione ottanta

Italian composers, like the Italian people, in general, have always had strong personality traits. Italian artists remain individual in their creativity even while seeking to establish an Italian school. Despite the difficulties, and there were many, the composers of the *generazione ottanta* (the generation born in the 1880s) were responsible for the emergence of a new musical consciousness in Italy and an Italian style, which was different from other European styles. And what is most important, the composers Franco Alfano, Ottorino Respighi, Ildebrando Pizzetti, Gian Francesco Malipiero, Alfredo Casella, and the next generation (Vincenzo Davico, Guido Guerini, Giorgio Federico Ghedini, Mario Castelnuovo-Tedesco, Goffredo Petrassi, Luigi Dallapiccola, and many others) were devoted to the composition of songs (*liriche da camera*) for voice and piano that followed the great European art songs of an earlier century and rank among the finest examples of the genre existing today.

Part I

The First-Generation Composers

The first generation of Italian art-song (*lirica da camera*) composers, those whose works were written and published in the twentieth century, were born around 1880. Many of them continued to follow the traditions into which they were born: Italian verism, French Impressionism, and German chromaticism. A few were not content with the *status quo* and consciously or unconsciously began to develop a new kind of Italianate music, which, although often influenced by Italy's northern neighbors, took on certain characteristics of its own. All these men wrote operas, but the opera form was not their first and only concern. They also composed instrumental music, chamber music, symphonies, choral music, and songs.

In the first generation of song composers Franco Alfano, Ottorino Respighi, and Ildebrando Pizzetti are considered traditionalists. They used the musical materials they had inherited, but they expanded them and developed new techniques. Co-existing with them were two equally fine composers—Gian Francesco Malipiero and Alfredo Casella—who more readily turned away from tradition and became conscious innovators in musical technique and style.

Franco Alfano

(1876–1954)

•

FRANCO ALFANO was born in Possillipo, a small town near Naples, on March 8, 1876. His first instruction in piano began in Naples with Alessandro Longo. Later he enrolled at the Conservatorio di San Pietro a Majella, where he studied harmony and composition. It was expected that young composers would go to Germany to complete their study, and in 1895 Alfano went to Leipzig to work with Hans Sitt and Solomon Jadassohn. The next year he went to Berlin to begin a career as a pianist, but he abandoned it rather early and appeared in public chiefly as an accompanist for singers and as a chamber music player. In Berlin he began writing his first operas, *Miranda* and *La Fonte di Enscir*. Neither has been published, but the latter was performed on November 8, 1898 at the Stadttheater in Breslau.

In 1900 Alfano went to Paris, where he composed two ballets for the Folies-Bergères and began a third opera, *Resurrezione,* with a libretto after Tolstoy, which was given its first performance in Turin at the Teatro Vittorio Emanuele in 1904. This work brought Alfano immediate recognition as a composer of opera, and he was hailed as a "verist" equal to Mascagni, Puccini, and Giordano. His success as an opera composer made it more difficult for Alfano to establish himself later as a composer of abstract forms of music.

In 1916 Alfano became professor of composition at the Conservatory of Bologna, and two years later he was appointed director. From 1923 until 1939 he was director of the Conservatory in Turin. After spending two years as manager of the Teatro Massimo in Palermo, he went to Rome as professor of operatic studies at the Conservatorio di Santa Cecilia; and from 1950 he was acting director of the Liceo Musicale Rossini at Pesaro. He died at the age of 78 at San Remo on October 27, 1954.

When Puccini died in 1925, leaving the third act of his opera *Turandot* unfinished, Alfano was recommended to Puccini's heirs by Toscanini as the composer best able to complete the writing of the last duet and finale. Aided in the task by some indications left by Puccini, Alfano composed a most effective ending, one that retains Puccini's style and intentions without imposing anything of Alfano.

Alfano composed twelve operas, all successful. He was most particular about his librettos, and when he could not find a satisfactory one for his opera *La Leggenda di Sakuntala,* he wrote his own. It was produced in Bologna in 1921, but the orchestral score was not published. The manuscript was destroyed during the Second World War, and it was necessary for Alfano to orchestrate it again for a new production at the Teatro dell'Opera in Rome in 1952.

Alfano's greatest contribution to Italian opera was the improvement of the orchestra. While Alfano was not an innovator, his approach to opera was quite different from that of the nineteenth-century composers. He was very much concerned about the need to improve all instrumental music in Italy. As Busoni had done, Alfano applied symphonic principles to the orchestral scores of his operas. The public was at first bewildered by the amount of musical material he used. The instruments were given lyrical contrapuntal lines equal to the vocal lines. Eventually polyphony and linear counterpoint became a predominant characteristic of twentieth-century Italian music.

Alfano scrupulously adhered to the verbal accent. Every word, every nuance is interpreted through the music. Nothing is left out. Almost every measure of his music contains directions for interpretation; nothing is left to chance. The music moves through a series of *rubati,* ritards, graded dynamics, and tempo changes all calculated by the composer. He did away with all ornamentation that did not come from a natural source of expression, and virtually nothing is left to the discretion of the performer.

Although Alfano began his career by writing operas, his prime interest was instrumental music. He composed four ballets; a symphonic suite; a symphonic poem; three symphonies (one is called *Sinfonia Breve,* for only 32 instruments); two *intermezzi* for strings; a divertimento for chamber orchestra and piano *obbligato;* two string quartets; one quintet; a concerto for violin, violoncello, and piano; two sonatas (one for violin and piano, the other for violoncello and piano); and pieces for piano solo.

Alfano's only work for chorus and orchestra, *Inno a Bolivar,* was performed at Caracas, Venezuela, on December 22, 1930, for the centenary of Bolivar's death. Of his more than 50 songs, the earliest that are preserved were written and published in Leipzig in 1896 while Alfano was attending Solomon Jadassohn's school. They are *Cinq Mélodies,* set to French texts by Alfred de Musset (Nos. 1, 2, 3, and 5) and Victor Hugo (No. 4). Most sources that mention Alfano say that his music was greatly influenced by Wagner, but a study of his songs does not bear this out. Instead of the Wagnerian motivic building of form, Alfano tends to use interpretive patterns of rhythm and harmony to express the ideas in the text; they are then developed with elaborations. His style can be compared to that of the French Impressionists. He uses dissonance without resolution and tone clusters born of polytonality for particular interpretive quality and color. Alfano's expressions of passion are as warm and Italianate as those in the melodramas of his immediate predecessors, but they are more classical, more controlled, and intentionally restrained by the composer.

Nearly half of Alfano's songs are settings of Italian translations of poems by Rabindranath Tagore. Others whose poetry he set are Bona, Colantuoni, Lipparini, DeLupis, Meano, Pastonchi, L'Orsini, Sappho, and one anonymous ancient poet. Four of his songs are wordless vocalises.

Thirty-seven of Alfano's songs are called *liriche,* seven are *mélodies,* six are *poemi,* two are *canti,* and one is a *poemetto.* Not one is called by the term used most frequently for the song form in the nineteenth century—*romanza.* Despite their unevenness, Alfano's songs have retained a firm place in the Italian repertory.

Tre poemi di Rabindranath Tagore

No. 1, Mamma, il giovane Principe

(*Rabindranath Tagore*)

1   Mamma il giovane Principe deve passare avanti la nostra porta.
2   Come vuoi che lavori stamane?
3   Insegnami come devo acconciare i miei capelli,
4   dimmi che vestito devo indossare.
5   Perchè mi guardi sgomenta, mamma?
6   So bene che il Principe non alzerà gli occhi alla mia finestra.
7   So che sparirà dalla mia vista in un baleno
8   e che solo il palpitar del flauto
9   giungerà singhiozzante di lontano sino a me!
10 Ma il giovane Principe deve passare avanti la nostra porta,
11 ed io voglio vestirmi per un momento con gli abiti più belli!
12 Mamma, il giovane Principe passò avanti la nostra porta,
13 e il sole mattutino scintillò sul suo cocchio!
14 Mi tolsi il velo dal viso,
15 mi strappai dal collo il vezzo di rubini
16 e lo lanciai sul suo cammin!
17 Perchè mi guardi piena di sgomento, mamma?
18 Lo so che non raccolse la mia collana,
19 vidi che s'infranse sotto le ruote
20 lasciando una macchia vermiglia ne la polvere
21 e nessuno comprese qual fosse il mio dono e per chi!
22 Ma il giovane Principe passò avanti la nostra porta
23 ed io gettai sui suoi passi il gioiello che portavo sul seno!

Three poems of Rabindranath Tagore

No. 1, Mamma, the young prince

1   Mamma, the young Prince must pass before our door.
2   How can you want me to work this morning?
3   Teach me how I should arrange my hair.
4   Tell me what dress I should put on.
5   Why do you look at me dismayed, mamma?
6   I well know that the Prince will not raise his eyes to my window.
7   I know that he will disappear from my sight in a flash of lightning
8   and that only the throb of the flute
9   will reach sobbing from a distance up to me!
10   But the young Prince must pass before our door,
11   and I want to dress myself for a moment in the most beautiful
       clothes!
12   Mamma, the young Prince passed before our door,
13   and the morning sun sparkled on his coach!
14   I took away the veil from my face,
15   I tore off from my neck the ruby necklace
16   and I threw it on his way!
17   Why do you look at me full of dismay, mamma?
18   I know that he did not pick up my necklace,
19   I saw that it was crushed under the wheels
20   leaving a brilliant red mark in the dust
21   and no one understood what my gift was and for whom!
22   But the young Prince passed before our door
23   and I threw upon his footsteps the jewels that I was wearing over my
       heart!

Mamma, il giovane Principe (Mamma, the young prince) is a charming, bittersweet narrative poem; and Alfano's setting of it is a simple musical enhancement of the story. The form of the song and the musical effects follow the action of the narrative. The two-measure piano introduction sets up a driving, syncopated rhythm on a repeated E, which points up the nervous anticipation of the waiting girl. The tempo is marked *mosso ma flessibile* (moving but flexible), and when the voice enters the direction in the accompaniment reads *seguire sempre il canto* (always following the song—voice). This instruction is extremely important, since there is considerable ebb and flow in the vocal line as the story progresses, and the accompaniment must not work against it. Also, there are a number of *staccati* and sharp accents at various points in the accompaniment while the voice is directed to be *espressivo e sempre legato* (expressive and always legato). The melodic line of the opening phrase of the poem reappears each time the word *principe* (prince) appears—once in a transposed variation and twice in exact repetition. It gives a sense of cohesion to the otherwise through-composed song.

There is a great deal of *rubato* throughout the song, and the composer uses a variety of musical terms to direct it—*indugiando* (holding back), *riprendendo* (retaking), *esitando* (hesitating). Each time there is a logic related to the telling of the story. When the protagonist questions her mother, such as in measure 18, *Perchè mi guardi sgomenta, mamma?* (Why do you look at me dismayed, Mamma?), the singer should attempt to describe the girl's discomfort with an appropriate vocal color. In measure 20 the composer writes *insensibilmente meno* (less insensible), another indication of his desire for subtle shifts of expression from phrase to phrase. A little tone-painting appears in measure 27, when the piano *tremolo* appears beneath the text *solo il palpitar del flauto giungerà singhiozzante di lontano* (only the throb of the flute will reach sobbing from a distance).

Although an *ostinato* of dotted sixteenth and 32d notes first appears in the accompaniment at measure 20, it is not until the *A tempo,* measure 37, that the composer states *come un trotto lontano* (like a distant trot) and makes its significance clear. The bass notes must be played *un po' pesante* (a little heavy), and there should be a gradual increase and decrease in dynamics. The prince literally comes and goes in the course of this six-measure piano interlude. Colorful arpeggiations in measures 46 and 47 comment on the splendor of the sight, and the series of ascending octaves in measure 49 indicates the reckless, rising excitement of the observer. The climax of the song comes with the *stentando* (labored) throwing of the necklace (measure 53) followed by a *precipitando* (headlong rushing) of descending octaves. The question *Perchè mi guardi piena di sgomento, mamma?* (Why do you look at me full of dismay, mamma?) should be sung *come spaventata* (as if frightened).

A degree of calm returns with the retaking of the initial tempo in measure 59, but it soon builds to the phrase *vidi che s'infranse sotto le ruote* (I saw that it was crushed under the wheels). Appropriate *tremolos,* marked *freddo* (cold), appear in the piano part at measure 63, as the voice, *come un brivido* (like a shiver), comments on the brilliant red necklace in the dust.

After an expressive return to the first theme, a series of breathless recitatives builds to a final outburst of emotion in measures 76–77. The sweeping energy must be maintained to the final *deciso* (decisive) chords. There are innumerable subtle accents and articulations in both the piano and the vocal parts of this grand song. The composer is generous with expression markings, indications of tempo change, and breath marks, all of which have the greatest impact when the subtleties of the story have been mastered and the performers understand exactly what the composer has done to bring the words to life.

No. 2, Egli mormorò: "Amor mio, alza i tuoi occhi"

(*Rabindranath Tagore*)

1 Egli mormorò: "Amor mio alza i tuoi occhi"
2 Lo rimproverai aspramente dicendo: "Parti!"
3 Ma egli non si mosse.
4 Stette davanti a me tenendomi per le mani.
5 Dissi: "Lasciami"
6 Ma egli non se ne andò.
7 Accostò il suo viso al mio orecchio
8 Le sue labbra sfiorarono il mio volto
9 Tremai e dissi: "Troppo ardisci"
10 Ma egli non si commosse . . .
11 Prese la ghirlanda ch'era al mio collo e mi lasciò.
12 Ora piango e domando al mio cor:
13 "Perchè non torna?"

No. 2, He murmured: "My love, raise your eyes"

1 He murmured: "My love, raise your eyes."
2 I reproached him sharply saying: "Leave!"
3 But he did not move.
4 He stood in front of me holding me by the hands.
5 I said: "Leave me"
6 But he did not go away.
7 He brought his face close to my ear.
8 His lips nearly touched my face.
9 I trembled and said: "You dare too much."
10 But he was not affected . . .
11 He took the garland that was around my neck and he left me.
12 Now I cry and ask my heart:
13 "Why does he not return?"

The first five notes of the vocal line in measure 1 outline the primary musical motive for *Egli mormorò: "Amor mio, alza i tuoi occhi"* (He murmured: "My love, raise your eyes"). Much emotion is compacted in this short, intense song, and the motive compacts it further. The poem involves dialogue, but everything is spoken with the voice of the narrator. Therefore, whatever contrasts are required must be achieved through changes in articulation, tempo, or dynamics rather than vocal color. The composer's specific accents are important, and his indications for breath are crucial. The latter can serve as expressive devices, as in measures 4–5—*Ma egli' non si mosse*

(But he' did not move); or to separate the narration from the direct quotation, as in the opening line, *Egli mormorò:' "Amor mio"* (He said:' "My love"). Alfano is consistent in his breath marks except in the second phrase, where the breath indication after *dicendo* (saying) is missing. (The slur indicated between these words does not solve the mystery since the composer uses both slur and breath indications later—see *Dissi: "Lasciami"* [I said: "Leave me"].) Since the second phrase is long, includes a *rubato,* and has a *fermata* on the last syllable, a breath could be taken after *dicendo* (saying). Directly beneath this line in the accompaniment is an unusual term, *strappato* (torn, ripped).

In measure 6 the piano part has the distinctive motive that opened the song, and the voice enters on the last half of it. It occurs again, with slight variation, in measure 11, and rather broadly (transposed) in measures 17 and 18. The motive comes to full flower in the final phrase of the song *"Perchè non torna?"* ("Why does he not return?"), and it is echoed immediately in the accompaniment *appassionato e angoscioso* (impassioned and anguished).

There are a number of colorful effects in the accompaniment throughout the song: the descending chords after *"Lasciami"* ("Leave me"), the *glissando*-like arpeggio before *Tremai* (I trembled), and the *tremolo* beneath *Ora piango* (Now I cry). All the tempo changes are clearly indicated, and there are many expression markings. The final four measures of the song, which return to the original tempo, contain the directions *cupo* (dark) and *triste e lontano* (sad and distant).

No. 3, Parlami amor mio

(*Rabindranath Tagore*)

1   Parlami amor mio, dimmi a parole quello che cantasti.
2   La notte è buia . . . Le stelle si smarriscono ne le nubi . . .
3   Il vento soffia tra le fronde.
4   Scioglierò i miei capelli . . .
5   Il mio mantello azzurro mi circonderà come la notte . . .
6   Stringerò la tua testa sul mio seno
7   e ne la dolce solitudine sospirerò sul tuo cuore!
8   Socchiuderò i miei occhi e ascolterò.
9   Quando le tue parole cesseranno
10 Staremo fermi e in silenzio . . .
11 La notte impallidirà.
12 Spunterà l'aurora . . .
13 Ci guarderemo negli occhi
14 e andremo pel nostro diverso cammin
15 Parlami amor mio . . .
16 dimmi a parole quello che cantasti . . .

No. 3, Speak to me, my love

1   Speak to me, my love, tell me in words that which you sang.
2   The night is dark . . . the stars become lost in the clouds . . .
3   the wind blows among the leafy branches.
4   I will loosen my hair . . .
5   My blue cloak will encircle me like the night . . .
6   I will press your head against my breast
7   and in the sweet solitude I will sigh on your heart!
8   I will half close my eyes and I will listen.
9   When your words will cease
10 We will remain still and in silence . . .
11 the night will grow pale.
12 The dawn will appear . . .
13 We will look each other in the eyes
14 and we will go our different ways
15 Speak to me, my love . . .
16 tell me in words that which you sang . . .

The impassioned excitement generated in *Mamma, il giovanne Principe* and the wrenching anxiety expressed in *Egli mormorò . . .* are relieved somewhat in *Parlami, amor mio* (Speak to me, my love), the third and final song of the set. The lovers have apparently consumated their passion, and, even though they must part at dawn, there is a sweet satisfaction expressed in Alfano's setting of the poetry. The 6/8 meter lends a gentleness to the opening; the introduction consists of four relatively consonant chords, which then break into a slightly rocking rhythm beneath the opening vocal line. The tempo is marked *lento e con dolce languore* (slow and with a sweet languor), and the dynamic level is *pp* and *dolcissimo*. In fact, the dynamic range of the entire song moves above *piano* only once, at the words *mi circonderà* (will encircle me) in measure 15, which is marked *poco f.* The introduction also carries the direction *come di lontano* (as if in the distance).

The opening vocal statement, carrying the words of the title, is melodically distinctive and creates a form of motive that appears later. Most of the song is in speech rhythms and is recitative-like in character. The melodic range is narrow, in keeping with the resigned, quiet mood of both the song and the text. The atmosphere is dark but not gloomy. Wonderful color effects are built into the piano part and are enhanced by directions such as *delicatamente* (delicately) in measure 7 and *cupo* (dark, covered) in measures 9–10, where the text speaks of stars covered by clouds. In the phrase that follows, *Il vento soffia tra le fronde* (the wind blows among the branches), the piano has four trilled notes marked *perdendosi* (dying away), which lead to very slow, quiet chords in measure 11.

As the poem moves away from a physical description of the scene and toward the expression of human emotion, the accompaniment rises in pitch and the phrases become longer, sometimes linking to form significantly stretched-out units. The composer gives many directions for this, such as *animando ancora—ma subito cedendo* (still more animated, but suddenly giving way). In short, a great deal of *rubato* is both necessary and called for.

The emotional climax of the poem is remarkably beautiful because of its understatement. First, at the phrase *e ne la dolce solitudine sospirerò sul tuo cuore* (and in the sweet solitude I will sigh on your heart) the composer thins the texture of the accompaniment and calls for *un filo di voce* (a thread of voice). Then, widely spaced ascending chords build from measure 21, marked *un po' meno del tempo initiale* (a little less than the initial tempo), to a hollow resolution on the first beat of measure 22. Over a very thin progression of octaves, the voice barely whispers the phrase *Socchiuderò i miei occhi e ascolterò* (I will half close my eyes and I will listen). Beneath the dying away of *ascolterò* the piano echoes the exact notes of that melody *ppppp profondamente expressivo penetrante* (as quiet as possible with profoundly penetrating expressiveness). Once again, Alfano calls for the utmost synthesis of voice and piano to create a moment of unearthly beauty. The piano arpeggio that follows brings the song back to the initial tempo, and the melody of the opening measures returns in a slightly varied rhythmic configuration. The accompaniment is more active and widely spaced.

After the word *silenzio* (silence) the activity in the piano is reduced again. While no *fermata* is indicated in the score, there should be a *tenuto* stretch to the word *silenzio* and a pause before the next chord is struck. The touching moment when the lovers gaze into each other's eyes carries quiet cascading arpeggiations, and the resignation of the final parting is set with repeated unison pitches over a subdued, but sustained, augmented chord.

The final measures of the song repeat the opening statement with an exact recapitulation of the initial musical material, creating a loose ABA structure. The quality here should be *come sognando* (dreamlike), and the music should be *calando insino all fine* (dropping away to the end), which is marked *massimo p* (utmost quiet).

This song "sings itself"; it is so carefully constructed and so expressive of the poem that little comment need be made once the structure of the song has been examined. The composer has indicated breath marks, and every possible descriptive word for color, articulation, and pedaling has been given. The song is of the finest quality and provides a fitting conclusion to this superb and relatively little known set of *liriche*.

Tre poemi di Rabindranath Tagore: G. Ricordi, 1919; Repr. 1950.
    1. *Mamma, il giovane Principe*   128167
    2. *Egli mormorò: "Amor mio, alza i tuoi occhi"*   128168
    3. *Parlami amor mio*   128028

Tre liriche (1928)

No. 1, Perchè, allo spuntar del giorno

(*Rabindranath Tagore*)

1 Perchè allo spuntar del giorno
2 venne il giovine errabondo alla mia porta?
3 Ogni volta che entro e esco gli passo daccanto
4 e i miei occhi lo fissano in volto . . .
5 Non so se devo parlargli o tacere . . .
6 Oh! Perchè venne alla mia porta?
7 Le notti nuvolose di luglio sono oscure . .
8 Il cielo d'autunno è soavemente azzurro
9 I giorni primaverili son turbati dai venti del sud . . .
10 Egli canta le sue canzoni
11 Con nuove melodie ogni volta.
12 Io lascio di lavorare
13 e i miei occhi s'empiono di larcrime.
14 Oh! Perchè venne alla mia porta? Perchè?

Three lyrics

No. 1, Why, at daybreak

1 Why at daybreak
2 did the wandering youth come to my door?
3 Every time I come in or go out I pass close to him
4 and my eyes stare into his face . . .
5 I don't know whether I should speak to him or keep silent . . .
6 Oh! Why did he come to my door?
7 The cloudy nights of July are dark . . .
8 The autumn sky is softly blue
9 the days of springtime are agitated by the south winds . . .
10 He sings his songs
11 with new melodies each time.
12 I stop working
13 and my eyes fill up with tears.
14 Oh! Why did he come to my door? Why?

Tre liriche (1928), setting poems by Rabindranath Tagore, share the element of frustrated love. In each, a mysterious figure appears bringing a melancholy presence that forever haunts the protagonist. Technically, the songs are quite accessible for both singer and pianist, but they require considerable interpretive skill and emotional maturity. Although all three are basically sad songs, they are varied enough to be performed as a set.

Perchè allo spuntar del giorno (Why, at daybreak) has a very Impressionistic quality. Each note of the initial piano figuration is held down after being struck and is additionally blurred through the use of the damper pedal. (The composer also requires the use of the soft pedal.) The piano part carries most of the musical interest in the song. The initial figuration is repeated under colorful slow-moving chords when the voice enters in measure 2. The figuration appears again later in the composition.

The vocal line is recitative-like during most of the song, following the speech rhythms of the poetry. The extremely slow tempo ($\flat$ = 52, counted eight to the measure) allows ample time for clean word articulation and syllable stress, but the composer additionally indicates his preferred accents with *tenuto* markings. The vocal entrance is marked *misterioso e dolente* (mysterious and sad) and *sempre sotto voce* (always half voice). The dynamic level remains extremely quiet until the anguished climax of the song in measures 10–11, *Oh! Perchè venne alla mia porta?* (Oh! Why did he come to my door?), which is prepared by a striking motive in the piano part in measure 9. Initiated with the interval of a fourth, it relates to the motive that opened the composition, but it is more forceful. When it comes to full flower, in octaves under the vocal line, the Puccini influence on Alfano is very much in evidence. Measure 12 repeats the motive from measure 1 in a lower register, effectively bringing down the emotion of the climax and preparing for the next section of the poem.

At the phrase *Egli canta le sue canzoni* (He sings his songs), the composer writes *come imitando un canto popolare* (as if imitating a popular song) and *con abbandono* (with abandon). Some theatrical effects are called for in measure 19: after *Io lascio di lavorare* (I stop working), where the rest after *lascio* is crucial, there is an expressive "sigh" in the piano part. When the voice enters at the end of the measure it is *con voce di pianto* (with weeping voice).

The final climax of the song is preceded by the same motive used earlier, but the phrase itself reaches one pitch higher. The tempo must broaden here, and there should be a slight hesitation before the last two measures of the composition. The last word *Perchè* (Why) should almost be whispered; the *tremolo* beneath it *molto fuso ed estinquendosi* (very blurred and dying away). The last piano note should not be struck until the voice has released its note and the *tremolo* has finished, rather like a period punctuating a sentence.

No. 2, Finisci l'ultimo canto

(*Rabindranath Tagore*)

1 Finisci l'ultimo canto e dividiamoci . . .
2 Dimentica questa notte or che la notte non è più!
3 Che provai a stringere fra le mie braccia?
4 I sogni non possono imprigionarsi!
5 Le mie avide mani stringono al cuore il vuoto
6 ed il mio petto ne resta ferito.
7 Finisci l'ultimo canto e dividiamoci!

No. 2, Finish your final song

1 Finish your final song and let us part . . .
2 Forget this night now that the night is over!
3 What did I prove by hugging within my arms?
4 Dreams can not imprison themselves!
5 My greedy hands press emptiness to my heart
6 and my heart remains wounded from it.
7 Finish your final song and let us part!

Finisci l'ultimo canto (Finish your final song), a poem of bitter pain and disappointment, is given a simple setting of feverish intensity. As in the opening of Puccini's *Tosca*, the piano sets the mood for the song with a startling chord progression in a slow tempo ($\quarternote = 42$), marked *lento e grave*. A folk-like melody for the voice sets the first phrase of poetry. The supporting chords are uncluttered, culminating in a series of dissonance-resolutions beneath the climactic held note on *dividiamoci* (let us part). The pianist should give a slight accent to the first and third beats in this passage while still observing the *decrescendo* to *pp*. The singer should breathe where indicated after *canto* (song) in order to control the dynamics of this phrase. While mildly dissonant chords continue in the accompaniment, the voice breaks into a more recitative-like pattern on pitches paralleling the top voice in the chord progression. A feverish outburst occurs in measure 12. The chord that initiates this measure should be prepared by a slight *crescendo* of accented bass notes in the measure immediately preceding. The vocal line here, *Che provai a stringere fra le mie braccia?* (What did I prove by hugging within my arms?) is in free speech rhythm and need not be metronomic, providing the pianist and the singer are together at the word *braccia*. The tempo can be reestablished in measure 14.

Beginning with the text *Le mie avide mani* (My greedy hands), marked *doloroso* (sadly), a slow *crescendo* builds in the ascending chord progression of the piano part to join with the voice in achieving the greatest intensity of the song, *stringono al cuore il vuoto* (press emptiness to my heart). This climax should be very broad; there is an important stress mark on the final syllable of *vuoto* (emptiness) and a *fermata* on the bass chord beneath it. A pause should occur with the breath taken immediately after *vuoto,* and *ed* (and) should be held while the *sforzando* octave A♮ is struck in the bass. Thereafter, the tempo can be retaken.

A long, consonant piano interlude precedes the repetition of the poem's opening line, which is set almost identically to its first appearance. The descending octaves in the accompaniment under *dividiamoci* give a heightened finality to the phrase, and its bitterness is carried over even into the quiet but dissonant chords that close the composition.

No. 3, Giorno per giorno

(*Rabindranath Tagore*)

 1   Giorno per giorno egli viene,
 2   egli viene, e poi sen va!
 3   Tieni amica, dagli un fiore,
 4   Questo fior che ho tra i capelli!
 5   Se ti domanda chi glielo dona,
 6   Oh! No! non dirgli, no, non dirgli il nome mio, ti prego,
 7   perchè egli non fa che venir . . .
 8   che venire e andarsene!
 9   Si siede in terra sotto l'albero,
10   fagli un sedil di foglie e fiori!
11   I suoi occhi son tristi
12   e portan la malinconia nel cor.
13   Ei non rivela il suo pensiero,
14   vien soltanto, e poi sen va.

No. 3, Day by day

1   Day by day he comes,
2   he comes, and then goes away!
3   Here friend, give him a flower.
4   This flower that I have in my hair!
5   If he asks you who gives it to him
6   Oh! No! do not tell him, no, do not tell him my name, I beg you,
7   because all he does is come . . .
8   he comes and then goes away!
9   He sits on the ground under the tree,

10   make him a seat of leaves and flowers!
11   His eyes are sad
12   and they bring melancholy in my heart.
13   He does not disclose his thoughts,
14   he only comes and then goes away.

Taking a cue from the folk-like opening phrase of *Finisci l'ultimo canto* (Finish your final song), the entire vocal melody of the third poem, *Giorno per giorno* (Day by day), could have been drawn directly from the repertory of a shepherd. The song is a clear-cut ABA form with classical phrase structure within the sections. (The melodic material of part B is drawn from part A.) The accompaniment, however, makes full use of the dissonant harmonic vocabulary of the twentieth century and sometimes points up a particular aspect of the text within the seemingly conventional setting.

The composer's phrasing indications show an easy ebb and flow throughout the song. They are clearly marked in the score—*ritardando* (slowing down), *riprendendo il tempo* (retaking the tempo). The more expressive phrases are given extra directions, such as *poco stentando* (a little stretched out) at measures 52–55 on *I suoi occhi son tristi* (His eyes are sad), or they have an interesting change of harmony, such as the enharmonic treatment in measures 60–63 on *Ei non rivela il suo pensiero* (He does not disclose his thoughts).

When part A returns the accompaniment pattern is twice as fast and very soft, requiring both damper and soft pedals. In the final verse the line *Oh! No! Non dirgli, no, non dirgli il nome mio, ti prego* (Oh! No! do not tell him, no, do not tell him my name, I beg you) should be sung very expressively with a definite breath before *ti prego*. A very broad *ritardando* is required for the close of the song, and the final notes of the accompaniment should trail away to nothing.

Tre liriche (Rabindranath Tagore): Universal Edition, 1929; Repr. Carisch, 1955.   19538 (Set)
   1. *Perchè allo spuntar del giorno*
   2. *Finisci l'ultimo canto*
   3. *Giorno per giorno*

Nuove liriche Tagoriane

No. 1, Perchè siedi là

(*Rabindranath Tagore*)

1 Perchè siedi là e tintinni i tuoi braccialetti,
2 così per gioco?
3 Riempi la conca . . .
4 È tempo che ritorni a casa.
5 Perchè muovi l'acqua con le mani ed ogni tanto . . .
6 ogni tanto guardi nella via se qualcuno giunge,
7 così per gioco?
8 Riempi la conca e vieni a casa.
9 Le ore passano . . .
10 L'acqua oscura scorre,
11 le onde ridono e sussurrano tra loro
12 così per gioco.
13 Le nubi vaganti si son raccolte dietro la collina
14 e indugiano, ti guardano in viso
15 e sorridono per gioco.
16 Riempi la conca e vieni a casa.

New Tagorian lyrics

No. 1, Why do you sit there

1 Why do you sit there and jingle your bracelets,
2 in this manner in jest?
3 Fill the basin . . .
4 It is time that you return home.
5 Why do you move the water with your hands and every so often . . .
6 every so often you look toward the road as if someone is arriving
7 in this manner in jest?
8 Fill the basin and come home.
9 The hours pass . . .
10 The dark water flows,
11 the waves laugh and murmur among themselves
12 thus in jest.
13 The drifting clouds have gathered behind the hill
14 and they loiter, they look you in the face
15 and they laugh in jest.
16 Fill the basin and come home.

Indicative of his continued attraction to the poetry of Rabindranath Tagore, Alfano's 1934 (published 1936) settings of *Nuove liriche Tagoriane* (New Tagorian lyrics) form an excellent program group. There are good contrasts in tempo, mood, and keyboard style from song to song, and the finale of the third song is an exciting crowd pleaser. All three poems are from the Tagore collection *Il giardinere* (The Gardener).

Perchè siedi là (Why do you sit there) is a gentle song. The subject of the poem has gone to a fountain to fill a basin and lingers there with a vague sense of anticipation. The poet questions the waiting. A rhythmic *ostinato* of alternating eighth notes creates a constant feeling of motion throughout the song, probably depicting the gently flowing water. *Tenuto* markings and pedal indications on the chord changes mark the subtly shifting harmonic structure that underscores the *ostinato*. These markings must be observed carefully, and the *ostinato* itself should be played *dolce, discreto* (sweetly, discretely). The tempo should not be any slower than the recommended ♩ = 116, or too much attention will be drawn to it. The vocal line must float easily above the accompaniment, *dolce e legato*. It has a narrow range, few skips, and no major climaxes. Occasionally the composer uses the direction *esitante* or *esitando* (hesitantly) to achieve word emphasis.

As the song progresses a subtle melodic line emerges from the slow-moving supporting chord progression in the piano part. When the composer writes shorter note values the lines emerge from the texture with no need for additional emphasis. Interludes, such as measures 32–36 and 48–57 give the pianist an opportunity for soloistic playing. In the second interlude there is an important *ritardando* in measures 54–57, with strong accents on the E♮–G♮ intervals in the treble clef. In measures 58–59 a *reprendendo* (retaking) of the tempo leads to the return of part A. (The song may be categorized as an ABA form even though the final section contains considerable variation.) The final section demands careful control of the *tempi*. There is a long, gradual *ritardando* in measures 65–71, a very brief *a tempo* in measure 72, and a second *ritardando* in measures 72–82. The pianist bears the prime responsibility for controlling the *tempi;* and the singer must hear the accompaniment well enough to sense where the accented syllables should fall if the two parts are to fuse.

Most of the directions and markings are quite clear. In measure 70 the composer wants the voice to enter *come un soffio* (like a whisper). Breath indications are good, often adding expressive effect, such as those in measure 47 after *perchè* (why) and measure 66 after *indugiano* (loiter). The breath indication in measure 43 before *così* (thus) is crucial if the singer is to achieve the required *pianissimo* on *gioco* (jest); and a good breath will be needed before the final phrase of the song so that the tone floats away, literally to nothing.

No. 2, Non nascondere il secreto

(*Rabindranath Tagore*)

1   Non nasconder il secreto del tuo cuore.
2   Amico mio . . .
3   Dillo a me, a me soltanto in confidenza.
4   Tu che sorridi sí soavemente,
5   dimmelo con dolcezza.
6   Il mio cuore ascolterà,
7   le mie orecchie non udiranno.
8   La notte è profonda.
9   La casa è silenziosa.
10 I nidi degli uccelli tacciono nel sonno.
11 Rivelami fra lacrime d'incertezza,
12 tra sorrisi trementi
13 fra la pena d'una dolce menzogna
14 il secreto del tuo cuore.
15 Non nasconder il secreto del tuo cuore,
16 amico mio.

No. 2, Do not hide the secret

1   Do not hide the secret of your heart.
2   My friend . . .
3   Tell it to me, to me alone in confidence.
4   You who smile so sweetly,
5   tell me it with gentleness.
6   My heart will listen.
7   my ears will not hear.
8   The night is deep.
9   The house is silent.
10 The nests of the birds are hushed in sleep.
11 Reveal to me through tears of uncertainty,
12 through quivering smiles,
13 through the pain of a sweet falsehood,
14 the secret of your heart.
15 Do not hide the secret of your heart,
16 my friend.

The phrasing of *Non nascondere il secreto* (Do not hide the secret), an expressive and very tender, but dramatic, song, is carefully indicated by the composer. The time signatures change freely with the poetic meter, and the eighth notes are grouped into flowing, irregular lines. The long marks over some of the notes indicate subtle quantitative accents that divide the melody into segments within the longer phrases. The single melodic line of the accompaniment moves in counterpoint with the vocal line, yet each melody has its own distinct phrasing. This phrasing does not coincide until the *ritard* at measure 10 leading to the cadence on the downbeat of measure 11.

The entire first section must be sung very quietly. The eighth notes should be kept very exact within the flow of the melody, and at no time should either performer have to wait for the other. The *mezzo forte* at the words *Tu che sorridi* (You who smile) should be little more than a *mezzo piano* to allow a true *mezzo forte* at the beginning of the middle section of the song. Here, the tempo is slightly faster. The strong chordal support added to the continuing countermelody builds dynamic intensity as the vocal line rises, falls, and rises again through a broad ritard to the forceful *forte* climax of *tra sorrisi tremanti* (through quivering smiles).

The immediate return to *piano* and the tempo of the middle section— with its sparse two-voice accompaniment, strengthened with octave doubling—leads through a ritard and a cadence back to Tempo I°. The return of the two contrapuntal melodies must be performed very softly, *come un'eco* (like an echo), while gradually slowing down and diminishing to the final two measures which are *a tempo*. It is essential that the last vocal note be held through to the fourth eighth note of the last measure. The final chord must be played *pianissimo*. The singer must not move and the pianist must not release the pedal until the sound has died away.

No. 3, Corro come il cervo muschiato

(*Rabindranath Tagore*)

 1 Corro come il cervo muschiato
 2 che ebbro del suo profumo
 3 si slancia nell'ombra del bosco.
 4 È una notte di maggio,
 5 e la brezza vien dal sud!
 6 Smarrisco la via e cammino, cammino . . .
 7 Cerco quel che non trovo,
 8 trovo quel che non cerco.
 9 Corro! Corro! Corro! Corro!
10 Dal mio cuore esce e palpita
11 l'immagin del tuo desiderio
12 La visione sfolgorante corre, corre veloce

13 Provo a ghermirla fra le mie braccia,
14 ma essa mi sfugge, e smarrisco la via . . .
15 Cerco quel che non trovo,
16 trovo quel che non cerco.

No. 3, I run like the musk stag

1   I run like the musk stag
2   who intoxicated with his perfume
3   hurls himself into the darkness of the woods.
4   It is a night in May,
5   and the breeze comes from the south!
6   I lose the way and I walk and walk . . .
7   I seek that which I don't find,
8   I find that which I don't seek.
9   I run! I run! I run! I run!
10 From my heart goes out and palpitates
11 the image of your desire.
12 The blazing vision runs, runs quickly,
13 I try to clutch it within my arms,
14 but it escapes me and I lose my way . . .
15 I seek that which I don't find,
16 I find that which I don't seek.

Corro come il cervo muschiato (I run like the musk stag) requires a virtuoso pianist and a singer with a secure technique. There is constant motion in the piano part, either trill or tremolo; and the triple meter must be felt as one beat per measure. The vocal line, which rides above the frenzied accompaniment, should be equally rhythmic but not *marcato*. The composer's breath indications are crucial to the correct subdivisions of the long phrases, which must literally sweep through the song to the very end. The only interruption is in measures 76–77, on the words *e smarrisco la via* (and I lose my way). Whenever the singer has the word *Corro* (I run), the initial consonant should be very crisp and the double *r* really rolled. The final *accelerando* can be almost as fast as the viruosity of the performers will allow. The *appoggiatura* on the final trill should begin on the beat, not before it.

Nuove liriche Tagoriane: G. Ricordi, 1936; Repr. 1953.
    1. *Perchè siedi là*   123618
    2. *Non nascondere il secreto del tuo cuore*   123619
    3. *Corro come il cervo muschiato*   123620

Tre liriche (1936)

No. 1, Felicità

(*Francesco Pastonchi*)

1 Nel vento della sera odorano i rosai:
2 Godi l'ora che mai più non ritornerà!
3 Nel vento della sera baciami tra le rose.
4 Fatta di tenui cose è la felicità!

Three Lyrics

No. 1, Happiness

1 In the evening wind the rose bushes give scent:
2 Enjoy the hour that will never return!
3 In the evening wind kiss me among the roses.
4 Happiness is made of tenuous things!

Felicità (Happiness), written in 1914, was reprinted and published as No. 1 of *Tre liriche* in 1936. The poem has an Impressionistic airiness about it, and the musical setting has a clear, exposed texture. The piano begins with a long descending scale-based melodic theme supported by a few arpeggiated chords. It may or may not describe the evening wind of the first line, but it does create an appropriately wistful mood. Since this thematic material is the most important in the song, it should be played very expressively and the composer's accent marks should be noted carefully. The tempo marking is qualified with the adjective *elastico* (elastic). The vocal entrance is much less melodic, more or less a verbal description of what the piano has just suggested. Simple chords accompany it.

On the second poetic phrase, the vocal line rides above the original piano theme, transposed, and becomes part of the overall texture. This theme continues throughout the song in shifting variations and transpositions while the vocal line, speaking poetically of the tenuousness of happiness, weaves around it. It finally finds its way back to the tonic key in the last measure, preceded by two measures of shadowy trill. The final vocal utterance is cleverly set on the fifth of the chord, further enhancing the unfinished quality of the poem.

There are a few special effects for the singer: The phrase *baciami tra le rose* (kiss me among the roses) is to be sung *sospirato* (sighing), and *la felicità* (happiness) is to be *mormorato* (murmured). Because so much attention is focused on the piano in this composition, the balance between the singer and the piano must be carefully coordinated.

No. 3, Antica ninna-nanna partenopea

(*Autore ignoto*)

1   ... e nonna nonna nonna nunnarella
2   'O lupo s'ha magnata'a pecurella!
3   ... e pecurella mia comme faciste
4   quanne mmocc'a lu lupo te vediste?
5   ... e pecurella mia comme farraie
6   quanne mmocc'a lu lupo te vedarraie?

No. 3, An old Parthenopean lullaby

(*Author unknown*)

1   ... and lullaby lullaby, little one
2   the wolf has eaten the little lamb!
3   ... and my little lamb what did you do
4   when you found yourself in the mouth of the wolf?
5   ... and my little lamb what will you do
6   when you find yourself in the mouth of the wolf?

Antica ninna-nanna partenopea (An old Parthenopean lullaby) is written in old Neapolitan dialect (Parthenope is one of the ancient names for modern-day Naples). The song is strophic; the melodic line is identical for each two-line verse but the accompaniment changes, becoming more active rhythmically and slightly more dissonant as the song progresses. The augmented second in the melodic line gives a modal feeling to the work, and the dissonant accompaniment seems particularly appropriate given the almost threatening quality of the poem. As with most simple songs, the phrasing is most important. The tempo must be fast enough for the singer to carry through the phrase lines as marked, without a breath. The performers should also be aware that the phrasing of singer and pianist do not always coincide. In verse two, for example, the singer's phrase is 4 + 5 measures, while the harmonic movement in the piano is really 6 + 4. There should be no *ritardando* in the song until the end, and the last notes in the vocal line should sound *lontano* (distant).

Tre liriche: G. Ricordi, 1936; Repr. 1953.
    1. *Felicità* (1914)   123621
    3. *Antica ninna-nanna partenopea* (1935)   123623

Tre nuovi poemi

No. 2, Melodia

(*Cesare Meano*)

1   Cammineremo nel bosco io e te!
2   Andremo a vedere la luna io e te!
3   La luna nella gabbia dei rami!
4   Ma c'è una cosa che non so dir, ahimè . . .
5   Nella luna che splende sul fiume. Ahimè!
6   Sul fiume in mezzo al bosco . . .
7   Come nel fischio del treno . . . Laggiù . . .
8   Che corre alla città ove la luna . . . Laggiù . . .
9   Si smarrisce tra le lampade!

Three new poems

No. 2, Melody

1   We will walk in the woods you and I!
2   We will go to see the moon you and I!
3   The moon in the cage of the branches!
4   But there is something that I don't know how to say, alas . . .
5   In the moon that shines on the river. Alas!
6   On the river in the middle of the woods . . .
7   As in the whistle of the train . . . Down there . . .
8   That runs to the city where the moon . . . Down there . . .
9   Loses its way among the lamps!

Although it seems a strange title for the subject of the poem, *Melodia* (Melody) *is* the subject of this semistrophic song. Each of the three verses of the poem (which seem to concern an awkward or reluctant lover) is set with the same folk-like, lyrical melody. The first and third verses are virtually identical melodically and harmonically, except for alterations in the final phrase that are necessary to create the climax of the song. The second verse is recognizably similar except for the opening minor tonality and modulations, which tend to set off the emotions of the narrator from the descriptions of the surroundings.

The tempo indication for the song is *largo,* but it should have a casual walking feeling with ample elasticity to produce the frequent *rubando* effects the composer has carefully marked. The chromatic chord movement and gentle 6/8 pattern in the piano introduction continue as accompaniment after the entrance of the voice. It should be played very *legato,* and the dynamics should rise and fall to delineate the phrase. There are *tenuto* markings on most of the chord changes, enhancing the forward movement of the harmony.

There are an unusual number of *fermate* in this song, but each one permits a savoring of the beautiful harmony; the performers should not ignore or rush any of them.

The accompaniment for the third verse, relating to the interlude that precedes it, is somewhat more active than it was in the first verse, but the harmony is the same. After the broad climax at *Si smarrisce tra le lampade* (Loses its way among the lamps), the tempo of the piano postlude should pick up noticeably, *quasi presto* (somewhat fast), and the dynamic level should remain loud through the final chord. It is as though the narrator–lover has had a sudden burst of confidence.

The song is gentle and quite accessible for less-advanced singers.

No. 3, Preghiera alla Madonna

(*Luigi Orsini*)

1 Madonna, io ti conobbi
2 quando mia madre congiunse la prima volta
3 le mie mani nella preghiera;
4 E ti vidi nel volto di lei
5 quando, raccolta sulla mia infanzia serena,
6 celava in un mite sorriso
7 la sua intima pena
8 E poi crebbi alla vita
9 e invidiai la lòdola che spazia e canta
10 e riempie del suo canto il Cielo.
11 Ti chiesi allora una grazia:
12 sciogliere un inno che avesse volo
13 e tintinno per te, Maria!
14 La grazia non venne mai.
15 Passaron gli anni.
16 E mia madre anche passò.
17 Ma tu con la tua tenerezza
18 rimanesti consolatrice alla mia dura fatica.

19 O palpito di gemme nella notte,
20 o chiarità dorata . . . la tua luce mi fu dolcezza!
21 Così possa io un giorno trovarti in cima
22 della percorsa via tese le mani ad offerirti in dono
23 fiore di puro Ciel la poesia!
24 E rivedera in te dolce Maria
25 il volto di mia madre.
26 E così sia!

No. 3, Prayer to the Madonna

1   Madonna, I knew you
2   when my mother joined for the first time
3   my hands in prayer;
4   And I saw you in her face
5   when, absorbed with my tranquil childhood,
6   she used to hide with a gentle smile
7   her innermost pain
8   And then I believed in life
9   and I envied the lark that soars and sings
10 and fills the sky with song.
11 I asked of you then one favor:
12 to release a hymn that would have flight
13 and I will ring it out for you, Maria!
14 The favor never came.
15 The years passed.
16 And my mother also passed on.
17 But you with your tenderness
18 remained a comforter in my bitter travail.
19 O jewelled palpitation in the night,
20 O golden splendor . . . your light for me was sweetness!
21 Thus may I one day find you at the summit
22 of the completed journey (with my) hands outstretched to offer to
        you as a gift
23 poetry the flower of the clear sky!
24 And to see again in you, sweet Mary,
25 the face of my mother.
26 And thus it will be!

The conceptual framework of the text of *Preghiera alla Madonna* (Prayer to the Madonna) is interesting and unusual. In contrast to the Marian *laude,* which attracted other Italian *liriche* composers, this poem is a combination of intimate prayer and autobiography addressed to *Maria, Mater Dolorosa* (Mary, mother of sorrows) rather than *Maria, Regina Coeli* (Mary, queen of heaven). It celebrates the intimate connection between Mary, the mother of God, and all mothers. And, for the author at least, the ultimate offering to this exalted being is poetry.

Alfano's setting of the rather long text is through-composed, following the mood changes and imagery of the poetry. Three devices, however, give unity to the song: 1. Although the range of the song is rather wide, most pitch movement within the phrases is stepwise or in small intervals, contributing a prayer-like quality to the setting. 2. Many phrases seem to feature the interval of a minor third, the traditional motive associated with sorrow. 3. A pattern of repeated single pitches (introduced in measure 5) reappears many times throughout the composition.

The song opens with three Tosca-like chords, followed by the first appearance of the repeated unison. The latter is marked *tenuto,* and the composer is consistent with this marking whenever the pattern appears, regardless of how disguised it may be within the texture of the song. (Although we give some examples, the pianist should make his/her own study of the score to discover how motives thus marked help to hold the total work together.) For instance, it appears in measures 23–24, introducing the second poetic phrase, and again at the climax of the phrase as the top voice in the chords at measures 35–36. Almost every phrase within the work requires some *rubato,* and these places are clearly indicated.

A change of accompaniment from the processional-sounding opening occurs in measure 49—again the repeated tones—and the melody is more lyrical. A wonderful effect occurs in measure 71 as the accompaniment pattern releases into an arpeggiated C♯ major chord. The *fermata* immediately preceding it is very important, as is the *pianissimo* dynamic on the chord itself. The arpeggiations beneath *volo* (flight) in measures 75–76 should sound like a *glissando.*

The continuation of the narration in measure 90 is preceded by several repetitions of the note F♮ which continues to sound in longer note values as the phrase moves on. The melody becomes prominent at Tempo I° (measure 98), with the direction *con molto commozione* (with much emotion) and the piano often doubling the line in octaves.

The heart of the song (measures 121–160) is preceded by a piano interlude in which repetitions of the note B♭ are clearly distinguishable and are varied by octave displacement. The broad sweeping vocal phrases of the whole following section, plus the much more active accompaniment, leave no doubt as to the emotional climax of the poem. It is important in this section to keep to the *animato* ($\bullet$ = 112) that opened the song. Alfano marks the breathing indications with his customary care, and several of the phrases are quite long. An additional breath will probably be needed in measure 148, before *ad offerirti* (to offer to you), or in measure 152, after *dono* (gift), but the phrase should feel continuous.

Since the climax of the section is really *la poesia* (poetry) in measures 157–158, the *fortissimo* intensity of the first part of the phrase should not let down very much. The singer, with a deep breath, should spring from the *fortissimo* chord on the first beat of measure 157 and stress the word.

The final section of the song sees the return of the repeated unisons, this time forming a pedal beneath a processional harmony and a recitative-like text. In measures 183–185 the chords that opened the composition appear in exact repetition, as does the pattern of F's, marked *tenuto,* in measures 187–188. A minor third, dissonant to the hollow open chord in the accompaniment, closes the composition.

Tre nuovi poemi: G. Ricordi, 1943.
    2. *Melodia*   125748 Repr. 1953
    3. *Preghiera alla Madonna*   125749 Repr. 1949

È giunto il nostro ultimo autunno

(*Miranda Bona*)

1   È giunto il nostro ultimo autunno!
2   Tieni le mie mani nell'ultima stretta terrena
3   e dimmi dove andrai.
4   Non guardarmi con occhi tristi . . .
5   Dopo l'estate della mia vita
6   ci ritroveremo nell'eterna Primavera!
7   Fuggi l'inverno quando io non ci sarò più
8   per fondere il ghiaccio intorno al tuo cuore . . .
9   Conserva il tuo cuore fra le rose profumate . . .
10   e cingilo con una rete di spine,
11   chè nessuno lo tocchi . . .
12   Quando verrò a te dopo l'ultima estate
13   ne conterò i palpiti.
14   Nessuno dovrà mancare . . .
15   Andranno a due a due coi miei palpiti
16   camminando con ritmo uguale.
17   Cantiamo il nostro ultimo duetto d'amore . . .
18   Raccogliamo le ultime rose per coronare il sogno . . .
19   Io resterò ferma presso la fontana del bosco
20   e ascolterò i tuoi passi allontanarsi.
21   Ti volgerai per l'ultima volta verso di me
22   e diremo insieme:
23   "Arrivederci nella eterna Primavera."

Our last autumn has arrived!

1   Our last autumn has arrived!
2   Hold my hands in this last earthly embrace
3   and tell me where you will go.
4   Do not look at me with sad eyes . . .
5   After the summer of my life
6   we will meet each other again in the eternal Spring!
7   You escape the winter when I will not be there any longer
8   in order to melt the ice around your heart . . .
9   Preserve your heart among the fragrant roses . . .
10 and gird it with a net of thorns,
11 so that no one may touch it . . .
12 When I will come to you after the final summer
13 I will count its beats.
14 Not one must be missing . . .
15 they will go two by two with my own heartbeats
16 pacing with equal rhythm.
17 Let us sing our final duet of love . . .
18 Let us gather the last roses to crown our dream . . .
19 I will remain steady near the fountain in the forest
20 and I will listen to your steps as they turn away.
21 You will turn for the last time towards me
22 and we will say together:
23 "Goodbye, (until we meet again) in the eternal spring!"

The sadness of separation expressed in *È giunto il nostro ultimo autunno* (Our last autumn has arrived) is offset by the optimism of ultimate reunion. Alfano chooses not to oversentimentalize the setting. The accompaniment is simple, the vocal line direct. The melodic lines are propelled by harmonic movement and by the regular triplet alternation of the 6/8 meter. A metronome marking is not supplied, but $\downarrow. = 44$–48 should be slow enough to allow the vocal lines to be expressive and fast enough to convey the rhythm of the chord changes. The structure of the song is really through-composed, even though the final measures are a variation of the opening.

The composer has specified an accent on the B♭ and A♮ in the right hand of the piano introduction; this accent should continue throughout the first page, where the pattern beneath the vocal line is repeated, and wherever else the pattern appears in the song. A slight *ritardando* at the end of measure 4 will enhance the syncopation and prepare for the vocal entrance, but this figure should not be slowed down when it appears later under the voice unless a *ritard* is specifically marked. As with other Alfano songs, the singer should read through the poem for proper word and syllable accents. Sometimes the composer's interest in other aspects of the musical fabric causes a normally unaccented syllable to receive undue stress. In measure 6, for example, the article *il* should not be accented even though it falls on the first beat of the measure. The phrase should move toward the accented second syllable of *autunno* (autumn), which falls on the first beat of measure 7.

The delicate polytonal melody in the piano interlude in measures 17–19, which seems to comment on the demand *dimmi dove andrai* (tell me where you will go), should be stretched out with a broad *ritardando*. The second section of the song, like the first, depends on dissonant chord movement in the accompaniment to shape the vocal phrase. The harmonic resolution in measure 26, for example, would produce a climax even if the dynamic level remained constant. The slight, but noticeable, rhythmic change in the arpeggios in measures 33–36 provides a sprightly reference to *Primavera* (Spring).

The third section is less dissonant. It begins entirely in the treble clef and contains much doubling between voice and piano. A feeling of sequential progression permeates the section. The fourth section, *Quando verrò a te* (When I will come to you), measure 53, should begin very quietly and *lontano* (distant). The syncopated rhythm of the octaves that support the climax of the section (measures 59–60) requires a strong accent. After several measures of rather narrow melodic range and slowed harmonic movement, the song bursts forth at the word *Cantiamo* (Let us sing) in measure 70. The accompaniment may or may not represent the heavenly harps, but the sheer musical effect of contrast at this point is stunning and should be performed *con abbandono* (with abandon), as indicated. At the end of the verse, at *per coronare il sogno* (to crown our dream), the piano interlude in measures 78–79 imitates the immediately preceding vocal line.

The last five lines of the poem are set in speech rhythms. In measures 80–87 the vocal line consists of a series of consecutive descending pitches, while the piano plays supporting chords above a pedal bass. The resulting polytonality is an effective means of retreating from the climactic point of the song. At Tempo I° (measure 96) the accompaniment pattern is very similar to the opening section of the song, except that the number of measures is doubled, thus creating a slower harmonic movement. The polytonal feeling continues through the final chords.

Throughout the song expression marks are clear, tempo and *rubati* are plainly indicated, and the composer is liberal with his breath indications.

È giunto il nostro ultimo autunno: G. Ricordi, 1943; Repr. 1953.   125532

Tre liriche (1943)

No. 1, Lungo la via del mare

(*Miranda Bona*)

1 Lungo la via del mare, il mio amore ed io,
2 creammo i primi canti del nostro gran poema.
3 Eran parole leggere
4 Come l'onde azzurre dai riflessi di perla.
5 Il lieve percuotersi dell'acqua sulla rena
6 accompagnava con tenue melodia
7 la poesia sommessa
8 che saliva dai nostri cuori
9 nell'estasi dell'amore novello.
10 Sulla spiaggia raccoglievamo conchiglie
11 per sentire nelle rosee cavità
12 avvicinate agli orecchi,
13 il fragore lontano dell'Oceano. Oh!
14 L'Oceano ha strade infinite.
15 Noi cercammo nel mare aperto la nostra via.
16 E i gorghi ci travolsero. Oh!

Three lyrics

No. 1, Along the road by the sea

1 Along the road by the sea, my love and I,
2 created the first lyrics of our great poem.
3 They were light words
4 like the blue waves due to the reflections of pearl.
5 The light breaking of the water on the sand
6 accompanied with tenuous melody
7 the subdued poetry
8 that arose from our hearts
9 in the ecstasy of new love.
10 On the beach we used to collect shells
11 to hear within their rosy cavities
12 close to our ears,
13 the distant roar of the Ocean. Oh!
14 The Ocean has infinite roads.
15 We searched for our way in the open sea.
16 And the whirlpools swept us away. Oh!

Two popular Italian subjects—love and the sea—are the central focus of the three poems by Miranda Bona that provide the texts for Alfano's *Tre liriche* (1943). The music is astonishingly lyrical for the difficult wartime period in which it was written and a considerable contrast to the bitter, more dissonant writing produced by many of Alfano's contemporaries. The poems are ambiguous mixtures of tentative emotion—trust and mistrust—related to the ever-changing forces of nature. Although the *tempi* are uniformly slow in all three songs, the rhythmic movement is not, and other contrasts in the musical texture provide enough interest for the songs to be performed consecutively as a set.

Lungo la via del mare (Along the road by the sea) is a broad three-part song form. The piano introduction bears some resemblance to Debussy's *La Mer,* with its sustained chords and sweeping 6/4 meter (which should be felt in two). In measures 4 and 5, to achieve a clean grace note before the first beat, the pianist should not neglect the sixth beat in the preceding measures, for it propels the rhythm forward. The vocal line, which begins in measure 5, is doubled by the chord progression in the accompaniment and establishes a clearly defined lyrical melody. In the interest of the forward rhythmic motion Alfano has sacrificed some word and syllable accents; the singer should read through these lines independently while preparing for performance. The three-staff organization of the first section of the accompaniment clarifies the texture beautifully; pedaling is left to the discretion of the performer, but it is clear from the scoring how much needs to be sustained. Some blurring would be desirable in this rather Impressionistic texture. A slight *fermata* on the word *poema* (poem) marks the end of the first phrase. The second phrase begins almost identically (except that it is reduced to the conventional two staves) and builds to a climax at *dell'amore novello* (of new love). The climax is marked *subito più caldo* (suddenly warmer) and is preceded by the direction *massimo p* (maximum soft). Since the phrase is rather long, a breath could be taken after *sommessa* (subdued) and again quickly after *cuori* (hearts). From there the phrase should not break, a feat made easier by the *rubato* direction in the score.

Part B, returning to Tempo I°, carries the direction *più scorrevole* (more flowing). The texture is lighter, the piano is completely in the treble clef, and the dynamic is *pp dolcissimo*. The accompaniment should be very *legato,* and special attention should be given to the *tenuto* markings in the repeated Eb and later Ab pedal tones. The tempo should pick up as the section climaxes at *dell'Oceano* (of the ocean). The dynamic marking here is *forte,* but it should not overpower the delicate texture. The roar is that of a *distant* ocean, and after the *fermata* there is a drop to *ppp*. The direction *come un'eco lontano* (like a distant echo) marks the exclamation Oh! The repeated bass notes in the piano part of these measures should be slightly detached. The sustained, expressive chords that provide a bridge to the return of part A are quite slow, but must still be felt in two.

The return of part A is marked by increased rhythmic activity (shorter note values) in the octave pattern. The sweep of the sea is again evident. The quiet ending, with minimal rhythmic movement, leaves this otherwise optimistic text and setting with a slightly ambiguous feeling. The composer introduces very specific pedal markings in the final measures of the piano part.

No. 2, I miei piedi son stanchi

(*Miranda Bona*)

1 I miei piedi son stanchi e doloranti:
2 "Dove mi conduci, Amore?"
3 I miei occhi son velati di sonno:
4 "Che c'è in questo buio?"
5 Le mie mani tese brancolano nel buio:
6 "Dove siamo?"
7 Ho paura della notte;
8 fantasmi giganteschi s'alzan dinnanzi a noi.
9 Sento urli di belve.
10 Un vento gelido sferza il volto.
11 Tu non rispondi alle mie domande:
12 ti fermi, sorridi, mi baci.
13 Io ti sorrido e ti seguo senza più parlare.

No. 2, My feet are tired

1 My feet are tired and aching:
2 "Where are you leading me, Love?"
3 My eyes are veiled with sleep:
4 "What is there in this darkness?"
5 My tense hands grope in the darkness;
6 "Where are we?"
7 I am afraid of the night;
8 gigantic phantoms rise up before us.
9 I hear howls of wild beasts.
10 A cold wind whips my face.
11 You do not answer my questions:
12 you stop, you smile, you kiss me.
13 I smile at you and follow you without speaking any longer.

The correct interpretation of the opening of *I miei piedi son stanchi* (My feet are tired) depends on two essential features: a plodding regularity in the repeated eighth notes of the left hand of the accompaniment, and the alternating expressive markings *indugiando* (hesitantly) and *a tempo* (back to tempo). The first establishes the underlying "walk" of the poem, the second the physical and psychological weariness and doubt of the central character. The erratic, angular melody in the treble of the introduction and in the accompaniment contributes an additional nervousness. The vocal phrases are short, and the composer adds breath markings to fragment them further. The weary phrases that open the song are narrow in range, and the second phrase—over a slightly altered harmony—almost duplicates the first. Otherwise, the song is through-composed, and many musical devices are used to illustrate the various aspects of the poem. The purely musical "answers" to the poet's questions vary. The first question, *Dove mi conduci, Amore?* (Where are you leading me, Love?), is answered with silence (a *fermata* on the final note—a break—and then a return to the original accompaniment pattern). The second question, *Che c'è in questo buio?* (What is there in this darkness?), is answered with an impatient rising scale and trill. The broadened accompaniment beginning in measure 13 anticipates the answer to the third question, *Dove siamo?* (Where are we?), but the answer, in measures 16–21, is capricious.

Substantial supporting chords underscore the increasing agitation at measure 22, marked *più concitato* (more excited), and build through the octave arpeggiation in measure 24, marked *poco stentando* (a little labored), to climax at *Sento urli di belve* (I hear howls of wild beasts). The C♯ octave, marked *lontano* (distant), and the supporting bass *tremolo,* which retreats from this climax, should be sustained and allowed to clear before the final *più calmo* (calmer) section begins. The last part of the song is a reaffirmation of trust. The long, sustained chords should be very *legato* while the voice, *dolcissimo,* speaks the short phrases *ti fermi* (you stop), *sorridi* (you smile), *mi baci* (you kiss me). The rests between these utterances are essential.

Even greater calm marks the optimistic resignation of the final phrase. A short breath before *parlare* (speaking) and the quick 32d-note figure in the accompaniment emphasize the cleverness of the ending of the poem. The chord resolutions through E major to C major and the final C major ninth chord should be savored. Music and poetry are completely fused in this superb setting.

No. 3, Scrivimi, amor mio

(*Miranda Bona*)

1 Scrivimi, amor mio, la parola del perdono.
2 Che la mia pena tocchi il tuo cuore!
3 Sono la tua piccola donna smarrita.
4 Ti cerco nelle notti insonni.
5 Nel sogno ti rivedo.

6   Mi parli col tuo dolce sorriso,
7   mi guardi coi tuoi teneri occhi,
8   quando l'ira non li riempie
9   di lucidi spigoli d'acciaio.
10 I tuoi occhi sembrano due diamanti gelidi,
11 ma se sorridono hanno il tremulo riflesso
12 delle acque marine.
13 I miei occhi hanno il colore del mar
14 disteso ai piedi d'una rupe;
15 la pupilla affoga nella tempesta;
16 le onde sfuggono dal loro letto e precipitano:
17 son le lacrime del mio dolore!
18 Scrivimi, amor mio, la parola del perdono!
19 Se il tuo viso sereno si chinerà sul mio viso,
20 presto si asciugherà il mio pianto,
21 come un rivolo d'acqua
22 sotto l'improvviso abbagliante sole, dopo la tempesta.
23 Oh! Scrivimi, amor mio, la parola del perdono.

No. 3, Write to me, my love

1   Write to me, my love, a word of forgiveness.
2   Let my suffering touch your heart!
3   I am your little lost beloved.
4   I search for you in the sleepless nights.
5   In my dreams I see you again.
6   You speak to me with your sweet smile,
7   you look at me with your tender eyes,
8   when anger does not fill them
9   with bright edges of steel.
10 Your eyes look like two icy diamonds,
11 but if they smile they have the tremulous reflection
12 of seawaters.
13 My eyes have the color of the sea
14 stretched out to the foot of a cliff;
15 my pupils drown in the storm;
16 the waves escape from their bed and rush down:
17 they are the tears of my grief!
18 Write to me, my love, a word of forgiveness!
19 If your serene face will bend down over my face,
20 quickly my tears will dry up
21 like a rivulet of water
22 under the unexpected and dazzling sun, after the storm.
23 Oh! Write to me, my love, a word of forgiveness.

Scrivimi, amor mio (Write to me, my love) moves at a slightly faster tempo than do the first two songs of the set, and structurally it seems to combine features of both. It shares a broad ABA structure with No. 1, but the central section has a through-composed quality like that of No. 2. After a four-measure chordal introduction the voice enters over a chord progression faintly reminiscent of the opening vocal line of No. 1. Again, there is a clearly defined lyrical melody on which the words ride in speech rhythms. Piano interludes between phrases tend to reflect on the meaning of the words in the preceding phrase, such as the accented rising notes of measure 11 indicating the anxiety of lost love. An expressive bridge (measures 17–18) leads to section B.

The middle portion of the song starts quietly with a key change and a broader, less talky, melodic line. The repetitious, arpeggiated accompaniment is sequential and builds steadily through increased dynamics, rhythmic changes, and a faster tempo to climax on the phrase *son le lacrime del mio dolore* (they are the tears of my grief). The accents on the first note of each falling arpeggio in the measure immediately preceding the climax are essential to underscore the word *precipitano* (rush down) and to set up the climax. This phrase is the one for which a true *forte* should be saved, making it the climax for the whole song set. (The full chords and octave doubling of the melodic line here leave no doubt of Alfano's admiration for Puccini.) After the release of *dolore* (grief), which may be held a bit—*rubato* is free throughout the section—the chords in the piano interlude reintroduce the melodic line that opened part A. The opening is exact, but the melody wanders soon thereafter. A two-measure reduction of the original four-measure piano introduction precedes a final quotation of the principal melody, setting a repetition of the poem's initial lines. The tranquility of the ending and clear tonal resolution into Db major seem to mirror an optimism that emerges from the poem.

Some phrases are long, but the composer has indicated breathing places quite carefully. Also, this song must move rhythmically, especially if the three songs are performed as a set. The ambiguities of both text and setting should provoke interest rather than frustration. Expressive indications are clearly marked, and there are no unusual Italian terms.

Tre liriche: Edizioni Servini Zerboni, 1946.   S. 4262 Z. (Set)
  1. *Lungo la via del mare*
  2. *I miei piedi son stanchi*
  3. *Scrivimi, amor mio*

Ottorino Respighi

(1879–1936)

•

OTTORINO RESPIGHI was born in Bologna on July 9, 1879 of educated and cultured parents. His father was an excellent pianist, and his paternal grandfather was a violinist who also served as organist in the cathedral of Fidenza. His mother's father and grandfather, Massimiliano and Giovanni Putti, were well-known sculptors. In 1891, at the age of twelve, Respighi entered the Liceo Musicale of Bologna to study violin and viola with Federico Sarti and composition with Luigi Torchi. Bologna was then one of the main centers of avant-garde musical activity. Giuseppe Martucci, director of the Liceo from 1886 to 1902, was responsible for Respighi's first love of orchestral and instrumental music. Martucci recognized his pupil's talent and claimed that he sometimes thought of Respighi as a master rather than a pupil.

In 1900 Respighi went to St. Petersburg as first violist for the Italian opera season at the Teatro Imperiale. There he was able to study composition and orchestration with Rimsky-Korsakov for five months. Under his guidance Respighi wrote and orchestrated *Prelude, Chorale and Fugue,* which he used for his diploma in composition from Bologna in 1901 and which later won wide acclaim. Rimsky-Korsakov's influence manifested itself in many of Respighi's orchestral compositions.

After finishing his diploma in composition at Bologna, Respighi returned to Russia for another nine months to play with the opera and with the Bolshoi Ballet. On his return to Italy he tried to reform Italian ballet productions but had no success. He played violin with the Quintetto Mugellini for a few months in 1906. In 1908 he went to Berlin as an accompanist in Frau Gerster's School of Singing in order to learn more about the German Romantic style and the active musical life in Germany. This experience also gave him invaluable training in the use of the human voice. In Berlin Respighi met the composer Max Bruch and was influenced by the latter's German chromaticism, and he frequently saw the great Ferruccio Busoni.

The next few years were occupied with composition. In 1913 Respighi accepted a position teaching composition at the Conservatorio di Santa Cecilia in Rome. Although he often returned to his studio in his family's home in Bologna, Rome became his permanent home and the inspiration for his most important orchestral compositions. It was here that he met and married one of his students, the talented Elsa Olivieri-Sangiacomo. An accomplished composer, pianist, and singer, she joined Respighi on most of his concert tours and together they performed his songs. His concerts were well received in North and South America and in Europe.

Respighi was fascinated with the rediscovery of early Italian music, part of the twentieth-century renaissance of Italian musical life. He became well known for his transcriptions, especially of Monteverdi's *Lamento d'Arianna* and of three suites of *Antiche Arie e Danze per Liuto,* which he arranged for orchestra. Characteristics of the early works he transcribed invaded much of his own writing, in which the open parallel fifths of medieval music moved easily to those of Impressionism. Medieval modes and Eastern scales are very much a part of Respighi's compositions.

In 1924 Respighi was made director of the Conservatory, but the position took so much of his time that he resigned after two years in order to devote himself exclusively to teaching, composing, and concertizing. Many of his compositions were performed at the Augusteo Concert Hall in Rome. Bernardino Molinari, a good friend of Respighi, was then the artistic director of the Augusteo Orchestra Association, one of the most important organizations in Europe for the performance of compositions by contemporary composers.

As a child Respighi had suffered rheumatic fever, which developed into endocarditis later in his life. In January 1936 he was stricken with a severe attack, and three months later he died while composing his opera *Lucrezia.* His wife was able to complete the work, and it was performed the following year. Bologna, the city of his birth, honored Respighi by naming a street after him and erecting a monument.

Among Respighi's vocal works are more than 60 compositions for solo voice. Two of these, *Aretusa* and *La Sensitiva,* are for mezzo-soprano and orchestra. His chamber music includes *Il Tramonto,* for mezzo-soprano and string quartet, and *Deità Silvane,* originally written for voice and piano, but soon rewritten for voice and eleven instruments. Respighi also wrote two choral works for soloists and chorus: *La Primavera,* with orchestra, and a more intimate work, *Lauda per la natività del Signore,* accompanied by eight instruments.

Respighi won his first acclaim as an opera composer; his operas were immediate successes but none lasted very long in the repertory. Although he excelled in large orchestral forms, he was most effective in smaller, more intimate works, in which his lovely lyrical lines are most apparent. Among his songs are several such chamber-type compositions.

Respighi's early songs are completely tonal with some chromaticism and modal scales. They do not foretell the Impressionistic traits that developed later. The forms are all ABA or strophic. One characteristic that is already apparent in his early songs and is typical of all of his vocal music is his treating the voice as if it were an instrument, with the vocal line conceived as part of the whole composition. The music expresses the overall feeling of the poem, and the poetic meter and meaning of individual words are not permitted to change the concept of the phrase line as a musical entity. The later Respighi songs show an increase in Impressionistic techniques with greater use of polytonality, parallel triads, and seventh chords used chromatically with less feeling of progression or tonal center.

Respighi was a linguist and felt at ease with either French or Italian texts. His songs are published as groups, but they are not song cycles, and there is no musical or poetic connection linking the individual songs.

Scherzo

(*Carlo Zangarini*)

1   Una notte, al davanzale,
2   ero sola, o pur non ero?
3   ben mi parve un soffio d'ale
4   che giungesse dal sentiero
5   chi la guancia mi sfiorò?
6   Se fu un bacio io non lo so.
7   Fu la tenda, è ver, rammento,
8   che la guancia mi percosse:
9   la carezza fu del vento,
10   pur vorrei che non lo fosse . . .
11   più ci penso e più rammento
12   che fu un bacio e non il vento!

Joke

1   One night, at the window sill,
2   I was alone, and yet wasn't?
3   It really seemed to me a breath of air of wings
4   that reached from the path,
5   that grazed my cheek?
6   If it was a kiss I do not know it.
7   It was the curtain, it is true, I recall,
8   that struck me on the cheek:
9   the caress was by the wind,
10   still I wish that it were not so.
11   The more I think about it the more I recall
12   that it was a kiss and not the wind!

In *Scherzo* (Joke) the mood of this charming poem is captured immediately by the irregular phrasing indicated in the bass line of the piano
accompaniment. The *allegretto* tempo should maximize the subtle mood
shifts in the text, and the song should be "spoken" rather than "sung." The
strength and meaning of the words govern the dynamics, *rubati,* and vocal
color. This song is essentially a "conversation with oneself" and should be
acted out as such.

Scherzo: Bongiovanni, 1906; Repr. 1966.   F. 238 B.

Contrasto

(Carlo Zangarini)

 1   Piange lenta la luna
 2   sue rugiade gemmanti:
 3   or lieto all'aria bruna
 4   sia l'oblio de li amanti,
 5   però che dolce è il riso
 6   tra il pianto de le cose.
 7   Ben la luna compose
 8   a la mestizia il viso.
 9   O amica, a quando a quando
10   giova l'oblio: scordare
11   l'altrui doglianze amare,
12   intorno andar cantando,
13   mentre piange la luna.

Contrast

 1   The moon weeps slowly
 2   its bejewelled dew drops:
 3   now happy in the dark air
 4   is the oblivion of lovers,
 5   However how sweet is the laughter
 6   between the weeping over things.
 7   The moon composes well
 8   in sadness its face.
 9   O friend, sometimes
10   oblivion is useful: to forget
11   other bitter pains,
12   go around singing,
13   while the moon weeps.

Composed before Respighi's involvement with French Impressionism, *Contrasto* (Contrast) shows the composer's gift for lyrical writing and affinity for the voice as an instrument. The style of this early song is similar to the Neapolitan songs popular at the time, and simplicity is the key to its construction and interpretation. It is written in ABA form but does not follow the versification of the poem; rather the B section begins in the middle of the second verse with an effective modulation from B♭ major to G♭ major and continues into the first line of the third verse. The "contrast" between the sadness of the moon and the happy oblivion of lovers appears throughout the poem, and the ABA song structure reflects this general concept. The vocal line is part of the fabric of the work and often appears in parallel sixths with the bass line of the accompaniment. There is no attempt to "set" specific words or meanings, although the dynamics sometimes underscore a particular feeling, such as at the phrase *O amica, a quando a quando giova l'oblio* (O friend, sometimes oblivion is useful). The pianist should be aware here of the change from duple to triple meter for two measures of accompaniment. In general, the meter of the song should be felt in two at approximately ♩. = 66 so that vocal phrases can be sung on one breath. The composer indicates an extra breath in the last phrase of the song to serve the final *ritardando*. All the dynamic changes and *rubati* are logical and clearly marked. The initial directions to the pianist—*leggerissimo* (very light) and *armonioso* (harmonious)—should be observed to highlight the charm of the song. Since the song is not primarily concerned with rhythmic word-setting, the singer must be careful not to accent unaccented syllables, particularly as they appear at the end of each phrase.

Contrasto: Bongiovanni, 1906.   F. 253 B.

Invito alla danza

(*Carlo Zangarini*)

1   Madonna, d'un braccio soave
2   ch'io cinga l'orgoglio dell'anca:
3   voi siete d'amore la nave;
4   la vela, madonna, vi manca:
5   io sono la vela a vogare
6   intorno pel cerulo mare.
7   Voi siete la mobile fusta
8   che il mar della musica sfiora:
9   io sono la vela robusta
10 che il viaggio dirige e rincora:
11 la nave risale, discende,
12 la vela ammaina, distende.

13 Volete che l'onda si svolga
14 in suon di gavotta gentile?
15 volete che il valzer disciolga
16 la larga sua corsa febbrile?
17 Io faccio l'inchino di rito,
18 madonna, e alla danza v'invito.

Invitation to the dance

1   My lady, with gentle arms
2   may I embrace the pride of the ship's quarters:
3   you are the ship of love;
4   the sail, my lady, you are lacking:
5   I am the sail for navigating
6   around the blue sea.
7   You are the moving galley
8   that the sea touches lightly with music:
9   I am the strong sail
10 that steers and encourages the journey:
11 the ship rises, descends,
12 the sail furls, distends
13 Do you want that the wave unrolls
14 in the sound of a gentle gavotte?
15 Do you want that the waltz unwinds
16 its broad feverish course?
17 I make the ritual bow,
18 my lady, and invite you to the dance.

Invito alla danza (Invitation to the dance), an early song, carries a
certain youthful eroticism, hinted at in the double meanings of the poetry's
nautical terminology and the music's rollicking waltz rhythm. The influence
of popular Italian song can be seen throughout the work, but it is tempered
by the experienced hand of the classically trained composer.

Lacking an introduction, this song is difficult to start. A slight hesitation
on the first note may help to establish the strong waltz rhythm from which
the song derives such character. As with later Respighi songs, the accompaniment and voice lines are equally interesting and, while interrelated, are
quite independent. The vocal part begins with a long seven-measure phrase
that should be sung on one breath, if possible. The accompaniment is phrased
2 + 2 + 3. The gentle *crescendo* of the vocal line climaxes in measure 6.
A dynamic rise and fall governs each of the subphrases of the accompaniment.
As the voice line continues with *voi siete d'amore la nave* (you are the ship
of love), the piano begins a long phrase of ascending eighth-notes that move

right through the completion of the consequent half of the vocal phrase and into the beginning of the next. The cleverness of this overlapping reflects the enthusiasm of the poetry and elevates the pedestrian vocal melody to art-song caliber.

The second section of the song, beginning *Voi siete la mobile fusta* (You are the moving galley) is more conventionally waltz-like. The vocal melody is doubled in the upper line of the accompaniment, and the phrases are synchronized. The setting allows all attention to center on the singer's words, which, given the male-female imagery of ship and sail, should be most expressively sung. The waltz tempo must remain steady until the measure marked *Tempo di Gavotta,* which should be slower than that of the waltz and very strict. Here again, the piano has the melodic interest (the music of the gavotte), while the vocal line is not much more than a recitative. A slight *ritenuto* and very definite *fermati* for both voice and piano conclude the section.

The return of the waltz tempo brings back the original accompaniment line, with the voice joining only on the second half of the phrase. The final words of text, *madonna, e alla danza v'invito* (my lady, and invite you to the dance), should be rhythmically free up to the word *danza,* which is marked *ritardando molto,* and suddenly and enthusiastically *a tempo* at the words *v'invito* (invite you). The accompaniment must continue with crisp *staccato* articulation and strict tempo to the end. The final rolled chords, with only a little stretch of the imagination, might picture the brash protagonist's fervent bow. This appealing song is a charming addition to any program but is particularly effective as an encore.

Invito alla danza: Bongiovanni, 1906.   F. 288 B. (T-S); F. 254 B. (Br-Ms)

Nebbie

(*Ada Negri*)

1 Soffro,
2 Lontan lontano
3 Le nebbie sonnolente
4 Salgono dal tacente
5 Piano
6 Alto gracchiando, i corvi,
7 Fidati all'ali nere,
8 Traversan le brughiere
9 Torvi.
10 Dell'aere ai morsi crudi
11 Gli addolorati tronchi

12 Offron, pregando, i bronchi nudi.
13 Come ho freddo!
14 Son sola;
15 Pel grigio ciel sospinto
16 Un gemito d'estinto
17 Vola;
18 E mi ripete:
19 Vieni;
20 È buia la vallata.
21 O triste, o disamata,
22 Vieni!
23 Vieni!

Mists

1 I suffer
2 Far, far away
3 The sleepy mists
4 Rise from the silent
5 Plain.
6 Shrilly cawing, the crows
7 Trusting their black wings
8 Fly across the heaths
9 Grimly
10 To the harsh weathering of the air
11 The grieving tree trunks
12 Offer, praying, their nude branches.
13 How cold I am!
14 I am alone;
15 Driven through the grey sky
16 An extinct wail
17 Flies;
18 And repeats to me:
19 Come,
20 Dark is the valley.
21 O sad, O unloved one,
22 Come!
23 Come!

Nebbie (Mists) is one example of the Italian art-song genre to achieve extensive international recognition. It is without doubt Respighi's best-known and most frequently performed song. Elsa Respighi's biography of her husband relates an extraordinary story about its composition. According to the composer, a melancholy mood had rendered him incapable of working, until suddenly one morning he awoke with an irresistible urge to compose. He sat at the piano and filled four pages with music. Later that day a friend arrived with a gift volume of poems by Ada Negri. Opening the book, Respighi glanced at the title *Nebbie,* read the poem, and thought of the music he had just composed. Singing Negri's verses to the music, he realized that they fit together as if composed simultaneously. Not one note needed to be changed, and a superb song came into being.

The anguish central to the poem is anticipated in the cold, repeated minor chords and hollow-fifth pedal tones of the opening measures. In most printings *tenuto* markings appear only under the first eight of the dirgelike chords that support the composition, but this direction should be extended throughout the work; each chord should feel as though it is literally being pulled from the piano. The *lento* tempo, however, must be relentlessly steady. The chord movement should be *legato,* but not to the extent that one chord melts into another. The downward drop of the hands on each chord is essential to establishing the world weariness of the poet and the bleakness of the landscape. Every chord, regardless of stretch, must be fingered so that it is played simultaneously, never rolled. Specific pedal directions are given only at two points, *tronchi* (tree trunks) and *offron* (offer), where grace notes in the bass precede the chord; however, pedal may be used as an aid to sonority throughout the composition provided the plodding quality of the movement is not obscured. The *crescendi* and *decrescendi* following the movement of the long block-chord scales must be almost imperceptible in order to focus attention on the singer's words.

The vocal line is completely integrated into the fabric of the composition, frequently paralleling the top note of the underlying chord movement. It is distinguished from it by the rhythmic flow of the word accents and the sound qualities of the expressive words. An extremely smooth vocal line must be drawn from the beginning to the end of the song, but the words should have the effect of being declaimed much as an intense dramatic soliloquy would be in classical theater. The dynamics of the vocal line, following those of the accompaniment, must be adjusted to allow for secondary accents on more important words and syllables. Also, the composer usually allows the beginning of the vocal phrase to enter one dynamic level higher than that of the corresponding accompaniment. The vocal phrase should give the impression of great length. In the first stanza a breath may be taken after *lontano* (far away). If at all possible no break should occur between *sonolente* (sleepy) and *Salgono* (Rise). In the second stanza, breaks may be taken after *corvi* (crows) and *nere* (black); in the third stanza, after *crudi* (harsh).

Although dramatic climaxes at *fortissimo* levels are called for twice within Respighi's setting of the first three stanzas of poetry, the greatest intensity in the poem comes in the fourth stanza, at *Come ho freddo! Son sola* (How cold I am! I am alone). The voice must maintain intensity here, allowing the outward resolution of the augmented chord in the piano part to provide dynamic contrast. A slight break is needed before the recitative, which follows; the rhythm can be more flexible and the words should have a *mormorato* (murmuring) quality. A breath may be taken after *sospinto* (driven), and the accompanying chords in this two-measure phrase should have a seamless quality.

At the resumption of the descending chord pattern beneath *Vola* (Flies), the tempo must return to its strict and relentless movement toward the final measure. Breaks in the phrase are clearly indicated in the punctuation . The final *Vieni! Vieni!* (Come! Come!) should be separated; and at the climax of the final *crescendo,* singer and pianist must release the last note together. There are few songs in the art-song repertory that call for greater dramatic expression from both singer and pianist in so short a time frame. The reputation of the song is well deserved.

Nebbie: Bongiovanni, 1906.   F. 255 B. (S-T); F. 251 B. (Br-Ms-orig); F. 550 B. (C);
© G. Schirmer, 1939

Nevicata

(*Ada Negri*)

1   Sui campi e sulle strade
2   Silenziosa e lieve,
3   Volteggiando, la neve
4   Cade.
5   Danza la falda bianca
6   Ne l'ampio ciel scherzosa,
7   Poi sul terren si posa
8   Stanca.
9   In mille immote forme
10 Sui tetti e sui camini,
11 Sui cippi e nei giardini
12 Dorme.
13 Tutto dintorno è pace:
14 Chiuso in oblìo profondo,
15 Indifferente il mondo
16 Tace . . .
17 Ma ne la calma immensa
18 Torna ai ricordi il core,
19 E ad un sopito amore
20 Pensa.

Snowfall

1 On the fields and on the streets
2 Silently and lightly,
3 Whirling, the snow
4 Falls.
5 The white flake dances
6 In the broad sky playfully,
7 then on the ground it rests
8 Tired.
9 In a thousand motionless forms
10 On the roofs and on the paths
11 On the stone boundaries and in the gardens
12 It sleeps.
13 Everything all around is peace:
14 Locked in deep oblivion,
15 Indifferent the world
16 is silent.
17 But in the immense calm
18 the heart turns to its memories,
19 and upon a quieted love
20 It meditates.

The mood for *Nevicata* (Snowfall), a simple three-part song, is established and maintained by the piano accompaniment, which must be played as *legato* as possible. Some blurring with the pedal is preferred as long as it does not interfere with the underlying harmonic movement. The tempo should be slow enough to create the atmosphere of gently falling snow, but fast enough to permit the singer to phrase with the punctuation in the text ($\downarrow$ = 44). A very slight *ritardando* in the last measure of section B will smooth out the return to Tempo I°, and a broadening of the final phrase brings the song to a more satisfying conclusion. The singer should be careful not to stress the final syllable of *bianca* (white) in the first section of the song, even though the phrase appears to lead to it.

Nevicata: Bongiovanni, 1906.   256 (S-T); 252 (Br-Ms-orig)

Stornellatrice

(1st verse, Carlo Zangarini; 2d verse, Alberto Donini)

1   Che mi giova cantar: "Fior di betulla:
2   vorrei tu fossi il sole ed io la stella,
3   e andar pel cielo e non pensare a nulla!"
4   quando poi l'eco mi risponde: nulla?
5   Che mi vale cantar: "Fiore dei fiori:
6   tu sei l'amore mio d'oggi e di ieri:
7   tu sei l'amore mio che mai non muori!"
8   quando poi l'eco mi risponde: muori?
9   (Che mi giova cantar: "Fior di frumento,
10 tu sei la mia ricchezza ed il mio vanto,
11 tu sei la mia speranza e il mio tormento:
12 quando poi l'eco mi risponde: mento?
13 Che mi giova cantar: "Fior de' ghiacciai,
14 si spegnerà nel gel la fiamma mia,
15 e tanto t'odierò quanto t'amai"
16 quando poi l'eco mi risponde: mai?)

The stornello singer

1   What is the use of my singing: "Flower of birch:
2   I wish you were the sun and I the star,
3   and we could go through the sky and not think of anything!"
4   When afterwards the echo answers me: nothing?
5   How worthwhile is my singing: "Flower of flowers:
6   you are my love of today and of yesterday:
7   you are my love because you never die!"
8   Afterwards the echo answers me: are you dying?
9   (What is the use of my singing: "Flower of wheat,
10 You are my wealth and my pride,
11 You are my hope and my torment."
12 Afterwards the echo answers me: Am I lying?
13 What is the use of my singing: "Flower of ice,
14 In the freezing cold my flame will die out,
15 and I will loathe you as much as I loved you."
16 Afterwards the echo answers me: Never?)

The poem of *Stornellatrice* (The stornello singer) is essentially a play on words (a stornello is a poetry form similar to a madrigal). The echo returns only the final portion of the initial phrase so that the meaning of the phrase is contradicted or altered. The musical setting is one of utmost simplicity. After the introductory question, chanted on a single pitch, the melody takes on an arched line similar to that associated with Neapolitan song. It is important that the accents and the *forte* dynamic level are observed at the end of the third phrase, since it sets up the ironic response. A definite breath break must be taken each time before that response, which also demands a change of vocal color. As with most strophic songs, the singer, while observing all the markings, should subtly adjust expressive devices to achieve variety from verse to verse. The rolled chords in the accompaniment imitate the strum of a stringed instrument and should follow the direction of the singer.

Stornellatrice: Bongiovanni, 1906.   F. 267 B. (S-T); F. 268 B. (Br-Ms)

Sei melodie

No. 1, In alto mare

(*Enrico Panzacchi*)

1 È sdruscito il navil l'ira del flotto
2 tregua non da.
3 Ecco l'ultima antenna il nembo ha rotto.
4 Signor, pietà!
5 Per le saette il ciel rimbomba, scisso
6 Di qua e di là;
7 Le sue gole mugghiando apre l'abisso;
8 Signor, pietà!
9 Fugge dai cori l'ultima speranza,
10 la morte è qua
11 Non un'ombra di vela in lontananza;
12 Signor, pietà!

Six melodies

No. 1, On the high sea

1 The ship is smashed in, the fury to the fleet
2 Gives no respite.
3 Here is the last aerial the squall has broken.

4   Lord, have pity!
5   The heavens roar with thunder bolts, divided
6   From here and from there;
7   The sea bottom opens up its howling throat.
8   Lord, have pity!
9   The last hope flees from our hearts,
10 Death is here
11 Not a shadow of a sail in the distance;
12 Lord, have pity!

Respighi's *Sei melodie* (Six melodies; 1910) are typical of the composer's early work. Although published in a set, they are independent songs, not intended as a cycle, and they bear no special musical relationship to each other. The fifth and sixth songs are to French texts and are not included in this analysis.

In alto mare (On the high sea) is a vivid musical description of a ship-wreck in which the pianist supplies the fury of the elements while the singer, thoroughly integrated into the musical texture, portrays the terror of the protagonist.

The character of the song is established in the opening chord and the agitated figuration in the accompaniment. The accented half notes, phrased across four measures, create a rising chromatic figure that heightens the excitement toward the climactic cry *Signor, pietà!* (Lord, have pity!). At many points the vocal line is in octaves with the piano line even though it is phrased in longer units. The accented half notes in the piano part should be played forcefully at all the dynamic levels called for throughout the song, and with the help of the pedal they should always be sustained throughout the measure.

After the singer's first cry for mercy, the accented half notes begin a sixteen-measure descending chromatic scale. Together with the *diminuendo,* it creates a graphic description of the sinking of the ship. Again, the vocal line sometimes duplicates it or simply speaks above it. There is a very important accent above the first syllable of the second plea, *pietà!* (have pity!).

At the *a tempo* the piano begins an exact duplicate of the first sixteen measures of the song and then breaks into a diatonic scale from the keynote to the fifth, creating a sense of uncertainty. The abandonment of hope and the approach of death are effectively set vocally with repetitions of the same note—*Fugge dai cori l'ultima speranza* (The last hope flees from our hearts), *la morte è qua* (Death is here). This despair must be expressed with a colorless, almost flat quality. The third and final plea, duplicating the rising scale in the accompaniment, should be truly terrifying, and the piano must surge to the end without *decrescendo* or *ritard.*

No. 2, Abbandono

(*Annie Vivanti*)

1 Io sono tanto stanca di lottare,
2 Dammi la pace tu che solo il puoi.
3 Io sono tanto stanca di pensare
4 Dammi il sereno de' grand' occhi tuoi.
5 Io sono tanto stanca di sognare
6 Tu mi risveglia a giorno glorioso.
7 Io sono tanto stanca di vagare
8 Legami l'ale e chiamami al riposo.

No. 2, Abandon

1 I am so tired of struggling,
2 Give me the peace that only you can (give).
3 I am so tired of thinking
4 Give me the serenity of your large eyes.
5 I am so tired of dreaming
6 Awaken me to a glorious day.
7 I am so tired of wandering
8 Bind my wings and call me to my resting place.

The words *tanto stanca* (so tired) are the central focus of the poem *Abbandono* (Abandon), but the song interprets them in a restless manner. The slow tempo (approximately ♩. = 54) must permit the alternation of eighth notes in the accompaniment to create this mood. The *rallentando* after the first verse can start one measure earlier, at the words *de' grand' occhi tuoi* (of your large eyes), and the ascending bass notes in the piano part of the following measure should be brought out. The vocal line phrases naturally in two-measure units, allowing for breath with or without punctuation in the text. In the last phrase a breath may be taken after *chiamami* (call me) to allow for a *crescendo-decrescendo* on the word *riposa* (resting place) and for the final note to be held full length. A slight *rallentando* should be observed in the next to the last measure of the accompaniment, and the final chord should be arpeggiated slowly in the same tempo as the alternating eighth notes.

No. 3, Mattinata

(*Gabriele d'Annunzio*)

1   Spandono le campane
2   a la prim' alba l'ave
3   spandono questa mane
4   un suon grave e soave
5   le campane lontane.
6   Nivea come neve
7   la nebbia copre il mare
8   Fluttua lieve lieve;
9   è rosea; scompare.
10 Bocca d'oro la beve
11 E neve e rose ed oro
12 il mattin fresco mesce.
13 Un alto inno sonoro
14 fanno come il dì cresce
15 ond' e campane in coro.
16 Salve, Ianua coeli.
17 Co 'l dì la nostra bella
18 fuor de' sogni e de' veli
19 balza Ave, maris stella!
20 Salve, Regina coeli!

No. 3, Morning time

1   The bells disperse
2   greetings at break of day
3   they disperse this morning
4   a deep and soft sound
5   the bells far off
6   White as snow
7   the fog covers the sea
8   It undulates very slightly;
9   It is rose-colored; it disappears
10 A golden opening drinks it up
11 And white and rose and gold
12 the cool morning pours
13 a sublime resonant hymn
14 they chant as the day grows
15 waves and bells in chorus
16 Hail, entrance of the heavens
17 with the arrival of day, our beautiful one

18 beyond dreams and veils
19 Rebound Hail, star (Queen) of the sea.
20 Hail, Queen of the heavens!

The ever-present bells in *Mattinata* (Morning) allow Respighi to indulge his love for the sounds of early church music; the resulting colors forecast his later involvement with Impressionism. The bell motive appears in the opening measure of the introduction and is clearly indicated with *tenuto* markings. The entire song is organized around this pattern, and it should be clearly heard within the fabric of whatever melodic and harmonic events are occurring at the same time. This is true whether the pattern is marked *tenuto,* or with accent marks, or unmarked. The pattern should be phrased over four measures, and they should be linked to form units of eight. A tempo of approximately ♩ = 60 satisfies the *allegretto* indication and still keeps the leisurely character of an early morning scene. The eighth-note pattern in the upper treble of the piano part, always played *legato,* should complement the basic bell motive and never obscure it. The longer notes in the accompaniment should be sustained as much as possible, and pedal may be used whenever needed to achieve bell-like sonority. The vocal line weaves through the texture even when emotions reach the higher levels toward the end of the poem. In the beginning the singer "reads" the poem, or describes the scene often in a chantlike style with dynamics ranging from *pp* to *mp.* The *pp* called for at the phrase *Bocca d'oro la beve* (A golden opening drinks it up) should be prepared with a *decrescendo* in the preceding measure at *scompare* (disappears). The pianist should be sure to bring out the accented B♮ underneath *lieve* (slightly), since this word begins a new four-measure phrase of the bell motive.

The third section of the poem is set with a modulation to what appears to be a modified, transposed Lydian mode (Respighi had a lifelong interest in early church modes). The bell motive here is marked with accents. At this point the vocal line becomes more prominent and rises to a climax on *coro* (chorus). While most of the vocal phrases have also fallen into four-measure groupings, allowing for ample breath at ♩ = 60, the singer may need to break the climactic phrase before *onde* (waves) to prepare for the high A♭ and to prepare the *crescendo* leading to the key change.

The final section of the song should be performed at a full *ff* as the bells become almost deafening. This intensity must also be present in the vocal line, even though it is quasi-Gregorian in its simplicity. The optional bass line for a third hand at the piano would contribute some needed depth in the texture but is certainly not necessary. At any rate, the *ff* volume and intensity should be maintained until the release of the final notes. The accented eighth-note motive in the final measures of the accompaniment is the composer's important final comment on the poem.

No. 4, Povero core

(A. Graf)

1   O mio povero cor, morta è la pace,
2   morto è l'amor, di novo a che sussulti?
3   Morta è la fede; a che più la vorace
4   fiamma di vita nel tuo grembo occulti?
5   O mio povero cor, quando più tace
6   La fredda notte e dei patiti insulti
7   Grave su te la rimembranza giace,
8   Udirmi sembra i tuoi sordi singulti.
9   O mio povero cor, fossi tu morto!
10 Così di gel così d'angoscia stretto
11 Onde vuo' tu sperar gioia o conforto?
12 O mio povero cor, non rinvenire;
13 O mio povero cor del chiuso petto
14 Fatti una tomba e lasciati morire!

No. 4, Poor heart

1   O my poor heart, dead is peace
2   love is dead again, what makes you tremble?
3   Dead is faith; to what more the voracious
4   flame of life do you conceal in your bosom?
5   O my poor heart, when will it be still
6   the cold nights and suffered insults
7   Heavy on you the remembrance lies,
8   It seems that your mute sobs hear me
9   O my poor heart, are you perhaps dead!
10 So tight with cold and anguish
11 Where do you hope for joy or comfort?
12 O my poor heart, do not revive;
13 O my poor heart, in my closed breast
14 make yourself a tomb and let yourself die!

In *Povero cor* (Poor heart) Respighi shows another of his major historical influences, seventeenth- and eighteenth-century *Arie italiane*. In fact, this song bears a remarkable resemblance to the well-known *Come raggio di sol*

(Like the rays of the sun) by Antonio Caldara (1670–1736). The interest is clearly in the vocal line, supported by constantly pulsating chords whose changing harmonies underscore key words in the text. A tempo of approximately ♩ = 60 will keep the rhythm moving and still allow the singer to connect some of the longer phrases on one breath. Phrasing is about the only interpretive problem in this song, for the dynamic markings, accents, and *rubati* are clearly marked and logical. The piano part should be conceived as one long phrase that moves inexorably to the final cadence. The vocal phrases are irregular musically but closely linked to the phrasing of the text. At times the phrasing requires the singer to breathe quickly between eighth notes, such as before *Morta è la fede* (Dead is faith) and *a che più la vorace fiamma* (to what more the voracious flame). The entire phrase, *a che più la vorace fiamma di vita nel tuo grembo occulti?* (to what more the voracious flame of life do you conceal in your bosom?), becomes very long at the *lento* tempo. If the singer cannot manage all of it on one breath, a short catch breath could be taken immediately before the prepositional phrase *nel tuo grembo,* providing an attempt is made to give the impression of one phrase dynamically. The pianist can help by not altering the forward movement. Similar choices at later points in the song must be made according to the capabilities of the individual singer. Many readings of the text should be made before such choices are executed.

Sei melodie: Bongiovanni, 1910

1. *In alto mare*	F. 381 B.
2. *Abbandono*	F. 382 B.
3. *Mattinata*	F. 383 B.
4. *Povero core*	F. 384 B.

Cinque canti all'antica

No. 1, L'udir talvolta

(*Giovanni Boccaccio*)

1 L'udir talvolta nominare il loco
2 Dove dimori, o talvolta vedere
3 Chi di là venga mi riaccende il fuoco
4 Nel cor mancato per troppo dolere.
5 E par ch'io senta alcun nascoso gioco
6 Nell'anima legata dal piacere,
7 E meco dico: quindi venissi io
8 Onde quel viene, o dolce mio disio!

Five old songs

No. 1, On hearing sometimes

1   On hearing sometimes the mentioning of the place
2   where you live, or sometimes seeing
3   who comes from there rekindles within me the fire
4   lacking in my heart because of too much grieving.
5   And it seems that I feel some hidden game
6   in my soul bound by pleasure,
7   And to myself I say: so I came
8   from where that one comes, O my sweet desire.

Giovanni Boccaccio (1313–1375) is best known as the author of *Deca-meron,* the brilliant collection of stories that mark the beginning of the literary transition from medieval courtliness to modern society. He was enormously active throughout his life as poet, scholar, lecturer, and biographer and included among his works a number of pastoral songs. In the first three songs of *Cinque canti all'antica* (Five old songs) Respighi serves the emotionally moving, unpretentious Boccaccio poetry with equally unpretentious musical settings. In all five songs (the fourth and fifth are by other poets) there are several twentieth-century touches, but the style is derived from earlier Italian music, especially that of Monteverdi, whom Respighi studied and greatly admired.

L'udir talvolta (On hearing sometimes) requires a moving *andante* tempo (approximately ♩ = 104–108) to propel the flow of the phrase and to express the gentle, sweet sentiment of the poetry. At this tempo it would be necessary to breathe after *dimori* (you live), *di là venga* (literally, "from there comes"), and *dolere* (grieving), thereby connecting the text grammatically, properly observing the dynamics, and accounting for the resolution of the suspensions with one technical solution. Phrasing in the second half of the song is easier. The *forte* dynamic and accent marks on *E par ch'io senta* (And it seems that I feel) should spring from the *crescendo* indicated in the preceding phrase. The short phrase *E meco dico* (And to myself I say) should be somewhat hushed, with a slight stretch on the word *dico.* However, the last note of that measure (low D in the piano bass) must act as a pick-up for a flowing *a tempo* at the key change. A breath should be taken before the final address, *o dolce mio disio!* (my sweet desire), and the *rallentando* must be observed.

No. 2, Ma come potrei

(*Giovanni Boccaccio*)

1 Ma come potrei io mai soffrire
2 Di partirmi da te che t'amo tanto
3 Che senza te mi par ognor morire?
4 Essendo teco, non so giammai quanto
5 più ben mi possa avere o più disire.
6 Ma sallo bene amore in quanto pianto
7 ista la vita mia la notte e 'l giorno
8 mentre non veggo questo viso adorno.

No. 2, But how could I

1 But how could I ever bear
2 to depart from you whom I love so much
3 Because without you I seem always dying?
4 Being with you, I do not know how much
5 more love I could have or more desire.
6 But I know (it) well love in so much weeping
7 my life persists night and day
8 when I don't see this beautiful face.

The declamatory nature of the lament *Ma come potrei* (But how could I) requires a departure from strict metric rhythm. The syllabic rhythmic setting and expressiveness of individual words should govern the ebb and flow of the phrase. Even a rather slow *adagio* ($\quarternote = 66$) permits the singing of phrases such as *Di partirmi da te che t'amo tanto* (to depart from you whom I love so much) and *in quanto pianto ista la vita mia la notte e 'l giorno* (in so much weeping my life persists night and day) on one breath for maximum connection. The phrase *non so giammai quanto più ben mi possa avere o più disire* (I do not know how much more love I could have or more desire) should not be broken until after *avere*. The dynamic range of the song is narrow, and the final phrase, in which the composer allows ample breathing for control, should have a quiet radiance.

No. 3, Ballata

(*Giovanni Boccaccio*)

1 Non so qual io mi voglia,
2 O viver o morir, per minor doglia,
3 Morir vorrei, che 'l viver m'è gravoso
4 Veggendomi da voi esser lasciato;
5 E morir non vorrei, che trapassato
6 più non vedrei il bel viso amoroso
7 Per cui io piango invidioso
8 Di chi l'ha fatto suo e me ne spoglia!

No. 3, Ballad

1 I know not what I desire,
2 Whether to live, or to die, for the least pain
3 I would wish to die, since to live is burdensome
4 seeing myself left alone by you;
5 and I would not wish to die, because dead
6 I would no longer see your beautiful loving face
7 For which I cry envious
8 of who has made it his and deprives me of it.

The relatively short phrases in *Ballata* (Ballad) permit a very slow *lento* ($\downarrow$ = 44) to express the poignancy of the introspective poetry. As in the previous song, the vocal melody is the most important element in the composition, with the piano accompaniment providing harmonic support. The dynamic range of the song is somewhat greater than that of the previous song, reflecting the poetic intensity of the text. The *tenuto* and accent marks must be observed very carefully, particularly on repeated notes. In fact, every *crescendo-decrescendo* and dynamic change is related to the meaning of the text. The *crescendo e stringendo* (growing louder and faster) on the second half of the phrase *che trapassato più non vedrei* (because dead, I would no longer see) helps to point up its sequential relationship to the following phrase. Each of these phrases should be sung on one breath. Although *forte* appears three times in this song, a little more volume should be saved for the final two measures to underscore the poet's emotional torment.

No. 4, Bella porta di rubini

(*Autore ignoto*)

1   Bella porta di rubini
2   Ch'apri il varco ai dolci accenti,
3   Se nei risi peregrini
4   scopri perle rilucenti,
5   tu d'amor dolce aura spiri
6   refrigerio a' miei martiri.
7   Vezzosetta e fresca rosa,
8   Umidetto e dolce labbro,
9   ch'hai la manna rugiadosa
10   sul bellissimo cinabro,
11   non parlar ma ridi e taci;
12   sien gli accenti i nostri baci.
13   Occhietti amati che m'incendiate
14   perchè spietati omai più siete
15   splendan sereni
16   di gioia pieni
17   vostri splendori
18   fiamme de' cori,
19   Bocca vermiglia ch'hai per confini,
20   O meraviglia, perle e rubini,
21   quando ridente
22   quando clemente
23   dirai: ben mio
24   ardo anch'io.

No. 4, Beautiful portal of rubies

(*Author unknown*)

1   Beautiful portal of rubies
2   You who open the way for sweet accents,
3   If in precious smiles
4   you disclose lustrous pearls,
5   you breathe out a sweet aura of love,
6   solace to my suffering.
7   Charming and fresh rose,
8   Moist and sweet lips,
9   because you have dewy manna
10   on your beautiful red lips,
11   do not talk but smile and be still;

12   let the accents be our kisses.
13   Beloved little eyes that inflame me
14   because you are ever more merciless
15   they shine brightly
16   full of joy
17   your brilliance
18   (in)flames all hearts.
19   Brilliant red mouth that you have for a border,
20   O marvelous pearls and rubies,
21   when smiling
22   when gentle
23   will you say "my darling
24   I also burn (with love)?"

To achieve the proper madrigal character of *Bella porta di rubini* (Beautiful portal of rubies), bar lines must be negated, as they would in true Renaissance style, and the vocal lines must move with the accentuation and meaning of the words. A tempo of approximately ♩ = 76 must be set so that breaths are taken only where logically indicated and do not interrupt the flow of the phrase. Although not marked specifically by the composer, a breath may be taken before the command *non parlar ma ride e taci* (do not talk but smile and be still) and before *Occhietti amati* (Beloved little eyes) each time these words introduce a phrase. Other breathing places not marked are before the second occurrence of *Bocca vermiglia* (Brilliant red mouth) and before *quando ridente* (when smiling). The final phrase, even with two *fermati,* should be sung in one breath, if possible; and, although it is not printed in most scores, the composer added the expressive marking *affettuoso* (with affection, warmth) to the final section of the song.

No. 5, Canzone di Re Enzo

(*Parole attribuite a Re Enzo*)

1   Amor mi fa sovente
2   Lo meo core penare
3   Dammi pene e sospiri
4   E son forte temente
5   per lunga dimorare
6   Ciò che poria aveniri:
7   Non ch'aggia dubitanza
8   de la dolze speranza
9   che 'n ver' di me fallanza

10 ne facesse, ma te nem' in dottanza
11 la lunga a dimoranza
12 di ciòe che venirne potesse.
13 Va, canzonetta mia,
14 E saluta messere,
15 Dilli lo mal ch'i aggio:
16 Quelli che m'an' bailia
17 si distretto mi tene
18 Ch'eo viver non poraggio
19 Salutami toscana
20 quella ched è sovrana
21 In cui regna tutta cortesia
22 E vanne in puglia piana,
23 Lamagna, capitana,
24 la dove lo mio core è nott'e dia.

No. 5, Song of King Enzo

(*Words attributed to King Enzo*)

1   Love often makes
2   My heart suffer
3   It gives me pains and sighs
4   and I am very fearful
5   throughout a long sojourn
6   of what could happen.
7   Not that I have my doubts
8   about the sweet hope
9   that in truth by me deception
10 of it is made, but you do not fear
11 the lengthy stay
12 of whatever might happen.
13 Go, my little song,
14 and greet the master.
15 Tell him the trouble that I have:
16 Those who have ruled over me
17 keep me in such anguish
18 that I can no longer live.
19 Give my best to the Tuscan woman
20 That one who is queen
21 In whom reigns every courtesy,
22 And go into the battlefield,
23 Great one, captain,
24 There where my heart is night and day.

Canzone di Re Enzo is set in the style of a medieval or early Renaissance court ballad. With a little stretch of imagination the piano accompaniment suggests the strumming of a lute or guitar, and the composer's unusually specific pedal indications enhance this idea. The *andante* tempo should be approximately ♩. = 84, and there should be a lilting quality to the 6/8 meter. The song is strophic with two stanzas, and the musical phrases are of unequal length. The pianist should follow the logic of the musical phrase while the singer phrases according to the text. When not indicated by punctuation, breaths may be taken before conjunctions or prepositional phrases, taking care to keep nouns and modifiers together and making maximum sense of the text phrase. The climax comes at the end of each verse, and the dynamics are logical and clearly indicated. A sixteenth-note triplet figure in the vocal line at measure 20 is written somewhat awkwardly to conform with the division of the syllables in the text. This figure should be kept rhythmically strict to match the accompaniment figure below it. After the *fermata* in measure 23 the accompaniment should return to a strict *a tempo* for the interlude leading to the second verse. The short postlude also requires a return to *a tempo*. The song should be performed with the simplicity a troubadour or minstrel might have given it.

Although the song is from an opera and technically outside the scope of this book, the composition stands as a "song" within the opera, the composer, himself, made the transcription for voice and piano, and it was published as part of the *Cinque canti all'antica* set.

Cinque canti all'antica: Bongiovanni, 1907–1910.

1. *L'udir talvolta*	F. 387 B. Repr. 1967
2. *Ma come potrei*	F. 388 B.
3. *Ballata*	F. 389 B. Repr. 1966
4. *Bella porta di rubini*	F. 390 B.
5. *Canzone di Re Enzo*	F. 391 B. Repr. 1967

Deità silvane

No. 1, I fauni

(*Antonio Rubino*)

1   S'odono al monte i saltellanti rivi
2   murmureggiare per le forre astruse:
3   s'odono al bosco gemer cornamuse
4   con garrito di pifferi giulivi.
5   E i fauni in corsa per dumeti e clivi,
6   erti le corna sulle fronti ottuse,

7 bevono per lor nari camuse
8 filtri sottili e zefiri lascivi.
9 E, mentre in fondo al gran coro alberato
10 piange d'amore per la vita bella la sampogna
11 dell'arcade pastore,
12 contenta e paurosa dell'agguato
13 fugge ogni ninfa più che fiera snella,
14 ardendo in bocca come ardente fiore.

Sylvan deities

No. 1, Fauns

1 One hears on the mountain the cascading brooks
2 murmuring through the hidden ravines:
3 one hears in the woods wailing bagpipes
4 with the shrillness of festive pipes.
5 And the fauns running through the little thorny shrubs and hillocks,
6 steep, their horns on their blunt foreheads,
7 (they) drink through their snub-nosed nostrils
8 subtle filters and lascivious zephyrs.
9 And, while at the bottom of a great chorus of trees
10 weeps for love for the beautiful life, the rustic bagpipe
11 of the Arcadian shepherd,
12 happy and fearful of being ambushed
13 every nymph flees quicker than a wild animal
14 burning at the mouth like a bright flower.

No. 2, Musica in horto

(*Antonio Rubino*)

1 Uno squillo di cròtali clangenti
2 rompe in ritmo il silenzio dei roseti,
3 mentre in fondo agli aulenti orti segreti
4 gorgheggia un flauto liquidi lamenti.
5 La melodia con tintinnìo d'argenti
6 par che a vicenda s'attristi e s'allieti,
7 ora luce di tremiti inquieti,
8 or diffondendo lunghe ombre dolenti:
9 Cròtali arguti e canne variotocche!
10 una gioia di càntici inespressi

11   per voi par che dai chiusi orti rampolli,
12   e in sommo dei rosai,
13   che cingon molli ghirlande
14   al cuor degli intimi recessi,
15   s'apron le rose come molli bocche.

No. 2, Music in the garden

1   The sound of a rattlesnake rattling
2   breaks in rhythm the silence of the rose gardens,
3   while at the far end of the fragrant hidden gardens
4   a flute warbles fluid laments.
5   The melody with silvery tinkling
6   it seems that it comes alive and it grows sad or rejoices in each other,
7   now shining with restless tremblings,
8   now diffusing long drawn-out sorrowful shadows:
9   Ringing rattlesnakes and various-toned reeds!
10   A joy of unexpressed songs
11   for you it seems that from the enclosed gardens spring forth,
12   and at the top of the rosebushes
13   that gird moist garlands
14   to the heart of the innermost recesses,
15   the roses open like moist mouths.

No. 3, Egle

(*Antonio Rubino*)

1   Frondeggia il bosco d'uberi verzure,
2   volgendo i rii zaffiro e margherita:
3   per gli archi verdi un'anima romita
4   cinge pallidi fuochi a ridde oscure.
5   E in te ristretta con le mani pure
6   come le pure fonti della vita,
7   di sole e d'ombre mobili vestita tu danzi,
8   Egle, con languide misure.
9   E a te candida e bionda tra le ninfe,
10   d'ilari ambagi descrivendo il verde,
11   sotto i segreti ombràcoli del verde,
12   ove la più inquieta ombra s'attrista,
13   perle squillanti e liquido ametista
14   volge la gioia roca delle linfe.

No. 3, Egle

1   The forest leafs out with fertile green foliage
2   turning the streams into sapphires and pearls:
3   through the green arches a solitary spirit
4   girds pale fires like obscure dances (reels).
5   And confined in you with pure hands
6   like the pure fountains of life,
7   dressed with sun and moving shadows you dance,
8   Egle, with languid steps.
9   And to you white and blond among the nymphs
10 of cheerful ambages describing the green,
11 beneath the hidden shady branches of foliage
12 where the most restless shadow languishes,
13 into brilliant pearls and clear amethysts
14 turns the raucous joy of the sap.

No. 4, Acqua

(*Antonio Rubino*)

1   Acqua, e tu ancora sul tuo flauto lene
2   intonami un tuo canto variolungo,
3   di cui le note abbian l'odor del fungo,
4   del musco e dell'esiguo capelvenere,
5   sì che per tutte le sottili vene,
6   onde irrighi la fresca solitudine,
7   il tuo riscintillio rida e subludii
8   al gemmar delle musiche serene.
9   Acqua, e lungh'essi i calami volubili
10 movendo in gioco le cerulee dita,
11 avvicenda più lunghe ombre alle luci,
12 tu che con modi labili deduci
13 sulla mia fronte intenta
14 e sulla vita del verde
15 fuggitive ombre di nubi.

No. 4, Water

1   Water, and you once again on your mellow flute
2   intone for me one of your variously slow songs,
3   of which the notes have the smell of the mushroom,
4   of moss and of slender maidenhair fern,

5   so that through all the thin veins
6   where you irrigate the cool solitude,
7   your brilliance returns and flows
8   at the unfolding of the serene music.
9   Water, and alongside of them the twining reeds
10   moving in clay the pale blue fingers
11   alternating longer shadows with lights,
12   you who with fleeting ways drew forth
13   over my tense forehead
14   and over the living foliage
15   fleeting shadows of clouds.

No. 5, Crepuscolo

(*Antonio Rubino*)

1   Nell'orto abbandonato
2   ora l'edace muschio
3   contende all'ellere i recessi,
4   e tra il coro snelletto dei cipressi
5   s'addorme in grembo dell'antica pace
6   Pan.
7   Sul vasto marmoreo torace,
8   che i convolvoli infiorano d'amplessi,
9   un tempo forse con canti sommessi
10   piegò una ninfa il bel torso procace.
11   Deità della terra, forza lieta!
12   troppo pensiero è nella tua vecchiezza:
13   per sempre inaridita è la tua fonte.
14   Muore il giorno, e per l'alta ombra inquieta
15   trema e s'attrista un canto d'allegrezza:
16   lunghe ombre azzurre scendono dal monte.

No. 5, Twilight

1   In the abandoned garden
2   Now the destructive moss
3   competes with the ivy in the recesses,
4   and amid the slender columns of cypresses
5   falls asleep in the bosom of peaceful antiquity
6   Pan.
7   On the wide marble thorax
8   that the bindweeds adorn with embraces,

9   once perhaps with soft singing
10 a nymph bent her beautiful torso provokingly
11 God of the earth, joyous force!
12 There is too much concern in your old age:
13 forever dried up is your fountain.
14 The day dies and through the deep quiet shadow
15 a song of joy quavers and grows sad:
16 long blue shadows descend from the mountain.

The five songs of *Deità Silvane* (Sylvan deities) were sent to the publisher Ricordi on March 1, 1917. Thus they were composed shortly after the completion (but before the great success) of *The Fountains of Rome*. Although Respighi's letters of these months indicate one of his many melancholy moods, the songs are lively, Impressionistic settings of picturesque forest scenes, full of the sounds of murmuring brooks, rustling leaves, and solitary flutes—which the compositional devices of Impressionism capture so beautifully.

I fauni (Fauns) begins *scherzoso* (playfully) with a melody built on intervals of fourths describing the pipes of Pan, the Arcadian shepherd; god of flocks, forests, and wildlife; and lecherous pursuer of wood nymphs. The marking *vivace* should be observed, but the initial tempo of the underlying quarter-note pulse should not be too fast. An important pentatonic melodic figure (representing the actual sound of the pipes) appears first in the accompaniment under the word *rivi* (brooks) and recurs at several key points in the song, sometimes in transposition. This figure must be heard clearly each time it appears. The first entrance of the vocal line is declamatory, but it becomes lyrical almost immediately. Sometimes the melody is supported by the accompaniment, as under the word *murmureggiare* (murmuring); at other times it is in equal partnership, as in the phrase *s'odono al bosco gemer cornamuse* (one hears in the woods wailing bagpipes), where the introductory piano melody appears in counterpoint. The character of the accompaniment should change at the *vivace* preceding the phrase *E i fauni in corsa* (And the fauns running), and the vocal line here should be more *staccato*. Similar changes of mood are clearly indicated throughout the song. The vocal phrase lines indicate suitable breathing places except at the phrase beginning *piange d'amore* (weeps for love), which should be carried through the word *sampogna* (rustic bagpipe). The marking *stringendo* (quickening) must be observed at the phrase *contenta e paurosa* (happy and fearful) to support the first climax at the word *fugge* (flees). The singer may breathe before this word. The forward rhythmic momentum must continue through the final *più vivace* section of the song. The concluding bars of arpeggiated fourths in the accompaniment should continue to build dynamically to the very last note, and the pedal should be sustained throughout.

The fourths that served as intervals of melodic organization in *I fauni* now appear in block chords in the lively, *staccato* introductory piano figure of *Musica in horto* (Music in the garden). The entrance of the voice part should be similarly *staccato,* achieved primarily through the crisp articulation of the consonants. The accompaniment, however, begins to *diminuendo* almost immediately, and the second vocal entrance should be more *legato*— specifically as it describes the "fluid lamenting" of the flute. Each vocal phrase in the song should be sung through on the initial breath whenever possible. Even at the slowest metronome marking for *moderato* ($\quarternote$ = 108), this should not be difficult.

At the key change, the *staccato* markings should be observed very carefully in the piano interlude, and the vocal entrance should maintain that character—again through consonant articulation. In the final section of the song, beginning *e in sommo dei rosai* (and at the top of the rosebushes), the melody in the left hand of the piano part should be brought out whether it is in counterpoint or in unison with the voice. The singer should breathe after *recessi* (recesses), the better to observe the *allargando* in the following measure and to *crescendo* through the final note of *bocche* (mouths). At this point the piano should rush to the final climactic chord.

Egle is the name of one of the numerous dryads, or wood nymphs, of classical mythology. The character of the song is derived from a reference in the middle of the poem to the languid dance steps of this delicate creature. It is important to establish a tempo in the introduction (approximately $\quarternote$ = 96) that permits the singer to move through each phrase as marked, without breaking for breath, and yet creates a lazy undulating beat. The quality thus achieved can also be enhanced by observing that, from the beginning through the middle of the song, every phrase begins on an upbeat. The singer must be careful not to accent them.

Tempo fluctuations, clearly indicated in common musical terminology by the composer, provide contrast in the overall Impressionistic fabric of the piece rather than underscore a particular aspect of the poem. The sixteenth-note triplet figures in the piano part supply the sparkling color of light on water and should be played as lightly as possible. Special attention should be paid to the inner voices of the piano part, beginning with the phrase *perle squillanti* (brilliant pearls) and continuing through the postlude. Absolute *legato* by both singer and pianist is essential for the mood of innocent sensuality implied in the song.

The *moderato* tempo marking for *Acqua* (Water) should not be interpreted as a strict metronomic definition (108–120). References to *canto variolungo* (variously slow songs), *fresca solitudine* (cool solitude), and *musiche serene* (serene music), along with images of *esiguo capelvenere* (slender maidenhair fern), suggest a much less hurried pulse (approximately $\quarternote\!\!.$ = 69). The constantly moving eighth notes in the melodic line and the flowing sixteenth-note accompaniment create a *moderato* feeling, even at this admittedly slower pulse, which seems more in keeping with the texture of the song. The vocal phrases can still be sung on one breath, according to the composer's indications; and a quickening of the tempo, *vivo,* is called for at the climax of the song, *subludii* (flows), the one place where sustaining the phrase might be difficult. A breath should be taken before *al gemmar* (at the unfolding).

While the final lines of the poem flow without punctuation, the clear rise and fall of the melodic line and the phrase markings indicate logical places for breathing. The piano postlude begins beneath the final phrase of the vocal line, at the word *nubi* (clouds), and contains the direction *poco tratt. a tempo* (a little drawing out of the tempo). The composer also calls for the use of soft pedal on the final line.

The title of the final song, *Crepuscolo* (Twilight), became a label for a whole group of Italian poets in the early twentieth century who were caught up in the shades and images of twilight. In this particular poem the reference is as much to the twilight of an age (classical mythology) or of life itself as it is to a time of day. The construction of the song closely follows the contrasting images of the poem. In the beginning all is desolation and decay, richly described in the E-minor tonality; the repetitive accompaniment patterns; the long, slow-flowing melodic lines in the voice part; and in a very important countermelody in the bass clef of the piano part. The pedal may be used as much as needed for this countermelody to form an unbroken duet with the voice, giving special attention to the overlapping phrases. Setting the tempo around $\downarrow$ = 76 will satisfy the *lento e triste* (slow and sad) qualification of the *andante* marking.

The image of Pan in the song is twofold. On the surface he is seen as a decaying, cold, marble fountain statue; in the poet's imagination he still lives the life of a mischievous seducer. The second image is captured by the change of tempo and distinctly more playful accompaniment pattern, which appears at the first statement of the god's name. The singer should note the composer's direction for a breath immediately before *Pan* to maximize the contrast. A wonderful musical reference to *Egle,* the third song of the set, occurs in the *Tempo languido di Valzer* (languid waltz tempo) section, which sees the torso of Pan bent over a wood nymph. This passage should be performed in the style of the third song.

The climax of the song should be less strict in tempo and follow the declarative nature of the words and contrasting tempo markings literally from measure to measure. There are poetic and musical ambiguities as the two images of Pan clash in the phrase *Deità della terra, forza lieta! troppo pensiero è nella tua vecchiezza:* (God of the earth, joyous force! There is too much concern in your old age). The tempo and accompaniment pattern of the opening measures of the song return to describe the twilight of the day and the image of the dried-up fountain, but they quickly give way after the singer's final phrase to the eternal playfulness associated with this favorite of sylvan deities. In the twilight the eyes play tricks and many things are possible!

The songs of *Deità Silvane* may be sung independently but are most effective when programmed as a set.

Deità silvane: G. Ricordi, 1917; Repr. 1949.   117086 (Set)
    1. *I fauni*   117081
    2. *Musica in horto*   117082
    3. *Egle*   117083
    4. *Acqua*   117084
    5. *Crepuscolo*   117085

Cinque liriche

No. 1, Tempi assai lontani

(*Percy Bysshe Shelley, trascrizione di Roberto Ascoli*)

1   Come l'ombra di cara estinta vita
2   sono i giorni lontani:
3   un'armonia per sempre omai fuggita,
4   una speme per sempre omai vanita,
5   un dolce amor che non avrà domani
6   sono i giorni lontani.
7   E quanti sogni nella notte fonda
8   di quel tempo passato!
9   Ogni giorno parea triste o gioconda ombra
10 che si proietti e si diffonda,
11 illudendo che a lungo avria durato:
12 tale il tempo passato!
13 Che mordente rammarico e che duolo
14 pei dì lontani tanto!
15 Son come un esil morto corpicciuolo
16 che il padre veglia,
17 e infin gli resta, solo di sua grazia,
18 il ricordo ed il rimpianto dei dì lontani tanto.

Five lyrics

No. 1, Times very long ago

(*[Italian] translation by Roberto Ascoli*)

1   Like the shadow of precious extinguished life
2   are the days long past:

3   a harmony by now forever fleeing,
4   a hope by now forever vanished,
5   a sweet love that will have no tomorrow
6   are the days long past.
7   And how many dreams in the deep night
8   of that time gone by!
9   Each day appears a sad or joyful shadow
10 that projects and diffuses itself,
11 illuding that it will last a long time:
12 such (is) time gone by!
13 What caustic regret and what grief
14 for the days so long ago!
15 They are like a thin, dead little child's body
16 that the father watches over,
17 and at last there remains for him, alone by his mercy,
18 the memory and the grieving of the days so long ago.

The first two songs of *Cinque liriche* (Five lyrics, 1918) are settings of the poetry of Percy Bysshe Shelley, whose long sojourn in Italy placed him very close to Italian sentiment. The third and fourth songs are to French texts and are not included in this discussion; and the final song sets a narrative poem by the famous Indian poet Rabindranath Tagore. The three poems originally in English were set by Respighi in Italian translation.

In *Tempi assai lontani* (Times very long ago) the composer creates, somewhat unusually for him, a prominent vocal line that is almost aria-like in its broad arch. To avoid impeding the forward flow of the melody the *andante lento* tempo should not be too slow ($\quarternote = 76$). The melody is supported by a series of chords phrased across the bar lines in units of four or five, and these, in turn, are connected by an underlying pattern of triplet eighth notes. The *dolce* quality of this flowing, *legato* background must be established in the opening measures of the song and continued under the vocal line throughout all of section A. The movement and phrasing of the chords should be seen as a countermelody to the vocal line. The pianist must maintain an even rhythmic flow, but the singer can allow a slight rhythmic flexibility to observe syllabic accents and the *tenuto* and accent marks emphasizing or leading to key words.

The change of key and tempo, *largamente* (slowly), marks the beginning of the contrasting B section, where melodic interest shifts to the piano. Throughout this section the primary melodic emphasis moves from piano to voice and back. One very long phrase, *Ogni giorno parea triste o gioconda ombra che si proietti e si siffonda* (Each day appears a sad or joyful shadow that projects and diffuses itself), may be broken for breath after *parea* or *ombra* or at both places. At the end of the section the *rallentando* must be observed so that the triplet eighth-note measure, marked *ppp* and *più lento* has a *déja vu* quality. A complete break, marked with a *fermata,* must be observed before playing the final measure; and the final chord should be held over with the pedal into the Tempo I°, the return of section A (the pedal is released on the third beat of the measure). This beautiful effect is quite deliberate on the part of the composer. The return of section A adheres closely to the expression used in its first appearance, and some material from section B brings the song to a close. A complete break must be made again (marked with *fermati*) before the piano postlude, which should evoke a thematic echo "of days so long ago."

No. 2, Canto funebre

(*Percy Bysshe Shelley, trascrizione di Roberto Ascoli*)

1   Rude vento, che diffondi in suon di pianto
2   un dolore troppo triste per un canto;
3   fiero vento che, se il ciel di nubi è fosco,
4   fai suonar di notte a morto le campane;
5   uragano, le cui lagrime son vane;
6   e tu, cupo dalle nude rame o bosco;
7   o spelonche funerarie, o mar profondo,
8   voi piangete, voi piangete il mal del mondo.

No. 2, Funeral song

(*[Italian] translation by Roberto Ascoli*)

1   Rough wind, you who diffuse with a mournful sound
2   a grief too sad for a song;
3   Fierce wind, you who, if the sky is dark with clouds,
4   make the bells toll the knell at night;
5   hurricane, whose tears are in vain;
6   and you, dark with your naked branches, O woods;
7   O funereal caverns, O deep sea,
8   you weep, you weep, for the evil of the world.

Respighi's attempt to create fiery hurricane winds in *Canto funebre* (Funeral song) requires the technique of a virtuoso pianist. The ominous, rumbling chromatic *ostinato* bass should be as fast as comfortable without losing the accents that define the phrasing of the pattern. The tempo, *allegro cupo* (fast, dark), should be set by the pianist. The vocal line of the song is through-composed, but the return of the initial piano *ostinato* at the end of the composition creates the impression of an ABA structure. In order to project the vocal line above the very active accompaniment the diction must be exceedingly clear, and the singer should choose vocal colors that enable expressive words to stand out in relief. The line should never be forced dynamically or vocally. Singers without a secure resonant low range should avoid this song.

At the proper tempo the first phrase can probably be sung on one breath. If additional breath is needed it can be taken after *pianto* (mournful). Later in the 7/4 measures—*fai suonar di notte a morto le campane* (literally, "make sound at night for the dead the bells")—a breath can be taken after *morto*. The same measures introduce the "bell motive": C♮ or B♯, F♯, and G♯ octaves in the bass line of the piano part. These tones must be accented as marked; and the *ffp* effects that precede them in the treble are equally important. When the chromatic *ostinato* returns in the final section of the song, the broader treble melodic line should be phrased in relation to the vocal line it partners. Punctuation in the text of the last section provides ample space for breathing, although the singer who feels the need for an additional breath in the last phrase may take one after *mal* (evil). There should be no slackening of the forward rhythmic drive in the last line of the piano part. The *fff* to *pp decrescendo* can be achieved at the very end of the last measure just by observing the composer's *fermata*.

No. 5, La fine

(Rabindranath Tagore, traduzione di Clary Zannoni Chaunet)

1 È tempo per me d'andare, mamma, me ne vado.
2 Quando nell'oscurità pallente dell'alba solitaria
3 tu stenderai le braccia al tuo piccino che è nel letto,
4 io ti dirò: "Il bimbo non c'è! Mamma, me ne vado."
5 Diventerò un delicato soffio d'aria e ti carezzerò
6 e incresperò l'acqua mentre ti bagni e ti bacerò,
7 ti bacerò ancora.
8 Nella notte tempestosa mentre la pioggia batte sulle foglie
9 tu m'udrai bisbigliare nel tuo letto,
10 e il mio riso splenderà
11 con il lampo attraverso la finestra aperta
12 nella tua stanza.
13 Se tu veglierai fin tardi nella notte
14 pensando al tuo piccino
15 io ti canterò dalle stelle:
16 "Dormi, mamma, dormi."
17 Sugli erranti raggi lunari io verrò pian piano
18 sul tuo letto e giacerò sul tuo cuore mentre tu dormi.
19 Diverrò un sogno e attraverso le tue palpebre socchiuse

20 scenderò nel profondo del tuo sonno
21 e quando ti sveglierai e guarderai intorno angosciata,
22 come una lucciola scintillante m'involerò nell'oscurità.
23 Quando nel giorno della gran festa
24 i bimbi del villaggio verranno.
25 e giocheranno intorno alla casa,
26 mi fonderò nella musica del flauto
27 e palpiterò nel tuo cuore tutto il giorno
28 La cara zia verrà coi doni della festa
29 e domanderà:
30 "Dov'è il nostro piccino, sorella?"
31 Mamma, tu le dirai dolcemente:
32 "È nelle pupille dei miei occhi,
33 in me stessa e nell'anima mia!"

No. 5, The end

([Italian] translation by Clary Zannoni Chaunet)

1   It is time for me to leave, Mamma, I am leaving.
2   When in the pale darkness of the lonely dawn
3   you will extend your arms to your little one who is in bed,
4   I will say to you: "The baby is not there! Mamma, I am leaving"
5   I will become a soft breath of air and I will caress you
6   and I will ripple the water while you bathe and I will kiss you,
7   I will kiss you again.
8   In the stormy night while the rain beats on the leaves
9   You will hear me whispering in your bed,
10 and my smile will shine
11 with the lightning through the open window
12 into your room.
13 If you stay awake until late in the night
14 thinking of your little one
15 I will sing to you from the stars:
16 "Sleep, Mamma, sleep"
17 on the wandering lunar rays I will come very softly
18 to your bed and I will lie on your heart while you sleep
19 I will become a dream and across your closed eyelids
20 I will descend into the depth of your sleep
21 and when you wake up and look about in anguish
22 like a sparkling firefly I will fly around in the darkness
23 When in the day of the great festival
24 the children of the village come,
25 and they will play around the house,

26   I will blend myself in the music of the flute
27   and I will palpitate in your heart all day long.
28   My dear aunt will come with holiday gifts
29   and she will ask:
30   "Where is our little one, sister?"
31   Mamma, you will tell her gently:
32   He is in the pupils of my eyes,
33   in my very self and in my soul.

La fine, the translation of "The End," a long, poignant narrative poem by Rabindranath Tagore, provides Respighi with the material for many colorful compositional effects. The song is constructed in sections, divided according to the background images the composer selects for special treatment. The story is threaded through this structure, at times in recitative style, at other times with aria-like melody.

The descending octaves underlying the opening recitative immediately establish a mournful mood. (The pianist should be aware that Respighi indicates very specific pedaling to carry through particular harmonies at several places in this song.) The dying child is the narrator, but the singer should not attempt a childlike quality except in direct quotations, as in measures 10–12, *"Il bimbo non c'è! Mamma, me ne vado"* ("The baby is not there! Mamma, I am leaving").

The changing piano figurations in measure 13 describe the movement of air, just as the alternating sixteenth notes in measure 16, marked *mormorando* (murmuring), describe the movement of water. The *forte* dynamic and the rumbling bass of the piano in measure 20 anticipate the storm that is the focus of the next section of the song. The repetitious major seconds in triplets in measure 23 should be as relentless as raindrops, while the highest notes of the treble are linked to create a countermelody to the vocal line. (If punctuation does not provide logical breaks in the phrase, the singer should look for subordinate clauses and breathe before them.) The *crescendo* throughout the "storm" section should build very gradually to the smashing *ff* climax at the word *stanza* (room). The energy from this climax should be carried through by the pianist into the bridge to the "lullaby" section, beginning in measure 38. The pianist should emphasize the countermelody, which appears here in the treble, and pay special attention to the bass-line countermelody, which begins in the *calmo* (calm) section at measure 43. The pedal markings are also important at this point.

The next section of the song, beginning in measure 63, describes a dreamlike state with shimmering treble chords and octaves against a repetitive G♯ octave figure in the bass. The vocal line, which was lyrical in the lullaby section, is once again speechlike. It descends on the phrase *scenderò nel profondo del tuo sonno* (I will descend into the depth of your sleep) and rises with the phrase *e guarderai intorno angosciata* (and look about in anguish). The firefly mentioned in the text in measure 78 is described musically by the piano in measures 82–83.

Measure 84 marks the beginning of the new "play" section. The tempo is *allegretto scherzo,* and the left hand of the piano part represents the bouncy movements of the children during the feast. There should be no change of tempo as this section passes to the following "flute" episode.

Most of the activity dies down with the introduction of the aunt into the story, and the vocal line returns to a *parlato* (spoken) style. The words of the aunt and the mother—as spoken by the narrator—should have a change of color. The mother's final lines should express her heartbreaking resignation. The final piano chords, repeating the opening measures of the song, bring the composition to full cycle. They should die away and peacefully resolve to the final C-major chord.

In essence this song is a short *scena,* but care should be taken not to overdramatize it. The singer's delivery should be simple and direct, and the pianist should provide unobtrusive background or comment on the action.

Cinque liriche: G. Ricordi, 1918; Repr. 1950.   117196 (Set)
    1. *Tempi assai lontani*
    2. *Canto funebre*
    5. *La fine*

Sei liriche (prima serie)

No. 6, Pioggia

(*Vittoria Aganoor Pompilj*)

1   Piovea: per le finestre spalancate
2   A quella tregua di ostinati odori
3   saliano dal giardin fresche folate
4   d'erbe risorte e di risorti fiori
5   S'acchettava il tumulto dei colori
6   sotto il vel delle gocciole implorate;
7   E intorno ai pioppi ai frassini agli allori
8   Beveano ingorde le zolle assetate.
9   Esser pianta, esser foglia, esser stelo
10 E nell'angoscia dell'ardor (pensavo)
11 Così largo ristoro aver dal cielo!
12 Sul davanzal protesa io gli arboscelli,
13 I fiori, l'erbe guardavo guardavo
14 E mi battea la pioggia sui capelli.

Six lyrics (first series)

No. 6, Rain

1 It rained; through the windows thrown open
2 to that respite of persistent ardors
3 rose from the garden fresh abundances
4 of revived grasses and of revived flowers.
5 The tumult of colors was appeased
6 under the veil of implored raindrops;
7 and around the poplars, the ash trees, the laurels,
8 the thirsty roots were drinking greedily.
9 To be a plant, to be a leaf, to be a stem
10 and in the anguish of ardor (I was thinking)
11 such great relief to have from heaven!
12 Over the windowsill, outstretched, I . . . at the trees,
13 the flowers, the grass kept on staring
14 and the rain kept beating upon my hair.

Pioggia (Rain), one of Respighi's best-known songs, has been published in several anthologies. A printing error occurs in most, if not all, editions of the song.* In the final word, *capelli,* the melody on the syllable *pel* ascends by two whole steps in half-note values to the final syllable, *li.* The slur then functions correctly in indicating that the syllable is sung through both half notes. Also, the final note for the pianist is in the bass clef; the change of clef is missing in some editions.

The greatest difficulty in performing this piece is anticipating the steady tempo, which must be set by both performers right at the downbeat. The singer must be ready before the pianist begins and must follow the tempo established on the first beat of the accompaniment. The incessant patter of rain is expressed by the accompanying figure, while the vocal line must be well articulated within a *legato* line. If the tempo is felt in two half-note beats per measure, the smoothness continues easily as three impulses in the 6/4 measure, giving the effect of slowing down and taking the place of an actual *ritard.* The piano continues in a burst of speed and dynamics that has its own rhythmic slow-down with the half-measure triplet divisions. With a gradual *diminuendo* and *rallentando* in the last measure of the triplet figure, the rhythmic fervor ends in a sustained *pianissimo* chord over which the voice enters very quietly and contemplatively. It then moves quickly through a passionate crescendo to the much-broadened *E nell'angoscia dell'ardor*

---

*This error was pointed out to author Lakeway by her voice teacher in Italy, Alba Zurlo Anzellotti, who had been personally coached by Respighi in the performance of his songs.

(and in the anguish of ardor). The interpretive breath before *pensavo* (I was thinking) is intended by the composer. With a *rallentando* and *diminuendo,* the piano phrase complements the vocal expression of wonder and longing. The mood changes again suddenly with the dynamic and tempo recapitulation of the patter figure in the accompaniment. The voice entrance is similar to the beginning and should continue in light and flowing phrases. A slight *ritard* may be made on the repetition of the word *guardavo* (I kept on staring), but the downbeat of the next measure is *a tempo,* which must be observed strictly through the final vocal phrase. The last four measures of the accompaniment are faster and should be articulated very lightly.

The Dorian modality and melodic minor tonality used in this song may cause the singer some difficulty with intonation. The sequence of whole and half steps must be established carefully.

Sei liriche (prima serie): Bongiovanni, 1912–1919.
    6. *Pioggia*   F. 486a B.

Sei liriche (Seconda serie)

No. 1, Notte

(*Ada Negri*)

1   Sul giardino fantastico
2   Profumato di rosa
3   La carezza de l'ombra posa
4   Pure ha un pensiero e un palpito
5   La quiete suprema
6   L'aria come per brivido trema.
7   La luttuosa tenebra
8   Una storia di morte
9   Racconta alle cardenie
10 Smorte?
11 Forse perchè una pioggia
12 Di soavi rugiade
13 Entro i socchiusi petali
14 Cade su l'ascose miserie e su l'ebbrezze perdute,
15 Sui muti sogni e l'ansie mute.
16 Su le fugaci gioie
17 Che il disinganno infrange
18 La notte le sue lacrime
19 Piange.

Six lyrics (Second series)

No. 1, Night

1   Over the fantastic garden
2   Rose-scented
3   The caress of darkness settles down
4   Still it has a thought and a palpitation
5   The supreme quiet
6   The air trembles as if shivering.
7   The mournful darkness
8   A story of death
9   It tells to the gardenias
10 Lifeless?
11 Perhaps because a rain
12 Of light dews
13 Within the half-closed petals
14 Falls on the hidden miseries and on lost elations
15 On mute dreams and mute longings
16 On the short-lived joys
17 That shatter disillusion
18 The night its tears
19 Weeps.

The second series (1919) of *Sei liriche* (Six lyrics) shows many elements of Respighi's mature style and the increasing influence of Impressionism. The first song of the set, *Notte* (Night), has become one of his best-known songs. It has a simple ABA + Coda structure in which the central, questioning lines of the poem, beginning at *La luttuosa tenebra* (The mournful darkness), constitute the contrasting B section.

Much of the vague, ethereal quality of the poetry is carried over into the music by Respighi's melodic cadencing on the fifth of the scale at the end of each section. At the end of section B this fifth becomes enharmonically the fifth of the returning A section key, and it is not until the final note of the coda that the voice cadences on the tonic. The *lento tranquillo* tempo should not be too slow ($\quarternote = 76$–80) or the accompaniment will plod and it will be difficult to connect phrases. The accompaniment pattern presented in the introduction should be played as directed *dolcissimo e molto legato,* and the pianist should be aware of a secondary but recognizable counter-melody indicated by quarter notes on the second, third, and fourth beats of the left-hand pattern.

Vocal phrasing poses some problems since Respighi, as usual, places greater emphasis on musical than on textual considerations. For example,

Sul giardino fantastico/Profumato di rosa (literally, "Over the garden fantastic/Perfumed with roses") should be sung on one breath for maximum text sense, yet the composer chooses to see the poem as it is laid out in poetic lines and creates two phrases. These can still be connected providing the chosen tempo does not tax the breath resources of the singer. An even greater problem is caused by inverse word order; *La quiete suprema* (literally, "The quiet supreme") is the subject of *Pure ha un pensiero e un palpito* (Still it has a thought and a palpitation). The singer is aided here, however, by the directions *un poco mosso* and the ascending scale passage in the accompaniment. Again, if the phrase is not sung on one breath the singer should at least attempt to connect the meaning. The alternating eighth notes at the close of section A make a picturesque accompaniment beneath the words *per brivido trema* (trembles as if shivering) and carry over expressively into the bass line of the next section. The change of key to C♯ minor, greater use of chromatic harmony, and the more aggressive accompaniment all serve the more ominous thoughts in the poetry. The singer might use a slightly darker vocal color here, but the piano part, while less *dolce,* must still observe the *legato.*

The returning A section with the triplet variation in the accompaniment takes its interpretive character from the direction *mormorando* (murmuring) and the *ppp* dynamic marking. A dynamic marking may be missing at the beginning of the song, but it should obviously be *p* or *mp* to permit later contrast in the final A section. The problem phrase here is *Sui muti sogni e l'ansie mute* (On mute dreams and mute longings). A breath could be taken after *sogni.*

In the coda all melodic interest shifts to the piano while the voice intones one long phrase above it on the fifth tone of the scale. Possible breathing places are after *gioie* (joys) and *notte* (night) if textual considerations are paramount. The final *Piange* (Weeps) should be quietly expressive, not dramatic, and released with the piano after the last note of the sustained arpeggio (again the fifth of the scale).

No. 2, Su una violetta morta

(*Percy Bysshe Shelley* [*translator not known*])

1 È vanito l'odor di questo fiore,
2 che, come il bacio tuo,
3 tenero ardente respirava su me.
4 Anche di questo fior fuggì il colore,
5 che rilucea deliziosamente di te,
6 solo di te.
7 Forma languida e vana ella riposa
8 sul mio povero cuor, che non oblia,

9   povero stanco cuor; immobile, di gel, silenziosa
10 ella irride così l'anima mia,
11 l'anima calda ancor.
12 Invano invano io piango a lei d'accanto;
13 e sospirando invan su lei mi chino:
14 oh! tutto in lei finì!
15 Il suo destino è muto, senza pianto.
16 Oh! il mio destino dovrebbe esser così.

No. 2, On a dead violet

1   The fragrance of this flower has vanished,
2   that, like your kiss,
3   tender ardor used to breathe on me.
4   Even from this flower the color has gone,
5   which shone delightfully, after you,
6   only from you.
7   Her languid and useless form she reposes
8   on my poor heart, which does not forget,
9   poor tired heart; motionless, cold, silently
10 she laughs like this at my soul,
11 my soul still warm.
12 In vain, in vain I cry to her beside me;
13 and sighing in vain stoop over her:
14 Oh! everything ends in her!
15 Her destiny is silent, without weeping.
16 Oh! My destiny should be thus.

The sadness of the poem *Su una violetta morta* (On a dead violet) can be felt in the descending minor and chromatic chords in the left hand of the accompaniment. The tied-over rhythms within the 12/8 triplet groupings prevent the scales from cascading too rapidly and contribute a languid character. The pianist should attempt to pull these scales through their full two octave length without breaking the phrase, and the chords that accompany the melodic scales should virtually melt together. Since the vocal line often parallels the scales at the unison or octave, the singer should depend on the words and their changing vowel colors rather than stress to distinguish it from the piano line. At an *andante expressivo* tempo the text phrases fall rather well within their punctuation. The long phrase at *poco più mosso e animando* (a little more motion and more animated), which reads *Forma languida e vana ella riposa sul mio povero cuor* (Her languid and useless form she reposes on my poor heart), could be broken for a breath immediately after *reposa*. The climax of the song comes at *povero stanco cuor* (poor tired heart). Respighi builds to this nicely through the use of a series of shorter descending scale lines, which burst into longer units at the climax.

The recitative-style section, starting at *immobile, di gel, silenziosa* (motionless, cold, silently), should be sung at a much slower tempo, following the accent of the word rhythms and avoiding a strict metric feeling.

The song is an ABA form, but only enough of the original material comes back at the end to identify that structure. Otherwise, there are many differences and bits of new material in the latter part of the song. The low chords in the bass clef of the accompaniment should have a somewhat ominous sound on the final page and the final vocal phrases *and* the short final piano motive should be performed quite emphatically.

(Nos. 3 and 4 of this series are settings of French texts.)

No. 5, Piccola mano bianca

(*Francesco Rocchi*)

1   Piccola mano bianca,
2   che tanto destino racchiudi,
3   porgi l'esili dita
4   sul mio tumido cuore.
5   Senti? il palpito preme
6   frequente con rapidi balzi.
7   Porgi l'orecchio:
8   suona d'amore il canto.
9   Suona le brevi gioie,
10 che limpide teco suggeva
11 ne la purezza d'oro
12 del meriggio d'estate,
13 suona la lunga pena
14 de l'animo laborioso,
15 che ti brama ti adora e ti venera e teme.
16 Oh ne le chiome lunghe,
17 fluenti su l'alabastro de le nitide spalle,
18 premere il bacio mio!
19 Oh a la piccola mano,
20 che tanto destino racchiude.
21 dare l'ultima gioia
22 de l'esistenza vana!

No. 5, Little white hand

1   Little white hand,
2   that holds so much destiny,
3   Place your thin fingers
4   on my swollen heart.
5   Do you feel? The palpitation presses
6   frequently with rapid leaps.
7   Place your ear (to my heart):
8   the song of love resounds.
9   It sounds of brief joys,
10 which clearly it used to absorb with you
11 in the golden purity
12 of a midday in the summer,
13 it sounds of the deep suffering
14 of the wearisome mind,
15 which longs for you, adores you, and reveres and fears you.
16 Oh, in your long hair
17 Flowing over the alabaster of your distinct shoulders,
18 On pressing my kiss!
19 Oh, to the little hand,
20 that holds so much destiny,
21 on giving it its last joy
22 of useless existence.

Although the poem speaks of "lost joys" it is the "remembered joys" that govern the mood of *Piccola mano bianca* (Little white hand). The structure of the song is ABA, with a coda in which some thematic material from section B returns. Respighi does not relate the structure of the music to the structure of the poem (in fact, the final A section returns in the middle of a phrase of text), but uses the meaning of the poetry as inspiration for the song. Because of the more frequent pauses in the text, the vocal phrasing in this song is less problematic than in *Notte*.

In the opening section the piano accompaniment must be played *legato* with emphasis on the sustained half note, on the pedal tone F♯, and especially on the phrasing of the chords in units as marked: a nine-chord unit, an interruption of eighth notes, a four-chord unit, two three-chord units, and so forth. The vocal line can be phrased according to the text, making sure to connect the phrase *dita sul mio tumido cuore* (fingers on my swollen heart). The following *agitato* section also achieves its character through the phrasing of the accompaniment. The re-attack on the second-beat chord creates a mild syncopation. Coupled with the sequential arrangement of the chords, it creates an excellent transition to the sweeping melody of section

B. The *poco ritardando* is very important in the measure before Tempo I°,
for the new melody, bearing a remarkable resemblance to Rimsky-Korsakov's
Sheherezade, should be played broadly.

The main interest throughout section B is in the piano part. The opening
melody is followed by two sequential patterns, and while the voice part is
essential, it is a lesser ingredient in the total texture of the section. The long
vocal phrase that closes the section could be broken for a breath after *pena*
(suffering).

The return of section A parallels the opening of the song except that it
does not modulate. Respighi's only concession to the greater intensity of the
poetry here is the direction *agitato* and later *con passione.* The coda begins
with a clear statement of the principal B section theme, this time for both
piano and voice, which trails off after six measures into a chromatic chord
progression resolving clearly to D major.

No. 6, Il giardino

(*Francesco Rocchi*)

1   Mormora nel giardino
2   a piè del colle una musica dolce,
3   un'armonia di note gravi
4   ne la sera pia;
5   mentre l'effluvio de le pie corolle
6   sommessamente in lievi onde,
7   in lievi onde si estolle
8   balsamando di sè tutta la via.
9   Muore nel cielo
10 e palpita una stria ultima d'oro;
11 e su da l'erba molle
12 i mille trilli tremano dal lago,
13 dove l'acqua specchiante
14 abbrividisce tacita
15 al suono vanescente e vago
16 di quella triste musica di sera.
17 Il giardino nel sonno
18 illanguidisce voluttuoso
19 de la primavera.

No. 6. The garden

1   (It) murmurs in the garden
2   at the foot of the hill a sweet music,

3   a harmony of deep-toned notes
4   in the pious evening,
5   while the effluence from the pious corollas
6   softly in light waves,
7   in light waves it rises
8   embalming the air with itself along the way.
9   It dies in the sky
10 and palpitates a last thin streak of gold;
11 and from above the soft grass
12 thousands of vibrations tremble from the lake,
13 where the reflecting water
14 quietly shivers to the sound
15 fading and vague
16 of that sad evening music.
17 The garden in sleep
18 languishes voluptuous
19 in the springtime.

Crepuscolo, or "twilight," imagery, so admired by the composers of Respighi's generation, is the inspiration for the through-composed song *Il giardino* (The garden). The piano part and the vocal line are totally integrated to create a subtly shifting atmosphere reflecting the sounds and colors described or implied in the poetry. A tempo of approximately ♩ = 84 will permit the pianist to achieve the Impressionistic effects, which depend on rapid finger articulation, and still allow the singer's lines to move languidly. The use of pedal in achieving these effects is left to the discretion of the performer, with the exception of four places where Respighi indicates that sounds are to be carried through the rests (see measures 16–17, 20–21, 22–23, and the final four).

The melodic phrases are based on musical rather than textual considerations. In the first section the singer may breathe after *giardino* (garden), *colle* (hill), *armonia* (harmony), *pia* (holy), *corolle* (corollas), and *onde* (waves) without distorting the text. However, these phrases should be sung in longer units whenever the singer can connect them comfortably.

The *a tempo* marking in measure 20 implies a *ritardando* in the preceding measures. It should begin on the phrase *in lievi onde si estolle* (in light waves it rises), thereby emphasizing the words *si estolle* while giving the pianist more time for the colorful but technically difficult figuration that underscores them. Respighi also indicates that a breath may be taken before *si estolle.* The changing accompaniment beginning with the phrase *Muore nel cielo* (It dies in the sky) still requires a *legato* approach, and the tempo should not change until the *poco animando* six measures later. When the original accompaniment figure returns at the final section of the song it should be slightly slower than the Tempo I°.

Both singer and pianist should be aware at the outset that the overall dynamic levels of the song vary only between *ppp* and *mf,* with a preponderance of *p*. A few words are given colorful effects, such as *si estolle,* discussed earlier; *palpita* (palpitates) is given a rapid rhythmic pattern; and *vanescente e vago* (fading and vague) is set with a *decrescendo*. However, Respighi's objective is to capture the overall mood of the poem rather than to depict specific word images.

Sei liriche (seconda serie): Bongiovanni, 1919; Repr. 1966.

1. *Notte*	F. 521 B.
2. *Su una violetta morta*	F. 522 B.
5. *Piccola mano bianca*	F. 525 B.
6. *Il giardino*	F. 526 B.

E se un giorno tornasse

(*Vittoria Aganoor Pompilj*)

1 E se un giorno tornasse che dovrei dirgli?
2 Digli che lo si attese fino a morirne.
3 E se ancora interrogasse senza riconoscermi?
4 Parla a lui come farebbe una sorella; forse egli soffre.
5 E se chiede dove siete, che debbo dirgli?
6 Dagli il mio anello d'oro, senza parole.
7 E se vorrà sapere perchè la sala è vota?
8 Mostragli che la lampada è spenta e l'uscio aperto.
9 Ma se poi mi richiede dell'ultima ora?
10 Digli che in quell'ora ho sorriso per non far ch'egli pianga.

And if one day he returns

1 And if one day he returns what should I say to him?
2 Say to him that you waited for him until death.
3 And if he still questions without recognizing me?
4 Speak to him as a sister would; perhaps he suffers
5 And if he asks where you are, what do I tell him?
6 Give him my gold ring, without words.
7 And if he wants to know why the room is empty?
8 Show him that the lamp is extinguished and the door is open.
9 But if he then asks again about the final hour?
10 Tell him that in that hour I smiled so as not to make him weep.

The tortured intensity of the poetry of *E se un giorno tornasse* (And if one day he returns) is well served by the *recitativo* setting, but the lack of a meter signature should not be interpreted as the absence of a regular rhythmic pulse. In fact, the success of the *parlando* vocal line depends on the underlying harmonic changes falling with definite regularity under the proper word accents in the text. With equal quarter notes supplying the pulse, the *molto lento e triste* tempo should be just that—very slow and sad, but not so slow that the phrases cannot be felt in long, one-line units. Except for the two places where *fermati* are indicated over rests (and are at the discretion of the singer), this recitative has a forward movement and a consequent emotional buildup that does not end until the release of the final note. Even the *largo* at the climax of the song and the following *rallentando* are a broadening of the basic pulse. The *crescendo ed incalzando a poco a poco* (louder and more pressing, little by little) must begin where indicated, and the other dynamic markings must clearly elucidate the words. The accompaniment should be very *legato;* some pedal blurring would help to create the Impressionistic mood. The singer should capitalize on the one major chord in the entire composition, at the words *ho sorriso* (I smiled), to bring about the necessary change of vocal color at this point. It is followed by an immediate return to the mournful mood of the rest of the song. Although not difficult technically, this song demands extraordinary emotional control and sensitive artistry.

E se un giorno tornasse: G. Ricordi, 1919; Repr. 1949.   117459

Quattro liriche: Antica poesia popolare armena

No. 1, No, non è morto il figlio tuo

(*Constant Zarian*)

1   No, non è morto il figlio tuo;
2   oh, non è morto, non è morto.
3   Se n'è andato pel giardino:
4   ha raccolto tante rose;
5   se n'è inghirlandata la fronte:
6   ed ora dorme al loro dolce odore.

Four lyrics: Old popular Armenian poetry

No. 1, No, your son is not dead

1   No, your son is not dead;
2   oh, he is not dead, he is not dead.
3   He (has) left through the garden:
4   he gathered many roses;
5   he wreathed his (own) forehead:
6   and now he sleeps in their sweet fragrance.

No. 2, La mamma è come il pane caldo

(*Constant Zarian*)

1   La mamma è come il pane caldo:
2   chi ne mangia si sente pago.
3   Il babbo è come il vino schietto:
4   chi ne beve si sente ebbro.
5   Il fratello è come il sole:
6   Esso schiara monti e valli.

No. 2, A mother is like hot bread

1   A mother is like hot bread:
2   whoever eats some of it feels contented.
3   A father is like pure wine:
4   whoever drinks some of it feels inebriated.
5   A brother is like the sun:
6   It brightens mountains and valleys.

No. 3, Io sono la Madre

(*Constant Zarian*)

1   Io sono la Madre . . .
2   Per sempre, per sempre è partito
3   il Figliuolo mio crocefisso.
4   Io sono la Madre . . .
5   Ho le pupille, ho le pupille fisse
6   su la strada senza fine,

7   dov'è passato il mio Signore.
8   Io sono il Cuore, dolore e lagrima,
9   il pianto di colui ch'è morto.
10 Io sono la Madre, Mariam,
11 l'ora dell'angoscia che freme d'intorno,
12 la mano lucente del mio Figliuolo
13 che si è crocefisso.
14 Io sono la Madre.

No. 3, I am the Mother

1   I am the Mother. . .
2   forever, forever (he) is gone
3   my crucified Son.
4   I am the Mother . . .
5   My eyes, my eyes are fixed
6   on the endless road,
7   where my Lord has passed.
8   I am the Heart, grief and weeping
9   the tears of him who is dead.
10 I am the Mother, Miriam,
11 the hour of anguish that throbs all around,
12 the shining hand of my loving Son
13 who is crucified.
14 I am His Mother.

No. 4, Mattino di luce

(Nersès)

1   Mattino di luce, sole di giustizia,
2   il tuo lume si levi dentro me.
3   Destati, o Signore, ad assisterci:
4   desta me assopito:
5   fa ch'io divenga simigliante agli angioli.
6   Destati, o Signore.
7   Fatti vita di me che son morto,
8   fatti luce per me ottenebrato,
9   lenisci il mio dolore!
10 Io ti prego con la mia voce,
11 Io ti supplico con le mie mani:
12 concedimi il dono della tua Benevolenza.

13 Dà ai miei occhi l'acqua perchè io pianga,
14 perchè io pianga a grosse lagrime,
15 e così cancelli i miei peccati.
16 Gesù in nome dell'amore,
17 intenerisci nel tuo amore il mio cuore di pietra.
18 Versa, o Signore, nella mia anima
19 la rugiada del tuo sangue,
20 e la mia anima si rallegrerà.

No. 4, A morning of light

1   A morning of light, sun of justice,
2   Lift up your light within me.
3   Awaken, O Lord, to help us:
4   Awaken me (from) drowsiness
5   make me become like the angels.
6   Awaken, O Lord.
7   Make me alive who is dead.
8   Make light for me in darkness,
9   Soothe my grief!
10 I pray to you with my voice,
11 I implore you with my hands:
12 Grant me the gift of your Benevolence.
13 Give to my eyes water so that I may weep
14 So that I may weep large tears,
15 and thus erase my sins.
16 Jesus, in the name of love,
17 soften in your love my heart of stone.
18 Pour, O Lord, into my soul
19 the dew of your blood,
20 and my soul will rejoice.

The unifying elements in Respighi's settings of four old popular Armenian poems are simplicity and modality. The former underscores the direct emotional content of the poetry, and the latter, while not strictly observed, gives the songs a middle-European flavor, separating them from the composer's usual Italianate idiom.

The first song, *No, non è morto il figlio tuo* (No, your son is not dead), is in the Phrygian mode transposed. The repetitive accompaniment, narrow melodic range, and *lento* tempo create the effect of a lullaby. The subdued dynamic range (*pp* to *mf*) should be observed strictly. Most of the phrasing falls in line with the punctuation in the poetry, but the singer could take a breath, if needed, after *ed ora dorme* (and now he sleeps) so that the rest of the phrase remains unbroken. The pianist should bring out the echo of the opening melody, which overlaps the singer's final phrase.

The second song, *La mamma è come il pane caldo* (A mother is like hot bread), sets the happiest of the poems in F major, but even here clear-cut scales are avoided (the fourth degree is often skipped), and a modal feeling results. The repetitive rhythm of the accompaniment and shifting accents in the vocal line evoke medieval dance music. The singer may need a breath after *Esso schiara* (It brightens) to complete the lengthened final phrase.

The third song, *Io sono la madre* (I am the Mother), uses the same melodic motive each time the words of the title are repeated. The varying levels of intensity in the text are reflected in clearly marked dynamic and tempo changes in the music. There is a change of key signature in the B section of the song, but the composer's avoidance of the crucial third degree of the scale and chromatic alterations in the accompaniment create the same ambiguous modality that is felt throughout the other songs. The descending fourths in the accompaniment of this song bears some resemblance to the accompaniment pattern of the first song. In order to build to the *fortissimo* intensity of the climactic phrase, the singer may need a breath after *del mio Figliuolo* (of my loving Son). The pianist completes the song with an augmentation of the title motive.

The final song, *Mattino di luce* (A morning of light), is set to a prayer by the Armenian poet Nersès (d. 1165). The moods of the supplicant vary from quiet contemplation to fiery outbursts. As in the opening song of the set, the melody is basically in the Phrygian mode, transposed, with an excursion to an altered parallel major in the final section and a harmonic understructure that shifts rather freely. The effect is similar to Gregorian chant, and the solemn *andante* tempo should be fast enough to permit a chantlike flow in the phrasing ($\downarrow$ = 76). All the accompanying chords in the first section must be arpeggiated; the accompanying chords at the key change should stress the hollow effect of the absent thirds. The clearly marked dynamics differentiate the shifting moods. The singer might need additional breath after *Fatti vita di me* (Make me alive) to achieve the first *fortissimo* climax at *che son morto* (who is dead), and after *e la mia anima* (and my soul) to achieve the final climax at *si rallegrerà* (will rejoice). The beginning of the final section—marked *ancora più largo* (even slower)—is an exact repetition of the melodic line that opens the composition. The overall problem in this song is to contain the overt emotional intensity within the boundaries of a solemn prayer. The songs need not be performed as a set, but they call for similar emotional and musical expression.

Quattro liriche: Antica poesia popolare armena: G. Ricordi, 1922
    1. *No, non è morto il figlio tuo*   118784, Repr. 1949
    2. *La mamma è come il pane caldo*   118785, Repr. 1949

Quattro liriche

No. 1, Un sogno

(*Gabriele d'Annunzio*)

 1 Io non odo i miei passi nel viale muto
 2 per ove il Sogno mi conduce
 3 È l'ora del silenzio e della luce.
 4 Un velario di perle è il cielo, equale.
 5 Attingono i cipressi con le oscure punte quel cielo:
 6 immoti, senza pianto; ma sono tristi,
 7 ma non sono tanto tristi i cipressi
 8 de le sepolture.
 9 Il paese d'intorno è sconosciuto, quasi informe,
10 abitato da un mistero antichissimo,
11 dove il mio pensiero si perde
12 Andando pel viale muto.
13 Io non odo i miei passi,
14 Io sono come un'ombra;
15 il mio dolore è come un'ombra;
16 è tutta la mia vita come un'ombra vaga,
17 incerta, indistinta, senza nome.

Four lyrics

No. 1, A Dream

 1 I do not hear my footsteps in the mute avenue
 2 to wherever the dream leads me.
 3 It is the hour of silence and of light.
 4 The sky is like a curtain of pearls.
 5 The cypresses reach with their dark tops to that sky,
 6 Motionless, without weeping; but they are sad,
 7 still they are not as sad as the cypresses
 8 of the sepulchres.
 9 The countryside around is unknown, almost formless,
10 inhabited by a very ancient mystery,

11   where my thought loses itself
12   while going through the silent avenue.
13   I do not hear my footsteps,
14   I am like a shadow;
15   my grief is like a shadow;
16   all my life is like a vague shadow,
17   uncertain, indistinct, nameless.

The verses of *Quattro liriche* (Four lyrics, 1920) are all by Gabriele d'Annunzio, the world-famous Italian poet. On this basis they may be programmed as a group, although each song is complete on its own.

Respighi sets No. 1, *Un sogno* (A dream) with sweeping arpeggios supporting a melodic line that seems to wander as aimlessly as the steps of the poet wander through his dream. In actuality, the song starts and ends clearly in the tonality of E major, but it modulates freely along the way and shows occasional glimpses of polytonality in the arpeggiations. The rhythmic hesitancy of dreamlike steps is cleverly evoked through the use of the grouping ♩ ♩ ♩. in the unusual and irregular 11/8 meter. The *lento* tempo should be interpreted freely at approximately ♩ = 40.

The song is through-composed, although a slight sense of a returning A section is felt in the *a tempo* at the phrase *Il paese d'intorno è sconosciuto* (The countryside around is unknown). There is little if any attempt at specific word-painting in the song, but word-rhythms are carefully set, and at times the dynamic indications *evoke* the proper color for a particular word, such as *sepolture* (sepulchres). These should be followed strictly. For the most part phrases break conveniently for punctuation about the time the singer needs breath. The opening phrase does not, however, and the singer will need to take a breath after *muto* (mute). The only other problem places are the phrases *attingono i cipressi con le oscure punte quel cielo* (literally, "reach the cypresses with their dark tops to that sky"), where the breath may be taken after *cipressi;* and, on the same page, *ma non sono tanto tristi i cipressi de le sepolture* (still they are not as sad as the cypresses of the sepulchres), where the breath should come after *tristi.*

Much of the effectiveness of the last few lines of poetry comes from the recitative style. They should be "spoken" as much as possible and be somewhat free rhythmically. There are a few scattered indications of *ritardando* or *rallentando* throughout the song, but it is important to keep a steady forward momentum throughout this composition to ensure that the powerful effect of its irregular meter is not lost.

No. 2, La najade

(*Gabriele d'Annunzio*)

1 Pullula ne l'opaco bosco e lene tremula e si dilata
2 in suoi leggeri cerchi l'acqua;
3 ed or vela i suoi misteri,
4 ora per tutte le sue chiare vene ha un brivido
5 scoprendo all'imo arene nuziali
6 ove ancor restano interi i vestigi dei corpi
7 che in piaceri d'amor commisti riguardò Selene.
8 Morta è Selene; morte son le Argire; i talami, deserti;
9 nel sovrano silenzio de la notte l'acqua tace;
10 ma pur sembrami a quando a quando udire
11 il gorgoglìo d'un'urna che una mano invisibile affonda,
12 in quella pace.

No. 2, The water nymph

1 It springs up in the shady woods and softly trembles and expands
2 in its light circles of water;
3 and now hides its mysteries,
4 now through all its clear veins it has a shiver
5 discovering at the deepest part nuptial sands
6 where still remain intact the remains of bodies
7 who, joined in the pleasures of love, were looked at intensely by
     Selene.
8 Dead is Selene; dead are the Argirs; the bridal beds, deserted;
9 in the supreme silence of the night the water is silent;
10 but yet it seems to me every now and then that I hear
11 the gurgle of an urn sunk by an invisible hand,
12 into that peacefulness.

La najade (The water nymph), also written in an irregular meter, appears to be through-composed, but the song is organized around the repetitions of two-measure chord progressions in the piano part. For example, the opening two-measure phrase is repeated twice, interrupted by a contrasting pattern, repeated again, then followed once more by the contrasting pattern. After four measures of a chordal motive in sequence, beginning with the first appearance of the proper name *Selene,* the opening pattern appears again beneath the phrase *nel sovrano silenzio de la notte* (in the supreme silence of the night) and finally at the beginning of the last page in the middle of the word *gorgoglio* (gurgle). This ascending and descending pattern, which must be played *legato,* may represent the motion of a forest spring. Certainly, the alternating 32d notes create a traditionally watery effect when they appear toward the end of the song. The vocal line rides freely through all this with asymmetric phrases overlapping the phrases of the accompaniment. A tempo of $\quad$ = 104–108 seems a little fast for the sections of the vocal line with sixteenth notes, but anything slower makes the all-important piano part too plodding. Some vocal phrases are long but contain enough subordinate clauses to be phrased for clarity of text.

The name Selene is one of many used for the Greek goddess of the moon. The reference to the Argirs is unclear, perhaps referring to the 50 daughters said to have been born to Selene and Endymion. After a repetition of Selene's motive, which begins at the final word *pace* (peacefulness), the song trails off to conclude in a bitonally influenced A major.

No. 3, La sera

(*Gabriele d'Annunzio*)

1   Rimanete, vi prego, rimanete qui.
2   Non vi alzate!
3   Avete voi bisogno di luce?
4   No.
5   Fate che questo sogno duri ancora.
6   Vi prego: rimanete!
7   Ci ferirebbe forse, come un dardo, la luce.
8   Troppo lungo è stato il giorno: oh, troppo.
9   Ed io già penso al suo ritorno con orrore.
10 La luce è come un dardo!
11 Anche voi non l'amate; è vero?
12 Gli occhi vostri, nel giorno, sono stanchi.
13 Pare quasi che non possiate sollevare le palpebre,
14 su quei dolorosi occhi;
15 e nulla, veramente, nulla è più triste
16 de l'ombra che le ciglia immote
17 fanno talvolta a sommo de le gote
18 quando la bocca non sorride più.

No. 3, The evening

1   Stay, I beg you, stay here.
2   Don't get up!
3   Do you need light?
4   No.

5   Make that this dream still lasts.
6   I beg you: stay!
7   It might perhaps wound us, like a dart, the light.
8   Too long has been the day, oh, too long.
9   And I already am thinking about its return with dread.
10 Light is like a dart!
11 You also, do not like it; is it true?
12 Your eyes, in the daytime, are tired.
13 It seems almost that you cannot raise
14 your eyelids, on those doleful eyes;
15 and nothing, truly, nothing is more woeful
16 than the shadow that your motionless eyelashes
17 make sometimes at the top of your cheeks
18 when your mouth no longer smiles.

The nervous anxiety of the poetry of *La sera* (The evening) is captured immediately by the insistent rhythmic repetition of a single E♮ in the left hand of the piano part. The articulation indicated in the first measure (accent-*tenuto*) should be followed consistently through the pattern, both here and at its reappearance later in the song. The structure of the song is a rather free ABA. The B section, however, is derived from and closely connected to the initial A section. It is defined as contrasting primarily because of the clear-cut return of the A section at the end of the song. The vocal line is neatly integrated into the texture of the complete work, but the phrases are short, further contributing to the nervous quality that permeates the poem and the song. At a tempo of ♩ = 66 most long phrases can be connected on one breath. In two places additional breaks might be needed: after *penso,* in *Ed io già penso al suo ritorno con orrore* (And I already am thinking about its return with dread), and after *quasi,* in *Pare quasi che non possiate sollevare le palpebre* (It seems almost that you cannot raise your eyelids).

The chords that provide harmonic background for the repetitious unison should progress smoothly and be phrased to form a countermelody to the vocal line. When the chord pattern begins to ascend in measure 11, it should *crescendo* very slightly toward measure 17, then *decrescendo* as it descends. The rolled chord beneath *luce* (light) should have a translucent quality to underscore this word.

Harmonic motion stops completely in measure 27, when the insistent dotted pattern returns on C♯ in the bass of the piano part. Through this section all attention is on the vocal line, and a *crescendo* must be made toward the climactic phrase of the song, *Pare quasi che non possiate solevare le palpebre, su quei dolorosi occhi* (It seems almost that you cannot raise your eyelids, on those doleful eyes). A complete break after this phrase and a real pause before the return of section A are required; the absence of sound will thus anticipate the next words, *e nulla* (and nothing).

The extremely long concluding phrase has several possibilities for breaks before subordinate clauses; ideally, it should sound as if it were being spoken. No *ritardando* is necessary in the short piano postlude since one is written into the rhythm. The final note should be held until it dies away.

No. 4, Sopra un'aria antica

(*Gabriele d'Annunzio*)

1   Non sorgono (ascolta ascolta) le nostre parole
2   da quell'aria antica?
3   Io t'ho dissepolta.
4   E alfine rivedi tu il sole,
5   tu mi parli, o amica!
6   Queste tu parlavi parole.
7   Non odi? Non odi? Ma chi le raccolse?
8   Dagli alvei cavi del legno i tuoi modi sorgono,
9   che il vento disciolse.
10   Dicevi: "Io ti leggo nel cuore.
11   Non mi ami.
12   Tu pensi che è l'ultima volta!"
13   La bocca riveggo un poco appassita.
14   "Non m'ami. È l'ultima volta
15   Ma prima che tu m'abbandoni
16   il voto s'adempia.
17   Oh! fa che sul cuore io ti manchi!
18   Tu non mi perdoni se già su la tempia baciata
19   i capelli son bianchi?"
20   Guardai que' capelli, su quel collo pallido
21   i segni degli anni;
22   e ti dissi: "Ma taci! Io t'amo."
23   I tuoi begli occhi erano pregni di lacrime
24   sotto i miei baci.
25   "M'inganni, m'inganni" rispondevi tu,
26   le mie mani baciando.
27   "Che importa? Io so che m'inganni;
28   ma forse domani tu m'amerai morta."
29   Profondo era il cielo del letto;
30   ed il letto profondo come tomba, oscuro.
31   Era senza velo il corpo;
32   e nel letto profondo parea già impuro.
33   Vidi per l'aperto balcone un paese lontano
34   solcato da un fiume volubile,
35   chiuso da un serto di rupi

36   che accese ardeano d'un lume vermiglio,
37   nel giorno estivo; ed i venti recavano odori
38   degli orti remoti
39   ove intorno andavano donne possenti
40   cantando tra cupidi fiori.

No. 4, On an old aria

1   (Listen! listen!) do not our words emerge
2   from that old aria?
3   I have unearthed you.
4   And at last you again see the sun,
5   you talk to me, O friend!
6   These words you used to speak.
7   Do you not hear? Do you not hear? But who collected them?
8   From the riverbeds hollowed from wood your modes rise up,
9   which the wind released.
10   You used to say: "I read within your heart.
11   You do not love me.
12   You think that it is the last time!"
13   I see your mouth again a little drooped.
14   "You do not love me. It is the last time."
15   But before you abandon me
16   the vow will be fulfilled.
17   Oh! let me be out of your heart!
18   Do you not forgive me if on my kissed temple
19   my hair is already white?
20   Look at that hair, on that pale neck
21   the signs of the years; and I said to you
22   "But be quiet! I love you."
23   Your beautiful eyes were filled with tears
24   under my kisses.
25   "You deceive me, you deceive me," you replied,
26   Kissing my hands.
27   "What does it matter? I know that you deceive me;
28   but perhaps tomorrow you will love me (when I am) dead."
29   Deep was the canopy of the bed;
30   and the bed deep and dark as a tomb.
31   The body was without a veil;
32   and in the deep bed it seemed already impure.
33   I saw through the open balcony a land far away
34   furrowed by a meandering stream,
35   enclosed by a wreath of rocks
36   while lit up they were burning with a red light,

37   in the summer day; and the winds used to bring about scents
38   from the distant gardens
39   around which used to go powerful women
40   singing among the covetous flowers.

Following a practice common among the early Italian composers he so admired, Respighi "borrows" a melody (an aria by Marcantonio Cesti, 1620–1689) to serve as a foundation for *Sopra un'aria antica* (On an old air). In the poem the rediscovery of an old aria, like Proust's *Madeleine,* recalls images and words from the past: a vague, ambiguous love affair related to passing years and death. Respighi's distinctive borrowed melody appears only in the piano part. It weaves in and out as if being heard from a distance or in the mind, while the vocal part, with negligible melodic interest, tells the story in speech-inflected rhythms.

The opening measures of the accompaniment are marked *pp* and *come in lontananza* (as if far away), but the latter direction should not be confined to the softer dynamics. Throughout the composition the Cesti melody must seem distant and dreamlike, even as it moves dynamically to its own internal phrase climax. The vocal line is related only harmonically to the piano melody, and for the most part it can be thought of as completely independent. True to form, Respighi does not set individual words very often; instead he creates a fusion of the Cesti melody, the speech rhythms of the poem, and his own harmonic language. Images in the poem govern choices in the structure of the song—the length of the returning theme, for example—but the relationship to the overall structure of the poem is loose.

The song is in a quasi-rondo form; the *aria antica* appears three times, with contrasting material in the intervals and a postlude. The theme's first appearance is in the piano introduction, and it is the longest of the three statements. The voice enters well into this melody as though someone were speaking over a background; voice and piano phrases are independent and frequently overlap. However, subtle relationships exist within the seemingly independent textures. For example, the Db, Gb, Db motivic interval, which appears in the piano melody in measure 14, is imitated by the voice one measure later; and the climax of the piano's melodic phrase in measure 19 coincides with the greater intensity of the poem in the words *Non odi? Non odi?* (Do you not hear? Do you not hear?). The Cesti melody seems to end with the cadence in measure 31, but fragmentary melodic motives based on it continue to underscore the text until measure 43. These motives move to chords completely out of the key beneath the poetic phrase of greatest intensity, *Oh! fa che sul cuore io ti manchi!* (Oh, let me be out of your heart!). The reverse word order here places the active verb *ti manchi* (let me be out) at the end of the phrase and therefore at the height of the climax.

The first clearly contrasting section of the song occurs with measure 44, an unmetric phrase in which the voice is of paramount importance and the piano provides a supportive harmonic accompaniment. Nothing in the poem indicates a particular need for contrast at this point. At the end of the section the Cesti melody reappears, but in a much shorter quotation of only thirteen measures. At the words *ed il letto profondo come tomba, oscuro* (and the bed deep and dark as a tomb), Respighi *is* influenced directly by the text; the Cesti melody breaks off, and new material, highly chromatic, builds toward a climax at *parea già impuro* (it seemed already impure), an image Respighi obviously found too vivid to ignore. The descent from this climax requires eight measures. Calm returns with the Tempo I° and the final statement of the Cesti theme accompanied with flowing triplets in the inner voices. In describing the bucolic scene the voice for the first time parallels some of the melodic contour of the Cesti theme and climaxes with it at the words *che accese* (while lit up). The piano melody ends at the word *estivo* (summer), and the melodic interest shifts to the voice through the completion of the final phrase, *cantando tra cupidi fiori* (singing among the covetous flowers). The piano postlude makes use of thematic fragments.

A thorough understanding of the construction of this song is the key to its interpretation. The pianist must be immersed in the Cesti melody and feel its inner phrasing independently of the singer. The singer must speak the words as if delivering a monologue superimposed on the musical background. Only then can those points of juncture between the two elements be brought together to create the complete artistic entity Respighi envisioned.

Quattro liriche: Bongiovanni, 1927.

1. *Un sogno*	F. 1272 B.
2. *La najade*	F. 1273 B.
3. *La sera*	F. 1274 B.
4. *Sopra un'aria antica*	F. 1275 B.

Ildebrando Pizzetti

(1880–1968)

•

ILDEBRANDO PIZZETTI was born in Parma on September 20, 1880. His father, Edoardo, taught piano and theory at the Scuola Musicale di Reggio Emila. Pizzetti had a lifelong interest in the theater, and as a child he wrote plays for his schoolmates. His formal musical training was begun at age fifteen when he entered the Conservatory of Parma. There he had six years of rigorous training in harmony and counterpoint with Telesforo Righi and Giovanni Tebaldini. During these early years Pizzetti experimented with religious music and compositions based on the writings of Shakespeare, Corneille, Byron, Pushkin, Ovid, Victor Hugo, and Ossian. These works reflected his preference for heroic subjects and large-scale constructions. They were not successful, and many were never completed. Pizzetti realized that he was not ready psychologically to cope with the inner meaning of these literary works. He began to develop a personal philosophy that made itself felt in all his compositions—the affirmation of a divine law of love present in all of creation.

In 1905 Pizzetti wrote incidental music for Gabriele d'Annunzio's tragedy *La Nave* and began a close friendship with the poet, from whom he received the nickname Ildebrando da Parma. From 1901 Pizzetti had been earning a living by giving private piano lessons, and for two seasons had also been the assistant conductor at the Teatro Regio of Parma. After a year as professor of composition at the Conservatory of Parma, he became professor of harmony and counterpoint at the Istituto Musicale "L. Cherubini" of Florence. He was appointed director in 1917 and remained there until 1924. These years were important in his development as a composer and in the shaping of his personal philosophy. Florence was a strong cultural center, and Pizzetti enjoyed the company of the leading Italian philosophers, writers, and artists. He became known for his critical studies of both early and contemporary music, and many of his articles were published in the important periodicals of the day.

In 1924 Pizzetti was nominated director of the Conservatory of Milan, at which post he remained for thirteen years. Many of his major operas and orchestral works were composed and performed during this period. He undertook a concert tour of North America in 1929, giving programs of his own music. In 1936 he taught a master class in composition at the Accademia di Santa Cecilia in Rome. He was nominated Accademico d'Italia in 1939, and from 1947 to 1952 he was president of the Accademia Nazionale di Santa Cecilia. In 1950 he won the Premio Italia with his first radio opera, *Ifigenia*. His fame as an opera composer increased with the success of each new production, and his output did not decline with his advancing years. *Figlia di Iorio* was given at Naples in 1954, *Assassinio nella cattedrale* in Milan in 1958, and *Il Calzare d'argento* in 1961, when Pizzetti was 81 years old.

Pizzetti believed that true art was a constant seeking for perfection. He had acquired a profound knowledge of the music of the greatest Italians of the three centuries preceding his own time and had studied the musical theory of the Greeks, Gregorian chant, the development of polyphony, the music of the Camerata Fiorentina, and the instrumental music of the seventeenth and eighteenth centuries. He knew and appreciated the music of Verdi, Wagner, and Debussy. He felt that from an assimilation of all these a new musical language would inevitably evolve for Italy. It would not be a mere imitation of these techniques, but would be eminently Italian—the natural outgrowth of the Italian heritage. Pizzetti always felt inhibited when he was bound to words written by others. By writing his own libretti he was able to choose words and create a drama in which he could blend the musical ideas and the text so that neither dominated. His operas contain no recitative as such and few developed song forms. His style is rather that of intoned speech in the Italian language.

Pizzetti's conservatism led him to join with Respighi and eight other signers of a manifesto dated December 17, 1932, deploring the "cerebralism" of modern music, but Pizzetti partly recanted at a later date. His ideal was to express in music the brotherhood and love of mankind. His music returns to the art of Gregorian chant, church modes, and polyphony—not as superficial "gimmicks" of the times but as a natural outgrowth of his training in early music. In his enthusiasm for its revival he applied all the resources of modern orchestral and vocal techniques without the limitations of outdated formulas and rules.

Pizzetti felt a strong relation between vocal expression and his sense of religion as applied to life. Even his instrumental works are marked by themes that are vocal in nature. Besides a large quantity of instrumental music in all genres, he wrote twelve operas, two for radio performance; incidental music to plays and other stage productions; music for four films; more than twenty choral works, including a *Messa di Requiem* for four to twelve solo voices; and six volumes of transcriptions of Gesualdo's Madrigals for five voices.

Pizzetti's music for solo voice and orchestra includes *Due liriche drammatiche napoletane* for tenor, to poems by Salvatore di Giacomo, written in 1916–1918; a cantata for bass, *Oritur sol et occidit* (1943); and several songs

Pizzetti had originally written for voice and piano, including *Vocalizzo* for mezzo-soprano (1957, orchestrated 1960). His vocal chamber music consists of *Tre Canzoni* to popular Italian poetry for tenor or soprano and string quartet, written in 1926; and *Due poesie di Giuseppe Ungaretti,* written in 1935 for baritone, violin, viola, violoncello, and piano.

Pizzetti's songs with piano accompaniment number more than 30, including several vocalises. Some of the songs are characterized by unexpected modulations, often brought about chromatically or by the use of polychordal writing that makes the tonality indecisive. His music contains no new chordal constructions, no new coloristic techniques, no showy impressions of external objects. Pizzetti tolerated composers who wrote in the new techniques but personally felt there was still much to be said in tonal music with tonal techniques.

Pizzetti's most moving moments are in the final measures of the songs that end in a contemplative mood. The accompaniment stops and the voice alone expresses the ultimate height of emotion. The tension does not cease, but is enhanced by the suspension of movement. Many of his effects are achieved by understatement. Pizzetti believed that the words and the music should express only as much as absolutely necessary, that too much verbosity or musical complexity decreases the inner psychological expression.

Pizzetti's songs range over a span of 60 years. It is difficult to single out any change or development of techniques or any phases in his work from a musical standpoint, although a reference is sometimes made to phases by subject matter: first d'Annunzio, then the Bible, and finally Italian history. The same facility for writing was with Pizzetti throughout his life. Since he did not indulge in passing fads and artificialities, his style does not evidence much change. It could be said of his later songs that they are more homogeneous, with fewer instances in which the text has a momentary rather than overall influence on the music.

Pizzetti died in Rome on February 13, 1968, a conservative but one of the most respected Italian musicians of his generation.

Cinque liriche

No. 1, I past*o*ri

(Gabriele d'Annunzio)

1 Settembre, andiamo. È tempo di migrare.
2 *O*ra in terra d'Abruzzi i miei past*o*ri
3 lascian gli stazzi e vanno verso il mare:
4 sc*e*ndono all'Adriàtico selvaggio
5 che v*e*rde è c*o*me i pascoli d*e*i m*o*nti.

6   Han bevuto profondamente ai fonti
7   alpestri, che sapor d'acqua natìa
8   rimanga nei cuori esuli a conforto,
9   che lungo illuda la lor sete in via.
10   Rinnovato hanno verga d'avellano.
11   E vanno pel tratturo antico al piano,
12   quasi per un erbal fiume silente,
13   su le vestigia degli antichi padri.
14   O voce di colui che primamente
15   conosce il tremolar della marina!
16   Ora lungh'esso il litoral cammina
17   la greggia. Senza mutamento è l'aria.
18   Il sole imbionda sì la viva lana
19   che quasi dalla sabbia non divaria.
20   Isciacquìo, calpestìo, dolci romori.
21   Ah perchè non son io co' miei pastori?

Five lyrics

No. 1, The shepherds

1   September, let us go. It is time to migrate.
2   Now in the land of Abruzzi my shepherds
3   leave their sheepfolds and go toward the sea:
4   they descend to the wild Adriatic,
5   which is green like the pastures of the mountains.
6   They have drunk profoundly at the alpine fountains,
7   so that the taste of water from their homeland
8   may remain in their exiled hearts as comfort,
9   it may long delude their thirst on the way.
10   They have renewed their rods of hazelwood.
11   And they go over the ancient sheep tracks to the plain,
12   almost like a silent grassy river,
13   over the footprints of the ancient fathers.
14   O voice of him who first
15   sees the glistening of the seashore!
16   Now along the shore walks
17   the flock. Without change is the air.
18   The sun makes the living wool so blond
19   that almost from the sand it doesn't vary.
20   Washing of waves, trample of hoofs, sweet sounds.
21   Ah, why am I not with my shepherds?

Although published as a set, Pizzetti's *Cinque liriche,* (Five lyrics) were written over a period of five years and are quite independent works. The texts range from d'Annunzio to popular Greek poetry, and the settings are equally contrasting. Although they are rather long to program as a complete set (there are no cyclical intentions), a group selected from the set would show the genius of the young Pizzetti as well as the emerging twentieth-century Italian style.

Pizzetti's best-known song, *I pastori* (The shepherds), written in 1908, is called a *lirica.* The text is taken from Gabriele d'Annunzio's *Sogni di terre lontane.* The pastoral mood is set immediately by the parallel octaves and Aeolian modality in 6/8 time, which reflect Pizzetti's training in early Italian music and Gregorian chant. The vocal line is freely set with rhythmic changes following the natural accents of the flowing poetic meter. The feeling of no bar lines in the text is in accord with the more conventional meters of the accompaniment. The division of the beats into two or three parts allows complete fluidity of the Italian accents. The vocal melodies must be sung with a very smooth *legato,* especially in the ornamental melismas occurring on the words *selvaggio* (wild), *piano* (plain), and *silente* (silent).

The long accents beginning on the words *su le vestigia* (over the footprints) suggest a warmth and reverence for antiquity. The mood then changes as the piano anticipates the coming view of the sea with its rising and falling syncopated arpeggios. The voice enters with a soft but very pure, round and close vowel on the words *O voce* (O voice), with no hint of a diphthong between the *o* and *v* of *voce.* In the unexpected change to C major the piano has a bright shimmering pattern; it dies away and the piano returns to a soft recapitulation of the initial recitative style. The sustained repeated note in the accompaniment over the undulating chordal patterns brings to mind the tolling of a bell. The final vocal statement is that of the poet wishing he were with his shepherds. There is a little *crescendo* on the ascending vocal line and the slightest broadening of tempo before a *diminuendo* into the final, unaccented syllable.

Both the singer and the accompanist should follow very carefully the phrasing, accents, and dynamics, which are meticulously indicated by the composer throughout the song. Other subtleties of expression will come with a thorough understanding of the text and the knowledge and practice of spoken Italian.

No. 2, La madre al figlio lontano

(*Romualdo Pàntini*)

1   O figlio, figlio, in che mondo ti trovi?
2   Da quanti mesi qua sola t'aspetto!
3   Ogni mattina riguardo il tuo letto:

4   è sempre intatto coi lenzoli novi
5   ed ogni sera mi rimetto a farlo
6   e lungamente ti sorrido e parlo.
7   E come spiego i candidi lenzoli,
8   dico che tanta pace ti consoli.
9   Scuoto i cuscini, li dispongo e dico:
10 l'amor più bello e il più fedele amico!
11 E poi rincalzo sotto le coperte:
12 così d'argento sette sacchi e sette!
13 O figlio, figlio, nel tuo letto bianco
14 torna una notte sola a riposare:
15 forse dormi sui monti o lungo il mare:
16 ti manca un letto quando sei più stanco.
17 E il tuo bel letto lo ritrovo intatto,
18 e dentro il petto mi ribevo il pianto.
19 Ma questa sera son tranquilla,
20 sento che torni a casa e dormi nel tuo letto.
21 Accendi il lume, fermati un momento,
22 guarda il cuscino bello di merletto.
23 L'ho rinnovato quando mi sei nato:
24 pel tuo ritorno, figlio, l'ho serbato.

No. 2, The mother to her faraway son

1   O son, son, in what world do you find yourself?
2   For how many months here alone have I been waiting for you!
3   Every morning I look again at your bed:
4   it is always intact with new sheets
5   and every evening I go to make it up again
6   and for a long time I smile at you and talk to you
7   and I smooth out the white sheets,
8   I say that so much peace may console you.
9   I shake up the pillows, I arrange them and say:
10 the most beautiful love and the most faithful friend!
11 And then I tuck under the blankets:
12 thus seven sacks of silver and seven!
13 O son, son, in your white bed
14 return at least one night to rest:
15 perhaps you sleep in the mountains or beside the sea:
16 you lack a bed when you are most tired.
17 And your beautiful bed I find it intact,
18 and within my breast I again drink my tears.
19 But this evening I am tranquil,
20 I feel that you are returning home and you will sleep in your bed.

21 Turn on the light, stop a moment,
22 look at the beautiful pillow of lace.
23 I renewed it when you were born:
24 for your return, son, I have kept it.

Pizzetti shows a strong influence of early church music in the devices
he chooses to express the quiet pain of the lonely mother in *La madre al
figlio lontano* (The mother to her faraway son). A poignant melodic motive:

sets the opening address, *O figlio, figlio* (Oh son, son), and reappears throughout the composition to recall the mood and to unify the work. After the
motive, the vocal line continues in primarily stepwise movement similar to
that of Gregorian chant. At the same time a slower-moving stepwise melodic
line appears in dotted quarter notes in the accompaniment. The effect is that
of a *cantus firmus* with a freer chant elaboration above it. The whole mood
structure is underscored by a mysterious *tremolo* low in the bass of the
accompaniment. There are slight shifts of rhythmic accent in the melodic
line when the 6/8 meter is grouped in two and then three, but the eighth
note should remain constant to preserve the chantlike quality. The accompaniment remains in 6/8 throughout the section, with the chord changes
unobtrusive and unaccented.

The accompaniment pattern changes in measure 20 with the mother's
increased activity—smoothing the sheets, shaking the pillows—but the vocal
line retains its chantlike outline, now broken into shorter phrases. At the
end of the section it becomes pure recitative, at *E poi rincalzo sotto le coperte:
così d'argento sette sacchie e sette!* (And then I tuck under the blankets: thus
seven sacks of silver and seven!), and anticipates the increased activity that
initiates the next section.

The alternating triplets in the accompaniment at measure 41 underscore
the increasing emotion that leads to the climax at the phrase *ti manca un
letto quando sei più stanco* (you lack a bed when you are most tired). A
slow *crescendo* should build through the entire section, observing an internal
rise and fall within the phrases. (The pianist should note the *mezzo-forte* to
piano indications that mark the chord resolutions as this section progresses.)
The *forte* reached at the vocal climax continues past the release of the word
stanco (tired), retreating slightly over the page in the only measure in which
the accompaniment also shifts into 2/4. (The composer indicates the eighth
notes as equal, taking the pulse from the preceding measure.) A *subito piano*
is indicated when the tremolo begins in measure 58 beneath a repetition of
the initial vocal motive. It becomes quieter at the word *pianto* (tears), which
is effectively set with a shift to a Neapolitan sixth chord.

The final lines of the song, beginning *Ma questa sera son tranquilla* (But this evening I am tranquil), show a slower-moving accompaniment pattern, which should be quite sustained. When the mother says *sento che torni a casa e dormi nel tuo letto* (I feel that you are returning home and you will sleep in your bed), the opening motive appears for the first time in major mode (transposed) and should be brought out dynamically in the overall texture. The final page of the song is literally a duet for voice and piano—the piano "sings" the original vocal line while the voice does a quasi-canonic variation on it. The two parts are equal and *intensamente expressivo* (intensely expressive). There should be a slight holding back of the tempo in the final four measures of the song.

No. 3, San Basilio

(*Poesia popolare greca tradotta da Niccolò Tommasèo*)

1   San Basilio viene di Cesarea:
2   porta scarpe di bronzo e ferree vesti.
3   "Basilio mio, donde vieni, e ove scendi?"
4   "Dal maestro vengo, e a mia madre vo,"
5   "Se vieni dal maestro, dicci l'abbiccì."
6   Sul pastorale s'appoggiò per dire l'abbiccì.
7   E il pastorale era verde, e gettò un ramo,
8   un ramo con fronde d'oro, trapunto in argento.

No. 3, Saint Basil

(*Popular Greek poetry translated [into Italian] by Niccolò Tommasèo*)

1   Saint Basil comes from Caesarea:
2   he wears shoes of bronze and iron garments.
3   "My Basil, whence do you come and where do you go?"
4   "I come from the master, and I go to my mother,"
5   "If you come from the master, say the alphabet to us."
6   He leaned on his pastoral staff, in order to say the alphabet.
7   And the staff was green, and it sprouted a branch,
8   a branch with leaves of gold, embroidered in silver.

Saint Basil the Great (c.330–379) was a Greek prelate, bishop of Caesarea in Cappadocia, a Doctor of the Church, and one of the Four Fathers of the Greek Church. His revision of the liturgy is occasionally used in the Byzantine rite. His appearance in this popular Greek verse is obviously awesome to the protagonist, and this quality is captured in the dignity of the setting.

The song is through-composed, but two short melodic motives:

and

appear in the accompaniment in various transpositions as a link between sections. Much of the processional quality of the composition comes from the rising scales that permeate the work. Sometimes they are repeated within the accompaniment (see measures 3–4 and 8–9), sometimes imitated from voice to accompaniment (see measures 16, 18, and 24).

The song should begin *pesante* (heavy) but not *forte*. The question *"Basilio mio, donde vieni e dove scendi?"* ("My Basil, whence do you come and where do you go?") should be asked very quietly. The reply can be a little louder, with a slight change of vocal color and a more elaborate articulation for contrast.

There are two misprints in lines 6 and 7 of the text underlay of this song (however, the poetry is quoted correctly in the front of the score and in the present volume). In line 6, with the words *per dire l'abbiccì* (in order to say the alphabet), the tempo should be held back slightly. The vocal climax at *argento* (silver) requires considerable vocal agility, given the rhythmic complexity of the measure, but the effect is as important as the precision. The short motive in the final measure of the accompaniment should be played quietly, but held back a little in tempo. It should be related to the opening measure of the song and also act as a final punctuation mark.

No. 4, Il clefta prigione

(*Poesia popolare greca tradotta da Niccolò Tommasèo*)

1   Oggi, Demo, gli è pasqua, oggi fiera:
2   i prodi fan festa, e tirano al bersaglio:
3   e tu, Demo mio, a Giànnina, alla porta del visire,
4   in catene, in ceppi, in trista carcere.
5   E tutto il mondo tel dicevano, e Turchi e Romei:
6   Demo caro, sta savio, se ti tocchi l'armatolato.
7   "E che mal vi fec'io, che piangete su me?
8   Faccia Iddio e la Vergine e sire san Giorgio,
9   che guarisca la mia mano, ch'io cinga la spada,
10   e alfin venga la primavera, venga la state,
11   che s'infrondino i rami e chiudano le viottole,
12   ch'io prenda il mio fucile, ch'io cinga la mia spada,
13   ch'io pigli l'opposto lato dei monti, dell'alte cime,

14   ch'io faccia arrosto pecore pingui e grossi montoni,
15   ch'io lasci madri senza figliuoli, spose senza mariti."

No. 4, The imprisoned brigand

(Popular Greek poetry translated [into Italian] by Niccolò Tommasèo)

1   Today, Demo, it is Easter, today, a fair:
2   the valiant take a holiday, and go target shooting:
3   and you, my Demo, at Giànnina at the gateway of the vizier,
4   in chains, in shackles in deplorable imprisonment.
5   And all the world said it to you, both Turks and Romans:
6   Demo dear, be good, if you face the artillery:
7   "And what evil did I cause you, that you weep over me?
8   May God and the Virgin and Sire Saint George,
9   heal my hand, so that I may gird my sword,
10   and at last may spring come, may the summer come,
11   so that the branches become leafy and close the narrow pathways
12   so that I may take my rifle, so that I may gird my sword
13   so that I may take the opposite side of the mountain, from the high
          summits
14   so that I may roast fat sheep and big rams,
15   so that I may leave mothers without sons, brides without husbands."

Il clefta prigione (The imprisoned brigand) was written at the same time as *San Basilio* and also sets popular Greek poetry as translated by *Niccolò Tommasèo*. In essence these two songs are a set within a set and form a good program group of their own. The word *clefta* comes from the Greek *klepht*, which translates as "brigand" or "bandit."

The character of the brigand is established immediately in the opening motive of the piano introduction:

It is vigorous and energetic and provides the central building block on which the rest of the composition is structured. The initial tempo should not be faster than the recommended ♩ = 96–100 even if it seems a bit slow when the voice enters. The masculinity of the motive is lost to frenzy if the 32d notes become blurred.

The first phrase of the vocal line reveals the composer's use of the Dorian mode, which remains throughout the song despite many transpositions and chromatic excursions. With the exception of this initial phrase and its almost exact repetition at *Faccia Iddio e la Vergine e sire san Giorgio* (May God and the Virgin and Sire Saint George), the vocal line is less interesting than the very active accompaniment. The story is told in speech rhythms with an occasional chromatic alteration or disjunct interval to create an expressive word accent. At the first climax, *"E che mal vi fec'io che piangete su me?"* ("And what evil did I cause you that you weep over me?"), the voice and piano join effectively in widely spaced octaves.

There should be a change of mood and a softer dynamic at *Faccia Iddio e la Vergine e sire san Giorgio,* as the brigand recalls the freedom of his earlier, outdoor life, but fragments of the central motive in the piano part must maintain an energetic undercurrent. The phrases lengthen and the accompaniment activity increases as the song moves to its final climax. The unrepentant brigand is brutal; the singer's tone quality and the pianist's articulation and tone quality must convey this brutality. At the phrase *ch'io faccia arrosto pecore pingui e grossi montoni* (so that I may roast fat sheep and big rams) the pianist should bring out the long ascending scale in the accompaniment (a similar device is used in *San Basilio*). Since this phrase is long and the singer must build a *crescendo,* a breath may be taken, if needed, after *pingui.* The singer should give the impression of the *crescendo* continuing through the rest before *ch'io lasci* (so that I may leave). The dynamic level of the final two lines should remain *fortissimo,* and the composer has marked a broadening and then a surging of tempo on each line. The energy must drive through to the final note, which singer and pianist should release together.

In preparing this song the singer must find a way to convey the energy and brutality without becoming overly strident; and the pianist should examine the score for all the permutations of the motive, which exists to create the energy and support the singer.

No. 5, Passeggiata

(*Giovanni Papini*)

1   Due in confidenza, dritti come re,
2   s'andava per le strade, fuor delle poesie,
3   un fiore per te e una foglia per me
4   e sleghiamo le fantasie!
5   S'era in due—soli fra muro e muro,
6   senza badare a chi passa, a chi vede,
7   occhio vuoto ma passo sicuro
8   imperatori in buona fede.

 9 S'incontravano i monti ad uno ad uno,
10 i tralci salutavano in giallo altalenìo
11 ma non si parlava a nessuno:
12 ognuno era all'altro il suo dio.
13 Per quanto era largo il mondo dintorno
14 fiatava per l'aria odore d'amore.
15 Noi, quasi amanti del primo giorno,
16 si sentiva alle gote un bruciore.
17 Ma s'era così felici, sudati, affannati,
18 brilli d'egoismo perfetto,
19 ci pareva ormai d'esser soldati
20 con dieci medaglie sul petto.
21 Alla fine, alla fine della salita,
22 nell'ultima baia dell'orizzonte,
23 una luna di velo senza vita
24 si stacca leggera da un monte.
25 Tutto è uguale e compagno all'infinito,
26 colmo è il cuore: per nulla rintocca;
27 eppure, un momento, ho sentito
28 l'umido bacio della tua bocca.

No. 5, Walk

 1 Two in confidence, straight as a king,
 2 were going along the road, beyond poetry,
 3 a flower for you and a leaf for me—
 4 and we release our fantasies!
 5 It was the two of us alone between wall and wall,
 6 without paying attention to who was passing, to who was looking,
 7 eyes vague but steps confident,
 8 emperors in good faith.
 9 They encountered mountains one after another,
10 the vine branches saluted in varying yellow
11 but they spoke to no one:
12 each was to the other his god.
13 As far as was wide the world around
14 (it) breathed through the air the scent of love.
15 We, almost lovers from the first day,
16 we felt on our cheeks a burning sensation.
17 But we were so happy; sweaty, exhausted,
18 half-drunk with perfect egoism,
19 we seemed by now to be soldiers
20 with ten medals on our chests.
21 At the end, at the end of the ascent,

22 in the last bay of the horizon,
23 a veiled moon without life
24 detaches itself lightly from a mountain.
25 Everything is equal and companion to infinity,
26 overflowing is the heart: it tolls for nothing;
27 and yet, for a moment, I felt
28 the moist kiss of your mouth.

The final song of the *Cinque liriche, Passeggiata* (Walk), was written in 1915, three years after Nos. 3 and 4. The poetry is more sophisticated and ambiguous than the Greek lyrics but it shares some of their earthiness. The musical devices are not very different.

The long piano introduction begins with the motive:

to which Pizzetti makes many references throughout the rambling, through-composed song. The widely spaced octave doubling creates an open, "outdoor" quality. The composer's pedal markings are quite specific. The introduction should begin with a firm *forte* attack and establish a brisk walking tempo (♩ = 94–100). The voice enters in measure 13 with the opening notes of the motive while the accompaniment plays it almost entirely within the chord structure. The climax at *sleghiamo* (release) in measure 26 should have a very slight broadening of the tempo, but the motive, which returns in sixteenth notes at measures 28–30, should be played strictly *a tempo*.

The climax of the second section (measure 42) should also remain strictly *a tempo*, and the upper notes of the accompanying chords should be accented in unison with the vocal line. After a fragmentary hesitation in measure 44, the motive appears again in measures 45–46 with a chromatic alteration. There is even greater alteration of the motive in measures 48–49, which should be played very softly but *chiaro* (clear).

In the author's score a quarter rest is missing from the first beat of the accompaniment in measure 50. A slight *crescendo* should lead to the phrase *giallo altalenìo* (varying yellow), but the quality should remain *dolce* and the dynamic should not go above *piano*. The chords in these measures, doubling the vocal line, should be slightly held back—the *a tempo* not beginning until measure 56. Another *rallentando,* not marked in the score but recommended by the composer in performance, is required at the phrase *ognuno era all'altro il suo dio* (each was to the other his god). *Tenuto* markings should be added to the score above *altro il suo dio.* The motive appears again in the interlude immediately after this phrase (measures 65–67).

In the next section of the song the phrase *fiatava per l'aria odore d'a-*
more (breathed through the air the scent of love) is too long to be sung on
one breath. It should be divided according to the phrase marking after *l'aria*
in measure 76. The pianist's phrasing is different here, but allowances must
be made for the breath. The measures beginning with *Noi, quasi amanti del*
primo giorno (We, almost lovers from the first day) should be sung a little
slower, with a breath taken after *giorno.* The half notes in the bass of the
accompaniment should be stressed and very sustained in measures 85–87,
and a return to *a tempo* occurs with the octaves in measure 88. These indications are not given in the score but were designated by the composer
in performance. A bright figuration in the accompaniment in measures 91–
94 accentuates the word *felici* (happy) in measure 91. The motive (with
chromatic alteration) appears immediately before (measures 89–90) and after
it (measures 95–96) in full chords. The succeeding phrases build to the
climax at *soldati* (soldiers) in measure 102. A breath may be taken, if needed,
to sustain the *fortissimo* after the word *ormai* (now). Although *a tempo* is
indicated right at the climax, this whole section should be somewhat broad
with a real *ritardando* in measure 108 leading to the *fermata.*

The motive appears in measures 109–110 to initiate the final section of
the song. The vocal phrases are shorter and more speechlike. At measure
127 a real *largo* is indicated with a notation that the eighth note should now
almost equal the quarter note from the preceding section. Fragments of the
motive appear in the piano part between vocal phrases and should be brought
out. In the final vocal phrase a breath may be taken after *bacio* (kiss) to
execute the difficult *mezzo piano dolce ma molto expressivo* (medium soft,
sweet, but very expressive) indicated in the score. Some Impressionistic
figurations in the accompaniment complete the composition in keeping with
the sentiment of the final line of poetry.

Cinque liriche: A. Forlivesi, 1916.
  1. *I pastori*   10614
  2. *La madre al figlio lontano*   10615
  3. *San Basilio*   10616
  4. *Il clefta prigione*   10617
  5. *Passeggiata*   10618

Tre sonetti del Petrarca: In morte di Madonna Laura

No. 1, La vita fugge e non s'arresta un'ora

1   La vita fugge e non s'arresta un'ora;
2   E la morte vien dietro a gran giornate;
3   E le cose presenti e le passate

4 Mi danno guerra, e le future ancora.
5 E 'l rimembrar e l'aspettar m'accora
6 Or quinci or quindi sì, che 'n veritate,
7 Se non ch'i' ho di me stesso pietate,
8 I' sarei già di questi pensier fôra.
9 Tornami avanti s'alcun dolce mai
10 Ebbe 'l cor tristo; e poi dall'altra parte
11 Veggio al mio navigar turbati i venti:
12 Veggio fortuna in porto, e stanco omai
13 Il mio nocchier, e rotte àrbore e sarte,
14 E i lumi bei, che mirar soglio, spenti.

Three sonnets of Petrarch:
On the death of Madonna Laura

No. 1, Life flees and does not stop an hour

1 Life flees and does not stop an hour;
2 And death follows closely behind;
3 And things present and past
4 Give me conflict, and future ones also.
5 And the remembering and the waiting grieve me
6 Now here now there in such a way, that in truth,
7 If it were not that I have pity for myself,
8 I would already be overcome by these thoughts.
9 Come back to me if some joy was ever
10 Felt by a sad heart; and then on the other hand
11 I see my navigating beset by turbulent winds
12 I see fortune at the harbor, and tired at last
13 My boatman, and broken masts and rigging,
14 And the beautiful eyes, that I am accustomed to watch, are spent.

Francesco Petrarca (Petrarch, 1304–1374), poet and humanist, was one of the greatest figures of Italian literature. In 1327, a year after taking minor ecclesiastical orders, Petrarch first saw Laura at Avignon, then the seat of the Papacy. She became the inspiration for his greatest love lyrics, in which the medieval portrait of woman as a spiritual creation gave way to the modern notion of a flesh-and-blood emotional being. Laura's death during the plague epidemic of 1348 inspired some of the poet's most poignant writing. Pizzetti's conservative, almost classical settings underscore the plaintive emotions of the texts. Each of the songs is independently effective, but their common inspiration creates a greater impact when they are performed as a group.

The first song, *La vita fugge e non s'arresta un'ora* (Life flees and does not stop an hour), establishes the subject and mood of the poems with its opening motive:

As the through-composed song progresses the motive appears at several points. Musical interest is rather evenly divided between voice and piano. The vocal line is moderate in range and primarily stepwise in motion. The rhythms follow speech accentuation while the piano provides chordal support and maintains the metric flow. The harmonies are conventional except for occasional polytonal chords, which do not jar the listener but allow the progressions to move in unexpected directions. No tempo indication is given; a *largo* or *larghetto* of approximately ♩ = 60 allows a proper melancholy mood to be established without impeding the rhythmic flow. Both the piano and the voice should be *assai sostenuto*.

The key to the interpretation of this song lies in enhancing the appearance of the initial motive, which reiterates musically the "fleeting" quality of life. It appears first as an echo in the bass line of the accompaniment in measures 4 and 5. (The incomplete measure at the beginning of the song is counted as No. 1, since it is not "made up" at the end of the song.) The most prominent use of the motive occurs in measure 15, at the musical climax of the song. In full, rich chords the transposed motive comments on the poet's overwhelming, but dignified, grief. The ascending stepwise movement of the harmony and the sixteenth-note figurations in the preceding measures help to build toward this climax, but the tempo should be increased also— *più mosso*. In an extremely clever device in measure 18, the response to the call for the departed lover to return is met by the incomplete motive. The *fermata* over the suspended A♯ should be a long time.

As the poet's disillusionment settles and the song moves toward a close, a triplet pattern, loosely drawn from the motive, appears three times in octaves in the piano part. In the final phrase the motive is stated exactly, but divided between piano and voice, and it is delayed just long enough to set the word *spenti* (spent). The song ends clearly in the tonality of E minor.

No. 2, Quel rosignuol che sì soave piagne

1 Quel rosignuol che sì soave piagne
2 Forse suoi figli o sua cara consorte,
3 Di dolcezza empie il cielo e le campagne
4 Con tante note sì pietose e scorte;

5   E tutta notte par che m'accompagne
6   E mi rammente la mia dura sorte:
7   Ch'altri che me non ho di cui mi lagne:
8   Che 'n Dee non credev'io regnasse Morte
9   O che lieve è ingannar chi s'assecura!
10 Que' duo bei lumi, assai più che 'l Sol chiari
11 Chi pensò mai veder far terra oscura?
12 Or conosch'io che mia fera ventura
13 vuol che vivendo e lagrimando impari
14 Come nulla quaggiù diletta e dura.

No. 2, That nightingale that so softly cries

1   That nightingale that so softly cries
2   perhaps for his children or his dear wife,
3   With sweetness he fills the sky and the countryside
5   with so many notes so compassionately and caring;
5   and all night it seems to accompany me
6   and it reminds me of my bitter fate:
7   that I have no other than myself with whom to complain:
8   among Goddesses I did not believe that Death could reign.
9   O how easy it is to deceive one who feels secure!
10 Those two beautiful eyes, much brighter than the sun
11 Whoever could have thought of seeing the earth (made) dark?
12 Now I know that my difficult future
13 wants that living and weeping I learn
14 how nothing in this life pleases and endures.

The hauntingly beautiful song *Quel rosignuol che sì soave piagne* (That nightingale that so softly cries) begins with a literal description of the nightingale in the piano introduction. The composer specifically directs that soft pedal be used throughout. Although the written rhythms should be observed, the spontaneity and freedom of the melody should be encouraged. Overall directions for the song indicate *sostenuto e triste* (sustained and sad), but the opening verse describing the nightingale and his life hovers more in major tonality than in minor. The sweetness of the section should be emphasized in vocal color and in such figures as the sweeping piano arpeggio underlying the word *cielo* (sky). A breath could be taken immediately after this, if needed, to observe the *tratt.* (stretched) direction, which occurs at this point in the phrase. The 32d-note piano figurations should be as birdlike as possible.

The second section begins with the same melodic motive as the first, but the story is changing, and the minor tonality is evidenced sooner, calling for a more plaintive vocal color. In the authors' copy of the score a quarter rest and an eighth rest are missing in the measure immediately after the word *m'accompagne* (accompany me). The *tenuto* markings above *dura* (bitter), *Dee* (Goddesses), and *Morte* (Death) must be observed; and a strong attempt should be made to sing through the phrase *Ch'altri che me non ho di cui mi lagne* (that I have no other than myself with whom to complain) on one breath.

While observing the rhythms accurately, the pianist should make the most of the fluttering hesitations on and after the word *Morte* (Death). From this point on the nightingale's song is narrower in range and less spontaneous. In the final line of poetry the word *nulla* (nothing) deserves attention, and the pianist should stress the hollowness of the final chords, marking only the quick alternation of major third to minor third. The nightingale has stopped singing.

No. 3, Levommi il mio pensier in parte ov'era

1 Levommi il mio pensier in parte
2 ov'era quella ch'io cerco e non ritrovo in terra:
3 Ivi, fra lor che 'l terzo cerchio serra,
4 La rividi più bella e meno altera.
5 Per man mi prese e disse: In questa spera
6 Sarai ancor meco, se 'l desir non erra:
7 I' son colei che ti die' tanta guerra,
8 E compie' mia giornata innanzi sera
9 Mio ben non cape in intelletto umano:
10 Te solo aspetto e quel che tanto amasti,
11 E laggiuso è rimaso, il mio bel velo.
12 Deh, perchè tacque ed allargò la mano?
13 Ch'al suon di detti sì pietosi e casti
14 Poco mancò ch'io non rimasi in cielo.

No. 3, I lift up my thoughts to the place where she was

1 I lift up my thoughts to the place
2 Where she was whom I am looking for and I do not find on earth:
3 There, among those whom the third circle encloses,
4 I saw her again more beautiful and less proud.
5 She took me by the hand and said: In this sphere
6 You will again be with me, if your desire does not err:
7 I am the one who gave you so much strife,
8 And completed my day's journey before evening
9 My virtue is not understood by human intellect:

10   You alone I await and that one whom you loved so much
11   and there below has remained my beautiful veil.
12   Alas, why does she remain silent and why does she extend her hand?
13   Because at the sound of the words so piteous and pure
14   there was little chance that I did not remain in heaven.

The final song of this set, *Levommi il mio pensier in parte ov'era* (I lift up my thoughts to the place where she was), begins with a repetition of bell-like chords in the treble of the piano part. The opening vocal line, which follows, has a strong Gregorian quality; and the combination creates a musical atmosphere very much like that of the traditional *In paradisum* (In paradise) finale of the Catholic Requiem Mass. Throughout the rest of the song the interval pattern of the first phrase can be found, in original pitch or transposition, every time a group of consecutive eighth notes appears in the accompaniment. They are obviously the structural underpinning of this through-composed song and, as such, should be heard clearly within the texture of the composition whenever they appear. In measures 24–25 the pattern is even marked *chiaro* (clear). With the exception of this recognizable melodic pattern, the rest of the accompaniment acts to support the vocal line with harmonic changes enhancing the text. The vocal line itself follows speech rhythms and maintains a chantlike quality throughout. As in chant, the climaxes are subtle rather than direct, with the focal point probably at the phrase *Te solo aspetto* (You alone, I await). The strange piano postlude, with its ambiguous harmony, seems to reflect the philosophical turn the poem takes in its final lines. The "third circle" mentioned in the third poetic phrase refers to Dante's *Paradiso.* The tempo for the song, unmarked except for the direction *largo,* should be about the same as for the first song of the set, $\quad$ = 60.

Tre sonetti del Petrarca: G. Ricordi, 1923; Repr. 1946.
1. *La vita fugge e non s'arresta un'ora*   119228
2. *Quel rosignuol che sì soave piagne*   119229
3. *Levommi il mio pensier in parte ov'era*   119230

Erotica

(*Gabriele d'Annunzio*)

1   Ondeggiano i letti di rose
2   ne li orti specchiati dal mare
3   In coro le spose con lento cantare
4   ne 'l talamo d'oro sopiscono il sir.
5   Da l'alto scintillan profonde

6   le stelle su 'l capo immortale;
7   ne 'l vento si effonde quel cantico
8   e sale pe 'l gran firmamento
9   che incurvasi a udir.
10 Ignudo le nobili forme
11 consparso d'un olio d'aroma,
12 l'amato s'addorme: la sua dolce chioma
13 par tutta di neri giacinti fiorir.
14 Discende dai cieli stellanti
15 un fiume soave d'oblio
16 Le spose, pieganti su 'l bel semidìo,
17 ne bevon con lungo piacere il respir.

Erotic

1   The beds are undulating with roses
2   in the gardens mirrored by the sea
3   with one voice the betrothed with slow singing
4   in the bridal bed of gold (they) sooth the sire.
5   From above shine deeply
6   the stars on the immortal head;
7   in the wind pours forth that canticle
8   and it rises through the great firmament
9   which bends to listen.
10 Naked as noble figures
11 covered with an aromatic oil
12 the beloved falls asleep: her soft hair
13 appears all flowered with black hyacinths.
14 From the starry skies descends
15 a gentle river of oblivion.
16 The brides, yielding to the beautiful demi-god,
17 (they) drink the breath with great pleasure.

In keeping with its title, *Erotica* (Erotic) is one of the most sensual of all the songs within the genre of Italian *liriche*. The poem is by Gabriele d'Annunzio, who was well known for his amorous pursuits, and the setting serves it admirably. It opens with an unusual scale, derived from Hungarian gypsy music, with lowered third and sixth and two leading tones—one to the dominant and one to the tonic—and consequently two augmented seconds. The resulting sound is definitely Eastern, and the strummed arpeggiations of the opening measures evoke an exotic stringed instrument. This piano introduction should be phrased over four measures, making a *crescendo* toward the high point of the melodic line in measure 3 and then tapering off before the entrance of the voice in measure 5. No tempo marking is given at the beginning of the song, and the metric markings are 3/4 for the accompaniment and 9/8 for the voice. Taking a cue from later markings in the score, an initial *lento* tempo (approximately $\downarrow = 60$) permits a languid stretch of the opening melody. The tempo should be reduced even further when the meter signature in the piano also changes to 6/8 in measure 9. It should never be rushed.

The slight rhythmic tug between voice and accompaniment and the repeated alternating seconds of the entering vocal line also contribute to the overall sensual mood. Although the treble line of the accompaniment becomes more active in measure 9, the bass line carries a repetition of the scale melody that introduced the song; this effect should emerge clearly from the texture. A little more motion is required beginning with measure 15. The excitement reaches a climax in measure 23, *con più vivo ardore* (with deeper passion). The composer indicates a breath in the vocal line in measure 22 to make the sustained G in measure 23 easier, but it should not be held longer than the indicated two counts. (In the author's copy of the score the dot is missing after the half note.) Essentially, the climax is carried in the long, lush piano interlude, reminiscent of Rimsky-Korsakov's *Sheherezade*. The upper notes of the bass clef again outline the melodic scale passage that opened the composition and should be brought out in the texture.

The vocal phrases are shorter in the opening measures of the new section, which begins in measure 27; again the voice and piano have different meter signatures, and this creates an uneasy restlessness. The tempo is slower and the dynamic level is much quieter, although the composer specifically draws attention to the scale theme in the bass of the piano (*pp ma molto in rilievo il tema nel basso;* very soft, but stressing the theme in the bass). This theme, transposed again, moves to the treble of the piano beneath *s'addorme* (falls asleep), and the following vocal phrase is quite long. A breath is required after *chioma* (hair) as it ties over to measure 33.

The motion increases in measure 37, and the song moves to a brilliant effect in measure 45. To set the word *piacere* (pleasure), the composer requires the softest, sweetest sound possible on a floating high Bb. It should literally tingle, while the piano repeats the scale theme in the bass and the dotted-rhythm countermelody in octaves and chords in the treble. The final words of the song should be whispered, with a long *fermata* over the first note and a considerable *rallentando* in the accompaniment. A languid feeling should continue in the final four measures of the accompaniment, leaving a quality of spent passion in the air.

Erotica: Bongiovanni, 1924,   F. 1299 B.

Tre canzoni

No. 1, Donna lombarda
(Poesia popolare italiana)

1   Amami tu, donna lombarda!
2   —Non posso amarti,
3   Sacra corona, non posso amarti
4   perchè ho marì'!
5   —Se tu hai marito, fallo morire!
6   T'insegnerò,
7   Va nel giardino del signor padre,
8   chè c'è un serpen',
9   Prendi la testa di quel serpente;
10 pèstala ben,
11 Quando l'avrai ben-ben pestata,
12 dannela a be',
13 Rivò il marito stanco assetato,
14 ni chiese da be',
15 —Di qualo vuole, signor marito,
16 del bianco o del ner?
17 —Del bianco che n'è, del meglio che c'è,
18 Parla un bambino di nove mesi
19 —Non ber quel vino, che c'è il velen!
20 —Che ha questo vino, donna lombarda,
21 che l'è torbè,
22 —Saranno i troni dell'altra sera,
23 che l'han fatto torbè.
24 —Bévelo tu, donna lombarda!
25 bévelo te,
26 —'Un posso beve', signor marito,
27 perchè 'un ho se',
28 —Con questa spada che tengo in mano
29 ti ucciderò,
30 —E per amore del Re di Francia,
31 io morirò, ah, io morirò.

Three songs

No. 1, Lombard woman
(Popular Italian poetry)

1   —Love me, Lombard woman!
2   —I cannot love you,

3   Holy monarch, I cannot love you
4   Because I have a husband.
5   —If you have a husband, make him die!
6   I will teach you how,
7   Go into the garden of the lord father,
8   Because there there is a serpent,
9   take the head of that serpent;
10 Crush it well
11 When you will have it completely crushed
12 Give it (to him) to drink.
13 The husband came back tired and thirsty,
14 he asked for a drink.
15 —Which one do you want, sir husband,
16 some light or some dark?
17 —Of the white wine that there is, some of the best that there is.
18 A child of nine months speaks
19 —Do not drink that wine because there is poison in it!
20 —What is wrong with this wine, Lombard woman,
21 Because it is cloudy?
22 —It must be the thrones of the other evening,
23 That made it cloudy.
24 —You drink it, Lombard woman!
25 You drink it!
26 —I cannot drink it, sir husband,
27 because I am not thirsty,
28 —With this sword which I hold in my hand
29 I will kill you,
30 —And for the love of the King of France,
31 I will die, ah, I will die!

Tre canzoni (Three songs), set to popular Italian poetry, were written originally for voice and string quartet and later transcribed by the composer for voice and piano. The songs are dedicated to the American patron Elizabeth Sprague Coolidge. Each of the three poems tells a story in which a woman is the central character.

Donna lombarda (Lombard woman) is a long narrative poem complete with infidelity, deception, and murder. It has many voices: the King of France, the Lombard woman, her husband, a child, and the narrator. There is a temptation with songs of this type to affect dramatic changes of vocal color. Pizzetti admirably underscores the emotions of his characters through compositional devices. Appropriate vocal colors may enhance the interpretation but should be subservient to phrasing, accent, harmonic movement, articulation, and the contrasts between voice and piano.

The song begins with a keyboard introduction marked *energico e rude* (energetic and rough), with a forceful dotted rhythm and a distinctive sixteenth-note motive:

The theme is decidedly masculine and serves both the character of the king and later that of the husband. The voice of the king is heard first, commanding the Lombard woman to love him. The accompaniment continues to develop the vigorous opening material beneath the vocal line, but the dynamics are different: *mezzo-forte* to *piano* in the accompaniment, *forte* in the voice part.

When the Lombard woman replies *Non posso amarti* (I cannot love you), the accompaniment pattern *più sostenuto* (more sustained) changes to widely spaced arpeggios. The effect is more graceful, although the sixteenth-note pattern

refers to the masculine theme of the song's opening. The vocal line is marked *dolce e accorato* (sweet and sorrowful). When the woman mentions her *marì'* (husband), the sixteenth-note pattern turns to the minor mode.

A repetition of the forceful opening measures of the song precedes the next section, which again presents the voice of the king. This section is divided into two parts. When the king suggests murdering the husband, the vocal melody is forceful and the accompaniment is rhythmically active and dissonant. When he describes the method of murder, the piano begins a lovely, lyrical melody accompanied by rather consonant harmonies. The music makes the projected act of violence seem almost seductive, less awesome. The dynamics throughout the section should be very quiet. At the end of the verse, *dannela a be'* (Give it to him to drink), the low **A♭** should be sung, if at all possible, in preference to the alternate octave. At this point the accompaniment introduces fragments of the song's opening masculine motive. The king departs, while the husband returns.

Another short motive, derived from the introduction, precedes the voice of the narrator as it describes the return of the tired, thirsty husband. The motive should project weariness as it continues as an *ostinato* beneath the narrator's words. The wife's response is marked *dolce*, but the fluttering sixteenth notes in the accompaniment betray some nervousness. The husband's request, marked *movimento* (moving), is set with a more angular vocal line and several repetitions of the rhythmic motive of four sixteenth notes and an eighth, which appeared in connection with his character earlier.

A completely new pattern of alternating eighth-note octaves over a spare, consonant harmony introduces the character of the baby. The pattern should be very sustained and the vocal entrance *pp* and *sotto voce*. At the command

Non ber quel vino (Do not drink that wine), which follows six measures of very consonant harmonic movement, Pizzetti simply introduces a seventh chord into the chord structure.

An agitated return to the husband's theme precedes his response. Here the vocal color is important since the composer writes above the husband's entrance *piano, ma duro e minaccioso* (soft, but hard and threatening)—as though through clenched teeth. An *ostinato* accompanies the section and continues with increasing activity in the inner voices beneath the wife's response. The composer indicates *rude e aspro ma pianissimo* (rude and harsh, but very quiet); the husband is not soothed by the wife's explanation. From here to the end of the song, the nervousness increases. The husband's lines are marked with *tenuto* indications and accents; and the wife's timid response is underscored by chromatic *ostinato* patterns building in intensity. The climax of the song is preceded by a *fortissimo* arpeggio, as the wife, accepting her death with passionate abandon, says, *E per amore del Re di Francia, io morirò* (And for the love of the King of France, I will die). Her response begins with the same notes (one octave higher) with which the king first commanded her love.

The piano postlude repeats the introduction with slight variation.

No. 2, La Prigioniera

(*Poesia popolare italiana*)

1 Manda a di' alla su' sorella che la cavi di prigionia
2 E le' ni manda a di' che in prigione ci puol marcì'
3 Manda a di' alla su' mamma che la cavi di prigionia
4 E le' ni manda a di' che in prigione ci puol marcì'
5 Manda a dire allo suo padre che la cavi di prigionia
6 E lu' ni manda a di' che in prigione ci puol marcì'
7 Manda a dire allo suo damo che la levi di prigionia
8 E lu' se la va a prende', e se la porta via.
9 —Morettina, 'un balla' più, chè l'è morta la tu' sorella.
10 —E se l'è morta, la ci stia!
11 Quando l'ero in prigionia, nun mi volse mai cavà'
12 Suona, violino, chè voglio ballà!
13 —Morettina, 'un balla' più chè l'è morta la tu' mamma.
14 —E se l'è morta, la ci stia!
15 Quando l'ero in prigionia, nun mi volse mai cavà'
16 Suona, violino, chè voglio ballà'!
17 —Morettina, 'un balla' più chè l'è morto lo tuo papà.
18 —E se l'è morto, lu' ci stia!
19 Quando l'ero in prigionia, nun mi volse mai cavà'
20 Suona, violino, chè voglio ballà'!

21   —Morettina, 'un balla' più, chè l'è morto lo tuo damo
22   —Se l'è morto di davero, mi farò il vestito nero,
23   e ballare io non vo' più.
24   Presto anch'io ne morirò.

No. 2, The woman prisoner

(*Popular Italian poetry*)

1   She sends word to her sister that she get her out of prison
2   And she sends word to say that in prison she can rot there.
3   She sends word to her mother that she get her out of prison
4   And she sends word to say that in prison she can rot there.
5   She sends word to her father that he get her out of prison
6   And he sends word to say that in prison she can rot there.
7   She sends word to her fiancé that he remove her from imprisonment
8   And he himself goes to get her and (he himself) takes her away.
9   —Little brunette, don't dance anymore, because your sister is dead.
10   —And if she is dead, let her stay there!
11   When I was in prison, she did not ever want to get me out.
12   Play, violin, because I want to dance!
13   —Little brunette, don't dance anymore because your mother is dead.
14   —And if she is dead, let her stay there!
15   When I was in prison, she did not ever want to get me out.
16   Play, violin, because I want to dance!
17   —Little brunette, don't dance anymore because your father is dead.
18   —And if he is dead, let him stay there!
19   When I was in prison, he did not ever want to get me out.
20   Play, violin, because I want to dance!
21   —Little brunette, don't dance anymore, because your fiancé is dead.
22   —If he is truly dead, I will make myself a black dress,
23   and I no longer wish to dance.
24   Soon I, too, because of that will die.

La prigioniera (The woman prisoner), like *Donna lombarda,* shows a
woman in despair. Even in her victorious dance there is a portent of disaster.
    The hollow open fifths of the first measures establish the starkness of
the prison scene. The vocal line enters above this at the end of the second
full measure and must establish the tempo—marked *andante mosso*. It must
not be too slow since the sing-song rhythm of the vocal line can easily plod
and there is a long story to tell. The emotional character of the line is *mal-
inconico* (melancholy, sad). Each of the prisoner's petitions for release be-

gins with a similar melodic pattern and each is set with the same 6/8 meter. However, the accompaniment pattern becomes increasingly active and the melodic range wider as the petitions progress. The climax is reached at *E lu' se la va a prende', e se la porta via* (And he himself goes to get her and takes her away). The voice should soar on the sustained line above the rapid sixteenth-note scales. The last words of the phrase should be held back a little before the change of rhythm that indicates the beginning of the dance.

The dance—a rather long interlude for solo piano—shifts from 6/8 to 3/4 with the direction *movimento di danza, moderato* (dancelike movement, moderate tempo), but it should be a little slower than the opening part of the song. Although theoretically representing the freedom of the prisoner, this dance is languid and trancelike rather than light-hearted, and it is interrupted by discordant octaves in the bass that break the flow of the rhythm.

When the song resumes in its 6/8 meter, the composer indicates a return to the slightly faster tempo of the initial 6/8 section. The melodic line is similar to that of the beginning of the song, and the dynamic level is *p ma intenso* (soft, but intense). Ignoring her sister's death because of an earlier rejection, the prisoner calls for the violin to begin the dance in a free two-measure section of recitative—*Suona, violino, chè voglio ballà!* (Play, violin, because I want to dance!). With a downward, sweeping scale and a sinister trill, the dance begins.

With each successive verse the dance becomes more frenzied, the texture thicker, the range wider, and the rhythmic activity greater, but the tempo remains the same.

The last verse, announcing the death of the fiancé, breaks in while the dance is in progress. It takes a few measures for the news to sink in. The dance disintegrates into fragments, and there are four measures of an ominous tremolo above a short *ostinato* of minor seconds.

The woman's final response is in the character of the song's opening measures, but the lines are fragmentary. The bass line of the piano part offers canonic imitation of the vocal line while the treble decorates with contrary motion. A clever shift in the rhythmic organization of the melodic line sets the words *e ballare io non vo' più* (and I no longer wish to dance). The final words, *Presto anch'io ne morirò* (Soon I, too, because of that will die), are uttered *col pianto nella gola* (with weeping in the throat). Two measures of the dance theme follow the singer's last word, with the composer's indication *stanco* (tired, weary); and the song ends as it began with open, hollow fifths.

Once again, Pizzetti has built into the construction of the setting the necessary devices for expressing the emotional state of the central character. Vocal phrases are generally short and no special breathing indications are needed. In some sections of the dance music small notes appear as indications of inner voices from the string quartet version of the work. These are for reference; the pianist is not obligated to include them.

No. 3, La pesca dell'anello

(*Poesia popolare italiana*)

1   Ell'eran tre sorelle, e tutt' e tre d'amò'
2   Rosetta, la più bella, si mise a naviga'
3   Nel navigar che fece, l'anello gli cascò
4   —O pescator dell'onde, vieni a pescar più qua
5   Pescami lo mio anello, che m'è cascato in mar
6   —Quando l'avrò pescato, cosa mi vuoi donà'?
7   —Cento zecchini d'oro, 'na borsa recamà.
8   —Non vo' tanti zecchini nè borsa recamà'
9   Solo un bacin d'amore, se tu me lo vo' da'
10 —Cosa dirà la gente che ci vedrà baciar?
11 —Dirà che l'è l'amore, che ce l'ha fatto fa'

No. 3, Fishing for a ring

(*Popular Italian poetry*)

1   There were three sisters and I loved all three of them.
2   Rosetta, the most beautiful went rowing.
3   While she was rowing she dropped her ring.
4   —O fisherman of the waves (sea) come and fish nearer to this place
5   catch for me my ring that has fallen into the sea.
6   —When I will have caught it, what will you give me?
7   —One hundred coins of gold, in an embroidered purse.
8   —I don't want so many coins or an embroidered purse
9   Only a kiss of love if you wish to give it to me.
10 —What will people say who will see us kissing?
11 —They will say that it is love, that made us do it!

La pesca dell'anello (Fishing for a ring), a wonderful narrative song, is like a miniature opera. The piano introduction, serving as an overture, has a built-in vitality in the folk-like rhythmic figures of the bass, so the composer's directions *arioso e sciolta* (airy and loose) should be carried out through articulation and phrasing. The piano seldom loses its melodic interest even under the vocal line. At the second appearance of the phrase *e tutt' e tre d'amò'* (and I loved all three), the pedal must hold the lower sustained notes while the charming polytonal figure is brought out in the treble.

The opening notes of the song appear in one variation or another at several points in the composition, and the singer should avoid accenting unaccented syllables when melodic considerations outweigh rhythmic word setting. A triplet figure introduced in the vocal line at the word *naviga'* (rowing) is later given to the piano to depict this activity thereafter. The pianist should also make the most of the colorful comments that punctuate the singer's phrase *l'anello gli cascò* (she dropped her ring).

The fisherman's response to the maid's request, *Quando l'avrò pescato* (When I will have caught it), is written at a lower pitch level, but it could still use a change of vocal color for further contrast. Throughout the rest of the song the identity of the speaker should never be in doubt. The rhythmic-melodic figure

in the accompaniment seems to anticipate the climax at *Solo un bacin* (Only a kiss), but it should not destroy the element of surprise. The *crescendo* should not start until exactly where it is indicated in the score, and the singer's entrance on the word *Solo* (Only) should be an abrupt *forte.* The piano trills that follow simulate a touch of trembling, and the interlude immediately after this phrase cleverly allows the stunned girl to think of a response.

The direction *p ma sentito* (quiet, but sincere) is the clue to the vocal character of the final phrase; an overclimactic treatment should be avoided. The last two lines of piano accompaniment serve as a curtain closer to the drama.

At several points in the song the direction *tratt.* is given. It translates as "stretch" and is an effective device to emphasize key phrases in the text.

Tre canzoni: G. Ricordi, 1927; Repr. 1944–45, 1953.
1. *Donna lombarda*   120236
2. *La prigioniera*   120237
3. *La pesca dell'anello*   120238

Due canti d'amore

No. 2, Oscuro è il ciel

(*Giacomo Leopardi*)

1 Oscuro è il ciel;
2 nell'onde la luna già s'asconde
3 e in seno al mar le Plejadi

4   già discendendo van.
5   È mezzanotte,
6   e l'ora passa frattanto,
7   e sola qui sulle piume
8   ancora veglio ed attendo in van.

Two songs of love

No. 2, Dark is the sky

1   Dark is the sky:
2   In the waves the moon already conceals itself
3   and in the bosom of the sea the Pleiades
4   already (they) go descending.
5   It is midnight,
6   and the hour passes in the meantime,
7   and alone here on my feather pillows
8   still I keep watch and I wait in vain.

The slow-moving open octaves that introduce *Oscuro è il ciel* (Dark is the sky) capture the vastness of the Aegean sky in this poem based on one by Sappho. Maintaining the same E–B octave pattern, Pizzetti cleverly changes the inner voices to create a moving harmony under the entrance of the voice, whose melodic motion in the initial phrases hovers between minor and major thirds. The texture remains open throughout this Impressionistic piece. Some text references are directly found in the music, such as the descending octave arpeggiation after the phrase *le Plejadi già discendendo van* (the Pleiades [stars in the constellation Taurus] already (they) go descending). For the most part, however, the keyboard and vocal parts fuse to create an overall mood for the text. The phrase introduced at measure 15, *e l'ora passa frattanto* (and the hour passes in the meantime), is repeated sequentially in measures 17–18, and a similar interval arrangement is then stretched out to create the climax at *e sola qui sulle piume* (and alone here on my feather pillows). The rapid figuration under the word *ancora* (still) in the next measure should be played as if the piano strings had been touched with a brush. The final vocal line returns to major–minor third alternation over some of Pizzetti's typical polytonal-sounding harmonies. The song ends clearly in E major. A slight break should occur before the singer's final utterance, *in van* (in vain).

Due canti d'amore: G. Ricordi, 1933; Repr. 1946, 1950.
    2. *Oscuro è il ciel*   122836

Tre canti greci

No. 1, Augurio

(*Traduzione di Pio Bondioli*)

1 In Rumelia c'è un albero frondoso
2 e di grande ombra;
3 alla radice ha una fresca polla
4 e sul tronco una croce.
5 Ci vanno i marinai per acqua
6 e fanno augurio sulla croce:
7 "Chi è amato e recusa amore
8 muoia svenato;
9 e chi ha due amanti
10 si abbia quaranta coltellate;
11 e chi n'ha tre o quattro
12 se n'abbia quarantaquattro;
13 e chi n'ha una, unica al mondo,
14 gioisca;
15 e chi non ne ha nemmeno una,
16 una palla lo colpisca al cuore."

Three Greek songs

No. 1, Wish

(*[Italian] translation by Pio Bondioli*)

1 In Rumelin there is a tree full of leaves
2 and very shady;
3 at its roots it has a fresh spring
4 and on its trunk a cross.
5 The sailors go there for water
6 and make a wish on the cross:
7 "Whoever is loved and rejects love
8 may he bleed to death;
9 and whoever has two lovers
10 may he have forty knife wounds;
11 and whoever has three or four of them
12 may he have forty-four;
13 and whoever has one of them, one only in the world,
14 may he rejoice:

15   and whoever has not even one of them,
16   may a bullet strike him in the heart."

Along with several of his contemporaries, Pizzetti was attracted to the popular songs and lyrics of Greece. The earthy, vital poetry translates well into Italian, and Pizzetti's well-crafted, conservative compositional style serves the poetry appropriately. Although each of the *Tre canti greci* (Three Greek songs) can stand as an independent song, their contrasting moods and tempo changes and the brilliant ending of the last song predispose their performance as a program group.

Augurio (Wish) begins *largo e disteso* (slow and stretched) with a four-measure piano introduction. The melodic line hovers between E♭ and E♮, creating a quasi-modal sound, and the rush of sixteenth and 32d notes in the final measure has the quality of a middle-European strummed instrument. As is often the case with Pizzetti, musical ideas presented in the introduction appear again throughout the work. The opening notes of the vocal line, while transposed, are closely related melodically and rhythmically to the opening measures of the composition; and the arpeggiated cluster chord in the accompaniment at measure 7 again recalls an ethnic instrumental sound. This "strumming" changes as the song progresses; a new pattern of six repeated sixteenth-note chords appears for the first time in measure 10 and leads into a countermelody for the piano. Although it is not specifically marked by the composer, these repeated sixteenth notes should *crescendo* very slightly toward the first beat of the following measure, and the countermelody should be phrased independently of the vocal line. An echo of the opening motive appears in the treble of the piano at measure 18 and closes the first section of the poem.

As each of the "wishes" of the poem is stated, beginning *chi è* or *chi ha* (whoever is, whoever has) in measures 19–20, Pizzetti embarks upon a clever and effective device. Each statement moves upward sequentially while the accompaniment follows one beat later with canonic imitation. In measures 22 and 26 there are even echoes of the song's opening motive, but by the third "wish" the momentum of the song requires more brilliant support, and a cascade of sixteenth notes provides it in measure 29. This *is* a climax, but not the true high point of the song.

A change of accompaniment in measure 31 signals the final wish, upon whose content the poet has placed an obviously higher value—*e chi n'ha una, unica al mondo, gioisca* (and whoever has one of them, one only in the world, may he rejoice). Here, the song's opening motive is stated exactly and the canonic imitation is just of that motive. The true climax comes with *gioisca* (may he rejoice), in measure 35. The song "comes down" from this climax with a series of short vocal phrases and fragmented phrases of accompaniment, including a few polytonal harmonies. This breaks off abruptly for the surprise ending. The joy of one true love is not the final point of the poem. Although treated as an afterthought, the last phrase must be forceful, almost brutal, and the chords that accompany it, sharp and brittle—including the final "shot."

No. 2, Mirologio per un bambino

(*Traduzione di Pio Bondioli*)

1 Non nella bella estate,
2 ma nel cuore dell'inverno,
3 proprio ora tu hai voluto andartene!
4 Mio bimbo, tu non hai voluto attendere
5 che a poco a poco le colline fiorissero,
6 rinverdissero i prati,
7 sbocciassero i garofani,
8 e crescessero i fiori.
9 Avresti potuto coglierne a piene mani,
10 e portarli nel basso mondo,
11 e i giovani li avrebbero messi sul berretto,
12 le giovanette sullo sparato della camicia,
13 e i piccoli li avrebbero tenuti in mano,
14 dimenticando la mamma.

No. 2, Lament for a child

(*[Italian] translation by Pio Bondioli*)

1 Not in the beautiful summertime,
2 but in the dead of winter,
3 just now you wished to go away!
4 My child, you did not wish to wait
5 until little by little the hills would bloom,
6 the fields would become green,
7 the carnations would blossom,
8 and the flowers would grow.
9 You could have picked them by handfuls;
10 and bring them into the underworld,
11 and the young boys could have put them on their berets,
12 the young girls on the front (opening) of their blouses,
13 and the little ones could have held them in their hands,
14 forgetting their mother.

Tension and anguish are established immediately in *Mirologio per un bambino* (Lament for a child) by the smear of 64th notes leading to an augmented fourth in the two-measure piano introduction. By the time this figuration is repeated five or six times the mood is all-pervasive. Much of the effectiveness of the song depends on the juxtaposition of the anxious, dirge-like accompaniment (to be played with damper and soft pedals) and the rambling, disoriented vocal line. The accompaniment does not resolve until the word *bimbo* (child), by which time the ear is crying for it. Harmonic movement increases in the accompaniment between dissonance and reso-lution in the next section, until another sense of peace is reached at the words *i fiori* (flowers) in measure 30. Further variation is achieved by octave displacement, and the addition of low bass reinforcement underscores the text as the protagonist (mother?) muses upon thoughts of the child carrying flowers to the underworld. At this point the composer warns *non forte, ma più intenso* (not loud, but more intense). As this poetic vision takes hold, the vocal line becomes more melodic and the repeated augmented fourth in the accompaniment ceases. This change should be gradual, as though it quietly comes over the mother, bringing her a brief respite from grief. The relief is short-lived, however, and the pattern returns in advance of the moth-er's final, most-tortured thought—that the dead child might forget her. The final repetitions should trail off in a blur over the bass notes, which are sustained with pedal. This song requires exceptional emotional maturity.

No. 3, Canzone per ballo

(*Traduzione di Pio Bondioli*)

1 Godete, giovani; godete, belle:
2 i giorni scemano e Caronte ce li conta,
3 ce li conta ad uno ad uno.
4 Incominciate il ballo, via!
5 poi la nera terra ci ingoi.
6 Caronte non ha giudizio nè riguardi;
7 strappa i figli dalle poppe e lascia i vecchi.
8 Ah! Balliamo dunque, poi che il ballo giova.
9 Sotto questa terra che calpestiamo,
10 tutti una volta andremo.
11 Questa terra verdeggiante divora giovani e pallicari;
12 questa terra fiorita divora giovanette, divora fanciulle
13 Divorerà anche noi questa terra che pur ci è madre;
14 Questa terra che ci divorerà, battetela col piede.

No. 3, Song for dancing

([Italian] translation by Pio Bondioli)

1   Enjoy, young men; enjoy, pretty girls:
2   the days shorten and Charon will count them,
3   he will count them one by one.
4   Begin the dance, be off!
5   After that the black earth will swallow us.
6   Charon has no judgment or considerations,
7   He snatches suckling babies and leaves the old people.
8   Ah! Let us dance therefore, since dancing gives delight.
9   Under this land which we are trampling,
10 One day we will all go.
11 This flourishing earth devours young men and old warriors,
12 this flowering earth devours maidens, devours little girls.
13 It will also devour us, this earth who also is mother to us;
14 this earth which will devour us, stamp on it with your feet.

The title *Canzone per ballo* (Song for dancing) is deceptive, since the real subject of the poem is death; the dancing alluded to is merely a prelude to it. The frenzied downward scale and angular melodic line of the piano introduction, combined with a vigorous folk rhythm and a minor modality, set the tone immediately. The composer also has qualified the *allegro* tempo with the adjective *rude* (harsh, rough). This is not a festive occasion.

The folk rhythm and crude harmonies from the introduction continue in the accompaniment beneath the entrance of the voice in measure 8. The first phrases stress the interval of a fifth, in effect heightening the poet's call to begin the macabre dance. The third phrase, *ce li conta ad uno ad uno* (he will count them one by one), is more sinuously chromatic, describing Charon, the mythological ferryman responsible for transporting the souls of the dead across the rivers Acheron and Styx and into the underworld. Immediately thereafter, the dance rhythms become prominent in the accompaniment, and the first climax of the song is reached in measure 27, *poi la nera terra ci ingoi* (After that the black earth will swallow us). In measure 30 Pizzetti restates the song's opening measures, and the voice follows in canonic imitation one measure later. The balances between singer and accompanist are crucial throughout this whole section, since so much of the text is elucidated by the musical structure.

The second section of the poem, beginning in measure 36, *Caronte non ha giudizio nè riguardi* (Charon has no judgment or consideration), is set similarly to the first, but with an even more active and more heavily textured accompaniment. There are also melodic changes in keeping with the modulations. The section culminates, as did the first, with the opening measures of the song, now in widely spaced chords with the vocal line in canonic imitation. The "retreat" from the second climax is longer and involves several echoes of the last few notes of the vocal line (see measures 68–69 and 71–72).

A new musical idea, using chromaticism drawn from earlier measures and prominently sounding an augmented fourth reminiscent of *Mirologio per un bambino,* sets the phrase *Sotto questa terra che calpestiamo* (Under this land which we are trampling). It is repeated quasi-sequentially. Patterns of octaves in the bass line of the piano part and contrary motion between piano and voice create increasing tension as the poet continues his catalog of death's victims.

In preparation for the finale of the song, the composer wisely decreases the musical activity (measures 119–134), centering the vocal line around one pitch over an *ostinato* bass. This quietly builds in intensity to the penultimate utterance *Questa terra che ci divorerà* (this earth which will devour us), brilliantly set in an augmented meter (measure 135). (The voice line here is barred differently than the accompaniment, but that in no way affects the coordination of the two parts.) A short fragment of the original dance motive interrupts (measures 140–142), and then the phrase is repeated sequentially. *Battetela* (stamp on it) is repeated three times with jarring intensity to draw the song back into a now frenzied, *fortissimo* repetition of the opening dance. A coda of sorts is produced as the singer repeats the dance rhythm over and over again on the same pitches while bell-like chords toll beneath in the accompaniment. The final scream (measures 174–175) should be quite abandoned and the final piano chords sharp and decisive.

Tre canti greci: G. Ricordi, 1933; Repr. 1946.

1. *Augurio*	122837
2. *Mirologio per un bambino*	122838
3. *Canzone per ballo*	122839

e il mio dolore io canto

(*Jacopo Bocchialini*)

1 Io sono un'arida fonte.
2 La state ferì la mia vena
3 che fluiva tranquilla e piena, un giorno.
4 Ora non più.
5 Una caduta di foglie quaggiù in fondo.
6 Un volo vano di piccole ali attorno.
7 Bocca assetata, non t'accostare.
8 Io sono una fonte dolente che langue
9 Ogni goccia è stilla di sangue,

10   ogni goccia è stilla di pianto.
11   E il mio dolore io canto.
12   Bocca assetata,
13   la mia vena di pianto non disseta.

and of my grief I sing

1   I am a dry fountain.
2   Summer wounded my vein
3   which flowed calmly and full, once upon a time.
4   Now no more.
5   Fallen leaves down here at the bottom
6   A useless flight of little wings around.
7   Thirsty mouth, do not come closer.
8   I am an unhappy fountain that languishes
9   Every drop is a drop of blood,
10   Every drop is a drop of tears.
11   And of my grief I sing,
12   thirsty mouth,
13   My tearful vein will not quench your thirst.

In *e il mio dolore io canto* (and of my grief I sing) the image of a dry fountain as a metaphor for a loveless life has an immediate impact. Pizzetti's setting of this short poem is dedicated to the poet, who was an old friend and companion. The compositional devices are similar to earlier Pizzetti settings. Again, a short, effective, easily recognizable motive,

is threaded through the work. It keeps the song within the framework of a single mood and allows the poetry to flow in speech rhythms. The form of the song freely follows the poetry. Most of the interpretive problems can be solved by careful observation of the scoring.

In the opening measures the rests between the notes of the ascending scale low in the bass highlight the motive, which is introduced in the treble. The latter figure should be very *legato*. The whole introduction is very quiet. The entrance of the voice should be one dynamic level higher than that of the accompaniment, but it should not get any additional stress. It is a statement of fact; the repetition of the falling motive immediately after it is the emotional comment.

Interestingly, the composer saves the use of the motive in the vocal line until the words *Ora non più* (Now no more) and alters it so that it falls a fourth, rather than a third. This effect is repeated at the climax, *Bocca assetata, non t'accostare* (Thirsty mouth, do not come closer). Even here the highest dynamic level is *mezzo-forte.*

The last page of the song is essentially a recitative for the voice, while the motive provides interest in the accompaniment. A broader melodic line sets the title words *E il mio dolore io canto* (And of my grief I sing), leading to a secondary climax at the repetition of the words *Bocca assetata* (thirsty mouth). The motive provides some final musical punctuation in the last measures of the accompaniment.

There are an unusual number of short rests in the vocal line of this song, and they must be scrupulously observed. The song should have a breathless, weary quality about it. The range and *tessitura* of the song make it especially suitable for baritone or bass voice without the need for transposition from the original key.

e il mio dolor io canto: Forlivesi, 1945.   11961

Gian Francesco Malipiero

(1882–1973)

•

GIAN FRANCESCO MALIPIERO was born in Venice on March 18, 1882 into an aristocratic Venetian family that had been prominent for many generations. The family was also very musical. Malipiero's grandfather Francesco Malipiero (1824–1887) had been an opera composer considered a rival to Giuseppe Verdi; and his father, Luigi, was a pianist and conductor. His mother, Emma Balbi, was a Venetian countess.

In 1893, after the break-up of his parent's marriage, Gian Francesco accompanied his father to Trieste, Berlin, and Vienna, where he often played in orchestras conducted by the elder Malipiero (he had begun violin lessons at the age of six). A stint at the Vienna Conservatory in 1898–1899 had mixed results: he failed violin but a transfer to harmony class proved successful.

In 1899 Malipiero returned to his mother's house in Venice and became a pupil of Marco Enrico Bossi at the Liceo Musicale Benedetto Marcello. When Bossi moved to Bologna in 1902 Malipiero continued his studies on his own. He spent considerable time in the Biblioteca Marciana copying, transcribing, and studying works of the early Italians that he had discovered— music by Frescobaldi, Cavalli, Del Cavalieri, Merulo, and, especially, Monteverdi.

In 1904 Malipiero moved to Bologna, where he resumed studies with Bossi and received a diploma from the Bologna Liceo Musicale. Soon after he worked as amanuensis for Antonio Smareglia, a blind composer who wrote in the style of Wagner. Malipiero later claimed to have learned most of his orchestration from this experience. A few classes with Max Bruch in Berlin (1908–1909) seemed not to have been of great value to him.

Returning to Venice in 1910, Malipiero married the daughter of a Venetian painter and sought solitude in the Veneto hill town of Aosolo. There he began to compose seriously, his music strongly influenced by his studies of early Italian composers. In 1911 he joined a group of rising Italian composers called I Cinque Italiani—the other members being Pizzetti, Respighi, Gianotto Bastianelli, and Renzo Bossi.

In 1913, feeling his work was stifled, Malipiero went to Paris. Alfredo Casella introduced him to Ravel, made him aware of current trends, and insisted on his attendance at a performance of Stravinsky's *Rite of Spring.* As a result of this profound experience, coupled with exposure to Debussy, Fauré, de Falla, and others, Malipiero absorbed new devices into his modal and contrapuntal writing, and he decided to suppress all compositions written before this time. However, most of them were not destroyed.

Shortly before or during his Paris visit, Malipiero submitted five compositions, each under a different name, to a competition organized by the Accademia di Santa Cecilia in Rome. He won four of the five prizes. This controversial situation created considerable hostility toward the composer and incited noisy disturbances at the public performances of his one-act opera, *Canossa,* and the tone poem, *Arione.*

Although Malipiero was secluded in Aosolo during much of World War I, the retreat of Caporetto brought the war to his doorstep and forced him and his family to flee to Rome in 1917. The anguish of this experience was reflected in *Pause di Silenzio I,* a major orchestral work consisting of seven pieces, each of which is introduced by a variation of the same fanfare. This structure, labeled "panel construction" by some critics, recurred in subsequent works.

Malipiero's first important opera, *Sette Canzoni,* written in 1919 to his own text, shows a break with the traditions of Verdi, Puccini, and the *verismo* composers. It consists of seven miniature operas, with no continuing plot, and lasts approximately 45 minutes. Each opera has a song as its musical center and is based on a personal experience of the composer. Although the melodic declamations show influences of Stravinsky and Debussy, they are very much in the style of Monteverdi.

While living in Rome, Malipiero worked with Casella's Società Italiana di Musica, and in 1923 he collaborated with Casella in founding Corporazione delle Nuove Musiche. From 1921 to 1923 he was professor of composition at the University of Parma Conservatory. He then returned to Aosolo, which remained his home until his death.

In the mid-1920s Malipiero's music lost some of the tormented restlessness of the war years and acquired greater serenity. It also shows more interconnection between early music styles and early twentieth-century compositional idioms. True to his interest in early music, in 1926 Malipiero began an edition of the complete works of Monteverdi, which was completed in 1942. Although controversial, Malipiero's work in this area was highly influential in the rediscovery of Monteverdi as well as many other early Italian composers.

In 1932 Malipiero became professor of composition at the Liceo Musicale Benedetto Marcello in Venice, and he was director of the institution from 1939 to 1952. He actually lived in the conservatory during the German occupation. Although Malipiero attempted to ignore political events, his opera *La Favola del Figlio Cambiata* was suppressed as "morally incongruous" with Fascist ideals soon after its premiere on March 26, 1934—an event from which Malipiero had to escape to avoid bodily harm. A later opera, *Julius Caesar* (1936), was successful with the Fascists, who came to honor Malipiero. During World War II the composer and his British-born second wife gave shelter to an escaped British aviator for several weeks until Italian partisans could arrange safe conduct to England.

World War II inspired Malipiero's Symphony No. 4, *In Memoriam,* which was commissioned by the Koussevitsky Foundation and introduced by the Boston Symphony Orchestra under Koussevitsky on February 27, 1948. In the postwar period, Malipiero's more lyrical, diatonic style of the 1930s and 40s turned more chromatic; an example of this development is the opera *Mondi celesti e infernali* (1948–49). His most powerful postwar opera is *Venere prigioniera* (1955), in which whole-tone and modal ideas interact extremely closely.

Malipiero retired from the Venice Conservatory in 1952 but continued to supervise the Istituto Italiano Antonio Vivaldi, which had begun to publish Vivaldi's complete instrumental works in 1947. He had an irrepressible urge to compose up to 1971, when he was 89. His one-act *Don Giovanni* was completed in 1962, and the *Quartetto per Elisabetta* was given its world premiere in Washington, D.C., in 1964.

Malipiero's overall style is basically one of free polyphony, with contemporary dissonances created by the interweaving of lines. Malipiero was influenced by his contemporaries in Italy and abroad, and he was typical of his generation in the need to rebel against the turn-of-the-century musical establishment. But he also owes a strong debt to plainsong, medieval and Renaissance music, and especially to the music of Monteverdi. His vocal melodies, in both opera and song, are closely molded on the speech inflections of the human voice, in which he showed great interest throughout his career.

Gian Francesco Malipiero died in Treviso, Italy, on August 1, 1973.

I sonetti delle fate

No. 1, Eliana

(*Gabriele d'Annunzio*)

1 Dorme a notte il palagio d'Eliana,
2 simile a un dòmo gotico d'argento.
3 Or, ne la luce senza mutamento,
4 pare un fragile incanto di Morgana.
5 Armoniosa come uno stromento
6 apresi a torno l'alta ombra silvana;

7 ed a piè de la scala una fontana
8 singhiozza in ritmo ne 'l silenzio intento.
9 A torme a torme candidi paoni
10 lenti, silenti come neve in aria,
11 discendono su l'agili ringhiere.
12 Sono le spose morte di piacere,
13 che tentan la dimora solitaria.
14 E il bosco è pieno d'implorazioni.

Sonnets of the fairies

No. 1, Eliana

1 Eliana's palace sleeps in the night,
2 like a Gothic cathedral (made) of silver.
3 Now, in the light without change,
4 it appears a fragile enchantment of Morgana.
5 As harmonious as an instrument
6 it opens up to the deep woodsy shadows;
7 and at the foot of the stairway a fountain
8 sobs rhythmically in the intense silence.
9 Swarm after swarm of snow-white peacocks
10 slow, silent like snow in the air,
11 they descend onto the slender banisters
12 they are the dead brides of pleasure,
13 who attempt the solitary life.
14 And the woods are full of supplications.

No. 2, Mirinda

(*Gabriele d'Annunzio*)

1 Mirinda e il fido, ne l'occulta stanza
2 adagiati su' troni orientali,
3 dilettansi a gittar lucidi strali
4 sotto i piè d'un fanciul nudo che danza.
5 Un grande e bianco augello, a passi equali,
6 carico d'otri, sparge in abondanza
7 acque d'ambra d'insolita fragranza
8 sui marmi che dan lume ai penetrali.
9 "Vedrem fiori, com' ampie urne fiorire;
10 berremo un vin ne' puri alvi de' frutti;

11 e guarderemo entro smeraldi il sole."
12 Dice Mirinda. E il termulo nitrire
13 de' liocorni e il murmure de' flutti
14 si mescono a le sue lente parole.

No. 2, Mirinda

1   Mirinda and her devoted one, in the secret room
2   reclining on oriental thrones,
3   Amuse themselves by throwing bright darts
4   under the feet of a young naked boy who is dancing.
5   A large, and white bird, with even steps,
6   loaded with bottles made of goat skins, he scatters in abundance
7   amber-colored waters of an extraordinary fragrance
8   on the marble statues which give light to the innermost recesses.
9   "We will see flowers blooming like large urns;
10 we will drink a wine from the pure hearts of the fruit;
11 and will look inside emeralds at the sun."
12 Mirinda says. And the tremulous neighing
13 of the unicorns and the murmuring of the waves
14 blend together with her slow words.

No. 3, Melusina

(Gabriele d'Annunzio)

1   Guarda, assisa, la vaga Melusina,
2   tenendo il capo tra le ceree mani,
3   la Luna in arco da' boschi lontani
4   salir vermiglia il ciel di Palestina.
5   Da l'alto de la torre saracina,
6   ella sogna il destin de' Lusignani;
7   e innanzi al tristo rosseg(g)iar de' piani,
8   sente de 'l suo finir l'ora vicina.
9   Già già, viscida e lunga, ella le braccia
10 vede coprirsi di pallida squama,
11 le braccia che fiorian sì dolcemente.
12 Scintilla inrigidita la sua faccia
13 e bilingue la sua bocca in van chiama
14 poi che a 'l cuor giunge il freddo de 'l serpente.

No. 3, Melusina

1 Observe, seated, the beautiful Melusina,
2 holding her head between her waxen hands,
3 the Moon in an arc from the distant woods
4 ascends brilliant red the Palestinian sky.
5 From the top of the Saracen tower,
6 she ponders the destiny of the Lusignani
7 and before the menacing reddening of the plains
8 she feels the hour of her death is near.
9 Yes, already, slimy and long, she sees
10 her arms covered with pale scales,
11 her arms that flower so gently.
12 Her face shines in rigidity
13 and bilingually her mouth calls in vain
14 before a serpentine coldness reaches her heart.

No. 4, Grasinda

(*Gabriele d'Annunzio*)

1 Dorme Grasinda in mezzo a' suoi tesori,
2 ove l'incanto un sonno alto le impose.
3 E l'intima dolcezza de le cose
4 ver lei migra in assai vaghi romori.
5 Fremono a torno li alberi canori,
6 da la grande armonia piovendo rose
7 quasi che per virtù misteriose
8 si rispandano i suoni in rari fiori.
9 Lento il corpo ne 'l sonno a 'l ritmo cede;
10 compongonsi le membra agili in arco
11 e prendon forma di lunata lira.
12 Si tendono le chiome argute al piede
13 facendo strano a' due pollici incarco;
14 e su tal corda l'anima sospira.

No. 4, Grasinda

1 Grasinda sleeps surrounded by her treasures,
2 Where a spell imposed on her a deep sleep.
3 And the intimate sweetness of the things
4 near her migrates in very lovely sounds.
5 They resound around the harmonious trees,

6   from the grand harmony raining roses
7   almost as by mysterious virtues
8   redisperse the sounds in rare flowers.
9   Slowly her body in her sleep yields to the rhythm;
10   Her limbs compose themselves with agility in an arc
11   and take the form of a crescent-shaped lyre.
12   Her tresses hold themselves out tautly strung to her feet
13   making a strange task for two big toes
14   and on such a chord her soul sighs.

No. 5, Morgana

(*Gabriele d'Annunzio*)

1   Or tremule, su i mar e su le arene,
2   crescon ne la lunare alba le imagi:
3   materiati d'oro alti palagi
4   e torri ingenti assai più che Pirene.
5   Salgono scale in luminose ambagi
6   con inteste di fior lunghe catene.
7   Come navi in balìa de le sirene,
8   ondeggiano le pendule compagi;
9   poi che Morgana, in dolce atto giacente
10   ne 'l letto de la nube solitaria,
11   quasi ebra di quel suo divin lavoro,
12   ama, seguendo un carme ne la mente,
13   cullare de le man languide a l'aria
14   la città da le mille scale d'oro.

No. 5, Morgana

1   Now tremulous, over the seas and over the sands,
2   they grow in the lunar dawn the images:
3   high palaces composed of gold
4   and towers very much more enormous than the Pyrenees.
5   They (the images) climb up staircases in luminous ambages
6   With long chains made with heads of flowers.
7   Like ships at the mercy of sirens,
8   the pendulous structures undulate;
9   so that Morgana, in a pleasant act lying down
10   in the bed of a solitary cloud,
11   almost intoxicated with her divine work,
12   loves, following a poem in her mind,

13 to rock, with her languid hands in the air,
14 the city of the thousand stairs of gold.

No. 6, Oriana—Oriana infedele

(*Gabriele d'Annunzio*)

1   Oriana tenea l'incantamento.
2   Giacean, ebri d'assai dolci veleni,
3   ne l'antro i prodi; e larga di sereni
4   sogni la Luna era a l'umano armento.
5   Pascean su 'l limitare i palafreni
6   meravigliosi, li èmuli de 'l vento:
7   battean la lunga coda in moto lento
8   a la coscia, e nitrian per li alti fieni.
9   Giunse Amadigi a l'antro solitario,
10 tutto de l'armi splendide vestito;
11 e tre volte sonò, ne 'l muto orrore.
12 Quindi, rompendo il magico velario
13 che l'edera tessea, con quell'ardito
14 gesto egli prese ad Oriana il cuore.

No. 6a, Oriana infedele

15 Quando Amadigi con l'eterna amante
16 giunse a l'isola Ferma (auree ne 'l giorno
17 lucean le mura ed i verzieri in torno
18 aulivano), le porte d'adamante
19 s'apriron mute e gravi, a 'l suon de 'l corno,
20 ma, lasciando Oriana a Floridante,
21 il Donzello del mare, almo e raggiante,
22 penetrò solo ne 'l divin soggiorno.
23 Disse a la donna il bel sir di Castiglia:
24 Ahi che troppo di te m'arse il desio!
25 Or tu m'odi! E la trasse ai labirinti
26 Mago ne l'aria odore di jacinti
27 vinse Oriana de 'l soave oblio.
28 Ridea Lurchetto in sua faccia vermiglia.

No. 6, Oriana—Oriana unfaithful

1   Oriana held the enchantment.
2   They (the brave men) were lying, intoxicated by very sweet poisons,

3   in a cave the brave men; and filled with serene
4   dreams the Moon appeared to the herdsmen.
5   The marvelous saddle horses were grazing
6   at the threshold, the emulators of the wind:
7   they were beating their long tails in slow motion
8   against their thighs, and were whinnying for the tall hay.
9   Amadigi arrived at the secluded cave,
10 all dressed in shining armor;
11 and three times he rang, in the silent awesomeness.
12 Hence, breaking the magic veil
13 that the ivy wove, with that daring
14 deed he took from Oriana her heart.

No. 6a, Oriana unfaithful

15 When Amadigi with his eternal love
16 reached the island Ferma (in the day the walls
17 of the city used to shine and the orchards surrounding
18 smelled sweetly), the massive doors
19 opened silently and slowly, at the sound of the horn.
20 But, leaving Oriana to Floridante
21 the noble youth of the sea, sublime and radiant
22 penetrated alone in the divine resort.
23 The handsome Sire from Castille said to the woman:
24 Alas, because my desire for you burned me too much!
25 Now you hate me! And he drew her into the labyrinths.
26 The sorcerer in the air perfumed with hyacinths
27 (he) overcame Oriana with gentle oblivion.
28 Lurchetto was laughing in her brilliant red face.

Gabriele d'Annunzio's *I sonetti delle fate* (Sonnets of the fairies) are remarkable for both their imagery and their intricate structure, including an unusual symmetrical rhyme scheme. Each sonnet consists of fourteen lines, grouped eight and six (see chart p. 168).

Malipiero's Impressionistic settings capture the elusive moods of the poems with equally interesting, but relatively uncomplicated, structures. The songs are strong enough to stand individually, but their shared subject matter and the composer's basic Impressionistic language call for their performance as a set. Also, there are many subtle references—a rhythmic echo, interval relationships, similar chord movements—that tie them together even without an obvious cyclical relationship. Musically and historically they represent important work in the *lirica da camera* form.

No. 1, *Eliana,* begins with the direction *con grande mistero* (with great

	1	2	3	4	5	6	6a
1	A	A	A	A	A	A	A
2	B	B	B	B	B	B	B
3	B	B	B	B	B	B	B
4	A	A	A	A	A	A	A
5	B	B	A	A	B	B	B
6	A	A	B	B	A	A	A
7	A	A	B	B	A	A	A
8	B	B	A	A	B	B	B
9	C	C	C	C	C	C	C
10	D	D	D	D	D	D	D
11	E	E	E	E	E	E	E
12	E	C	C	C	C	C	E
13	D	D	D	D	D	D	D
14	C	E	E	E	E	E	C

mystery)—an appropriate description for the entire set of sonnets. It is difficult to set a tempo for this song; there are several meter changes, and the accompaniment patterns vary from measures of sustained whole and half notes to measures of 32d notes. The quarter note should remain relatively constant throughout the changes, and a tempo of ♩ = 66–72 should make the accompaniment technically comfortable without distorting the phrasing of the vocal line.

The piano introduction is very quiet. The pattern of slowly rising diminished fifths establishes an Impressionistic color and bears a slight resemblance to Debussy's *La Cathédrale engloutie* (The sunken cathedral). The accents are grouped 2 + 2 + 2, and there is an increase of rhythmic movement at the meter change in measure 4. The composer gives no directions for pedaling, but the style obviously calls for the blurred effects favored by the Impressionist composers in general, and the pianist should approach this accompaniment in the same manner as a piano part by Debussy or Ravel.

The entrance of the vocal line in measure 5 poses no problem if the quarter note is kept constant; it should be possible to sing the opening phrase on one breath. (Pianist and singer may have to experiment with *tempi* until vocal phrasing according to text is achieved.) The vocal lines throughout the song are in speech rhythm but are broadly melodic rather than recitative-like. The slow, sustained opening chordal measures give way to more rapid rhythmic movement and quicker piano figurations by the third phrase, which describes the appearance of Morgana. The sixteenth-note patterns trace many of the chord tones from previous measures, and an almost exact replica of measures 2–3 appears in measures 17–18.

When the procession of quarter-note chords begins in measure 19, care should be given to achieving a good dynamic balance with the voice. The vocal line lies rather low, while the underlying chords ascend. The *tenuto* marks in the accompaniment should designate a slight hesitation rather than a dynamic accent. The singer will need a breath after the word *stromento* (instrument) in measure 20. A slight *rallentando* precedes the change in the accompaniment to a sextuplet pattern of sixteenth notes in measure 24. This should apply only to the octaves, which appear directly above the *rallentando,* and the opening of the vocal line. Measure 24 should be *a tempo,* with the quarter note again as the constant. Accent marks in the left hand of the accompaniment and the staccato indications (measures 24–27) should be observed carefully. The right hand, in part describing a fountain, should be suitably "watery." The singer should attempt to phrase through the word *ritmo* (rhythmically) in measure 26 before taking a breath.

The transition to the new pattern—32d notes grouped in fours—should be very smooth. The E-minor arpeggiation against the C-major pedal should be very quiet and murmuring, taking its color from the word *torme* (swarm) in the text. After the word *paoni* (peacocks), where the singer should take a breath, the accented notes in the accompaniment form an ascending chromatic scale that should emerge from the texture with a slight *crescendo*. The dynamic level drops back to *ppp tranquillissimo* in measure 32, as the peacocks begin their descending procession. Measure 35 introduces yet another pattern in the accompaniment—canonic imitation between the treble and bass lines—with the direction *voluttuosamente* (voluptuously). This section, which is preceded by a *rallentando,* could be slightly slower than the preceding one. It is also *mf,* so far the fullest dynamic level in the song, and it reaches a climax on the word *morte* (dead). The singer should not breathe until after the word *piacere* (pleasure). An accompaniment similar to the opening of the song introduces the final phrase, but it carries the direction *un poco agitato.* A second climax of sorts is reached at the final word *implorazioni* (supplications), and fragments of the last accompaniment pattern bring the song to a quiet conclusion in a clear C-major tonality.

In No. 2, *Mirinda,* the tempo indication *veloce* (quickly) again indicates character more than basic pulse. The dance rhythm, which begins in measure 7, works best at a moderate tempo ($\quarternote$ = 108–112), if the slightly languid oriental character of the piece is to be achieved. The composer wants a burst of sound and activity in the first six measures of the introduction, tapering to a light, crisp, rhythmic articulation of the dance, which appears before the entrance of the vocal line. Much of the opening of the piece is built around the F♯–B♭ interval, expressing the exoticism of the locale. The vocal lines are broadly melodic and in most instances can be phrased according to the commas in the text. A breath should be taken, however, in the third poetic phrase after *lucidi strali* (bright darts) in order to sing the fourth phrase without a break. The two parts, voice and piano, are quite independent in the opening section of the work, as though a narrator were describing the scene matter-of-factly over the sound of dance music.

When Mirinda speaks (measures 46–47) the tempo slows (*molto meno mosso*), and the accompaniment becomes an atmospheric, colorful background for the sensuous delights she describes. The fragments of the dotted-rhythm dance theme, which appear in the bass clef, should emerge from the texture but still sound far off. The dance theme appears in its entirety in the measures before the climactic phrase *e guarderemo entro smeraldi il sole* (and we will look inside emeralds at the sun). This phrase reaches the highest dynamic level in the song (*mf–f*) and carries the direction *ancora meno mosso* (even less motion). The return of the narrator to describe *tremulo nitrire de' liocorni* (tremulous neighing of the unicorns) and *murmure de' flutti* (murmuring of the waves) carries the direction *veloce* (quickly); here the sixteenth notes in sextuplet groupings should be a blur of sound beneath the vocal line. The return of the dance theme for the last two lines of the song requires a slightly slower, but strict, rhythm and crisp articulation. A decrease in both tempo and dynamics completes the short five-measure postlude.

Mid-point in the cycle, *Melusina* is a setting of a very direct poem, whose images are more concrete than those of the other poems. Malipiero chooses a simple three-part song form with a short coda. The first and third sections have virtually identical piano parts—a ground bass over which a series of chords, mostly minor, progress in parallel motion (a common Impressionistic device.) In the first occurrence of part A the vocal line consistently duplicates the upper voice of the chord line; in the return it does so in a more fragmentary manner.

The overall tempo for the song is *lento,* and the dynamic level of the A sections is *sempre pp.* The parallel chords should be heavy and ponderous, even though they are quiet. The *tenuto* markings should lend a labored quality to the line, and the voice should be dirgelike, in keeping with the close interval relationships and repetitions within the line.

The B section begins in measure 12 with the direction *strisciante* (creeping, crawling). Melusina's vision of her own dying body is graphically described in the poetry. The chords supporting the chromatic vocal line should be played very *legato* and should be phrased within the bar as well as over the full length of the six-measure unit. When the accompaniment changes to a more active line of sixteenth notes, special stress should be given to the accented notes that initiate each grouping. The climax comes in the phrase *le braccia che fiorian sì dolcemente* (her arms that flower so gently). The ascending eighth notes, countered by accented descending quarter notes, are marked *con slancio* (with a rush). The highest dynamic level is actually reached in the piano part in measure 35, one measure after the release of the vocal phrase. Measure 35, marked *rallentando,* with a *fermata* governing the chord tones within it, prepares the return of the pedal bass, which signals the recapitulation of section A.

The final section is very quiet and somewhat slower. While the chord patterns are identical to the opening of the composition, the vocal line is more fragmented. The final seven measures act as a coda; arpeggiations and block chords, still in parallel motion, progress in a continuing downward spiral to a quiet conclusion. The song is one of unrelieved sadness, appropriately hollow in color and quality.

Malipiero's interest in early Italian music is evident in the madrigal-inspired setting he chooses for the first and last sections of No. 4, the graceful sonnet *Grasinda*. The piano introduction consists of two long arpeggios—one *lentamente* (slowly), one *veloce* (quickly)—in the manner of a harp testing its tuning. When the vocal line enters, a regular meter should be established. Marked *non lento,* a moderate tempo of ♩ = 84–96 will keep the flow of the melodic line in section A while still permitting the rapid articulation of the arpeggiated accompaniment in section B. A delicate countermelody with the motive

and interesting inner-voice movement accompanies the opening vocal phrase but acts independently of it. Voice and piano must be carefully balanced in this *pp dolcissimo* dynamic so that the delicacy of the texture, appropriate to the poem, can be maximized. After the release of the word *romori* (sounds), the measured trill in the accompaniment anticipates the beginning of section B.

The indication *un poco più movimento* (a little more motion) appears at the beginning of part B, but the tempo has to be governed by the ability of the pianist to execute the very rapid arpeggios in the accompaniment. The effect should be of airy *glissandi* lightly supporting the broad vocal line. The rhythmic grouping of these figurations varies—9, 10, 11, and so forth—but the basic meter should remain constant. The dynamic level is still very quiet, and the pedaling should achieve an Impressionistic blur while still allowing the chord changes to be perceived. The last three measures of the section are marked *largo,* but the change should not be too abrupt, rather a broadening of the phrase and spacing to bring the section to a close. A *fermata* over the final F♯ serves as a transition back to section A.

Section A returns to the first tempo and a structure almost identical to that of its earlier counterpart. By the fourth measure, however, the composer has given the direction *animando* (animated), and both the vocal line and the accompaniment build to the setting of the climactic word *lira* (lyre), where the rapid *glissandi* from section B provide the accompaniment. In the measures immediately before the word *lira,* the ascending chromatic line in the inner voice of the bass-clef accompaniment should stand out from the overall texture.

The final lines of poetry are set with a combination of devices drawn from earlier sections. As the vocal melody broadens, the rippling arpeggiations in the treble of the accompaniment are joined in the bass by an extension of the motivic piano melody that opened the song. The dynamics remain quiet, and the texture should still seem transparent and diaphanous. A little more solidity is found in the octaves and rolled chords that double the vocal line on the final phrase, *e su tal corda l'anima sospira* (and on such a chord, her soul sighs). This phrase should be sung and played more broadly, as the composer directs, and at a full *forte*. Echoes of the madrigal-like accompaniment lead full circle to an arpeggio in the same tonality as the first chord of the song.

The other-worldly poetic imagery of the sonnets continues with No. 5, *Morgana*, in a musical setting filled with Impressionistic devices. The structure is a modified three-part song form, but the sections do not bear any direct relationship to the structure of the poem. Morgana, herself, is seen as the focal point of the poem, and the harmonic and rhythmic motion of the song build toward the statement of her name in measure 30. Again, no tempo indication is given, only the direction *leggermente mosso* (lightly moving), which primarily describes the opening measures. To some extent the tempo will be governed by the articulation of the ten-note grouping of 32d notes in the accompaniment. The whole measure-long accompaniment figure that introduces the work should be very quiet (*ppp–pp*) and *senza colore* (without color). No pedal indications are given, but the phrase lines point up the movement of the inner-voice chords, for which the pedal will probably be needed. The introduction is interesting. Over a G♭ pedal (the third of the chord is omitted), an inverted F-major chord is introduced. It moves in upward parallel motion to an inverted G♭ chord, which itself then "resolves" to E♭ minor. The composer uses a hollow pedal, polytonality, parallel harmony, a pentatonic scale (the ten-unit 32d-note grouping), and enharmonic resolution—a whole lexicon of Impressionist devices. The measure-long pattern becomes an *ostinato* over which the vocal line enters.

The vocal line follows the speech rhythms of the text, and the pitches are always derived from the underlying chords. It is not a particularly distinguished melodic line, serving rather as part of the overall texture of the song. At a tempo slow enough for good keyboard articulation, the vocal phrases become rather long, requiring careful examination of text for additional breaths. For example, the phrase *materiati d'oro alti palagi e torri ingenti assai più che Pirene* (literally: "composed of gold high palaces and towers very much more enormous than the Pyrenees") will probably need to be broken at the second syllable of *torri* and at the first syllable of *ingenti,* thus setting off the qualifying phrase from the subject.

The B section of the song, which starts in measure 12, has a meter change to 3/4, a more insistent accompaniment pattern, and the direction *un poco agitato*. Tensions build through the wonderful patterns of contrary motion toward the climax of the song in measures 30–33. The descending parallel chord patterns in the accompaniment in measures 19–29 carry careful markings for phrasing and *staccato* versus *tenuto* articulations, which must be carefully observed. Also, important accents are needed in the upper (inner-voice) line of the bass clef of the accompaniment. The dynamic level remains *p* throughout these measures, but the textural richness leads logically to the broad, sweeping octaves (continuing the contrary motion) that underscore the climactic vocal phrase. The slightly faster tempo should enable the singer to carry the phrases from comma to comma in this section. There should be as much connection as possible. The *ritenuto* in measure 30 should be interpreted as a stretching of the climactic phrase, and the dynamic levels in measures 30–33 are higher—*mf* and *f.*

Measure 34 marks the return of the accompaniment pattern that opened the song; the octave displacement creates an even more ethereal quality. The tempo should return to the languor of the opening measures, and similar attention should be paid to the phrasing of the chords in the inner-voice line. A *diminuendo* is called for in the final four measures of the accompaniment, and the short, two-measure "codetta" is marked *lento* and *ppp.*

The last two sonnets, Nos. 6 and 6a, although complete in themselves, concern the same subject, *Oriana,* and are set in one continuous song. A subtitle, *Oriana infedele* (Oriana unfaithful), marks the beginning of the second sonnet, but the structure of the song is governed by the subjective content of the poem rather than by its form.

The bulk of the song is organized around two musical ideas, one "feminine" and one "masculine." The first musical idea occurs with a series of polytonal chords in the piano introduction. The tempo indication is *alquanto ritenuto* (somewhat held back), and the dynamic level is *pp dolcemente.* The languid movement cadences on a C_7 chord approached through an appoggiatura just before the voice enters. Similar chord movements underscore the opening vocal melody, which doubles much of the treble piano line.

In measures 9–10 the second musical idea,

more robust in character, appears beneath the verb *giacean* (lying), whose implied subject is *i prodi* (brave men). Thereafter, much of the song refers to these musical ideas, combines them, or is derived from them. The appearance of the Moon in line 4 of the sonnet brings back the "feminine" motive in measure 18, while measure 22 uses the "masculine" motive in the bass line of the accompaniment in anticipation of the poetic description of *palafreni mervigliosi* (marvelous saddle horses).

There are several examples of specific tone-painting in this song. While the vocal melodic line tends toward stretched-out recitative, the accompaniment often comments graphically on the poetic text. In measure 28 *staccato* chords marked *un po' agitato* (a little agitated) set the word *vento* (wind), and a *rallentando* is directed at the words *moto lento* (slow motion), which describe the beating of the horses' long tails (measure 31). Trills in the inner-voice line of the accompaniment appear at the word *nitrian* (whin-nying) in measures 32–34.

A new section, of sorts, begins in measure 35. The "masculine" theme is stated with vigor, first in G major, then in an implied A major over a G-major bass. The theme shifts up an octave as the poem progresses. Even the poet's *e tre volte sonò* (and three times he rang) is found in the accented notes of the upper line of the bass-clef accompaniment in measure 42–44. These should emerge from the texture here and in the measures before the series of running staccato eighth notes that lead to the winning of Oriana's heart. The latter occurs in measures 54–58 with a return of the "feminine" theme. Aspects of this theme in the treble, coupled with the "masculine" theme in the bass, mark the lush piano interlude and transition to the second sonnet, *Oriana infedele* (Oriana unfaithful).

The musical "descriptiveness" of the first sonnet's setting continues into the second. A broad melodic line with fragmented references to earlier mo-tives and an arpeggiated accompaniment describe the shining city walls. A martial, trumpetlike statement of the "masculine" theme, marked *maesto-samente* (majestically) describes *le porte d'adamante* (the massive doors). A climax is reached in measure 101, with *Ahi che troppo di te m'arse il desio* (literally, "Alas, because too much for you burned me my desire") and the first *forte* dynamic in the song.

A new pattern of sixteenth-note sextuplets is introduced in measure 108 to evoke Oriana's oblivion. The melodic line in the lower line of the piano part is derived from the "feminine" theme and should be brought out in the texture. A broad *fortissimo* return to the "masculine" theme begins the piano postlude, marked *mosso* (motion or moving), but the atmospheric chords of the final two measures make a last reference to Oriana.

Most of the vocal phrases in this song can be achieved on one breath. The balances between voice and piano, however, require some attention since so much of the expression and organization of the work depends on recognizing the themes and their references, which occur chiefly in the piano part. Although the vocal part seems more like extended speech, the broad Italian melodies should not sound "talky."

I sonetti delle fate: A. and G. Carisch and C. Carisch and Jänichen, 1914.
C. 13357 J. (Set)

1. *Eliana*		C. 13351 J.
2. *Mirinda*		C. 13352 J.
3. *Melusina*		C. 13353 J.
4. *Grasinda*		C. 13354 J.
5. *Morgana*		C. 13355 J.
6. *Oriana—Oriana infedele*		C. 13356 J.

Tre poesie di Angelo Poliziano

No. 1, Inno a Maria Nostra Donna

1 Vergine santa, immacolata,
2 degno amor del vero Amore,
3 che partoristi il Re,
4 che nel Ciel regge creando il Creatore.
5 Vergine rilucente, per te sola
6 si sente quanto bene è nel mondo:
7 tu siei degl'affannati buon conforto,
8 e del nostro navil se' vento e porto.
9 O di schietta umiltà ferma colonna,
10 di carità coperta
11 accetta di pietà, gentil Madonna,
12 per cui la strada aperta
13 insino al Ciel si vede,
14 soccorri ai poverelli,
15 che son fra lupi agnelli,
16 e divorar ci crede
17 l'inquieto nemico, che ci svia,
18 se Tu non ci soccorri, Alma Maria.

Three poems of Angelo Poliziano

No. 1, Hymn to Mary, our lady

1 Virgin holy, immaculate,
2 worthy love of the true Love,
3 who gave birth to the King,
4 who in the Heavens reigns creating the Creator.
5 Virgin resplendent, through you alone
6 one feels how much good is in the world:
7 you are for those troubled good comfort,
8 and of our ship you are the wind and the harbor.
9 O, of sincere humility the pillar of strength,
10 covered with charity
11 appreciated with pity, kind Madonna,
12 for him who sees the open road
13 up to heaven,
14 give help to the poor,
15 who are sheep among wolves,
16 and believe the restless enemy
17 will devour us and lead us astray,
18 if you do not help us, Divine Mary.

The first song in the cycle *Tre poesie di Angelo Poliziano* (Three poems of Angelo Poliziano) is a hymn of supplication entitled *Inno a Maria Nostra Donna* (Hymn to Mary our lady). The first section is a simple address identifying and praising the Virgin as mother of the King of Heaven. The second is more personal, addressing the Madonna as the comforter of the troubled, the guide to those lost on the sea of life. The third part is a direct plea for help in destroying the enemies that beset the road to salvation. The musical contrasts differentiating these sections are subtle but clear. They are achieved primarily through tempo change and underlying harmonic and rhythmic movement while the voice maintains a simple speech-inflected line. The *lento* tempo works best at approximately $\quarternote = 44$, and the absence of a meter signature allows the phrasing to flow with the declarative nature of the poem. The accompaniment is modal in character and, although structured in block chords, is reminiscent of the implied chordal movement underlying Gregorian chant. The sequential nature of the accompaniment creates four-note phrases within each bar in section one, but the voice must carry over bar lines in accordance with the text. A breath should be taken after *il Re* (the King) to allow this to happen naturally.

The tempo change for the second section should be slight, just enough to underscore the more liberal declamation indicated by the composer. Sufficient contrast is provided by the augmentation of the accompanying chord sequence, with phrases now spanning two measures of music.

The tempo change at section three should carry with it a slightly more metrical feeling. Its greater intensity is achieved through wider range of melody and more rapid movement of the accompaniment figure. In the line *per cui la strada aperta* (for him who sees the open road), the singer should not breathe until after *si vede* in order to complete the first thought. Other breathing places are indicated consistently by rests or commas in the text.

At no time should the dynamic level rise above the indicated *mezzo piano,* and the final, most intense section must begin and end *pianissimo.* The singer must achieve intensity through heightened enunciation and tone quality rather than volume. Note that the final decorative vocal figure is an inversion of two earlier ones, now rising rather than falling, and thus expressing the optimism of the supplicant.

No. 2, L'eco

1   Che fai tu, Eco, mentre io ti chiamo?
2   Amo.
3   Ami tu due, o pur un solo?
4   Un solo.
5   Ed io te solo, e non altri amo
6   Altri amo.
7   Dunque non ami tu un solo?

 8   Un solo.
 9   Quest'è un dir io non t'amo.
10   Io non t'amo.
11   Quel che tu ami, amil' tu solo?
12   Solo.
13   Chi t'ha levato dal mio amore?
14   Amore.
15   Che fa quello a chi porti amore?
16   Ah, more.

No. 2, The echo

 1   What are you doing, Echo, while I call you?
 2   I love.
 3   Do you love two, or rather one alone?
 4   One alone.
 5   And I you alone, and no others do I love.
 6   Others do I love.
 7   So then do you not love one only?
 8   One only.
 9   This is saying I don't love you.
10   I don't love you.
11   The one that you love, do you love him alone?
12   Alone.
13   Who took you away from my love?
14   Love.
15   What does that one do to whom you bring love?
16   Ah, he dies.

A "play upon words" is the main device in *L'eco* (The echo). While the echo answers with the final words or syllables of the singer's phrase, the meaning is changed or reversed. As the conversation progresses a little story is pieced together. The repetitive accompaniment patterns provide an Impressionistic underpinning for the speechlike vocal line and are specifically marked *incolare* (colorless). They should be played lightly and *legato,* and care should be taken to observe the terraced dynamics as the voice differentiates the speaker from the echo. A change of vocal color is also called for at each appearance of the echo—in line with the composer's direction *lontano* (distant). The tempo (approximately ♩ = 88) should permit an unobtrusive movement of the accompaniment while allowing the singer enough freedom to achieve the conversation-like character of the song. Once established, the tempo remains steady except for the increasing agitation as the singer becomes more impatient with the echo's reply—*Dunque non ami tu un solo?* (So then you do not love one only?). A slight slackening of the tempo permits an easy transition to the accompanying sextuplet figure in the final five measures of the song. The dynamic range of this song is narrow—*mf* to *pp*—and should not be exceeded.

No. 3, Ballata

1 Donne mie, voi non sapete
2 ch'io ho il mal ch'avea quel prete:
3 fu un prete (questa è vera)
4 ch'avea morto il procellino.
5 Ben sapete che una sera
6 gliel rubò un contadino,
7 ch'era quivi suo vicino
8 altri dice suo compare,
9 poi s'andò a confessare,
10 e contò del porco al prete.
11 El messer se ne voleva
12 pur andare alla ragione,
13 ma pensò che non poteva,
14 chè l'avea in confessione:
15 dicea poi fra le persone,
16 Oimè, ch'io ho un male,
17 ch'io non posso dire avale,
18 e anch'io ho il mal del prete.

No. 3, Ballad

1 My ladies, you do not know
2 that I have the same misfortune that that priest had:
3 he was a priest (this is true)
4 who had killed the little pig.
5 Well you know that one evening
6 a peasant robbed him of it,
7 who was his next-door neighbor,
8 moreover, says his witness,
9 he then went to confession
10 and told about the pig to the priest.
11 The priest wanted
12 even to bring him to reason,
13 but he thought that he could not,
14 because he had heard it in confession:
15 He used to say then to the people.

16   O my, I have a misfortune
17   that I cannot talk about now,
18   and I, too, have the misfortune of that priest.

There is undoubtedly some *double entendre* in the poet's claim of having a misfortune like that of the confession-bound priest, but the overall character of *Ballata* (Ballad) is one of lament, real or imagined. The narrow, chromatic, weaving melodic line at the beginning of the song, repeated in sequential transposition at the Tempo I°, creates a whining effect, which the descending minor chords in the accompaniment reinforce, especially when heard against the droning pedal bass. (This pedal bass, although widely spaced, would sound best if it is not rolled.) The long section of sixteenth notes, which tell the bulk of the story, should increase in motion and dynamics as they move toward a quasi-Gregorian flourish on the word *prete* (priest). The 32d-note accompaniment figures in the final section of the song heighten the emotional content of the words, and the final block chords require firm accents. Throughout the song, word and syllable accents within the phrase should be shaped to convey the story in a clearly narrative way, and metronomical regularity should be avoided.

Tre poesie di Angelo Poliziano: London ed., Chester, 1921.   J. and W. C. 3857
  1. *Inno a Maria Nostra Donna*
  2. *L'eco*
  3. *Ballata*

Alfredo Casella

(1883–1947)

•

IF A DESIRE TO EFFECT REFORM AND CHANGE in an artistic climate requires the unswerving and enthusiastic support of at least one key figure, then the cause of modern Italian music must pay a debt of gratitude to the work of Alfredo Casella.

He was born in Turin on July 25, 1883 to a family with considerable musical talent. It is believed that the madrigalist Casella, mentioned in Dante's *Divine Comedy,* was an ancestor. In any case, Alfredo's father was a professor of cello at the Liceo Musicale, his uncle was a cello virtuoso, and his mother was a pianist. At age four Casella started studying the piano with his mother, and he made his public debut as a pianist in 1894.

In his early years Casella showed equal interest in music and in science, particularly chemistry and electricity, and a career in either area would have been possible. The urging of Giuseppe Martucci and Antonio Bazzini swung the young man toward music, although his scientifically oriented mind was in evidence throughout his life in his approach to musical composition.

In 1896 Casella went to Paris to attend the Conservatoire, and he remained in that city for the next nineteen years. He studied piano with Louis Diémer and composition with Xavier Leroux. He also attended Fauré's composition classes in 1900–1901. He quickly developed an interest in the music of Debussy, Ravel (with whom he had personal contact), Strauss, Mahler, the Russian nationalists, Bartók, Schoenberg, and Stravinsky. He was affected by the cubist and futurist movements in the visual arts, and he traveled extensively, even making trips to Russia in 1907 and 1909.

In 1915 Casella felt a need to return to Italy to create a musical art both Italian and European. He succeeded Sgambati as professor of piano at the Liceo di Santa Cecilia in Rome. In 1917, to further what had already become a deep and abiding concern, Casella founded the Società Nazionale di Musica, later renamed Società Italiana di Musica Moderna (SIMM). With his co-founders—Pizzetti, Respighi, G. F. Malipiero, Gui, Tommasini, and Castelnuovo-Tedesco—he organized and conducted concerts that brought the music of Ravel, Stravinsky, and many other modern European composers before the Italian public. Often these works were not received kindly; a riot broke out after a performance on January 21, 1917 of Casella's own *Elegia eroica,* dedicated to the war dead. *Ars Nova,* the magazine published by SIMM, often provoked attacks by the Italian musical press. Casella appeared as composer, pianist, and conductor at the SIMM concerts until the activities of the organization ceased in 1919.

Wide travels as both pianist and conductor were undertaken by Casella in the years immediately after World War I and eventually led to his resignation from the Liceo (renamed Conservatorio) di Santa Cecilia in 1922. In 1925 Casella performed the piano part in the first performance of his *Partita* in a concert given by the New York Philharmonic under Willem Mengelberg.

In Rome, on September 21, 1923, at a meeting in the villa of the influential poet Gabriele d'Annunzio, Casella, along with Gian Francesco Malipiero and Mario Labroca founded the Corporazione delle Nuove Musiche (CDNM). This organization became integrated almost from the beginning with the Italian section of the International Society for Contemporary Music (ISCM), although it maintained some autonomy until 1928. One of the corporation's first activities was a tour to introduce Schoenberg's *Pierrot lunaire* in Rome, Milan, Naples, Florence, Turin, Venice, and Padua. In addition to his activities in the corporation, Casella found time to issue new editions of keyboard masterworks by Bach, Mozart, and Beethoven and to write critical articles for Italian newspapers and magazines, including *Musica d'oggi,* which he edited and financed.

From 1930 to 1934 Casella turned his attention to the Venice Festival of Contemporary Music, which he directed in collaboration with Adriano Lualdi and Mario Labroca; and in 1932 he joined the Accademia di Santa Cecilia, in charge of the advanced piano class.

There is some controversy regarding Casella's involvement with Fascism. His opera (or lay oratorio) *Il deserto tentato,* reportedly written at the personal request of Mussolini, praised the Ethiopean campaign. It was first performed in Florence's Teatro Comunale on May 19, 1937 and was denounced by critics inside Italy for its music and outside Italy for its politics. There is no question that Casella lent himself to serve at Fascist festivals and celebrations. Yet, at the 1937 Venice Festival, he personally championed the cause of Arnold Schoenberg, whose music had been suppressed since 1930. As the alliance between Italy and Nazi Germany grew, Casella's family position was made difficult by the fact that his wife was a French Jew.

In 1939 Casella helped to found the Settimane Senesi at the Accademia Chigiana in Siena in support of early music. His interest in this area had begun as early as 1906–1909, when he had been the harpsichordist of the Société des Instruments Anciens in Paris.

In 1942 Casella suffered the first attack of the illness that eventually led to his death. He composed until 1944, conducted until 1946, and accompanied until shortly before he died, in Rome on March 5, 1947. One of his final compositions was the *Missa Solemnis pro Pace.*

Casella's scientific orientation and objective interest in the music of other composers has caused critics to see a reluctance on his part to develop a consistent musical style. However, his career in Italy can be divided into three periods in which the devices he chose for musical expression are similar.

The first period, up to 1913, shows the influence of his teacher Fauré and the German and Russian composers he admired. (The last came partially through the appearances of Diaghileff's Russian ballet.) However, his music is more Romantic than Impressionistic, and toward the end of the period he began to show self-conscious Italian influences. In fact, his first major success came with the rhapsody *Italia* (1909), which was introduced in Paris on April 23, 1910 in an all-Casella program conducted by the composer. Several popular Italian melodies, including Tosti's song *Amarecchiare*, are woven skillfully into a Romantic texture.

In 1913–1914 the composer moved toward the extreme avant-garde, showing influences of Bartók, Stravinsky, Schoenberg, and the later works of Debussy. There are individualistic uses of superimposed perfect fourths, chromatic chord counterpoint, and somewhat atonal writing, as seen in works such as *Notte di maggio* (1913), on a poem by Giosuè Carducci. Expressionist references to the horrors of war occur in *Pagine di guerra* (1919).

This period ended in 1920, almost as abruptly as it had begun, and chromaticism was replaced by dissonant diatonicism. Harmonic experimentation gave way to linear textures, and Italian folk influences returned. For the first time, Casella's music also showed influences of earlier Italian composers—Domenico Scarlatti and Niccolo Paganini, in particular—and the use of older Italian musical forms. The *Concerto for String Quartet* is generally considered as establishing Casella's "third manner"—Italian classicism with an extended tonal system. This neo-classicism, devoid of romantic chromaticism, remained as his mature musical style. Toward the end of his life, Casella occasionally used twelve-tone series.

Tre canzoni trecentesche

No. 1, Giovane bella, luce del mio core

(Cino da Pistoia)

1 Giovane bella, luce del mio core,
2 Perchè mi celi l'amoroso viso?
3 Tu sai che 'l dolce riso
4 E gli occhi tuoi mi fan sentire amore.
5 Sento nel core tanto di dolcezza,
6 Quando ti son davante,

7   Ch'io veggio quel ch'Amor di te ragiona.
8   Ma, poi che privo son di tua bellezza,
9   E de' tuoi be' sembianti,
10 Provo dolor che mai non m'abbandona.
11 Però chiedendo vo la tua persona,
12 Disioso di quella chiara luce
13 Che sempre mi conduce
14 Fidel soggetto de lo tuo splendore.

Three fourteenth-century songs

No. 1, Beautiful young woman, light of my heart

1   Beautiful young woman, light of my heart,
2   Why do you hide from me your affectionate face?
3   You know that your sweet smile
4   And your eyes make me feel love.
5   I feel in my heart so much sweetness,
6   When I am before you,
7   That I see what Love reasons about you.
8   But, since I am devoid of your beauty,
9   And of your beautiful semblance
10 I feel sorrow that never leaves me.
11 However, I go calling for your personage,
12 Desirous of that bright light
13 That always leads me,
14 Faithful subject of your splendor.

Tre canzoni trecentesche (Three fourteenth-century songs) were composed in 1923. They represent Casella's third period of compositional style, dissonant classicism, which occupied him up to the time of his death.

No. 1, *Giovane bella, luce del mio core* (Beautiful young woman, light of my heart), is written in sections according to the complete sentences of the poem—ABCDE—with each section given a subtle treatment corresponding to the meaning of the poetic phrase. However, the many thematic interrelationships among the phrases—repetition of complete sections of the accompaniment, motives appearing in transposition—give unity to the whole. Despite the frequent meter changes there is a processional, dancelike feeling to the rhythm, not unlike fourteenth-century court music (which also had irregular meters). The tempo should be a lively *allegretto,* and the composer warns that quarter notes must be equal at all times; there is absolutely no *rallentando* until the final measures of the song. In order to avoid a plodding quality, the pianist should strive for clean *legato* and follow the phrasing indications across bar lines. When the voice enters, the initial melody follows the upper voice of the accompaniment and sounds rather like a folk song. It is the most recognizably melodic material in the song. Phrase B, beginning in measure 12, follows the same procedure, but breaks into a slight melisma at the end on the word *amore* (love).

A new accompaniment pattern is introduced in measure 18, and throughout the third phrase of the song the vocal lines ride independently above the pattern. Interesting modulations at the end of the phrase become *marcato* as they lead into the fourth phrase. The accompaniment pattern here is almost an *ostinato*. There is a very important shift to minor modality in measure 34. In this fourth phrase, or section D, the poet speaks of feeling sorrow, and the composer's direction is *con intenso sentimento* (with intense feeling). The final word of the phrase, *m'abbandona* (leaves me), receives melismatic treatment, as did *amore* (love) earlier; and an accompaniment pattern similar to that of measure 18 (now transposed) makes a bridge to the last section of the song (measures 46–53).

In measure 53 the piano part begins an exact repetition of the opening measures of the song, but when the vocal melody enters in measure 55, it does not follow the top voice of the piano part, as it had earlier. The "singing" upper line of the accompaniment should be stressed in this section since it is the most melodic and it ties the end of the song with the opening. The exact duplication ends after a few measures, but the entire final section contains material reminiscent of the beginning. Another long melisma completes the phrase on the word *splendore* (splendor). The piano postlude is made up of the accompaniment pattern introduced in measure 18 and repeated in measure 46; it is transposed again here. This pattern, mostly running eighth notes over a procession of quarter notes in the bass, should remain perfectly steady. The *rallentando* must not occur until the final four measures of the song.

No. 2, Fuor de̲ la bella gaiba*

(Aut̲ore ignoto)

1   Fuor de̲ la bella gaiba
2   Fuge lo lusi̲gnuolo.
3   Plange lo fantino, poi che̲ no̲n trova
4   Lo̲ so osi̲lino ne̲ la gaiba nova;
5   E̲ dice cum dolo:
6   Chi gli avrì l'usolo?
7   E̲ dice cum dolo:
8   Chi gli avrì l'usolo?
9   En un busche̲tto se mi̲se ad andare;

* This poem is in a northern dialect; therefore there is no syntactic doubling.

10   Sentì l'ozletto* sì dolce cantare.
11   Oi bel lusignuolo, torna nel mio brolo.

No. 2, Out from the beautiful cage

(*Author unknown*)

1   Out from the beautiful cage
2   Flees the nightingale.
3   The little boy cries when he does not find
4   his little bird in the new cage;
5   And he says with grief:
6   Who will get him the bird?
7   And he says with grief
8   Who will get him the bird?
9   In a little wood he began to go;
10   He heard the little bird singing so sweetly.
11   O beautiful nightingale, return to my garden.

The quick piano figurations that introduce *Fuor de la bella gaiba* (Out from the beautiful cage) depict the flight of the bird; the singer's first phrase is a simple statement of what has happened. The emotional content of the song really begins with the *andante* ($\downarrow$ = 60) and the falling chromatic figure in the accompaniment. The composer's direction to the singer, *con grand' espressione e dolcezza* (with great expression and sweetness), is some justification for a childlike tone quality, if it can be achieved without artifice. If a breath is needed in the first phrase, the logical place for it is after *osilino* (little bird). A contrast in vocal color should definitely be made between the narrator's words, *E dice cum dolo* (And he says with grief), and the child's, *Chi gli avrì l'usolo?* (Who will get him the bird?), observing the composer's directions *ad libitum, con fantasia* (freely and with imagination). The meter in measure 15 is incorrect in the authors' copy of the score—it is 7/4 not 4/4. At the end of the measure, singer and pianist must come together on the syllable *lo,* and the *fermata* should be held only briefly, as marked.

A technically difficult passage of widely spaced chords introduces the next section. The composer indicates that the tempo must remain steady and the chords played without arpeggiation. (Both sustaining and soft pedals are to be used throughout this section.) The measure marked *perdendosi* (dying away) after *dolce cantare* (sweetly singing) prepares for the *come sognando* (dreamlike) final section of the song. Here, the tempo should be slower and the florid vocal line sung freely. In essence the child's plea for the return of the nightingale has become an imitation of the nightingale's song itself.

The tie into the rests on the final note of the vocal line simply indicates the lack of a fixed beat as the voice trails away. The piano should not enter

---

* ozletto is pronounced osletto.

until after the singer finishes, and the entire piano postlude should be held
by the pedal until it fades naturally.

No. 3, Amante sono, vaghiccia, di voi

(Autore ignoto)

1 Amante sono, vaghiccia, di voi;
2 Quando vi veggio tutto mi divoro.
3 Esco del campo, quando io lavoro,
4 E come pazzo vo gridando oi ... oi ...
5 Poi corro corro, e ò digiunto i buoi;
6 E vo pensando di voi, chè non lavoro.
7 Voi siete più luciente che l'oro.
8 E siete più bella ch'un fior di ginestra,
9 E siete più dolce che no è 'l cerconcello
10 Dè, fatevi un poco alla finestra;
11 Ch'io vi prometto ch'al vostro porcello
12 Drò delle ghiande una piena canestra,
13 E anche vi dico che al vostro vitello
14 Drò della paglia una piena canestra.
15 E a voi madonna cotanto dolciata,
16 Vi darò, Vi darò un ... un cesto d'insalata.

No. 3, I am in love, charming one, with you

(Author unknown)

1 I am in love, charming one, with you;
2 Whenever I see you I am completely devoured.
3 I go out of the field, when I work,
4 And like a madman I go crying oi ... oi ...
5 Then I run and I run and I have unyoked the cattle;
6 And I go on thinking about you, because I do not work.
7 You are more lustrous than gold.
8 And you are more beautiful than the broom flower,
9 And you are sweeter than watercress.
10 Pray, place yourself for a moment at the window;
11 Because I promise you that to your young pig
12 I will give a full basket of corn,
13 And also I tell you that to your calf
14 I will give a full basket of straw.
15 And to you my lady of such sweetness,
16 I will give you, I will give you ... a basket of salad.

Amante sono, vaghiccia, di voi (I am in love, charming one, with you) by an unknown fourteenth-century poet is proof that the madness of love transcends all centuries. The poem bursts with energy, and the song begins with an equally energetic fanfare for piano marked *vivace assai* and *chiassozo* (noisy, rowdy). In measure 6 a vamp-type accompaniment introduces the voice of the farmer-poet. The overall outline of the voice part resembles a folk song, but the subphrases are interrupted by frequent rests to give it a breathless, *agitazione* (agitated) quality.

When the farmer-poet stops his work to contemplate his beloved a complete change occurs in the music (measure 23). The tempo slows to *lento,* and the new eighth-note division now equals the previous quarter note. The vocal line, in recitative style, *appassionato ed insinuante* (impassioned and flattering), lauds the attributes of the beloved above slow-moving dissonant chords. Several *portamenti* are written in the vocal line, but the composer qualifies them with the adjective *lieve* (slight).

Another change of character occurs at measure 30, when, finished with his flattery, the poet in *voce forte* (strong voice) commands the beloved to come to the window. The rhythmic flow should be a little more regular through this section, as the poet reels off his projected gifts to the animals.

The final page of the song begins *risoluto* (resolute), as the poet comes to a gift specfically for the lady. He hesitates, in a lowered voice, almost as if looking around for something, until with decisive full voice he decides on a basket of salad. The piano immediately provides a concluding comment drawn from the vamp figure that introduced the poet-farmer.

This charming, funny song is set with simplicity and would lend itself to a spirited acting-out on the part of the performers. It provides an excellent close for the set or for any program group.

Tre canzoni trecentesche: Ricordi, 1923; Repr. 1950.   119505 (Set)
    1. *Giovane bella, luce del mio core*
    2. *Fuor de la bella gaiba*
    3. *Amante sono, vaghiccia, di voi*

Quattro favole romanesche di Trilussa

No. 1, Er coccodrillo

1   Ner mejo che un signore e 'na signora,
2   Marito e moje, staveno sdrajati
3   Su la riva der mare, scappò fora
4   un Coccodrillo co' la bocca aperta
5   E l'occhi spaventati.

6 La moje, ch'era sverta,
7 S'aggiustò li riccetti e scappò via:
8 Mentre ch' er Coccodrillo, inviperito,
9 Se masticava er povero marito
10 Come magnasse un pollo all'osteria.
11 Siccome er Coccodrillo, pe' natura,
12 Magna l'omo eppoi piagne,
13 puro quello se mésse a piagne' come 'na cratura,
14 Ogni cinque minuti
15 Ciaripensava come li cornuti
16 E risbottava un antro piantarello.
17 Tanto ch' er giorno appresso, a l'istess'ora,
18 Ner rivede' la povera signora
19 Riprincipiò le lagrime e li lagni;
20 Sperava forse che s'intenerisse:
21 Ma inveci, sì! la vedova je disse:
22 Dio mio, quanto sei scemo! Ancora piagni?

Four Roman fables by Trilussa

No. 1, The crocodile

1 In midday when a gentleman and a lady,
2 Husband and wife, were lying together
3 on the seashore, there ran out
4 a crocodile with his mouth open
5 and his eyes terrifying.
6 The wife, who was turned away,
7 Fixed her hair and ran off:
8 While the crocodile, enraged,
9 chewed up her poor husband
10 as he would eat a chicken at the tavern.
11 While the crocodile, by nature,
12 ate the man and then he wept.
13 That one also began to cry like a creature.
14 Every five minutes
15 He was again thinking of himself as a villain.
16 And burst out into another fit of weeping.
17 So much that the next day at the same time,
18 On seeing again the poor lady
19 He began once more the tears and the laments;
20 He was hoping perhaps that she would be moved to pity.
21 But instead, yes! The widow said to him:
22 My God, what an idiot you are! Are you still crying?

Quattro favole romanesche di Trilussa (Four Roman fables by Trilussi) provides an opportunity for Casella to express his feelings in the challenging and confusing years following the devastation of World War I. The songs work on more than one level—there is considerable humor in the text and the music, but there are also episodes of irony, and a detached bitterness is never far from the surface. The analogies between animal and human behavior must have been particularly applicable to the political situation at the time the songs were written and are, perhaps, just as apt today. The musical settings are descriptive of the poetry. They contain numerous meter changes, but are typical of the music-writing conventions of Casella's neo-classical style. Most of the measures are metrically equivalent, indicating only shifts of accent, and even these conform very well to the natural accent of the poetry or text. The look of the score is more difficult than the realization of it. The songs can be performed individually, but none are very long and the *tempi* are relatively quick. Changes of tempo, texture, and dynamics are more noticeable within songs than between them, but they still form an excellent program group and were probably intended as such by the composer.

Er coccodrillo (The crocodile) begins with a humorous tempo direction, *allegretto borghese* (ordinary, moderately fast). (*Borghese* also translates as *bourgeois,* or middle class; and capitalized it is the name of one of Italy's most famous historical families!) The five-measure piano introduction is quite light, and the melodic line has a "movie music" quality about it. Husband and wife enjoy an uneventful sojourn at the beach.

In measure 11 dramatic dissonant sevenths suddenly herald the approach of the crocodile. His sinister appearance should be maximized by the sharply *staccato* piano chords punctuating the description of his eyes in measures 14–15. The *fermata* at the end of measure 15 must be observed. The tempo then increases *sempre molto mosso* as the wife runs from the scene—depicted by single *staccato* chords in the accompaniment and a rapid descending scale after *via* (away). *Ferocemente* (ferocious) chords underscore the crocodile's consumption of the husband. Without losing the vocal line, the singer should stress each note in relating this horror, but the vocal color should change immediately to *giacoso* (playfully, jokingly) as the dinner is compared to *Come magnasse un pollo all'osteria* (as he would eat a chicken at a tavern).

A piano interlude effects the transition of moods to the unexpected remorse of the beast. A repeated motive in the accompaniment (measures 32 and 34) is marked *doloroso* (sadly), and the creature's regretful afterthoughts are marked *con gravità* (with seriousness) in the vocal line at measure 36. The motive introduced in measure 32 is expanded under a slightly longer, stretched phrase as the animal's emotional state builds in measures 38–39 and is echoed in measure 40.

At the *adagio melanconico* in measure 41, the sixteenth note of the new section is equivalent to the eighth note of the previous section, and the accompaniment (now on four staves) is played without pedal. The figure in the treble is actually marked *piangendo* (crying). This section is problematic because the accompaniment is designed to fit specific beats within the measure, yet the quasi-recitative character and emotional state of the words call for considerable flexibility.

A reflection of the opening measures of the song introduces the final section. The accompaniment, almost identical, is transposed, and the tempo is the same as the principal tempo. After the crocodile sees the now widowed wife, his emotional state is described by the falling fourths of the accompaniment in measure 52, *quasi singhiozzando* (almost sobbing). After an expressive dissonant chord in measure 56, the wife calmly expresses her total lack of concern with a series of short phrases over single, dissonant chords in the accompaniment. After a short pause, the opening measures of the song, with its jolly melodic line, return to complete the work.

This song needs to be acted out, not so much in terms of great changes of vocal color, but with the right tone and facial expression to fit the exaggerated character of the crocodile and the ironic response of the wife to the supposed tragedy. The pianist should be as much a part of the drama as the singer.

No. 2, La carità

 1 Er Presidente d'una Società
 2 Che protegge le Bestie martrattate
 3 S'intese domannà la carità:
 4 —Ho fame, ho fame, signorino mio,
 5 M'ariccomanno, nun m'abbandonate,
 6 Dateme un sòrdo pe' l'amor de Dio!
 7 —Nun te posso da' gnente:
 8 —Je fece er Presidente—
 9 —Io nun proteggo che le bestie sole . . .
10 —E allora
11 —je rispose er poverello cacciannose er cappello—
12 —Fatelo pe' 'ste povere bestiole . . .

No. 2, Charity

 1 The President of a Society
 2 that protects mistreated animals
 3 he intended to ask for charity:
 4 —I am hungry, I am hungry, my little master,
 5 Help me, do not abandon me.
 6 Give me some money for the love of God!
 7 —I can't give you anything!
 8 The President said—
 9 —I protect only the animals alone . . .

10   —And then—
11   —the poor man answered, removing his hat—
12   —Do that for those poor little creatures . . .

The opening measures of *La carità* (Charity, love) should be a bit pompous, with a blurred sweep to the ascending bass scale; the very *staccato* chords continue throughout. The vocal line should be phrased over the entire indicated phrase marking, with a short breath after Società (Society) only if needed. The character of the vocal line should be almost *marcato*.

A new section, beginning in measure 10, is much freer, with a distinct change of character and vocal color. The composer's direction is *stretto, affannosamente* (tight, painfully). All attention is in the anguished words of the singer; the piano merely provides dry support.

Measure 14 sees a return to the matter-of-fact movement that opened the composition; the vocal entrance is marked *con voce ruvida* (with rude, harsh voice). The President explains that his charity is for animals. Perhaps those who seek charity for themselves have not considered charity for lesser creatures. The final lines are spoken in recitative style. Casella carefully indicates which of the supporting chords are to be arpeggiated and which must not. The melodic notes of the recitative are usually contained in the supporting chords that follow them. An awareness of this device should help the pianist achieve the proper weight in the voicing of each chord.

A brief postlude of melodic material from the introduction concludes the song with the proper note of irony and continued pomposity.

No. 3, Er gatto e er cane

1   Un Gatto Soriano
2   Diceva a un Barbone:
3   Nun porto rispetto
4   Nemmanco ar padrone,
5   Perchè a l'occasione
6   Je sgraffio la mano;
7   Ma tu che lo lecchi
8   Te becchi le botte:
9   Te mena, te sfotte,
10   Te mette in catena
11   Cor muso rinchiuso
12   E un cerchio cor bollo
13   Sull'osso der collo.
14   Siconno la moda
15   Te taja li ricci,
16   Te spunta la coda . . .

17 Che belli capricci!
18 Io, guarda, so' un Gatto
19 So' un ladro, lo dico:
20 Ma a me nun s'azzarda
21 De famme 'ste cose . . .
22 Er cane rispose:
23 Ma io . . . je so' amico!

No. 3, The cat and the dog

1   A Cypress cat
2   Said to a French poodle:
3   I have no respect
4   Not even for my master,
5   Because on occasion
6   I scratch his hand;
7   But you who lick him
8   You earn beatings:
9   He hits you, he teases you,
10 He ties you up in chains
11 With your muzzle shut in
12 And a ring with the license
13 around the neck bone
14 According to fashion
15 he cuts off your curls,
16 he clips off the tip of your tail.
17 What beautiful caprices!
18 I, you see, I am a cat
19 I am a thief, I admit it:
20 But to me no one dares
21 to do these things.
22 The dog replies:
23 But I . . . I am a friend!

A decisive chord sets up the opening recitative of *Er gatto e er cane* (The cat and the dog), and it is punctuated by only one additional *staccato* chord, disconcertingly placed on the second half of the first beat of measure 2. The *fermata* over the last two beats of the measure is most important since the character of the song does not really begin until the second line of music. Here the change to 6/8 meter, the *vivacissimo* tempo, and the *sempre staccatissimo* accompaniment impart a *tarantella*, dancelike feeling to the composition. When the accompaniment figure is grouped in triplets it should be more *legato* and phrased, as marked, to lead to the second beat of the duple meter (or third beat when the meter shifts to 9/8). The vocal line cannot be as *staccato* as the accompaniment, but it should stress the word accents within the phrase, and above all, connect the vowels at this very fast tempo.

Not much attempt is made at word-painting, although the composer does indicate accents and writes rests separating the syllables of the words *lecchi* (lick) and *botte* (beatings). There should be no break in the forward momentum of the song, however, until measure 25, when the cat exclaims: *Che belli capricci!* (What beautiful caprices!). The indication is *molto allargando,* and each note must be accented. After the sharp, loud chord in the accompaniment (not arpeggiated, if possible), the high G should be held slightly longer, and a *portamento* should lead to the release a minor seventh below.

The new section, now in simple meter, is slower and less loud, *quasi confidenzialmente* (almost confidential) as the cat admits its deceits and then with cloying sweetness sings a free melismatic cadenza on *cose* (things). The composer indicates *goffamente* (clumsily, awkwardly) for the two measures preceding the dog's response (measures 35–36), but there is some dignity in the strictness of the *moderato* tempo. The answer *Ma io . . . je so' amico!* (But I . . . I am a friend!) is appropriately marked *con bonarietà rassegnata* (with good-natured resignation). The short postlude should be very fast and without *rallentare.* The last measure should be little more than a whisper.

Several measures within this song are simply marked *pausa* (pause). The length of these pauses is at the discretion of the performers, but some change of posture or expression is needed so that the drama and musical continuity do not disintegrate. It is also interesting that the construction of so many of the supporting chords on fourth and fifths impart a dry feeling.

No. 4, L'elezzione der presidente

1   Un giorno tutti quanti l'animali
2   Sottomessi ar lavoro
3   Decisero d'elegge 'un Presidente
4   Che je guardasse l'interessi loro.
5   C'era la Società de li Majali, La Società der Toro,
6   Er Circolo der Basto e de la Soma,
7   La Lega indipendente fra li Somari residenti a Roma;
8   C'era la Fratellanza de li Gatti Soriani, de li Cani,
9   De li Cavalli senza vetturini,
10   La Lega fra le Vacche, Bovi e affini . . .
11   Tutti pijorno parte a l'adunanza.
12   Un Somarello, che pe' l'ambizzione
13   De fasse elegge' s'era messo addosso
14   La pelle d'un leone, Disse:
15   —Bestie elettore, io so' commosso:

16   La civirtà, la libertà, er progresso . . .
17   Ecco er vero programma che ciò io,
18   Ch'è l'istesso der popolo!
19   Per cui voterete compatti er nome mio . . .
20   Defatti venne eletto proprio lui.
21   Er Somaro contento, fece un rajo,
22   E allora solo er popolo bestione s'accorse de lo sbajo.
23   D'avè' pijato un ciuccio p'un leone!
24   Miffarolo! . . . Imbrojone! . . . Buvattaro! . . .
25   —Ho pijato possesso,
26   Disse allora er Somaro
27   —E nu' la pianto Nemmanco si morite d'accidente;
28   Peggio pe' voi che me ciavete messo!
29   Silenzio! e rispettate er Presidente!

No. 4, The election of the President

1   One day every one of the animals,
2   subjected to work
3   decided to elect a President
4   who would watch over their interests.
5   There was the Society of the Pigs, the Society of the Bull,
6   the Circle of the Pack Horse and of the Beast of burden,
7   the independent Society of the Donkeys residing in Rome;
8   there was the Fraternity of the Cypress Cats, of the Dogs,
9   of the Horses without drivers.
10   The Society among the cows, the oxen and similarly
11   all would take part at the meeting.
12   A donkey, who because of his ambition
13   to be elected had placed upon his body
14   the skin of a lion, he said:
15   —Beasts, voters, I am moved:
16   civility, liberty, and progress . . .
17   Here is the true program that I have,
18   which is the same as for the people!
19   For which you will vote with indulgence my name . . .
20   In fact, it was indeed he who was elected.
21   The happy donkey, began to bray,
22   and only then were the beast-people aware of their mistake
23   of having taken an ass for a lion!
24   Liar! . . . Cheat! . . . Imposter!
25   —I have taken possession
26   said then the donkey
27   —And no crying even if by chance you die.

28   Too bad for you who elected me.
29   Silence! And respect the President!

Politics is rarely a predicatable phenomenon, but pomposity, deception, and disappointment are too frequently components of this so-called art. Within the boundaries of his neo-classical style Casella manages to illuminate all these elements in keeping with the poem *L'elezzione der presidente* (The election of the President). The overall structure is through-composed, sectionalized by the events and moods of the characters as the story progresses.

The opening of the song is in free recitative style over a chordal underpinning and marked *con fantasia* (with imagination, fancy). The precise rhythmic figures interspersed with the recitative anticipate similar figures that appear later in the march that initiates the first large section of the poem. It is marked *tempo di marcia eroicomico* (in the tempo of a mock-heroic march). Without attempting to describe specific animals musically, the march moves forward as the catalogue is recited over changing patterns in the accompaniment. Occasionaly, there is a brief reference in the accompaniment to a melodic figure or articulation that has appeared in a previous measure. A number of chords built on fourths, fifths, and octaves contribute to the quasi-heroic quality of the section. The tempo should be very strict throughout, and, while each phrase describing a group of animals should be internally connected, a *marcato* quality is called for in the enunciation of the text. Everything moves to the announcement of the "meeting" in measure 31.

A very different kind of accompaniment pattern appears in measure 34; the chromatic *ostinato* is somewhat stealthy in character. The vocal phrases here should be short and breathless, rising in pitch along with the rise in pitch of the accompaniment and broadening to measure 39. (The barring in these measures of changing meter is slightly different for the accompaniment and the vocal line, but it in no way affects the clarity of accent or coordination of the parts.)

A brief pause should precede the accented chords beneath the grandiose statement in the vocal line at measure 40. The pedal should sustain the chords beneath the melisma that opens the "pronouncement." As the donkey enumerates his political program the rhythms should be strict in both vocal line and accompaniment, including the two-measure postlude (measures 49–50), which indicates his confidence (or bravado).

In the new section (measures 51–52) the composer indicates a special expressivity for the falling thirds of the upper voice of the left-hand chord pattern. These notes, inverted, become the vocal line in measure 53. This passage has a cunning quality. The abrupt *allegro giocoso* and widely spaced dissonances herald the donkey's deceit, and his revealing, celebratory bray occurs with a melisma on *rajo* (bray). A doubling of the initial march figures and the chromatic sinuousness of the donkey's first theme provide an agitated accompaniment for the reaction of the deceived constituents. The words *Miffarolo!* . . . *Imbrojone!* . . . *Buvattaro!* (Liar! . . . Cheat! . . . Imposter!) should almost be shouted. A long pause should precede the final section.

The concluding portion of the song begins with a clever device in measure 72. The same motivic fragment that underscored the donkey's pre-election political promise now appears one tone lower, and the tempo is *largo e tragico.* The words are spoken *con voce forte* (with strong voice). The accompaniment under the phrase *e nu' la pianto Nemmanco si morite d'accidente* (And no crying even if by chance you die) should be very *legato,* and the singer should observe the indicated *portamento.* The word *Silenzio!* (Silence!) should be sung *forte* and *autocraticamente* (autocratically); the final words should rush to the accented syllable of *Presidente* (President). Either of the alternate pitches Casella provides here would be appropriate, and in fact might be more forceful than the ascent to the high Bb in the original line. The emotional point of the song has already been made in the setting of *Silenzio!* (Silence!).

The dissonant closing chords of the piano part should be decisive and dry. In politics, things are often not what they seem, and promises are most often broken once power has been achieved.

Quattro favole romanesche di Trilussa: Ricordi, 1923.   119554 (Set)

1. *Er coccodrillo*	119550
2. *La carità*	119551
3. *Er gatto e er cane*	119552
4. *L'elezzione der presidente*	119553

La sera fiesolana

(*Gabriele d'Annunzio*)

1   Fresche le mie parole ne la sera
2   ti sien come il fruscìo che fan le foglie
3   del gelso ne la man di chi le coglie silenzioso
4   e ancor s'attarda a l'opra lenta
5   su l'alta scala che s'annera
6   contro il fusto che s'inargenta
7   con le sue rame spoglie
8   mentre la Luna è prossima a le soglie cerule
9   e par che innanzi a sè distenda un velo
10 ove il nostro sogno si giace
11 e par che la campagna già si senta
12 da lei sommersa nel notturno gelo
13 e da lei beva la sperata pace
14 senza vederla.

15 Laudata sii pel tuo viso di perla, o Sera,
16 e pe' tuoi grandi umidi occhi ove si tace
17 l'acqua del cielo!
18 Dolci le mie parole ne la sera
19 ti sien come la pioggia che bruiva
20 tepida e fuggitiva,
21 commiato lacrimoso de la primavera,
22 su i gelsi e su gli olmi e su le viti
23 e su i pini dai novelli rosei diti
24 che giocano con l'aura che si perde,
25 e su 'l grano che non è biondo ancora
26 e non è verde,
27 e su 'l fieno che già patì la falce
28 e trascolora,
29 e su gli olivi, su i fratelli olivi
30 che fan di santità pallidi i clivi
31 e sorridenti!
32 Laudata sii per le tue vesti aulenti, o Sera,
33 e pel cinto che ti cinge come il salce
34 il fien che odora!
35 Io ti dirò verso quali reami
36 d'amor ci chiami il fiume, le cui fonti eterne
37 a l'ombra de gli antichi rami
38 parlano nel mistero sacro dei monti;
39 e ti dirò per qual segreto
40 le colline su i limpidi orizzonti
41 s'incurvino come labbra che un divieto chiuda,
42 e perchè la volantà di dire
43 le faccia belle
44 oltre ogni uman desire
45 e nel silenzio lor sempre novelle consolatrici,
46 sì che pare
47 che ogni sera l'anima le possa amare
48 d'amor più forte.
49 Laudata sii per la tua pura morte, o Sera,
50 e per l'attesa che in te fa palpitare
51 le prime stelle!

Evening at Fiesole

1 Refreshing are my words in the evening,
2 that they may be like the rustling made by the leaves
3 of the mulberry tree in the hand of one who picks them silently
4 and still tarries with the slow work

5   on the high staircase which is darkened
6   against the tree trunk that shines like silver
7   with its stripped branches
8   while the Moon is very near on the pale blue sills
9   and it appears that in front of her extends a veil
10   where our dream lies
11   and it seems that the countryside already feels
12   submerged by her in the nocturnal intense cold
13   and from her may drink the hoped-for peace
14   without seeing her.
15   Be praised for your face of pearl, o Evening,
16   and for your large humid eyes where is still
17   the water of the sky!
18   Sweet my words in the evening
19   may they be to you like the noise of the rain,
20   tepid and fleeting,
21   tearful departure of spring,
22   on the mulberry, and on the elms, and on the vines
23   and on the pines with the new rosy fingers
24   that play with the breeze that is dying away,
25   and on the wheat which is not yet blond
26   and is not green,
27   and on the hay that already suffers the scythe
28   and grows pale,
29   and on the olive trees, on the brethren olives
30   that sanctify the pale
31   and smiling slopes.
32   Be praised for your fragrant attire, o Evening,
33   and for the surrounding with which you gird yourself like the willow
34   (and like) the hay which scents!
35   I will tell you toward what kingdoms
36   of love the river calls us, whose eternal springs
37   in the shadows of ancient branches
38   speak in the sacred mystery of the mountains;
39   and I will tell you by what secret
40   the hills on their clear horizons
41   curve like lips closed by a prohibition,
42   and why the wish to tell
43   makes them beautiful
44   beyond every human desire
45   and in their silence ever new comforters,
46   thus it seems
47   that every evening the soul can love them
48   with a love more strong.
49   Be praised for your pure death, o Evening,

50   and for the wait that makes pulsate in you
51   the first stars!

Fiesole is a charming village in the hills overlooking the city of Florence. For centuries artists, writers, and musicians—Italian and foreign—have been enchanted by the almost magical quality of the place and by its superb views of one of Europe's most artistic cities. D'Annunzio's poem is a *laude,* or tribute, to Fiesole at evening, a special time that attracted the attention of many Italian poets at the turn of the century. Casella's song is quite free, following the "stream-of-consciousness" imagery of the poem and achieving structure by turning to the same musical material three times, at the words *Laudata sii* (Be praised).

At first glance *La sera fiesolana* (Evening at Fiesole) seems lengthy and rambling. However, it is only 101 measures long, and the repeated melodic-harmonic material that gives it structure appears precisely at measures 30, 61, and 91—an indication of Casella's mathematical mind. The piano intro-duction sets the *misterioso* (mysterious) atmosphere with an eight-measure *ostinato* bass of dissonant ascending chords. In measure 3 a folk-like melodic line in the treble creates a pastoral feeling, but it is to be played *mezzo confuso, con molte pedale* (somewhat indistinct, with much pedal). The irregular meter of 5/8 adds to the atmosphere. (There are many changes of meter throughout the song, but the relationships are always equal, and the composer is specific about the division within the measure.) A change in the accompaniment pattern in measure 9 anticipates the entrance of the voice in measure 10 in a *parlando* (speaking) style, with the direction *mezzo voce, quasi mormorando* (half voice, almost murmuring). This quality continues throughout the first "free association" section of the poem. There are subtle variations, such as the left-hand piano part in measures 16–18 and the jarring chord progression in measure 24, which support expressive sections of the text. An interruption of rhythmic flow and a short melodic motive in measures 27–29 signal a new section.

In measure 30 Casella presents the first of the three *Laudata sii* (Be praised) sections with the directions *grave, mistico,* and *appassionato.* A series of widely spaced dissonant chords (without arpeggiation) herald the word *laudata* (praised). The object of praise, *sera* (evening), is given a broader melodic arch and is supported by similar dissonant chords. The increased activity in all the musical elements continues through the end of the section.

The second stanza of the poem is set with a slightly faster tempo be-ginning in measure 39. The accompaniment, an alternation of dissonant in-tervals in even eighth notes, is *molto e lievemente confuso* (very light, in-distinct, blurred) with *molto pedale* (much pedal). The very lively melody in measure 40 bears a faint resemblance to the style of the melody that opened the composition, but it too is to be "indistinct"—a direction that continues to apply when the accompaniment doubles the entrance of the voice in measure 43. Measure 48 carries the direction *con grazia e freschezza* (with grace and freshness), in keeping with the pastoral scene being described in the poetry. A greater variety of accompaniment figures emerges as the stanza progresses.

In measure 61 the fanfare-like dissonant chords (in transposition) again announce the word *laudata* (praised), and *sera* (evening) again is the high point of the phrase. The dynamic level here, however, is *pianissimo*. The third stanza, which begins in measure 67, is lightly moving with a *stringendo* (gradually increasing tempo) indication. As the poem moves toward its climax, the initially murmuring accompaniment broadens to more widely spaced chords and there is considerable increase in activity. While there is much rise and fall of phrasing and dynamics in the section, everything should move toward the climactic measures 84–86. The composer cautions against too loud a dynamic level; the *largamente* tempo, high vocal *tessitura,* and extremely widely spaced keyboard activity create the climax effectively enough.

Measure 91 presents again the dissonant chords announcing the *Laudata sii* (Be praised). This time, however, the section is *calmato, quasi estatico* (calm, almost ecstatic), and the chords are *pp ma sostenuto.* The entrance of the voice is marked *a voce bassa ma con somma dolcezza di espressione* (with low voice, but with the highest degree of sweetness of expression). The word *sera* (evening) is treated *dolcissimo,* and the final measure of voice, in *parlando* style, is marked *rallentando e dilequando* (slowing down and dispersing). The piano postlude returns to the principal tempo and recalls the opening measures of the work with the direction *lontano* (distant).

La sera fiesolana is a song of atmosphere. Voice and piano are well integrated, and the composer is specific in his performance directions. Most phrase breaks are clearly indicated, but the "talkiness" of the poem would permit additional ones in places where the singer needs breath.

La sera fiesolana: Ricordi, 1924; Repr. 1947, 1979.   119549

Part II

The Second-Generation Composers

Some of the second generation of *liriche* composers were not very much younger than those of the first generation, but they had the advantage of a precedent-setting movement already under way. The renewed interest in Italian culture and literature, and the corresponding consideration of art song as a worthwhile compositional activity, had been established by the older composers, some of whom acted as teachers or mentors to the younger ones.

Although study and travel outside Italy were still considered desirable, the developments within Italy and the opportunities for performance and exposure provided by the newly formed societies for contemporary music made staying at home equally valuable.

Of the four principal second-generation *liriche* composers, two are best known within Italy—Vincenzo Davico and Giorgio Federico Ghedini. The others achieved true worldwide recognition. Mario Castelnuovo-Tedesco moved to the United States, where he trained several well-known American composers, particularly in the area of film scoring; and Goffredo Petrassi remains, as of this writing, the highly respected dean of living Italian composers.

Vincenzo Davico

(1889–1969)

•

VINCENZO DAVICO was born on January 14, 1889 in the Principality of Monaco of Italian parents from Piedmont. He was a precocious child and at eight years of age wrote a drama and set part of Dante's *Divine Comedy* to music. His earliest musical studies were undertaken in Turin, under Giovanni Cavero, and were followed by study at the Conservatory of Leipzig under Max Reger, with whom Davico continued to work after receiving his diploma in 1911. Shortly thereafter, his composition *Princess Lointane* won first place in the Concorso Nazionale di Roma, and his *Trois impressions symphoniques* (based on works of Rostand) were chosen to be played at the Augusteum of Rome. Davico was, reportedly, the youngest composer yet chosen for that honor. While still in his early twenties he made his debut as an orchestral conductor in Rome and had considerable success both in Italy and abroad in that capacity.

In 1918, the year Debussy died, Davico moved to Paris, where he remained until 1940, deeply under the influence of that master French Impressionist. It is probable that Davico's intensive study of strict contrapuntal techniques under Reger made the freedom of Impressionism even more attractive, but from the time of his childhood, the composer evidenced a distinct dislike for the romantic sentimentalism especially prevalent in Italy at that time. As he developed, Davico was able to combine the evanescent atmosphere of Impressionism and the French capacity for refined emotion with German discipline. Above all, he remained aware that melody was Italy's gift to the world of music; and the intrinsic beauty of melody was the conscious base on which all of his musical choices were made. Despite the overall Impressionist aesthetic, Davico shows a severity of line and a constant affirmation of the sense of tonality that is distinctly Italian.

The composer's one-act opera, *La Dogaressa,* created in 1920 for the Opera of Monte Carlo was successful, but his search for an elevated spiritual direction, away from theatricality, finds greater expression in the concert opera *La Tentation de Saint-Antoine,* first performed in 1921. While Davico wrote several works in the larger forms—three operas, a concert requiem (*Requiem per la morte d'un povero,* 1950), two ballets, and several compositions for orchestra—he found his most congenial expression in chamber works and especially songs. Throughout his life Davico was fascinated by the human voice. As early as 1909 his *Canti minimi,* three songs on verses by Lorenzo Stecchetti and the Hungarian poet Petőfi, showed an intimate chamber style based on German *Lied* and very different from the verist opera tradition then supreme in Italy. Davico's songs exhibit a welding of words and music quite different from the quasi-operatic songs with mere supporting accompaniments carried over from the nineteenth century. They even required a style of singing that returned to the principles of seventeenth- and eighteenth-century Italian vocal tradition. Davico searched for a condensation of poetical-musical emotion to its most fundamental elements, attempting to make the maximum effect from a minimum of composition. Accompaniments are often little more than a few arpeggiated chords in repeated rhythmic patterns, and melodies are often created around single motives without development or expansion. Davico's greatest talent seems to have been his ability to select out and define a state of mind with purely musical means. Each song represents a single mood based on the state of mind most representative of the specific words of the poem. Inflections and word rhythms are scrupulously observed. His texts are drawn from the French Symbolist poets and the *crepusculari* (twilight) poets of early twentieth-century Italy, who often focused on images of nature with reference to moonlight. Davico was very interested in oriental art and philosophy. Contemporary critics considered his *Liriche giapponese,* 1920, on Japanese *tanke* and *haiku* poetry, masterpieces of the song literature of the period.

Although Davico remained in Paris for 21 years—a not uncommon practice for the Italian musicians of the period—he was an untiring propagandist in the cause of modern Italian music and considered himself first and foremost an Italian composer. In 1940 he returned to Italy as a director for Italian radio. He carried on intensive activities as music critic, lecturer, and writer on modern music, both Italian and international. After World War II his compositions turned more in the direction of twelve-tone technique, as seen in the fifth song of *Cinque notturno.* Further experiments in avante-garde ideas are seen in *Canta un rosignol,* freely written for soprano voice with a flute taking the part of the nightingale; *Commiato,* a free elaboration of a thirteenth-century Persian couplet; and *Sera d'autunno,* in which the entire song is set without any of the usual indications of time. The vocal rhythms imitate those of the spoken language, and the accompaniment is instructed to follow the voice.

Vincenzo Davico died in Rome on December 8, 1969.

Liriche giapponesi

No. 1, Luna d'estate

(*Akiko Josano, traduzione di G. Marone*)

1   Barca d'argento guidata da una vergine nuda,
2   maliosa che naviga pianamente
3   fra le onde leggere delle nuvole

Japanese lyrics

No. 1, Summer moon

(*Akiko Josano, [Italian] translation by G. Marone*)

1   Boat made of silver steered by a nude virgin,
2   fascinating, who sails slowly
3   among the light waves of the clouds

No. 2, Pioggia

(*Akiko Josano, traduzione di Elpidio Jenco*)

1   Cadono i fiori di ciliegio
2   cadono insieme ai miei sogni
3   del passato
4   cadono a la rinfusa
5   lagrime e fiori

No. 2, Rain

(*Akiko Josano, [Italian] translation by Elpidio Jenco*)

1   The cherry blossoms are falling
2   they fall together with my dreams
3   of the past
4   they fall in confusion with
5   tears and flowers

No. 3, Gioia umana

(Nobutsuma Sasaki, traduzione di G. Marone)

1 Vorrei diventare la brezza dolce di primavera
2 e spingere la porta delle case dolorose
3 e portare in esse conforto e fiori

No. 3, Human Joy

(Nobutsuma Sasaki, [Italian] translation by G. Marone)

1 I would like to become the sweet breeze of springtime
2 and push open the door of sorrowful houses
3 and carry into them comfort and flowers

No. 4, * * *

(Suikei Maeta, traduzione di Elpidio Jenco)

1 Quando avrò restituito le ossa nude
2 al signore mio padre
3 e la carne putrida alla terra madre
4 che ci sarà mai che potrò chiamare mio

No. 4, * * *

(Suikei Maeta, [Italian] translation by Elpidio Jenco)

1 When I will have given back my bare bones
2 to my Lord my father
3 and my putrid flesh to mother earth
4 what will there ever be that I can call my own

No. 5, Sogno

(Suikei Maeta, traduzione di G. Marone)

1 Se pur il pensiero è peccato
2 perchè non custodite, Signore
3 voi stesso le porte del sogno
4 dalle quali io corro ogni notte
5 dalla mia dolce amante

No. 5, Dream

(Suikei Maeta, [Italian] translation by G. Marone)

1 If even the thought of it is sinful
2 why do you not guard, Lord,
3 yourself, the portals of dreams
4 by means of which I run each night
5 to my sweet mistress

Liriche giapponesi (Japanese lyrics) are settings of traditional Japanese poetry. While the translations alter the highly disciplined structure of the Japanese originals, they still evoke the original pastel colors and delicate shades of meaning. Davico's music attempts to establish a single, overall mood for each poem.

In No. 1, *Luna d'estate* (Summer moon), utter calm is achieved by using both the sustaining and the soft pedal throughout. In fact, the composer's own handwritten notes in a rehearsal copy of the score call for as much pedal blur as possible. Although no tempo indication is given, the melodic line should flow slowly over the gentle wavelike motion in the accompaniment. However, there are three clear phrases in the text, and the tempo must allow each phrase to be sung on one breath. A breath may be taken at the comma after *nuda* (nude) and at the composer's indication after *pianamente* (slowly). The voice should literally float through the climactic final phrase, *leggere* (light), and the whole song should be very quiet.

The mood of despair in No. 2, *Pioggia* (Rain), depends on the balance between voice and piano. The opening piano motive is marked *sfumate* (vanishing, or vague) and the second chord *lontano* (distant). There is no meter signature, and the tempo indication is also somewhat vague—*abbastanza adagio* (slow enough). The opening vocal statement should be sweetly speechlike. The repeated descending arpeggios in the piano part of the following measures should each *crescendo* in the downward direction, following the overall *crescendo* of the vocal line, but at one full dynamic level lower (*ppp* to *mf* for the piano, *pp* to *f* for the voice). This permits a more passionate expression in the vocal line while not exceeding the limits of Japanese sensibility. The *fermata* at the end of the third score should not be overlooked. The frequent rests in the vocal line of the final phrase create a built-in sigh effect, but they should not obscure the fact that it is still one phrase. The underlying chords in the accompaniment should be sonorous and *legato* and should *ritard* along with the voice on the final words *e fiori* (and flowers).

In No. 3, *Gioia umana* (Human joy), a descending arpeggio similar to the rainfall figure in the preceding song is altered by irregular rhythm and faster tempo to become a spirited spring breeze. Coordination with the sustained vocal line will be facilitated if singer and pianist feel the steady duple meter. Again, the composer calls for the use of two pedals and directs the accompanying figure to be *leggerissimo,* while the initial chord is allowed to vibrate underneath. The singer should observe the *tenuto* markings on *primavera* (springtime) and on the descriptive descending chromatic line *case dolorose* (sorrowful houses). The tempo indication again is vague— *abbastanza vivace* (fast enough). The song should not feel rushed; and the final arpeggio should not be played in tempo, but truly *squisitamente* (exquisitely), for the flowers of sadness that closed the second song have become flowers of happiness.

The lack of a title for the fourth song is significant since the answer to its question could be "nothing." The mood of foreboding is established with the first loud, somber chord and the ominous rhythmic figure in the bass. The voice must "speak" rather than "sing" above this accompaniment. The *tenuto* markings beneath each note of the first phrase should be carried through the whole song. In effect, the singer reluctantly drags forth these statements, moving from *tenuto* to *accento* as the final fearful question bursts forth. The "nothingness" of the answer is indicated by the *subito piano* in the measure immediately following the release of the voice and the even softer dynamics leading to the final chord.

The sweet innocence of dreams, in which even forbidden thoughts find release, is expressed in No. 5, *Sogno* (Dream), in the quiet rippling arpeggios of the accompaniment and the long *cantabile* lines for the voice. This song is definitely to be "sung," extending phrases across the bar line and smoothly over the asymmetric 5/4 meter. The slow initial tempo should remain steady until the slight *ritard* and *pianissimo* indications at *porte del sogno* (portals of dreams). The following phrase should move faster, in accordance with its meaning—*dalle quali io corro* (by means of which I run)—and be counteracted immediately with a sudden *ritard* at *ogni notte* (each night). The continued *ritard* in the vocal line, the broadening of the accompaniment, and the *pianissimo* dynamic cleverly set the furtive quality of the final words of the poem.

The *Japanese lyrics* are masterpieces of subtle mood and require sensitive artistry and attention to the tiniest details.

Liriche giapponesi: F. Bongiovanni, 1921.   F. 1265 B. (Set)
   1. *Luna d'estate*
   2. *Pioggia*
   3. *Gioia umana*
   4. * * *
   5. *Sogno*

Tre liriche

No. 3, Come un cipresso notturno

(*Gino Gori*)

1 Vorrei sentirmi lungo
2 come un cipresso notturno
3 per indicare col dito
4 l'osteria dell'infinito
5 dove una stella d'argento
6 si dondola sull'altalena del vento
7 per insegnare che il vin dell'oblio
8 si beve solamente nella casa di Dio
9 Ah oh! Ah oh!

Three lyrics

No. 3, Like a nocturnal cypress

1 I would like to feel tall
2 like a nocturnal cypress
3 in order to indicate with my finger
4 the inn of the infinite
5 where a silver star
6 swings on the swing of the wind
7 to show that the wine of oblivion
8 is drunk only in God's house
9 Ah oh! Ah oh!

The pentatonic figure in contrary motion that introduces *Come un cipresso notturno* (Like a nocturnal cypress) immediately establishes a sense of open space and mystery. The *tenuto* markings indicate the smoothest possible movement between notes rather than any *rubato,* and the liberal use of two pedals should create the *dolcemente lontano* (sweetly distant) effect that the composer calls for. The pedal tones must be sustained throughout each measure as indicated. The rhythmic motion of the song, probably derived from the text *stella d'argento si dondola sull'altalena del vento* (a silver star swings on the swing of the wind), should be established in the first measure of the introduction and remain steady throughout the entire song. The choice of tempo is somewhat flexible providing the character of the song is *calmo e sereno* (calm and serene); ♩. = 54 might provide a starting point.

The vocal line is simple and folk-like in character, and the phrasings are clearly indicated. Depending on the tempo, quick catch breaths could be taken after *d'argento* (silver) and *oblio* (oblivion), although the phrases would be more effective sung through. The grace notes on the words "Ah oh!" should not be rushed since they imitate segments of the accompaniment pattern; the release of these two final vocal utterances should be strictly as marked to allow the accompaniment to emerge. A *smorzando* (dying away) is called for on the final phrase, and there should be no *ritard*.

Tre liriche: Ricordi, 1926; Repr. 1947.
   3. *Come un cipresso notturno*   120941

Cinque canti popolari toscani

No. 1, Fiorin d'argento

1 Fiorin d'argento,
2 e per amarvi voi ho pianto tanto;
3 povero pianto mio gettato al vento.
4 Ah! Ah!

Five popular Tuscan songs

No. 1, Little flower of silver

1 Little flower of silver,
2 and for the love of you I have cried so much;
3 my poor tears thrown out to the wind.
4 Ah! Ah!

No. 2, Ninna-nanna

1 Fai la nanna, dolce lume,
2 fai la nanna, ninna-nanna na!
3 Le mie braccia per te son piume.
4 Fai la nanna, mio conforto.
5 Nel mio seno anch'io t'ho porto.

No. 2, Ninna-nanna

1 Go to sleep, sweet light,
2 Go to sleep, to sleep!

3   My arms for you are feathers,
4   Go to sleep, my comfort.
5   In my breast I also am your harbor.

No. 3, Fior di pepe

1   Fior di pepe!
2   Tutte le fontanelle son seccate,
3   povero amore mio,
4   muore di sete!

No. 3, Flower of pepper

1   Flower of pepper!
2   All the fountains have dried up,
3   my poor love,
4   he dies of thirst!

No. 4, O luna

1   O luna, che tu passi tanti monti,
2   passane uno, non ne passar tanti;
3   saluta 'l m' amor se tu l'incontri.

No. 4, O moon

1   O moon, since you pass by so many mountains,
2   pass by one of them, do not pass by so many of them;
3   give greeting to my love if you meet him.

No. 5, O maggio bello

1   O maggio bello, ch'hai tanta possanza,
2   che l'erbe secche le fai rinverdire,
3   ai pastorelli fai mutare stanza,
4   verso la casa sua li fai venire.
5   Ah! Ah!
6   Chi ama il pecoraro ama qualche cosa!
7   Torna di maggio che pare una rosa.
8   Chi ama il pecoraro ama un bel fiore.
9   Torna di maggio che pare un signore.
10 Ah! Ah!

No. 5, O beautiful May

1 O beautiful May, you have so much power,
2 that the dry grasses you make green again,
3 you cause the shepherds to change their place of residence,
4 toward your home you make them come.
5 Ah! Ah!
6 He who loves the shepherd loves something!
7 The return of May appears like a rose.
8 He who loves the shepherd loves a beautiful flower.
9 The return of May appears like a gentleman.
10 Ah! Ah!

Cinque canti popolari toscani (Five popular Tuscan songs) have no special thematic relationship other than the shared origin of their texts. However, there is enough variety of style and tempo among them to create an interesting program set.

The first song, *Fiorin d'argento* (Little flower of silver), deals with love of money. The setting makes use of a habanera-like rhythmic pattern in the piano part, but the alternation of triple and quadruple subdivisions of the beat creates a built-in feeling of hesitation, perhaps to underscore the lamentations of the protagonist. The printed score is marked *andante mosso,* but the composer wrote in *non troppo lento* in his own rehearsal copy of the score. Except for the short *ritard* at the first entrance of the vocal line and the *adagio* at the first "ah!" the tempo should remain steady until the *allargando* marking in the final line of the song. The *meno assai* (much less) and *ancora meno* (still less) on the second and third phrases refer to dynamics and character rather than tempo. Also from the composer's own handwritten markings, the *mf* at the *quasi adagio* "ah!" is changed to *p* followed by a *crescendo* to *forte* and a *decrescendo* to *pp* one bar before the cutoff. Although most of the phrases can be sung in one breath, the composer indicated possible breaks after *voi* (you) in the second phrase and *mio* (my) in the third. He also permits liberal use of pedal (a Davico trademark), especially to bring out countermelodies such as the upper line of the piano part at the beginning of the second verse, *e per amarvi voi* (and for the love of you). The last line of the piano part and the final chord should be allowed to vanish.

In *Ninna-nanna,* the swaying rhythmic pattern of the lullaby should remain relatively constant until the *allargando* marking toward the end of the verse. However, the composer, himself, when accompanying this song, allowed a slight *ritard* in the fifth measure of each verse to permit a stretching of the words and to prepare for the full realization of the important piano melodic line in the following measure. Whatever liberties are taken in the tempo should not interfere with the forward motion of the underlying pattern.

The successively quieter dynamic levels of the first three measures of the song (and its second verse) were considered crucial enough for the composer to circle these indications in his own rehearsal score. In measure 11 Davico added the indication *forte* diminishing to *piano* in the treble entrance of the piano countermelody; the same effect should be applied when this figure appears in the second verse, and, in fact, both singer and pianist should make the most of the lovely duet in thirds, which continues until the end of the verse. At the very end of the song Davico delayed the entrance of the treble piano figuration within the *ritenutissimo* section and released all sound on the first beat of the last measure. He did not allow the sound to continue as indicated in the printed score. Liberal use of pedal is permitted throughout the song.

In *Fior di pepe* (Flower of pepper) the composer added two *fermati* in performance: over the first syllable of *pepe* (pepper) in the opening statement of the song, and over the first syllable of *mio* (my) in the last phrase. He also indicated *molto legato* over each of the *portamenti*. After the dramatic beginning, the essential function of the piano, with liberal pedal use, is to provide a colorful Impressionistic background for the declarative vocal line. The term *bisbigliando* under the alternating chords, beginning in measure 3, translates as "whispering." If the phrase *Tutte le fontanelle son seccate* (All the fountains have dried up) cannot be sung in one breath, a break can be made after *fontanelle.* The indicated contrasts in dynamics and articulation are very important in the final four measures of the piano part, especially the expressive *staccatissimo* at the word *sete* (thirst). The song is short but rich in colorful effects, and it provides a good center for the group.

The directions *infinitamente calmo* (infinitely calm) provide the best description of *O luna* (O moon). The pedal must sustain the whole notes at the beginning of each measure through the gently rippling sextuplet figure. The *mezzo-forte* opening should *decrescendo* almost immediately to *pianissimo* and should not rise above this dynamic for the rest of the song. The long, lyrical vocal line should be one dynamic level above this, *piano* rather than *pianissimo,* following the rise and fall of the phrases as indicated, but within a very narrow range. In the final phrase the composer added a gentle *crescendo* toward the word *amor* (love) and a drop to *pianissimo* on the words *se tu l'incontri* (if you meet him), perhaps to emphasize the tentative quality of the text. The *allargando* should be stretched out through the last line of music. There should be an air of mystery about the song in both the vocal and the piano colors.

In *O maggio bello* (O beautiful May) the *allegro festoso* tempo (joyful, hearty *allegro*) must be set by the pianist so that the clarity and accent of the accompaniment pattern can be articulated; if possible, $\jmath$ = 120 should be the slowest. The pattern is always subordinate to the voice, but it provides all the rhythmic energy over which the flamenco-like vocal line rides, and it must be strictly *a tempo* through the end of the verse. The singer must observe every expressive marking, particularly *tenuto* and *staccato* indications.

A stunning dynamic and tempo effect can be achieved between the verses through the *diminuendo* and *allargando,* which begin after the second "Ah!" in measure 19 (Davico moved the indication for *piano* one beat later in his rehearsal copy of the score). The return to the *a tempo* and *forte* should be shockingly abrupt. The composer indicated several changes in the final page of the song: *Tenuto* markings should be added over the first two syllables of *un signore* (a gentleman); the dynamic markings for the final "Ah!" in measure 36 should be *ff*; and this note should be held to the beginning of the piano arpeggio in the final measure. The dynamic markings in the printed score (*f, ff, fff*) are at odds with the expressive indications *smorzando, diminuendo.* In performance Davico observed a *decrescendo* beginning in the middle of measure 37, with one more burst of energy (*fff*) in the attack of the final arpeggiated chord, which diminishes as it ascends. As the climactic song of the group, this earthy, celebratory poem requires a bright vocal color and passionate intensity.

Cinque canti popolari toscani: G. Ricordi, 1929; Repr. 1947.   121069 (Set)
    1. *Fiorin d'argento*
    2. *Ninna-nanna*
    3. *Fior di pepe*
    4. *O luna*
    5. *O maggio bello*

Quattro liriche

No. 1, Fior d'amaranto

(*da* Tre canti popolari toscani)

1 Fior d'amaranto
2 Mi son sognato non m'avami punto
3 quando mi son svegliato aveva pianto

Four lyrics

No. 1, Flower of amaranth

(*from* Three popular Tuscan songs)

1 Flower of amaranth
2 I dreamed that you would not have me at all
3 when I woke up I had cried.

No. 2, Q luna che fa' lume

(*da* Tre canti popolari toscani)

1 Q luna che fa' lume allo stellato
2 fa' lume all'amor mio valli di dreto
3 e digli con che core m'ha lasciato

No. 2, O moon that gives light

(*from* Three popular Tuscan songs)

1 O moon that gives light to the starry sky
2 give light to my love, go straight to him
3 and tell him with what love he has left me

No. 3, Acqua di rio

(*da* Tre canti popolari toscani)

1 Acqua di rio
2 Teco sarò di luglio e di gennaio
3 Dove tu muori te morirò anch'io

No. 3, Water of the river

(*from* Three popular Tuscan songs)

1 Water of the river
2 With you I will be in July and in January
3 Where you will die I will also die

No. 4, L'ultima notte

(*Gino Gori*)

1 La notte ultima sarà dolce e tranquilla
2 avrò spento la lampada d'argilla
3 come tutte le sere
4 avrò messo fuori la porta come sempre
5 i due sandali di feltro
6 Così la morte verrà non veduta e non sentita
7 e uscirò dalla vita in silenzio
8 senza svegliare nessuno

No. 4, The last night

1   The last night will be sweet and peaceful
2   I will have turned out the lamp of clay
3   as with every night
4   I will have put outside the door as always
5   my two sandals of felt
6   Thus death will come unseen and unheard
7   and I will depart from life in silence
8   without awakening anyone

Quattro liriche (Four lyrics), published in 1932, are not a cycle, but they work very effectively when programmed as a set. The first three have a common Tuscan origin; the fourth song, although unrelated, serves well as a finale. They each evidence Davico's compositional traits of repetitive accompaniment figures, dissonant tonal harmony, and lyrical melodic lines.

After a dramatic opening statement in which the piano arpeggiation is marked *stentate* (hard), *Fior d'amaranto* (Flower of amaranth) breaks into a habanera-like rhythm. According to the composer's direction at the end of measure 1, the last two octaves in each repetition of the pattern are to be delayed. This interesting rhythmic hesitation should not be allowed to influence the arch of the phrase when the voice enters *assai largamente* (rather slowly). The song itself is straightforward with some emphasis through *tenuto* markings on the words *non m'avami punto* (you would not have me at all) and a slight *ritard* on *aveva pianto* (I had cried). The repetition of *fior d'amaranto* (flower of amaranth) should be sung successively more quietly, with the final measure of piano like a whisper. The song was dedicated to the Spanish prima donna Conchita Supervia.

The second song, *O luna che fa' lume* (O moon that gives light), is an example of the composer's lifelong fascination with moonlight as a poetic topic. It is marked *tranquillo assai* (very tranquil) and should be performed with much *rubato*. Accents and *tenuto* markings very carefully emphasize key words or phrases. On the repetition of the phrase *e digli con che core* (and tell him with what love) the composer added a *fermata* on the syllable *di* above the high G in his rehearsal copy of the score. At the end of this phrase the singer should make a slight *crescendo* toward the second syllable of *lasciato* (left). The humming section (*bocca chiusa,* mouth closed), which so effectively completes the song, should be supported by a very delicate, Impressionistic color in the piano, allowing tones to vibrate freely with liberal use of pedal.

Liberal pedaling will help to achieve the *dolcemente mormorato* (sweetly murmuring) quality required for the third song, *Acqua di rio* (Water of the river). The picturesque pattern in the piano part should remain relentlessly steady to the end of the song, until it dies away dynamically with only the slightest *ritard* on the final arpeggiated figure. The vocal line should be stretched out above the accompaniment, observing the dynamic markings within the phrase. The flamenco-like vocal decorations at the ends of several phrases should be sung with flair and abandon as long as the forward motion of the song does not falter.

The touching poetry of *L'ultima notte.* (The last night) is set with utter simplicity. The directions are *molto calmo e sereno* (very calm and serene). The widely spaced block chords require some finger stretching but should not be arpeggiated unless actually written that way. The pedal can be used to sustain sound beneath the delicate triplet figure that appears at the *più mosso.* This song is totally unpretentious and must be sung with a vocal quality and delivery free of all mannerisms. The piano merely comments on this delivery or supports it, and the poem speaks for itself.

Quattro liriche: Carisch, 1932.
<table>
<tr><td>1. Fior d'amaranto</td><td>16491</td></tr>
<tr><td>2. O luna che fa' lume</td><td>16492</td></tr>
<tr><td>3. Acqua di rio</td><td>16493</td></tr>
<tr><td>4. L'ultima notte</td><td>16494</td></tr>
</table>

Cinque liriche romantiche

No. 1, Ho il cuor così greve di pianto

(*D. Valeri*)

1 Ho il cuor così greve di pianto
2 che non posso lagrimare
3 Ho il cuor così gonfio di pianto
4 che non posso più cantare
5 Ho il cuore così perduto in te
6 che non c'è più vita per me

Five romantic lyrics

No. 1, My heart is so heavy with tears

1 My heart is so heavy with tears
2 that I cannot weep
3 My heart is so filled with tears
4 that I can no longer sing
5 My heart is so lost in you
6 that there is no more life for me

The linking element in the poetry of Davico's *Cinque liriche romantiche* (Five romantic lyrics) is the loss of love, probably through death. As the songs progress, moods of acceptance, resignation, tranquility, and remembrance emerge from evocative descriptions of time, place, and object. The composer has captured these images with imagination and feeling.

The piano introduction to *Ho il cuor così greve di pianto* (My heart is so heavy with tears) consists of a melodic motive and some *Tristan*-like chords. Unresolved, shifting dissonances underline much of the speech-inflected vocal line with characteristic falling seconds on key words such as *pianto* (tears). Breathing places are marked where a break is necessary between phrases—even in the accompaniment after the word *lagrimare* (weep); but considering the slow tempo, an additional breath can be taken within each of the three phrases before the word *che* (that). (The composer has actually indicated this in the third phrase.) *Rubato* is essential in this song, and although the composer has indicated a series of *ritardandi* and *a tempi*, the singer's sensitivity to the precise meaning of the words should be the final determinant of this ebb and flow. Special attention should be paid to the colorful effect at the word *cantare* (sing), when the previous series of chord clusters resolves into a clearly defined arpeggiated minor triad. The despairing climax of the poem, *che non c'è più vita per me* (that there is no more life for me), is set with great intensity in a series of falling intervals marked *precipitando* (crashing, falling). The pianist should be aware that this motive is immediately repeated in transposition before the opening motive is restated at the original pitch to bring the song to a cyclical conclusion.

No. 2, Pioggia d'ottobre

(*G. Cevinini*)

1   Mormorano le gronde
2   della piccola corte
3   Sovra le foglie morte
4   canzoni moribonde
5   il cuore si nasconde
6   ha chiuso le sue porte
7   penso a le foglie morte
8   ascolta e non risponde
9   batte l'acqua tenace
10 un' alberella grama
11 altre foglie van giù
12 un bel sogno di pace
13 il cuor stanco ricama
14 nel ciel grigio lassù

No. 2, October rain

1 Murmuring are the eaves
3 of the small courtyard
3 Over the dead leaves
4 funereal songs
5 the heart conceals itself
6 it has closed its doors
7 I think about the dead leaves
8 it listens and does not respond
9 the water beats constantly
10 a little tree grieves
11 other leaves fall down
12 a beautiful dream of peace
12 the tired heart embroiders
14 in the grey sky above

The description of gently falling raindrops in the piano accompaniment, marked *leggero e cristallino* (light and crystalline), sets and maintains the mood of *Pioggia d'ottobre* (October rain). The vocal line, again in speech rhythm, simply tells the story—with words of greater intensity, such as *foglie morte* (dead leaves)—indicated only with *tenuto* markings. The break from the relentless rain in section B allows for the poet's increased introspection at this point and requires some change of vocal color. The directions *lasc. vibrare* under two ascending piano figurations mean "allow to vibrate"; and the final direction, *sfumatissime,* means "vanish to nothing."

No. 3, Plenilunio

(*E. Turalla*)

1 Un mar profondo
2 il cielo tutto azzurro
3 con poche stelle
4 e una bianca luna
5 quiete vette
6 pensierose aperte
7 ove tacite brillano le nevi
8 Su tutta l'Alpe
9 in chiarità notturna
10 vive la notte
11 ed un tranquillo ardore
12 piove dai cieli

13   sulle cime bianche
14   sui boschi e le montagne
15   e sul mio cuore

No. 3, Full moon

1   A deep sea
2   the sky all blue
3   with few stars
4   and a white moon
5   quiet treetops
6   pensive spaces
7   where silently shine the snows
8   On all the Alps
9   in the nocturnal brightness
10   lives the night
11   and a tranquil ardor
12   rains from the heavens
13   on the white peaks
14   on the forests and the mountains
15   and on my heart

In *Plenilunio* (Full moon) the composer leaves his usual recitative style for broader melodic writing. Coupled with the even, *legato,* repetitious arpeggiated accompaniment, it achieves the tranquility sought by the poet in his vision of moonlight and nature. The arpeggiated accompaniment figure should be played without accent anywhere but on the first note, so that the melodic line, which is phrased in both duple and triple meter, can ride effortlessly above. There is an actual or implied polytonality in the accompaniment figures, but its purpose is to provide background color for the vocal line rather than structural definition. Phrases are clearly marked in the song, and breath indications are given by the composer. One particularly long phrase, *Su tutta l'Alpe in chiarità notturna vive la notte* (On all the Alps in the nocturnal brightness lives the night) may require a breath after *notturna* (nocturnal). The frequent *tenuto* markings in the melodic line should not interfere with the steady tempo of the accompaniment. A *ritard* should be taken only where indicated in the score and, if possible, should be achieved by spacing out the eighth notes rather than actually changing the tempo.

No. 4, Fiori

(*V. Malpassuti*)

1   Se con troppi fiori dormi
2   nelle stanze tutte chiuse

3 t'addormenti nella morte
4 e ti svegli nell'oblio
5 pure teco i vo' dormire
6 nella stanza tutta chiusa
7 per svegliarmi nell'oblio
8 per dormire nella morte

No. 4, Flowers

1 If with too many flowers you sleep
2 in rooms entirely closed
3 you go to sleep in death
4 and you awaken in oblivion
5 yet with you I want to sleep
6 in a room entirely closed
7 in order to awaken in oblivion
8 in order to sleep in death

References to death return in *Fiori* (Flowers) with slow-moving dissonant chords and a melodic motive similar to the writing in the first song of the set. The song must be slow and rather nonmetrical, and it should be sung with great intensity at both *forte* and *pianissimo* levels. The poet's desire for oblivion is cleverly anticipated by the resolution to a major chord when the word *oblio* (oblivion) first appears; and there is a nice ambivalence between major and minor tonalities at the final word, *morte* (death). Every word of this text must be "spoken," and the accompaniment should be extremely *legato*. The muddiness of the low-register piano writing is an essential ingredient in the color; no attempt should be made to clear it.

No. 5, Rondini!

(*D. Valeri*)

1 Rondini allegre
2 Rondini leggere
3 in giro in giro
4 vorticosamente
5 ma nello specchio del mio cuor dolente
6 tante piccole croci nere nere.*

No. 5, Swallows!

1 Swallows merry
2 Swallows light-hearted

*The song text is erroneously written "nere neve."

3 around and around
4 vortically (whirling tumultuously)
5 but in the mirror of my sorrowful heart
6 (there are) many small very black crosses

The final song of the set, *Rondini!* (Swallows!), is one of sudden contrasts. The poet delights in the flight of the swallows, which is captured with great charm in the Impressionistic piano figurations, until they remind him of black crosses. As the tempo and the accompaniment pattern change the vocal color changes from "singing" to "speech." Each expression mark should be observed scrupulously, and the final two measures of the piano part should be brittle and abrupt.

Cinque liriche romantiche: Carisch, 1947.
   1. *Ho il cuor così greve di pianto*   20451
   2. *Pioggia d'ottobre*   20452
   3. *Plenilunio*   20453
   4. *Fiori*   20454
   5. *Rondini!*   20455

Ninna-nanna calabrese

(*Testo popolare calabrese*)

1 Durmiti bedda durmiti ch'è ura
2 che bedde comu a vui
3 Dormunu a st'ura
4 durmiti bedda mia faccia di rosa
5 se vui durmiti la mamma riposa
6 Durmiti vui amuri di la mamma
7 ch'a vui v'ama di core e non v'inganna

Calabrian lullaby

(*Popular Calabrian text*)

1 Sleep pretty one sleep because it is time
2 that pretty ones like you
3 are asleep by this hour
4 Sleep my pretty one face like a rose
5 if you sleep your mamma rests
6 Sleep, your mother's darling
7 who loves you sincerely and does not deceive you

Ninna-nanna calabrese (Calabrian lullaby) has none of the underlying weariness of the Abruzzi lullaby, which follows. It is simple, straightforward, and tender. The piano part imitates a strummed instrument, and the composer himself used an exaggerated pedal throughout. The vocal line is "sung," with no *parlando* effects, and it should be very *legato*. The accent marks over *ch'è* (because it is) in the first verse and *la* (literally, "the") in the last one should not be seen as emphasis on unimportant words but as an indication to move on through the phrase. The entire song should be sung quietly; the two indications of *forte,* occurring at the *fermati* on *durmiti* (sleep), are part of the *messa di voce* effect on these sustained high notes and do not signal an abstract dynamic level. The singer should also avoid accenting the final syllable of *durmiti* (sleep) when moving on from the *fermata.* At the duplets on the phrase *se vui durmiti* (if you sleep), the composer prefered a quasi-*portamento legato* each time they appear. Phrase lines, *rallentandi,* and *tenuti* are clearly marked at logical places. A break for breath is permissible between *la mamma* (literally, "the mamma") and *riposa* (rests) on the final *rallentando* to give extra attention to the *tenuto* markings. The song is written in Calabrian dialect.

Ninna-nanna calabrese: A. Corso, 1950.

Ninna-nanna abruzzese

(*su versi popolari*)

1 Nanna e nannarella
2 il lupo s'è mangiato la pecorella.
3 Se l'è mangiata e non se l'è finita
4 la pecorella ci ha person la vita.
5 O sonno che addormentasti il pastore
6 addormenta 'sto figlio mio alla buon'ora.
7 Ahi.

Lullaby of the Abruzzi

(*on popular verses*)

1 Go to bye-bye
2 the wolf has eaten the lamb.
3 He has eaten it and he has not finished it,
4 the lamb lost its life.
5 O sleep, you who made the shepherd fall asleep,
6 Let this son of mine fall asleep at an early hour.
7 Ahi.

The mother is very weary in *Ninna-nanna abruzzese* (Lullaby of the Abruzzi) and sings the strange verses almost absent mindedly, as much to herself as to the child she rocks. While marked *dolcemente* (sweetly) the slow tempo and heaviness of the repeated chord patterns should establish this weariness immediately, and the pedal should sustain the sounds to the point of blurring. The singer should observe each *tenuto* marking and the special *ritenutissimo* (great *ritard*) at the word *pecorella* (lamb).

The central section of the song begins *quasi parlato* (almost spoken), and the composer asks for a tempo that is not strict, but also not rushed. The subtle nuances depend on understanding each word of the text with a touch of special sadness at *perso la vita* (lost its life). The piano must follow the inflections of the voice totally in this section. The next phrases express most vividly the mother's frustration that the child has not yet fallen asleep. The arpeggios should be stretched out, and the vocal line should reach *forte* as the mother calls out for sleep to come to her aid. The short piano solo that provides the bridge to the return of section A should "sing" as much as possible. A definite break must be made at the end of it, before the rocking motion begins again. The final line of the accompaniment should broaden and die away; the final utterance of the singer should achieve a sighing effect through the indicated *messa di voce* on the cry *Ahi*. The song is a tender lullaby, but a feeling of weariness is the key to its interpretation as the singer tries to achieve the proper vocal color and inflections. The song text is printed in standard Italian and in the Abruzzi dialect.

Ninna-nanna abruzzese: Edizioni Curci, 1950.   5039

Cinque canzoni d'Isotta

No. 1, Il vascello

1   Geme la chiglia della nave mia
2   che lenta salpa su l'onda amara
3   verso la meta d'un crudo destin.

Five songs of Isolde

No. 1, The war vessel

1   The keel of my ship groans
2   as it slowly sails on the bitter waves
3   toward the goal of a harsh destiny.

No. 2, Il filtro

1 Non tremi la tua mano che mi porge la morte
2 E scenda la lunga notte con gelidi sogni
3 E tutta m'avvolga d'infinito oblio.

No. 2, The philtre

1 Do not tremble your hand that gives me death
2 And let the long night descend with icy dreams
3 And everything completely wraps me in infinite oblivion.

No. 3, L'incanto

1 Tu sei mio, ed io tua sono
2 E di questo tu devi avere certezza!
3 avvinto sei al mio cuore
4 con ferrea catena che infrangere mai potrai.

No. 3, The enchantment

1 You are mine, and I am yours
2 and of this you must be certain!
3 You have enthralled my heart
4 with an iron chain which you will never be able to shatter.

No. 4, La caccia di Re Marco

1 Ascolta, Brangània,
2 Ferve la caccia di Re Marco
3 che aspra fruga al selva!
4 E già lontan si spegne il suon del corno.
5 Ah! sola rimango
6 E forse invan l'attendo.

No. 4, The hunt of King Mark

1 Listen, Brangane,
2 Going full force is the hunt of King Mark
3 that roughly searches the forest!

4 And already in the distance dies away the sound of the horn.
5 Ah! alone I remain
6 And perhaps in vain I wait for him.

No. 5, La morte

1 Tristano,
2 Tu giaci già nell'ombra ed io ancora vivo,
3 ma non vita è questa mia,
4 ma sogno infinito di dolcissima morte nostra.

No. 5, Death

1 Tristan,
2 You lie already in the shade (in death) and I still live,
3 but this existence of mine is not life,
4 but an infinite dream of our very sweet death.

In *Cinque canzoni d'Isotta* (Five songs of Isolde), based on ancient French texts, Davico conveys the complete emotional framework of the legend of Tristan and Isolde with a remarkable economy of textual and musical means. Each song is complete in itself, yet unity throughout the cycle is achieved by the use of free atonality, lyrical melodies, speech rhythms, and many Davico compositional trademarks—repetitious accompaniment patterns, favorite interval relationships (leaping dissonances resolved a third downward), and full but translucent harmonies.

The saga begins with *Il vascello* (The war vessel), whose repetitive rocking accompaniment, marked *ondeggiando con infinita calma* (swaying or rolling with infinite calm), provides a background for the broad melodic line. The pedal should blur these dissonances further. The singer should not be hurried and should use long phrases to point up Isolde's stoic acceptance of her fate. If possible, the first breath should not be taken until after *mia* (my). The dynamics within phrases are clearly marked. A *crescendo* on the opening word, *geme* (groans), will provide additional color for this word, and the final phrase should *crescendo* toward *crudo* (harsh). If this phrase cannot be sung on one breath, a break may be taken after *meta* (goal), providing the *crescendo* is carried through it. The *morendo* (dying) indication in the two-measure piano postlude creates the effect of the ship sailing into the distance and out of sight.

In *Il filtro* (The philtre) Isolde welcomes what she believes is a death potion prepared at her request by Brangane, her attendant. Again, the mood is one of calm resignation. Each pitch of the opening piano arpeggio must be held through the measure, and all chord motion under the repeated treble octaves should be very *legato* and blurred by the pedal. The repeated octaves should not sound agitated but faintly ominous, and the movement of the vocal and the piano lines toward *morte* (death) should be broad rather than suddenly dramatic. In the final vocal phrase the singer can achieve a stunning effect by connecting, without a *portamento,* the final syllable of *'infinito* (infinite) with the first syllable of *oblio* (oblivion), at the same time making a *decrescendo* to *pianissimo.* This phrase describes the sweet oblivion Isolde hopes to find in death. The piano postlude is an exact repetition of the opening arpeggio, but at one dynamic level lower and with the marking *ritenutissimo* (very slowed down). The case for broad phrase connection in this song is supported by Davico's use of enharmonic tones at two phrase midpoints: *mano che mi porge* (hand that gives me) and *notte con gelidi sogni* (night with icy dreams).

Of course, Brangane has not prepared the death potion, but has substituted a love potion. *L'incanto* (The enchantment), with its ominously low opening notes and sinuous chromatic chords, creates a passionate Wagnerian intensity within a few measures. The opening statement should almost be spoken, but on one underlying vocal line, supported by *legato* chord movement in the accompaniment. In the measures marked *mosso deciso* (decisive motion), rhythmic precision is important in the vocal line while brittle detached chords provide punctuation in the piano part. Little or no pedal should be used here, although it can be applied again in the measure marked *calmo subito* (suddenly calm) to achieve connection between the chord and its resolution to an octave *pianissimo.* The "aria" begins after this, with the rising vocal line supported by the ascending arpeggiation in the piano. A breath may be taken after *cuore* (heart), but should be taken after *catena* (chain) to provide the power for the climactic *potrai* (be able)—passion given full reign. The word *mai* (never) deserves extra intensity along the way to this climax since it gives meaning to the verb. At the *molto largamente* the piano is scored on three staves to accommodate the now expanded repetition of the song's opening chord sequence. This should be played with as much orchestral effect as possible, observing the *allargando* and *ritenutissimo* effects before the final entrance of the voice. The final statement of the voice duplicates the opening statement exactly, but is transposed down one halfstep.

La caccia di Re Marco (The hunt of King Mark) is a miniature *scena.* Now married to King Mark, Isolde hears the horns of his hunting party recede into the forest. She realizes that she is finally alone, and with an outburst of passion, she anticipates a meeting with Tristan. The song should be performed with full dramatic intensity; the composer's markings are quite clear. Great contrasts in piano articulation and vocal color are required at the end of the song, beginning with the section marked *calmo senza misura* (calmly without measure). The *fortissimo* piano figure before the singer's climactic "ah!" requires a harsh, brittle accent; the singer's voice should sound "abandoned" rather then "beautiful."

A slowly rising figure in the piano introduction, faintly reminiscent of that which underscored the passionate aria of the third song, provides the mood for Isolde's inevitable death in *La morte* (Death). It is marked *estremamente lento e senza rigore di tempo* (extremely slow and without regularity of tempo). The color of the piano is *lontano* (distant), an echo of the intensity of the previous songs. Tristan is dead; Isolde is desolate and weary.

The vocal line is almost spoken until it leads to the climactic *vivo* (I live), with piano chords acting as commentary rather than support. The *messa di voce* (*p* to *f* to *p*) on *sogno* (dream) is very important, since it indicates Isolde's only hope for the fulfillment of her desire to be with Tristan. In the final moments of the phrase, voice and piano move together with the direction *ancora più lento che all'inizio* (still slower than the beginning) and the accompaniment marked *dolcissimo e armonioso* (very sweet and harmonious). The word *morte* (death) no longer conjures up fear, only sweet peace.

Cinque canzoni d'Isotta: G. Ricordi, 1955.   129049 (Set)
    1. *Il vascello*
    2. *Il filtro*
    3. *L'incanto*
    4. *La caccia di Re Marco*
    5. *La morte*

Commiato

(*Liberamente elaborato da un distico persiano del XIII secolo*)

1 Non parlare più
2 serba
3 sulle tue labbra mute
4 tutto il sapore
5 dell'ultimo bacio
6 perchè non ne vanisca il profumo
7 mormorando altre parole
8 d'amore

Leave

(*Freely elaborated from a fourteenth-century Persian distich*)

1 Don't talk anymore
2 keep
3 on your mute lips

4 all the flavor
5 of the last kiss
6 so that the perfume will not vanish
7 murmuring other words
8 of love

Sera d'autunno

(*Renato Fauroni*)

1 Un fantasma di luna
2 dietro agitate nuvole
3 stassera
4 Rabbrividenti foglie che il vento
5 poi in un attimo disperde
6 voce cupa del mare lontano
7 E in me tristezza
8 di un ricordo

Autumn evening

1 A moon phantom
2 behind agitated clouds
3 this evening
4 Shivering leaves that the wind
5 then in a moment disperses
6 the deep voice of the distant sea
7 And in me sadness
8 of a memory

Although the structural framework of *Commiato* (Leave) and *Sera d'au-tunno* (Autumn evening), both published in 1958, is atonal, an irrepressible Italian lyricism is still evident. At first glance *Commiato* appears to be a series of short speechlike phrases superimposed on cluster chords. However, each phrase is subtly linked to create a melodic arch not unlike verismo writing. Although rests appear in both the vocal and the piano part they never appear at the same time, and an unbroken thread of sonority must be maintained throughout the song. It is particularly important to observe the tie-lines written in the piano part and to assist with the pedal where necessary. The tempo of the piece must be slow enough to observe the expression markings: *dolcissimo* (very sweetly), *espressivo* (expressive), and *sentito* (heartfelt), but not too slow to negate the effect of the long line. The song calls for fine control of dynamics (as soft as *pppp*), extreme *legato,* and well-developed breath control.

The melody of *Sera d'autunno* is slightly more angular than that of *Commiato,* and the song has more descriptive effects in the music that reflect specific images in the text. Again, however, the sonorities are continuous, overlapping except for the break clearly indicated after the word *disperde* (disperses). This word is beautifully complemented by the small-note piano figuration, marked *sfumando e lasciando vibrare* (vanishing and allowed to vibrate). The notes literally disperse. The middle phrase, beginning *Rab-brividenti* (Shivering), is long, and the singer may need a breath after *vento* (wind), although the direction *mosso alquanto* (a certain amount of motion) indicates that the phrase should be propelled forward at this point. The composer is careful at the beginning of the song to use the terms *dolce ma sonoro* (sweetly, but sonorous). The more vigorous word images in this poem require this interpretive approach throughout, even though the song is slow, requires extreme *legato,* and calls for dynamic levels as soft as *pppp*.

Commiato: A. Forlivesi, 1958.   12331

Sera d'autunno: A. Forlivesi, 1958.   12330

Giorgio Federico Ghedini

(1892–1965)

•

THE LIFE OF GIORGIO FEDERICO GHEDINI is less documented than those of many of his contemporaries, in part because of the rather late recognition of his status as a composer. He was born in Cuneo in the province of Piedmont on July 11, 1892. In 1905 his family moved to Turin, the provincial capital, where young Giorgio studied piano and organ with Evasio Lovazzano. Later he entered the Liceo Musicale in order to study cello with Salvatore Grossi and composition with Giovanni Craveo. He moved on to study composition under Marco Enrico Bossi at the Liceo Musicale of Bologna and received a diploma from that institution in 1911.

In 1909, while still a student, Ghedini worked as a coach at the Teatro Regio in Turin; he eventually became an assistant conductor, responsible for directing both opera and concerts in the city and on tour. Although his association with the theater continued until 1920, Ghedini turned to teaching in 1918, obtaining a post at the Scuola Municipale di Canto Corale of Turin, under the direction of Vicenzo Veneziani. A little later he was entrusted with teaching piano and elementary harmony at the Liceo Musicale di Giuseppe Verdi in Turin; he moved on to teach courses in advanced harmony, counterpoint, fugue, and, finally, composition.

In 1938 Ghedini was appointed professor of composition at the Conservatory of Parma. In 1941, he left to accept a new position as professor of composition at the Conservatory of Milan; and from 1951 to 1962 he was director there. In addition to his teaching and administrative duties, Ghedini was active at various times as advisor to Teatro alla Scala and RAI (Italian radio) and as an organizer of Settimane Musicali Senesi and the Italian branch of the International Society for Contemporary Music. Ghedini died in Nervi, near Genoa, on March 25, 1965.

Although his creative activity began early and Ghedini was intensely dedicated from the beginning, his real fame and international recognition did not begin until around 1940. Until then he was a respected but cautious musician, distancing himself from the more innovative currents of contemporary music. Most of his early work was never published, and until the 1920s he was known only to a small circle of friends. His compositions of the late 1920s and early 1930s are uneven, showing the passing influences of neo-Romanticism, post-Impressionism, and finally, neo-Classicism. During this time Ghedini evidences an increasing involvement with early Italian music (he made many editions and transcriptions throughout his life of music by Frescobaldi, Gabrieli, Monteverdi, Bach, Schütz, and others) and a growing awareness of his contemporaries (particularly Franco Alfano, Andrea Della Corte, Romualdo Giani, Guido Gatti, and Alfredo Casella). Ghedini's orchestral *Partita* (1926) shows many neo-Classical characteristics and bears some relationship to Casella's *Partita* of 1925. Ghedini's *Concerto Grosso* of 1927 shows strong Baroque influences, which culminate in his adaptations of Baroque idioms in the 1940s.

Architettura, written in 1940, an orchestral work of seven sections that Ghedini called *edifici sonori* (literally, "buildings of sound") marks his emergence among the recognized leaders of Italian—and European—contemporary music. From here on his compositional style is established, and, while it shows the influence of Stravinsky and others, his original use of intervals and, especially, of orchestral timbre is purely personal.

Ghedini's early operas and vocal works, such as *Maria d'Alessandra* (1936) and *Re Hassan* (1937–38), are traditional, showing affinity for Wagner and Pizzetti, but *La baccanti* (1941–1944), first performed at La Scala in Milan on February 22, 1948, shows the achieved mastery of personal style. Based on the play by Euripides, the opera was hailed for the personification of the Greek spirit through timbral contrasts in voice and orchestration. The *Concerto dell'albatro* (1945) is regarded in Italy as a Ghedini masterpiece. It is a seascape with neo-Baroque outlines in which a speaking voice three-quarters of the way through the composition reads passages from Herman Melville's *Moby Dick.* The works of the late 1940s—*Musica notturna* (1947), *Canzoni* for orchestra (1947–1948), and *Concerto funebre per Duccio Galimberti* (1948)—confirmed Ghedini's position. The last-named work, an unorthodox requiem to a text from Ezekiel, was dedicated to the heroes of the resistance movement against Fascism.

In the 1950s and 60s Ghedini's work did not break much new ground, and some weakness in final sections has been attributed to a tendency to finish a work too rapidly. His interest in Gregorian and Baroque music continued, but some nineteenth-century idioms are evident as well. Some of Ghedini's music is self-imitative. His last work, *Sinfonia 1965,* was posthumously reconstructed by Giuseppe Sabretti.

Ghedini's songs reflect the various styles the composer was exploring at the time they were written, but they are superbly crafted and reflect a sincere attempt to create a fusion of word and music in the true art-song tradition. His choice of poetic material is always tasteful and interesting, and it is obvious that Ghedini could come close to his emotions in this intimate form—especially as reflected in the poignancy of *Tre liriche su testi di Bacchelli,* published in 1964, the year before he died.

Diletto e spavento del mare

(*da Mosco, traduzione di G. Mazzoni*)

1 Quando il ceruleo mare d'un'aria quieta s'increspa
2 Mi si commuove il core di placida gioia: la terra
3 Più non m'alletta e quella pace m'invita a la barca.
4 Ma se risuonan grigi i flutti e ribollono curve l'onde
5 ed i cavalloni spumeggiano lunghi rompendo,
6 guardo a la terra, guardo agli alberi, e fuggo dal mare.
7 Caro m'è allora il suolo, mi piace la selva tutt'ombre
8 Dove se il turbin soffia, pur sempre vi cantano i pini.
9 Misero il pescatore! Che in cambio di casa ha la barca,
10 Ha per travaglio il mare, ne' pesci vaganti ha le prede.
11 Dolce me prenda il sonno ne l'ombra d'un platano folto
12 E mi diletti il lene rumor d'una fonte vicina
13 che non spavento induce ma caro diletto al villano.

Delight and fear of the sea

(*from Mosco, translated [into Italian] by G. Mazzoni*)

1 When the sky-blue sea is rippled by a quiet breeze
2 My heart is moved with peaceful joy: the earth
3 No longer allures me and that peace invites me to the boat.
4 But if the grey billows resound and the curved waves boil
5 and the breakers foam high as they break,
6 I look at the land, I look at the trees, and I flee from the sea.
7 Dear to me then is the ground, I like the forest all shady
8 Where even though the whirlwind blows, yet always the pines sing to
   you.
9 Pitiable is the fisherman! Who instead of a house has a boat,
10 He has the sea for his work, some wandering fish are his prey.
11 Pleasantly sleep overcomes me in the shade of a dense plane tree
12 And I delight in the gentle sound of a nearby fountain
13 Which induces not fright but pleasure to the peasant.

Ghedini's fascination with early Italian music influenced his compositional style, especially during the period when *Diletto e spavento del mare* (Delight and fear of the sea) was written (1928). There are many neo-Classical traits in the setting, and given Ghedini's penchant for seeing the philosophy behind a poem as well as the vividness of the imagery within it, they are very appropriate.

The song begins very quietly in minor mode, with the voice entering above a pedal tone B♭ with the marking *come un racconto* (like a story).

When the accompaniment moves, it flows downward in octaves, in a recognizable motive that appears again and again throughout the song. Although harmonies are implied, the song is highly contrapuntal. The vocal line, in speech rhythms, is balanced against the octaves and single-line melodies in the accompaniment. The lines often converge, but more often work in contrary motion. The dynamic range is narrow (*pp–mf*), and even at times of busy rhythmic activity it does not rise much above *mezzo-piano*. While the accompanying lines should be distinguishable at all times, it is especially important for the pianist to bring out moving passages between vocal entrances (such as measure 10) or during sustained tones (such as measures 16–17). This effect of shifting melodic interest from voice to piano and back adds another dimension to the contrasting interplay of the two elements.

The first climax comes in measure 25, but it should not be louder than a *mezzo-forte*. The rising vocal line and forward movement of the octaves in the accompaniment create the *crescendo* automatically. The bass octaves could be seen as subtle tone-painting in measures 25–26 under the word *rompendo* (break), but, in general, musical references to the text should not receive additional emphasis; they are subtle. After the phrase *e fuggo dal mare* (and I flee from the sea) there is a downward progression of eighth notes, which the composer very carefully marks *dolcissimo e uguale* (very sweet and equal), avoiding the temptation to have them "run."

The second section of the song, beginning *Caro m'è allora il suolo* (Dear to me then is the ground), continues the sweet mood of the first, with such directions as *dolce, soave e profondo* (sweet, gentle and profound), *sommesso* (soft, meek), and *raddolcendo* (soothingly). After the phrase *pur sempre vi cantano i pini* (yet always the pines sing to you), a flutter of sixteenth notes in the accompaniment comments on the text, *lievemente* (breezily).

As the poet muses on the contrasts between "landed" life and the life of the fisherman, some very fine contrapuntal writing in contrary motion enhances the expression. Again, tempo fluctuations and dynamic ranges are slight. A clever triplet figure appears suddenly in the accompaniment beneath the phrase *E mi diletti lene rumor d'una fonte vicina* (And I delight in the gentle sound of a nearby fountain) to depict the fountain. The long lyrical piano postlude is in the major mode. The poem conveys the attitude of a person speaking to himself, musing on the choices he sees available for himself. The song captures this mood.

For the most part vocal phrases are short, or the composer indicates the best place for a breath. One phrase needs special attention; if possible no breath should be taken between measures 26 and 27, so that a seamless *decrescendo* is achieved between *rompendo* (break) and *guardo* (I look).

Diletto e spavento del mare: G. Ricordi, 1927; Repr. 1953.   120582.

La quiete della notte

(da Alcmane, traduzione di G. Mazzoni)

1 De le montagne dormono le cime;
2 E i dirupi e i burroni e le valli ime;
3 E quante foglie ha in selve,
4 Quante montane belve
5 E quante serpi mai nudre la terra;
6 E le api, e i mostri che l'abisso serra
7 del nereggiante mare,
8 E il popol degli augelli uso a volare.

The calm of night

(from Alcmane, translation [into Italian] by G. Mazzoni)

1 The peaks of the mountains sleep;
2 And crags and deep ravines and low valleys;
3 And as many leaves as are in the forests,
4 As many wild animals on the mountains,
5 and as many serpents ever nurtured on earth;
6 and bees, and monsters that the chasm shuts off
7 from the darkening sea,
8 And the multitudes of birds accustomed to fly.

Ghedini's musical setting of this unusual poem seems to imply an equation between night, sleep, and death. *La quiete della notte* (The calm of night) is a through-composed song, based freely on the Baroque *passacaglia* form, one of the many structures from earlier Italian music that Ghedini admired. The first four measures of the piano introduction establish the *ostinato* over which the rest of the song is constructed. Unlike a strict *passacaglia,* this *ostinato* modulates frequently and is sometimes fragmented, but it never loses its identity. The vocal melody has a low *tessitura,* narrow range, and speechlike rhythms that are often extended into longer note values. The dynamic range of the song is narrow (*ppp–mf*). The increase in rhythmic activity and the dynamic rise in measures 25–27 and 31–33 are the only indications of climax in the entire song, and each time they lead into measures marked *pp* and *ma espressivo* or *dolce.*

The crucial direction for the proper interpretation of this song occurs at the very beginning, with the composer's tempo setting *profondamente grave e molto lento* (deeply solemn and very slow, $\downarrow$ = 92) and the indication in the accompaniment *legatissimo e inesorabilmente in tempo sino all fine* (as *legato* as possible and inexorably in tempo up to the end). There is no *rallentando* or *ritardando* at any point in the work. Once begun the tempo should be metronomically regular until the final note; *tenuto* markings should be interpreted more as accents than as held notes, and if the singer delays a consonant or stresses a syllable for word emphasis it should in no way cause an interruption in the relentless forward motion of the accompaniment. The *tenuto* indications in measures 25–26 are intended for the pianist, who should hold the whole notes throughout the measure.

The composer is generous with breath indications, except for the phrase *e i mostri che l'abisso serra del nereggiante mare* (and monsters that the chasm shuts off from the darkening sea). While the singer should phrase it as a complete thought, the slow tempo requires a breath at some point, and the composer's phrasing indicates one after *serra*.

The extreme lowness of the accompaniment makes this song problematic for male voices, even though the vocal range is appropriate. When sung by a bass or a baritone, a light voice would be more effective than a dark one, and this suggestion is valid for mezzo-sopranos as well. An overly dark vocal production coupled with the muddiness of the lower end of the piano could destroy what is a rather clear structure within the somber, dark texture.

La quiete della notte: G. Ricordi, 1927; Repr. 1953.   120583

Di', Maria dolce

(*Giovanni Dominici*)

1   Di', Maria dolce con quanto desio
2   Miravi 'l tuo figliuol, Cristo mio Dio?
3   Quando tu il partoristi senza pena,
4   La prima cosa, credo, che facesti,
5   Tu l'adorasti, o di grazia piena,
6   Poi sopra il fien nel presepio il ponesti;
7   con pochi e pover panni lo involgesti,
8   Maravigliando e godendo, cred' io.
9   Oh quanto gaudio avevi, oh quanto bene,
10 quando tu lo tenevi nelle braccia!
11 Dimmi, Maria, chè forse si conviene
12 Che un poco per pietà mi sodisfaccia,
13 Baciavilo tu allora nella faccia?
14 Sì ben, credo, e dicei: "O figliol mio!"
15 Quando figliuol, quando padre e signore,
16 Quando Iddio, quando Gesù lo chiamavi;
17 Oh quanto dolce amor sentivi al core
18 Quando in gremio il tenevi e lo lattavi!
19 Oh quanti atti d'amore soavi

20 Avesti, essendo col tuo figliuol pio!
21 Quando talora un poco il dì dormìa,
22 E tu, destar volendo il paradiso,
23 Pian piano andavi, che non ti sentìa,
24 E poi ponevi il viso al santo viso;
25 Poi gli dicevi con materno viso:
26 "Non dormir più, che ti sarebbe rio"
27 Quando tu ti sentivi chiamar mamma?
28 Come non ti morivi di dolcezza?
29 Come d'amor non t'ardeva una fiamma,
30 Che t'avessi scoppiata d'allegrezza?
31 Daver che grande fu la tua fortezza
32 Poi che la vita allor non ti finìo
33 E lui figlio del sommo eterno padre,
34 E lui, Signor, la sua umile ancilla
35 Pietosamente la chiamava madre,
36 Che sol pensando il cor mi si distilla.
37 Chi vuol sentir qualche dolce favilla
38 Di quell'amore, il qual sempre disìo,
39 Ponga nel buon Gesù ogni disìo.

Tell me, sweet Mary

1   Tell me, sweet Mary with how much joy
2   you gazed upon your loving son, Christ my God?
3   When you gave birth to him painlessly,
4   The first thing, I believe, that you did,
5   You adored him, o full of grace,
6   Then on the hay in the manger you laid him;
7   With a few poor clothes you wrapped him,
8   marveling and rejoicing, I believe.
9   Oh how much happiness you had, oh how much pleasure,
10 Whenever you held him in your arms!
11 Tell me, Mary, because perhaps if you agree
12 Because a little through pity would satisfy me,
13 You kissed him then on his face?
14 So well, I believe, and you said: "O my loving son!"
15 At times loving son, at times father, at times Lord,
16 At times God, at times Jesus you used to call him;
17 Oh how much sweet love you felt in your heart
18 When you used to hold him on your lap and you used to nurse him!
19 Oh how many gentle acts of love
20 You had, being with your blessed son!
21 When sometimes he slept a while during the day,

22   and you, wishing to watch over the heavenly one,
23   Very slowly you moved about so that he would not hear you,
24   And then you used to place your face by his holy face;
25   Then you used to say to him with motherly advice
26   "Do not sleep any longer because it would be bad for you."
27   When you used to hear yourself called "mamma"
28   How did you not die from tenderness?
29   How were you not burned by a flame of love,
30   that would have made you burst with happiness?
31   Truly your strength was very great
32   Since your life did not end for you then.
33   And he, son of the highest eternal father,
34   And he, Lord, his humble handmaiden
35   Lovingly he used to call her mother.
36   Only thinking about this my heart dissolves.
37   Whoever wishes to feel some tender spark
38   of that love, who always desired it,
39   place in the good Jesus every desire.

Di', Maria dolce (Tell me, sweet Mary), a moving *Laude spirituale,* has roots deep in the Italian Catholic tradition, beginning with the activity of St. Francis of Assisi (1182–1226). Defined as hymns of praise and devotion in the Italian language, *laude* were often composed by and for congregations called Companie di Laudesi or Laudisti—fraternal organizations that cultivated devotional singing among the people. The tradition continued through the middle of the nineteenth century, and Ghedini's decision to set one of these hymns is an example of the interest contemporary Italian composers took in their own rich cultural tradition.

This particular Marian text is filled with tender maternal images and dwells on the intimacy of the relationship between Mary and the infant Jesus. Ghedini's setting is respectfully simple, allowing the words to create their own impact within a very lyrical musical ambience. It shares with Gregorian chant an overall stepwise movement and relatively narrow range within sections. When the range widens and skips occur, they point up the more emotional exclamations of the text and thus avoid the necessity for a dramatic change in dynamics.

The work is through-composed, but the motive

appearing first on the words *Christo mio Dio* (Christ my God), returns at several points throughout the composition in both the vocal line and the accompaniment. The tempo should be unhurried, but not too slow, and rather steady—*senza indugiare* (without delaying). The *rubati* are few and clearly marked. The irregular alternation of 3/4 and 2/4 is no problem if the quarter note is kept constant. If anything, the alternation permits greater freedom for the speech rhythms of much of the text. A forward momentum is crucial to the interplay between voice and piano. Balance is very important, since the accompaniment often carries a melodic interest equal to or greater than that of the vocal line. As long as the text can be clearly articulated, the piano should not play a subservient role. Whenever the climactic "Christo" motive appears, it should be brought out from the rest of the texture.

The composer's directions for expression are quite clear. There are a few unusual terms: in measure 105 *sommesso* (soft, meek), in measure 121 *ravvivato* (revived, brightened), and in measure 147 *rimettendosi in tempo* (put back in tempo).

If the words are fully understood and the composer's *tempi* are followed faithfully, the simplicity of the setting carries this song along, and the necessary vocal colors are self-evident.

Di', Maria dolce: G. Ricordi, 1927; Repr. 1954.   120585

Canta un augello in voce sì suave

(*Matteo Maria Boiardo*)

1 Canta uno augello in voce sì suave,
2 Ove Meandro il vado obliquo agira,
3 Che la sua morte prende con dilletto.
4 Lassar le usate ripe non gli è grave;
5 Ma con dolce armonia l'anima spira,
6 Nè voce cangia alfin, nè muta aspetto.
7 L'unda del fiume il novo canto ammira,
8 E lui, fra l'erbe fresche a la rivera,
9 Perchè nel suo zoir doglia non spera,
10 Segue cantando ove natura il tira.
11 Così me tragge questa bella fiera
12 A voluntaria morte e dolce tanto,
13 Che per lei moro, e, pur morendo, canto.

A bird is singing with voice so soft

1 A bird is singing with voice so soft,
2 Where the Meandro (river) proceeds on its winding way,
3 That he takes his own death with delight.

4   To leave his accustomed banks is for him not painful;
5   But with sweet harmony his soul breathes,
6   His voice doesn't change at the end, nor does it change appearance,
7   The waves of the river marvel at the new song,
8   And he, among the fresh grasses by the bank,
9   Because in his joy he does not expect pain,
10   He follows singing wherever nature draws him.
11   Thus this beautiful wild creature leads me
12   To death voluntarily and so sweetly,
13   That I die for her, and, even dying, I sing.

Canta uno augello in voce sì suave (A bird is singing with voice so soft) is a bittersweet song built around the motive:

which represents the voice of the bird. It alternates between major and minor tonality in accordance with the subtle, shifting moods of the poem. The dynamics must be similarly subtle, such as the *decrescendo* on the words *dolce armonia* (sweet harmony). The temptation to breath after *armonia* must be avoided, but the rest before *spira* (breathes) indicates a breath to point up the word-painting by the descending scale. At the phrase *Segue cantando ove natura il tira* (He follows singing wherever nature draws him) the expressive marking *raddolcendo* (soft and soothing) provides a good contrast for the sudden intensity of the next phrase. The breath mark after *fiera* (wild creature) should be observed to permit a secure accent on the word *tanto* (so) at the end of the phrase. The rests between *moro* (I die), *e pur* (and even), and *morendo* (dying) are integral elements in the expression of these significant words. The composer's alternate version of the last phrase permits the repetition of the word *canto* (I sing) and facilitates the holding of the vocal line as marked through the piano postlude. It is a sensible solution to what would otherwise require extraordinary breath control.

Canta un augello in voce sì suave: G. Ricordi, 1937; Repr. 1950.   123901

Datime a piena mano e rose e zigli
(*Matteo Maria Boiardo*)

1   Datime a piena mano e rose e zigli,
2   Spargeti intorno a me viole e fiori,
3   Ciascun che meco pianse e mei dolori,
4   Di mia leticia meco il frutto pigli.

5   Datime e fiori e candidi e vermigli:
6   Confano a questo giorno e bei colori;
7   Spargeti intorno d'amorosi odori,
8   Chè il loco a la mia voglia se assumigli.
9   Perdon m'ha dato et hami dato pace
10 La dolce mia nemica, e vuol ch'io campi.
11 Lei che sol di pietà se pregia e vanta.
12 Non vi maravigliati perch'io avampi,
13 Chè maraviglia è più che non se sface
14 Il cor in tutto d'alegreza tanta.

Give me a handful of roses and lilies

1   Give me a handful of roses and lilies,
2   Strew violets and flowers around me,
3   Each one who wept with me in my grief,
4   Now pick with me the fruits of my joy.
5   Give me flowers both white and red:
6   Beautiful colors are appropriate for this day.
7   Strew around their lovely odors,
8   So that the place will resemble my pleasure.
9   She has pardoned me and has given me peace
10 My sweet adversary and she wishes that I live.
11 She who only out of pity esteems herself and boasts.
12 Do not marvel that I am exuberant,
13 It is more the wonder that my heart is not
14 Bursting with so much happiness.

An accomplished pianist is required to achieve the fresh, joyous character of *Datime a piena mano e rose e zigli* (Give me a handful of roses and lilies). While the accompaniment looks simple, it does not fall under the fingers easily. The composer's suggested tempo ($\downarrow$ = 96) must be followed so that the singer can complete the long phrases in one breath and for the forward movement of the music—even cadences are marked *senza rall.* (without slowing down). Key words are generally emphasized through accents, grace-note decorations, or *tenuto* markings, all of which must be scrupulously observed by the singer. The phrase beginning *Perdon m'ha dato* (She has pardoned me) should be sung more sweetly, but not softer, and no breath should be taken between *pace* (peace) and *La dolce* (sweet). The composer permits a breath both before and after the climactic word *d'alegreza* (happiness), but the phrase is more effective if the first one can be eliminated. A slight *rallentando* is permitted on the final cadence, but not too much, and the piano postlude should be *a tempo* and rather sprightly in character.

Datime a piena mano e rose e zigli: G. Ricordi, 1937.   123902

Due liriche

No. 1, Candida mia colomba

(*Matteo Maria Boiardo*)

1 Candida mia colomba qual è toa forma degna?
2 Qual cosa più simiglia a la toa gran beltade?
3 Augello de l'Amor, segno di pace,
4 Come debio nomarti,
5 Che nulla cosa quanto te me piace?
6 Arboscel mio fronzuto,
7 Dal paradiso colto,
8 Qual forza di natura
9 Te ha fatto tanto adorno
10 Di schietto tronco e de odorate foglie,
11 E de tanta vaghezza,
12 Che in te racolte son tutte mie voglie?
13 Lucida perla colta ove se coglie
14 Di preziose gemme ogni richeza,
15 Dove l'unda vermiglia abunda in zoglie,
16 E sopra el lito suo le sparge intorno,
17 Serà già mai ventura
18 Che a me dimostri sì benigno il volto,
19 Che da te speri aiuto?
20 Candida mia colomba
21 Augella de l'Amor, segno di pace ...
22 Arboscel mio fronzuto,
23 Dal paradiso colto ...
24 Lucida perla ...

Two lyrics

No. 1, My snow-white dove

1 My snow-white dove what is your worthy form?
2 What thing most resembles your great beauty?
3 Bird of Love, symbol of peace,
4 What should I call you,
5 Since no other thing pleases me so much as you?
6 My leafy young tree,
7 Picked from paradise,

8   What force of nature
9   Has made you so adorned
10 With a pure trunk and with fragrant leaves,
11 And with so much gracefulness,
12 That in you are gathered all my desires?
13 Luminous pearl picked where they gather
14 Precious gems of every richness,
15 Where vermillion waves abound in leaves,
16 And above your shore he scatters them all around,
17 Will there ever be the chance
18 That you will show me so kind a visage,
19 That from you I hope for aid?
20 My snow-white dove
21 Bird of love, symbol of peace . . .
22 My leafy young tree,
23 Picked from paradise . . .
24 Luminous pearl . . .

Due liriche (Two lyrics, 1935) are settings of verses by Matteo Maria
Boiardo (1434–1494). The first is a buoyant love song comparing the loved
one to a snow-white dove, the second a lament for the loss of the loved one.
The set could form a program group except that the first is designated for
soprano or tenor while the second is for mezzo-soprano or baritone. Only a
wide-ranged female voice could perform both in their original keys.

Candida mia colomba (My snow-white dove) begins with the motive

which appears again and again throughout the song at the original pitch and
in transposition. The entrance of the voice with the title phrase in measure
2 likewise introduces a melodic motive,

which reappears in various guises. The form of the song is really through-
composed, but it is sectioned somewhat to conform with the poem. This
factor and the recurring motives create a broad ABA, if not *rondo,* feeling to
the overall architecture.

In typical Ghedini style, there is considerable interplay between piano
and voice. The keyboard activity virtually stops when the voice enters in

measure 2, and it remains purely supportive until the voice finishes in measure 4. As soon as the voice is released, part of the original keyboard motive
takes over. This shifting of interest between the two forces continues throughout the song; the forces come together with equal interest principally at the
climactic points (measures 26 and 37–39) and in the last section of the work
(mesures 41–52), where the vocal and keyboard motives overlap. There is
also some interesting overlap within the change to the key of D major in the
center of the song (measures 26–32). Finding a balance for these two elements in the composer's presentation is the primary problem in interpreting
the composition. For the most part the words are set clearly in speech rhythms
and should be relatively easy to project. Phrases break logically with commas
in the text, or the composer has marked places where breaths may be taken.
The phrase beginning in measure 17, *Qual forza di natura/Te ha fatto tanto
adorno* (What force of nature/Has made you so adorned) should not break
after *natura* but carry through to the breath indication after *adorno*. A good
breath should also be taken before the climactic *Lucida* (Luminous) in measure 26 and before *Che da te speri aiuto* (That from you I hope for aid) in
measure 37, especially if the alternate high B♭ is sung. This phrase, then,
should be sung on one breath.

The metronome indication ♩ = 80 comes with the qualification *liberamente* (liberally), and there are numerous indications for *rubati* throughout
the song, including a few unusual ones, such as *ampro* (broad, spacious) in
measure 29 and *riprendendo il movimento* (retaking the movement) in measures 33–34.

Special attention should be given to the composer's careful marking of
articulation on such phrases as *Che nulla cosa quanto te me piace* (Since
no other thing pleases me as much as you). The accent and *tenuto* markings
are quite deliberate for the proper expression of the words. Dynamic markings are clear and appropriate, and the whole song should have a *fresco e
sonoro* (fresh and resonant) quality, as the composer directs.

No. 2, Tu te ne vai

(*Matteo Maria Boiardo*)

1   Tu te ne vai, e teco vene Amore,
2   E teco la mia vita e ogni mio bene;
3   Et io soletto resto in tante pene,
4   Soletto sanza spirto e sanza core.
5   Debbio forsi soffrir questo dolore
6   Ch'io non venga con teco?
7   E chi me tene?

8   Ahi, lasso me! Che con tante catene
9   Me legò sempre e lega il nostro onore.
10 Oh, se io credesse pur che alcuna volta
11 Di me te sovenisse, anima mia,
12 Quanto minor sarebbe il mio martire!
13 Ma, quando io penso che me sarai tolta
14 Oggi, e sì presso è la partita ria,
15 Campar non posso, o di dolor morire.

No. 2, You are going away from here

1   You are going away from here, and with you goes Love,
2   And with you my life and my every goodness;
3   And I remain all alone in so much pain,
4   All alone without spirit and without heart.
5   Must I perhaps suffer this grief
6   Because I am not going with you?
7   And who holds me?
8   Ahi, wretched me! Because with so many chains
9   It always tied me, and it ties our honor.
10 Oh, if I believed still that sometimes
11 You could think of me, my love,
12 How much less would be my suffering!
13 But, when I think you will be taken from me
14 Today, and so near at hand is the wicked final parting,
15 I cannot live, or die of grief.

Although quite contrasting in subject matter and mood, the second song, *Tu te ne vai* (You are going away), also makes use of a repetitive motive,

in both the piano and the voice part. The melancholy mood of the text is expressed in the minor tonality of the song (it begins more or less in B minor and moves through several tonalities to cadence finally in F♯ minor), the slow tempo (♩ = 44), and the expression marking *raccolto, grave e pesante* (concentrated, solemn and heavy). Even the motive itself, which appears simultaneously in voice and piano at measure 2, has a heavy feeling because of its falling intervals, narrow range, and heavy rhythmic accent. The first four lines of poetry are set within a very narrow pitch range, hovering about or returning to F♯. The piano part is equally constricted, but the performer should attempt to create a line from the more rhythmically active inner voice; it duplicates the vocal line note-for-note throughout most of the song.

At the words *Ahi, lasso me!* (Ahi, wretched me!), changes in dynamics and texture lead toward the first climax of the song. It should not be over-stressed since the following phrase, beginning softer, leads to a second, more important climax on the word *martire* (suffering). The octave movement in the bass of the piano part creates an increase in forward momentum here. The more emotionally intense center of the poem is also set with wider intervals and greater rhythmic activity.

In the final six measures of the song the melodic doubling between voice and piano is less obvious. The final utterance *o di dolor morire* (or die of grief) should be stretched out rhythmically. The last note requires a smooth *messa di voce.*

Due liriche: G. Ricordi, 1946.
    1. *Candida mia colomba*   127119 (S-T)
    2. *Tu te ne vai*   127120 (Ms-Br)

Quattro strambotti di Giustiniani

No. 1, Se li arbori sapesser favellare

1 Se li arbori sapesser favellare,
2 e le lor foglie fusseno le lengue,
3 l'inchiostro fusse l'acqua dello mare,
4 la terra fusse carta e l'erbe penne
5 le tue bellezze non potria contare.
6 Quando nascesti gli angioli ci venne,
7 quando nascesti, colorito giglio,
8 tutti li santi furno a quel consiglio.

Four strambotti by Justinian

No. 1, If the trees knew how to talk

1 If the trees knew how to talk,
2 and their leaves were tongues,
3 ink were the water of the sea,
4 earth were paper and grass pens
5 your beauties could not be counted.
6 When you were born the angels came

7   when you were born, colored (white as a) lily
8   all the saints were at that council.

No. 2, Sia benedetto il giorno che nascesti

1   Sia benedetto il giorno che nascesti
2   e l'ora e il punto che fusti creata!
3   Sia benedetto il latte che bevesti,
4   e il fonte dove fusti battezzata!
5   Sia benedetto il letto ove giacesti,
6   e la tua madre che t'ha nutricata!
7   Sia benedetta tu sempre da Dio!
8   Quando farai contento lo cor mio?

No. 2, Blessed be the day that you were born

1   Blessed be the day that you were born
2   and the hour and the moment that you were created!
3   Blessed be the milk that you drank,
4   and the font where you were baptized!
5   Blessed be the bed where you lay,
6   and your mother who nursed you!
7   May you always be blessed by God!
8   When will you make my heart happy?

No. 3, Io mi viveva senza nullo amore

1   Io mi viveva senza nullo amore,
2   non era donna a cui volesse bene.
3   Denanti a me paristi, o nobel fiore,
4   per dare alla mia vita amare pene;
5   e sì presto m'entrasti tu nel core
6   come saetta che dall'arco vene,
7   e com'entrasti io presto serrai
8   perchè null'altra donna c'entri mai!

No. 3, I used to live without any love

1   I used to live without any love,
2   there was no woman whom I loved.
3   Before me you appeared, o noble flower,

4   In order to give to my love bitter pain;
5   and so quickly you entered into my heart
6   like an arrow coming from the bow,
7   and as you entered I quickly closed up
8   so that no other woman could ever enter there!

No. 4, E vengote a veder, perla lizadra

1   E vengote a veder, perla lizadra,
2   e vengote a veder, caro tesoro;
3   non sa'tu ben che tu se' quella ladra
4   che m'hai ferito il cor tanto che moro?
5   Quando io passo per la to contrada
6   deh lassati vedere, o viso adorno!
7   Quel giorno che ti vedo non potria
8   aver voglia nessuna, anima mia!

No. 4, And I come to see you, lustrous pearl

1   And I come to see you, lustrous pearl,
2   and I come to see you, my dear darling;
3   do you not know well that you are that thief
4   who has wounded my heart so much that I am dying?
5   Whenever I pass through your street
6   pray let me see you, O beautiful face!
7   That day that I see you I could
8   have no other desire, my beloved!

A *strambotto* is a folk lyric of six or eight lines, usually on a satirical or amorous subject, each line of which consists of eleven syllables. *Strambo,* itself, means twisted, odd, unusual. As song texts *strambotti* and *frottole* preceded the madrigal and were considered less-elegant forms.

The *Quattro strambotti di Giustiniani* (Four *strambotti* by Justinian) are a rarity among the Italian *liriche da camera* in that the composer gives clear indications for them to be performed as a cycle. They are related in key but contrasting in mood and tempo, and each bears the direction to *segue* (lead) into the next. Even more unusual is the repetition of melodic material in the last song, creating a cyclical reference to the opening song. All four poems center on love—actually adoration of the love object; and the four divisions of the composition are not individually titled.

The first song begins with a piano introduction reminiscent of folk music on a mandolin. The vocal line enters in the second measure in an equally folk-like manner and rides above a repetition of the opening measure. The tempo indication ($\quarternote = 63$) may seem slow for *andante,* but the basic motion is in eighth notes, and a faster tempo would create a brittle sound in the accompaniment. As the verses progress alterations and transposition of the opening material increase, but no really new material is introduced. The phrase *Quando nascesti gli angioli ci venne* (when you were born the angels came) calls for a considerably slower tempo, but the original tempo must be regained for the last phrase. This song sets up the subject for the cycle, and it should be performed simply. There is no real phrase climax, and the loudest dynamic indications occur in the piano "postlude," which in reality is the introduction to the next song.

Marked *un poco agitato* (somewhat agitated), the second song has an attitude of wonder about it. Short, choppy phrases ride over irregular meters, and a little breathiness in the vocal color would help to create the mood. The stretch of the melodic line into longer note values for the final phrase creates a natural climax. The tempo here should be a little faster, and the change can be prepared in the movement of the eighth-note accompaniment beneath *Dio* (God.) Only a very slight holding back should occur on the final words, *cor mio* (my heart), but the final *fermata* in the accompaniment should be held until the singer can establish the mood for the next song.

The greatest intensity in the cycle occurs in the third song. Here the poet expresses his deepest, most passionate thoughts, and the setting matches them. It begins with solo voice, and the change of intensity from the previous song should be felt immediately in the color of the sound. Once the rhythmic movement shows a consistent forward direction and the accompaniment activity increases, beginning with *Denanti a me paristi* (Before me you appeared), a *crescendo* should build all the way through to the climax at *e com'entrasti io presto serrai* (and as you entered I quickly closed up). There can be some dynamic gradation within this passage, but the buildup should be long and steady. As if there were not enough, the composer writes an additional outburst of passion for the piano in the brief, brilliant passage leading to the final song.

A calm happiness concludes the cycle. The tempo seems slow ($\quarternote = 66$), but the rapid rhythmic movement actually sounds quite lively. The accompaniment has an instrumental charm (the fluttering grace notes are important), and the vocal line has a folk-like sound once more. Immediately after the phrase *o viso adorno* (O beautiful face) there is a slow, quiet reference to the opening song; it is repeated with variation in the following measures. The cycle concludes very optimistically with a light accompaniment figure and a bright G-major arpeggio. All indications for *rubati,* tempo changes, and expression are carefully indicated in the score.

Quattro strambotti di Giustiniani: Suvini Zerboni, 1947.   S. 4188 Z. (Set)
   1. *Se li arbor i sapesser favellare*
   2. *Sia benedetto il giorno che nascesti*

3. *Io mi viveva senza nullo amore*
4. *E vengote a veder, perla lizadra*

Tre Canti di Shelley

No. 1, Pellegrini del mondo

(*Trascrizione di Augusta Guidetti*)

1 Dimmi, o Stella, che sull'ali di luce
2 affretti l'infuocato volo,
3 in qual grotta notturna ripiegherai le penne?
4 Dimmi, o Luna pallida e grigia,
5 delle strade solinghe del Cielo pellegrina,
6 in quale abisso del giorno o della notte,
7 vai cercando riposo?
8 O stanco Vento, che vai vagabondando
9 come il reietto ospite del mondo,
10 hai forse ancora un tuo riposto nido
11 sull'albero o sull'onda?

Three songs by Shelley

No. 1, Pilgrims of the world

([*Italian*] *translation by Augusta Guidetti*)

1 Tell me, O Star, who on wings of light
2 You hasten your burning flight,
3 in what nocturnal grotto will you fold up your wings?
4 Tell me, O pale and gray Moon,
5 pilgrim of the solitary ways of the Heaven,
6 in what abyss of the day or the night,
7 are you going to seek repose?
8 O weary Wind, who goes wandering about
9 like a rejected guest of the world,
10 do you have perhaps yet your secret nest
11 in a tree or on a wave?

Ghedini's three songs based on poems by Percy Bysshe Shelley form an interesting program group. Each poem deals in some way with the mysteries of light, wind, and sky; and each song exhibits some aspect of the composer's interest in *ostinato*, or repetitive figures.

The poem *Pellegrini del mondo* (Pilgrims of the world) is divided into three sections, centering respectively on images of a star, the moon, and the wind. The musical setting is a three-part form in which a key change provides the essential contrast for the middle section. A repeated third, established in the first measure of the introduction, appears in *ostinato*-like variation throughout the entire song. Melodic interest is clearly in the vocal line, which is through-composed. Its first three measures are repeated in the left hand of the piano bridge before the key change and again in the postlude. This reference to the opening phrase is marked *espressivo* each time it appears, and the pianist should weight the melody more heavily than the *ostinato* against which it is played. Likewise, the initial melody itself must stand out from the accompaniment as it begins in measure 2, marked *pp e chiaro* (very soft and clear). The tempo, *molto lento e contemplativo* (very slow and contemplative), should be relentlessly regular so that the plodding chords can achieve their full effect. A slight holding back is indicated in the measure immediately before the key change, and a more exaggerated slowing down is called for immediately before the third section of the song. Since the final words concern the "weary Wind," more freedom in the tempo is permitted; in fact, the composer uses the direction *poco indugio* (a little delayed).

The texture of the composition becomes a little thicker with each verse. At first the repeated thirds are balanced only against a pedal base or the melodic fragment taken from the opening vocal line. In the second verse a line of quarter notes creates a sense of suspension against the *ostinato* thirds, and the accompaniment becomes quite active by the end of the section. When the original key returns, the thirds have been expanded to include another voice, and a pattern of alternating eighth notes appears in the left hand. Each of the three sections has its own climax, but the most forceful dynamic is saved until the piano postlude, by which time the repeated chords have become more dissonant and hollow. The final measures, ending on a single tone, should be allowed to vibrate with the pedal until they die away. From Ghedini's setting, the protagonist seems almost angry that he cannot fathom these natural mysteries.

No. 2, Vento rude

(*Trascrizione di Augusta Guidetti*)

1 Vento rude, che forte lamenti un dolore
2 troppo triste per il canto;
3 Vento selvaggio, ove ostinate nubi
4 suonano a morto per la notte intera;
5 mesta bufera, che piangi inutilmente,
6 e nudi boschi dai rami tormentati;
7 grotte profonde, ed alto mar tremendo
8 sul male del mondo fate lamento . . .

No. 2, Severe wind

([*Italian*] *translation by Augusta Guidetti*)

1   Severe wind, loudly you bewail your grief
2   too sad for singing;
3   Wild wind, where persistent clouds
4   toll for death throughout the entire night;
5   sad gale, you cry uselessly,
6   and bare woods with tormented branches;
7   deep grottos, and tremendous high sea
8   for the wickedness of the world make your lamentation.

In *Vento rude* (Severe wind) the piano introduction establishes the character of the poem immediately with a "wind" motive. As is Ghedini's fashion it is repeated throughout the song. In measure 11 the dynamic marking *pp* also carries the direction *confuso* (muddled, indistinct), which should apply to all appearances of this motive. The tempo, as directed by the composer, should be *agitato* but not rushed. The vocal line initially "speaks" the poem either above or between the repetitious "wind" motive. The emotional climax is achieved not by the loudest dynamic but by a stretching out of the vocal line and a simplification of the accompaniment in measures 24–28. The accented rising arpeggio leading to the *fortissimo* chord before *lamento* (lamentation) provides a striking contrast to the repetitious sixteenth-note pattern. The singer should observe the breath indication before *lamento* in order to create the correct stress on this important word, and the pianist must observe the *ff–p* dynamic on each repetition of the "wind" motive, which closes the song so effectively. The tempo should remain strict to the very last measure.

No. 3, Mentre azzurri splendono i cieli

(*Trascrizione di Augusta Guidetti*)

1   Mentre azzurri splendono i cieli,
2   mentre i fiori sono giocondi,
3   mentre gli occhi che mutano anzi sera
4   fanno contento il giorno;
5   mentre scorrono ore di pace, sogna . . .
6   e dal tuo sogno poi ridestati al pianto.

No. 3, While the heavens shine blue

([*Italian*] *translation by Augusta Guidetti*)

1 While the heavens shine blue,
2 while the flowers are gay,
3 while eyes that change before evening
4 make the day happy;
5 while peaceful hours roll by, dream . . .
6 and then from your dream reawaken to sorrow.

In *Mentre azzuri splendono i cieli* (While the heavens shine blue) the melodic line of the first four measures of the piano introduction becomes the *ostinato* motive for the entire song. After the introduction the vocal line repeats much of this opening melody, doubled by the treble line of the accompaniment. There is some variation as the line progresses but the original melody appears again in the upper voice of the accompaniment, with a Brahmsian phrase overlap in measure 12. The voice joins this melody in measure 13. A variation of the motive, in transposition, appears in measure 16, and yet another repetition of the motive occurs in the piano postlude. The composer's directions for expression are explicit throughout this short, but extremely clever song. Special attention should be given to the accented line of descending eighth notes in the accompaniment beneath the final words *al pianto* (to sorrow). Breathing places not indicated specifically by the composer can be determined easily by the phrase markings.

Tre canti di Shelley: Suvini Zerboni, 1947.   S. 4189 Z. (Set)
  1. *Pellegrini del mondo*
  2. *Vento rude*
  3. *Mentre azzurri splendono i cieli*

Tre liriche su testi di R. Bacchelli

No. 1, Presenze naturali

1 Percepire presenze naturali remote,
2 pur certe benchè sol immaginate:
3 Su vaste terre e immensità di mare aleggiare,
4 alitar primo di venti sul nascere;
5 Primo densar di gacie delle acque piovane
6 in grembo delle gravi nubi erratiche,

7   germogliare, gemmare, germogliare di semi
8   e gemme e di germogli;
9   anzi sentir da scaturigini più arcane
10 l'effondersi delle forze feconde e fecondanti,
11 tutto ciò, quasi attratto in un'eco di silenzio,
12 chiama ed illude a simboli e figure
13 lo stess'atto che le inventa e le anulla.
14 Per capire presenze naturali remote . . .

Three lyrics on texts by R. Bacchelli

No. 1, Natural presences

1   To perceive natural remote presences,
2   Very real although only imagined;
3   to hover over the vast earth and the immensity of the sea,
4   To breathe the first time the winds on becoming born;
5   the first condensation of the drops of rainwater
6   into the bosom of heavy erratic clouds,
7   to germinate, to bud, to germinate from seeds
8   and buds, and from sprouts;
9   in fact to feel from the more mysterious sources
10 the spreading forth of the fertile and fertilizing forces,
11 all this, almost brought about in an echo of silence,
12 it summons and deceives by symbols and figures
13 the same act that devises them and nullifies them.
14 In order to understand natural remote presences . . .

Tre liriche su testi di R. Bacchelli (Three lyrics on texts by Riccardo Bacchelli [b. 1891]) carry deep philosophical implications, and their very choice by Ghedini, toward the end of his life, indicates the composer's inward contemplation of nature, mankind, creativity, and death. These lean settings incorporate many of the signature devices of his earlier works and attempt to elucidate the broader meanings of the texts as well as depict specific imagery within them.

Presenze naturali (Natural presences) opens with a rising arpeggiated chord that stretches out over five measures to reach three octaves above a dissonant Db pedal bass. This arpeggio, marked *molto fuso* (very fused or melted), appears with variation throughout the first section of the song. The vocal line enters above it in speech rhythm staying within the chord tones but in a much narrower pitch range. The effect enhances a sense of wonderment as the poet contemplates the mysteries of nature with such expressions as *vaste terre* (vast earth) and *immensità di mare* (immensity of the sea). Although the dynamic level remains low, the increasingly active accompaniment and greater melodic range create excitement as the poem moves toward the imagery of "sprouting seeds" and reaches its first mini-climax at *scaturigini più arcane* (more mysterious sources). The sudden drop to *pp* on *arcane* should also carry a hushed tone quality. The shift to a triplet figure in the accompaniment provides the perfect device to describe the spreading out of the mysterious life force, which builds to its final climax at *le inventa e le annulla* (devises them and nullifies them). The *ff* dynamic must remain through the descending octaves and the *marcato* chords that complete the phrase beneath *annulla.* A slight break should precede the final nine measures of the song. Here the Db pedal bass from the opening measures of the composition has been transposed to C♯, four octaves higher in the treble, while the rising arpeggio, also transposed, is played beneath it. The voice again stays narrowly within the chord tones, and the atmosphere of wide-eyed wonder is re-created with the repetition of the poem's first line. The singer should observe carefully the many short rests scattered throughout this song even though they seem to interrupt the flow of the phrase. The composer's effect, and it is masterful, is one of thoughts so deep, so searching, that they come in spurts and are verbalized with difficulty.

No. 2, A un muover d'aria

1   A un muover d'aria, per la costa folta,
2   Di pini e palme e fiori e di cipressi,
3   All'azzurro del mar scende l'ulivo
4   Col suo brivido argenteo, e vi si perde.
5   Poco che volti il vento, torna vivo
6   Quel verde argento a salir
7   verso l'altro azzurro del ciel prossimo e profondo.
8   E l'alterna vicenda sulla sponda luminosa e piacente,
9   con le rose volutuose e col funebre cipresso
10 Par che narri la favola dell'uomo.

No. 2, By a movement of the air

1   By a movement of the air, along the dense shoreline,
2   With pines and palms and flowers and cypresses,
3   to the blue of the sea the olive grove descends
4   With its shivering silver, and there it loses itself.
5   You turn back the wind but a little, it again becomes alive
6   that silvery green as it climbs
7   toward the other blue of the sky near and deep.

8   And the alternate succession of the bright and pleasing shore,
9   with the voluptuous roses and with the gloomy cypress.
10 It seems that it may be narrating the story of mankind.

A un muover d'aria (By a movement of the air), with its faster tempo
($\quad$ = 138) and *fresco e leggero* (fresh and light) texture, provides a nice
contrast to the first and third songs of the set. The vocal line is paramount,
sung against a solitary repetitive E♮ octave in the accompaniment. The left
hand introduces a melody in measure 16 that duplicates the vocal line; it is
then echoed in measures 23–24. The point of the poem—contrasts in imagery
such as *rose volutuose* (voluptuous roses) and *funebre cipresso* (gloomy
cypress) in measures 57–62—gets lost in the texture of the song. The singer
needs to develop color contrasts to enhance the imagery. The climax of the
song, at *favola dell'uomo* (the story of mankind), needs no special treatment
other than the *crescendo* that is built into the ascending pitch of the vocal
line. The *crescendo* must continue, however, through the long, held final
syllable of *uomo* as the piano ascends. There is a faint resemblance here to
the ascending arpeggiated chords that underlie so much of the first song of
the set. The final climax carries the same *f* dynamic as an earlier phrase, *verso
l'altro azzuro del ciel* (toward the other blue of the sky), measures 35–40,
but it must be louder than the earlier phrase.

The *parlato* (spoken) phrases that open the song return with minor
variations to close it. The accompaniment, however, is now in alternating
minor seconds. After one brief interruption—again reminiscent of *Presenze
naturali*—the seconds broaden in note values and trail away. The composer
specifically directs that these final measures be *sempre in tempo* (always in
tempo).

No. 3, Ọ grande spirito

1   Ọ grande spirito, animo creativo,
2   Adesso che̮ ti vuoi ritrar da me̮
3   intendo ciò̮ che̮ è stato, al tempo mio,
4   quando immane̮vi in me̮ diuturno e̮ forte!
5   Così anzi l'alba e̮ dopo se̮ra danno
6   sulle montagne e̮ in mar se̮gno di vento
7   palpitando le̮ ste̮lle in alto cielo.

No. 3, O great spirit

1   O great spirit, creative soul,
2   Now that you wish to withdraw from me

3   I understand what has happened during my time,
4   when you dwelt within me long-lasting and strongly!
5   Thus in fact the dawn and afterwards evening give
6   on the mountains and in the sea a sign of the wind
7   palpitating the stars in the high heaven.

In *O grande spirito* (O great spirit) the poet's deep appreciation for the creative spirit that has filled his life is given an expansive, almost heroic treatment by the composer. The organ-like opening chords and bold vocal address require an even *f* dynamic and full voice through to the exciting ascending eighth-note scale (measures 12–14). When the accompaniment pattern changes in measure 19 its dynamic is reduced to *piano,* but the voice remains *forte* and *marcato.* This boldness of statement should continue until measure 35, where the intensity of the song backs away in anticipation of the forthcoming major climax. Incidentally, in this same measure, the E♮ octave, which was so prominent in the second song, makes another insistent appearance. The word-painting and doubled accompaniment on *vento* (wind, measures 45–46) and the alternating sixteenth notes on *palpitando* (palpitating, measure 47) help to build toward the climax on *cielo* (heaven)—the poet's comparison of personal creativity with the creativity of nature. The sweeping piano accompaniment beneath *cielo* continues beyond the singer's release and leads to a slower and even grander musical restatement of the title line, *O grande spirito* (O great spirit). When the second ending is taken after the repeat, the ascending eighth notes in the accompaniment move relentlessly in tempo to the very end, and the final five octaves should be played with a flourish. Textually and musically the song is a broad affirmation of the creative life, and it provides a fitting climax to the searching observations of the earlier songs. The musical cross-references in these three songs create a much stronger cyclical sense than exists in most sets of *liriche da camera;* they should definitely be programmed together.

Tre liriche su testi di R. Bacchelli: Carisch, S.P.A., 1964.
1. *Presenze naturali*	21674
2. *A un muover d'aria*	21675
3. *O grande spirito*	21676

Mario Castelnuovo-Tedesco

(1895–1968)

•

MARIO CASTELNUOVO-TEDESCO was born April 3, 1895 in Florence. His family had come to Tuscany more than 400 years earlier as part of a group of emigré Jews from the Spanish province of Castilla Nueva, from which the family name probably derives. The addition of Tedesco came through a family alliance only two generations before Mario's birth. In Italy the composer was often known just as "Castelnuovo."

Throughout his life Castelnuovo-Tedesco credited his musical talent to his mother's family and to his maternal grandfather in particular. In 1925, many years after the older man's death, the composer found a small book of manuscripts containing musical settings his grandfather had made of several Hebrew prayers. This discovery became a source of both musical and philosophical inspiration for Castelnuovo-Tedesco and stimulated him to compose music on Jewish themes.

At the instigation of his grandfather, Mario began to study piano in secret at the age of nine under his mother's tutelage. A year later, when he played two Chopin pieces and one of his own compositions for his father, Mario dispelled the wealthy banker's earlier disapproval of musical pursuits.

Castelnuovo-Tedesco undertook more formal training at the Cherubini Royal Institute of Music in Florence, studying piano under Edgardo del Valle de Paz, a cousin of his mother, and composition under Ildebrando Pizzetti. He achieved diplomas in these areas in 1914 and 1918 respectively. From the beginning he composed prolifically and showed exceptional gifts. He was influenced at first by Pizzetti and Ravel, but he was later able to forge a personal brand of Impressionism with unconventional harmonic and rhythmic methods. Castelnuovo-Tedesco was most successful in the smaller forms, such as his settings of Spanish and Tuscan folk texts, although his first work in a larger form, *Tre fioretti di San Francesco* for mezzo-soprano and piano or orchestra (1919–20), a setting of verses by Saint Francis of Assissi, was also his first Florentine composition to gain widespread recognition. His opera *La Mandragola* was awarded first prize in the Concorso Lirico Nazionale of 1925 and was produced in Venice on May 4, 1926. Still, the best music of the 1920s are Castelnuovo-Tedesco's songs, especially the *Thirty-three Shakespeare Songs*. In the mid-1920s his style moved away from Impressionism and toward neo-Romanticism, adhering to basic tonality, but allowing some unresolved dissonances and consecutive fifths.

On March 6, 1924 Castelnuovo-Tedesco married Clara Porti. They and their two sons lived in Florence until 1939, while Castelnuovo-Tedesco worked as a free-lance composer. Some of his recognition in Italy and abroad came about through the efforts of Alfredo Casella and the Società Italiana di Musica. American audiences were introduced to his music through the world premiere of *Symphonic Variations* for violin and orchestra played by the New York Philharmonic under Arturo Toscanini on April 9, 1930. Jascha Heifetz played Castelnuovo-Tedesco's *Concerto italiano* in New York in 1931 and the world premiere of his second violin concerto, *The Prophets* (based on Jewish themes), at a concert of the New York Philharmonic, Toscanini conducting, on April 12, 1933.

In 1939 the anti-Semitic activity in Fascist Italy caused Castelnuovo-Tedesco and his family to flee to the United States. He first took up residence in Larchmont, New York, and on November 2, 1939 he appeared as soloist in the first performance of his *Second Concerto for Piano and Orchestra,* with the New York Philharmonic, Sir John Barbirolli conducting.

In 1940 the family moved to Beverly Hills, California. In 1946 Castelnuovo-Tedesco became an American citizen, and in the same year he accepted a position as teacher of composition at the Los Angeles Conservatory, which he maintained until his death. In the 1940s to the mid-1950s he was active as a film composer, often working under a pseudonym, although he acknowledged the scores for René Clair's *And Then There Were None* (1945), *The Loves of Carmen* (1948), and *The Mask of the Avenger* (1951). He had a major influence on other film composers and counted among his students André Previn, Henry Mancini, and Jerry Goldsmith.

From the 1930s onward Castelnuovo-Tedesco showed little stylistic change in his music. He tended toward neo-Classicism, often tried unusual experimentation with instrumentation, and even took some isolated excursions into dodecaphony. Four major influences can be seen in his work:

First, he had a passion for Shakespeare, as seen in *Thirty-three Shakespeare Songs* and the opera *The Merchant of Venice*. The latter took first prize in a contest sponsored by La Scala and was premiered on May 25, 1961 at the Florence May Music Festival.

Second, he loved old Jewish music, as seen in the *Sacred Service for Sabbath* (1943), the biblical opera *Saul* (1958–60), and a series of biblical oratorios.

Third, he never lost his affection for the hills of Tuscany. He maintained an apartment in Florence, overlooking the Arno, to which he returned in the summers. Tuscan folk songs and folk poetry appear at various times in his compositions.

Fourth, his devotion to his adopted country is reflected in such works as *Larchmont Hills* (1942) and *An American Rhapsody* (1945).

Castelnuovo-Tedesco always composed in ink and never at the piano. A large portion of his very prolific output has never been published, and several larger works have never been performed. He died at Mount Sinai Hospital in Hollywood, California, on March 15, 1968, of a heart attack.

stelle cadenti

(*Poesie popolari toscane*)

I.
1 Oh! quanto siete pallida nel viso!
2 parete un fior garofano nel vaso,
3 parete un angiolin di paradiso—
II.
1 Fior d'erba secca.
2 Non c'è più pettirossi nella macchia,
3 non c'è più pettirossi: Addio, civetta!
III.
1 Mi vo' far fare una casina in piazza
2 per sentir l'oriolo quando tocca,
3 per veder l'amor mio quando ci passa—
IV.
1 M'affaccio alla finestra e vedo l'onde,
2 e vedo le miserie che son grande,
3 e chiamo l'amor mio che non risponde!
V.
1 Fiorin di pepe.
2 Tutte le fontanelle son seccate.
3 Povero amore mio! muore di sete.
VI.
1 Sono stata all'appalto a pigliar sale,
2 e m'hanno detto "Con chi fai all'amore?"
3 e gli ho risposto: "Fo con chi mi pare!"
VII.
1 Fiorin d'alloro.
2 E per marito voglio un campanaro,
3 che mi suoni un bel doppio quando moro.
VIII.
1 Vado di notte come va la luna,
2 vado cercando lo mio innamorato;
3 e ritrovai la morte acerba e dura;
4 mi disse—"Non cercar: l'ho sotterrato!"

IX.

1 Oh! come fa la donna contadina,
2 quando la vede l'amante passare?
3 La va sull'uscio, e chiama la gallina,
4 finchè l'amante si viene a voltare—
5 Quando l'amante poi s'è rivoltato
6 "Sciò, sciò, gallina! che non t'ho chiamato."

  X.

1 Sono stato all'inferno, e son tornato:
2 (Misericordia! la gente che c'era!)
3 V'era una stanza tutta alluminata,
4 e dentro v'era la speranza mia.
5 Quando mi vedde, gran festa mi fece,
6 e poi mi disse "Dolce anima mia!
7 Non ti ricordi più di quella volta
8 ch'eramo innamorati tutti e dui?
9 Non ti ricordi più di que' bei giorni?
10 Tempo passato, perchè non ritorni?"

 XI.

1 Ho visto la Sirena in mezzo al mare;
2 sur uno scoglio gran pianto faceva:
3 i pesci gli faceva addolorare
4 dalle triste parole che diceva:
5 E disse, "Figlio non t'innamorare!
6 Chi s'innamora soffre una gran pena,
7 chi s'innamora, in una fiamma ardente,
8 fa cento morti il giorno e vive sempre!"
9 Ho visto tanti pesci stare in pianto . . .
10 Pensa: che farò io, che t'amo tanto!

XII.

1 Quando, bellino, al cielo salirai,
2 ti verrò incontro con il cuore in mano:
3 tu pien d'amore al sen m'abbraccerai
4 ed io ti menerò dal gran Soprano.
5 Il Soprano, veduto il nostro amore,
6 farà dei cuori innamorati un cuore;
7 un cuore solo farà di due cuori,
8 in Paradiso, in mezzo alli splendori!

Shooting stars

(*Popular Tuscan poetry*)

 I.

1 Oh! How pale your face is!
2 You seem a carnation flower in a vase,
3 you seem a little angel in paradise—

II.

1   Flower of dry grass.
2   There are no more robins in the bushes,
3   there are no more robins: Good-bye, little owl!

III.

1   I want to have made for myself a little house in the square
2   in order to hear the oriole when it sings,
3   in order to see my love when he passes there—

IV.

1   I look out the window and I see the waves,
2   and I see the misfortunes that are great,
3   and I call to my love who does not respond!

V.

1   Little flower of pepper.
2   All the fountains are dry.
3   My poor love! He is dying of thirst.

VI.

1   I was at the tobacconist's shop to get some salt,
2   and they said to me, "With whom do you make love?"
3   and I replied to them, "I make [love] with whomever I like!"

VII.

1   Little flower of laurel.
2   And for a husband I want a bell ringer,
3   who might play for me twice as long when I die.

VIII.

1   I go at night as goes the moon,
2   I go seeking my beloved;
3   and I find again death austere and harsh;
4   he said to me—"Seek not: I have buried him!"

IX.

1   Oh! What does the countrywoman do,
2   when she sees her lover passing by?
3   She goes to the door, and calls the hen,
4   until the lover begins to look back—
5   When the lover then has turned back
6   "Shoo, shoo, hen! I did not call you."

X.

1   I was in hell, and I returned:
2   (Mercy! The people that were there!)
3   There was a room all illuminated,
4   and within there was my hope.
5   When he saw me, he welcomed me with joy,
6   and then he said to me, "My sweet love!
7   Do you no longer remember that time
8   that we were in love with each other?

9 Do you no longer remember those beautiful days?
10 Time passed, why do you not return?"
   XI.
1 I saw the mermaid in the middle of the sea;
2 on a rock she was weeping loudly:
3 she was making the fish grieve
4 by the sad words that she was saying:
5 And she said, "Son, don't fall in love!
6 Whoever falls in love suffers great pain,
7 whoever falls in love, in a burning flame,
8 dies a hundred times a day and lives still!"
9 I saw so many fish who were weeping . . .
10 Think (of it): What will I do, since I love you so much!
   XII.
1 When, pretty one, you go up to heaven,
2 I will meet you with my heart in hand:
3 you, full of love, will embrace me to your breast
4 and I will lead you to the great Sovereign.
5 The Sovereign, on seeing our love,
6 will make of the hearts in love one heart;
7 one heart alone he will make of two hearts,
8 in Paradise, in the midst of the splendor!

stelle cadenti (Shooting stars), settings of twelve relatively short folk poems from the Italian province of Tuscany, were composed between 1915 and 1918 and published in 1919. They may be performed as a set, or selections may be made to form a program group. They are not linked as a conventional song cycle, but they share the composer's practice of developing a central musical device for each poem and their keys are logically related. The songs in the latter part of the set are longer than those at the beginning. The poems range from simple observations of nature to philosophical musings on life, death, and the afterlife. As the set progresses images move from earthly toward heavenly.

No. 1, *Oh! quanto siete pallida* (Oh! How pale your face is) opens with a "pallid" pattern of four sixteenth notes that alternate a minor second apart and then fall to a major third. The expression marking is *tranquillo,* the dynamic *pp senza sfumature* (very quiet, without nuance), and both sustaining and soft pedals are required. The pattern becomes the central motive of the song by reappearing at several points in the accompaniment, and with slight variation it sets the opening *Oh!* and closing *Paradiso* (Paradise) of the vocal line. The single-line treble melody in the last four measures of the accompaniment is a transposed echo of the first complete vocal phrase, and a final statement of the sixteenth-note motive appears beneath it in the penultimate measure. The song is a concise atmospheric setting of a simple poem.

No. 2, *Fior d'erba secca* (Flower of dry grass), depends on clean articulation for its interpretation. Taking its character from the word *secca* (dry),
the accompaniment consists of octaves and a superimposed pattern of triplets
marked *pizzicato* (plucked) and *staccato con spirito* (detached, with spirit).
The tempo must not be too fast, and the song should have an *ironico* (ironic)
character. The vocal phrases are short and should deliver the text in a dry,
matter-of-fact manner. The biggest accent occurs on the final word, *civetta*
(little owl), and on the three supporting chords in the accompaniment, which
are marked *strappate* (torn, jerked). The short piano postlude begins *forte
con brio* (loud with vivacity), but a *subito piano* occurs just before the final
three chords, which must be *leggerissimo* (as light as possible). The irregular
meters in this song also help to define its character; the basic pulse should
be kept constant to maximize the effect.

No. 3, *Mi vo' far fare una casina* (I want to have made for myself a little
house), carries an unusual expression mark, *spensieratamente* (carefree,
thoughtlessly). The lazy 6/8 meter, in which thirds and fourths alternate
above a ground bass with vague polytonal qualities, captures the whimsical
mood of the poem. The first phrase of the vocal line simply doubles the
upper notes of the accompaniment. A change of character takes place for the
second line of poetry: both the accompaniment and the vocal line seem to
imitate the sound of the oriole, and this motive is used to set the words
l'amor mio (my love), perhaps as an intended comparison. The repetition
of *l'amor mio* calls for a slight slowing down, but the remainder of the final
vocal line should return to the initial tempo.

No. 4, *M'affaccio alla finestra* (I look out the window), is the first somber
song of the set. The starkness of the emotional seascape is captured in the
opening measure by the wide spacing of the first chord and the contrary
motion between the treble and bass clefs. This wavelike pattern is enhanced
by the rise and fall within the sextuplet rhythmic figure in the treble. The
quarter notes in the upper line of the bass clef bear important *tenuto* accents,
indicating the necessary emergence of this line within the texture. The prin-
ciple of contrary motion remains important throughout the composition. In
measure 4, the vocal line takes on the falling sextuplet figure while the
accompaniment surges upward with an arpeggio of 32d notes. These effects
of ebb and flow are most evocative but remain at a very soft dynamic level.
The drama builds at the words *e chiamo* (and I call); again there are widely
spaced chords, and the sextuplet pattern appears in octaves. The vocal line
reaches a full climax at *l'amor mio* (my love) as the pitch rises to the highest
level yet reached in the entire song set. Here and in the remaining three
measures considerable dexterity is required to bring out the important inner
voicings of the piano part while maintaining the wide keyboard spacing. The
intensity of the last vocal phrase is indicated by the direction *soffocato*
(smothered, choked), and the song ends with the same quiet dynamic with
which it began. The rests in the vocal line should enable the singer to make
each phrase on a single breath, except for *e vedo le miserie che son grande*

(and I see the misfortunes that are great), which could be broken briefly after *e vedo*. When performing the songs as a set, a slightly longer pause might be needed before No. 4 to make the transition to the bleakness of the mood.

No. 5, *Fiorin di pepe* (Flower of pepper), uses a popular Tuscan lyric that was also set by Vincenzo Davico. Castelnuovo-Tedesco's setting is a gem of economy, capturing the sub-text of the poem; that is, the heat of love may create a thirst, but the fountains that quench it could be dry. The main musical theme does not appear until the second, and most important, line of poetry, beginning in measure 7. The two-measure piano introduction and the opening phrase of the voice part are anticipatory, made up of fragments of the theme to come. With the direction *tranquillo con semplicità* (tranquil with simplicity) and the irregular 5/8 meter, the light-textured theme captures the wistful regret implied in the poetry. The *staccato* articulation is very important in the piano part, as is the duplet phrasing of the sixteenth notes. In measure 9 there is a crucial rest on the sixth beat; this hesitation points up the meaning of *seccate* (dry) and prepares the new *lento* tempo for the most emotional line of the poem. The accompaniment beneath the words *muore di sete* (He is dying of thirst) should be played very *legato* as a contrast to the rest of the piano part; however, the last measure of the composition returns to *staccato* articulation.

No. 6, *Sono stata all'appalto* (I was at the tobacconist's shop) is a *scherzo*. There are two elements in the accompaniment; a pattern of alternating fifths and fourths in a steady progression of *staccato* eighth notes, which act as a type of *ostinato;* and a nimble pattern of dotted-sixteenth and 32d notes, which skip above the *ostinato*. Once the whimsical mood is established in the introduction, the vocal line needs only to convey the story as it builds to the indignant reply. Here, as in No. 5, the articulation is very important. The tone color established by the pianist in the introduction should indicate the humorous nature of the poem. The tempo is marked *con spirito, ma non troppo mosso* (with spirit, but not too much motion). The vocal color can afford to be a bit raucous, particularly at the phrase *Fo con chi mi pare!* (I make [love] with whomever I like!). Here, the first four sixteenth notes, marked *declamato* (declaimed, spoken), should be held back, but the *a tempo* should return at *pare* (I like). The entire last page of the song is for piano. It begins very loud, *quasi martellate* (rather hammered), with heavy accents on the alternating eighth notes. The pattern eventually becomes softer and *staccato* and fades away, *lontano* (distant). This charming song is a fitting mid-point for the set.

No. 7, *Fiorin d'alloro* (Little flower of laurel), begins with the direction *oscillando tranquillamente* (swinging peacefully). It has a soft but insistent triplet pattern of two sixteenth notes and a quarter note. The "bells" appear for the first time on the off beats of measure 2 and should be accented with the left hand. Despite the leanness of the introduction, there is an urgency about it that leads to the *squillante* (shrill) vocal entrance in measure 3. This should be made a real "cry," with the dynamic crest on the first syllable of *campanaro* (bell ringer). The dynamic rise and fall in the accompaniment should be phrased to give maximum support to the singer. Beginning with the fourth beat of measure 7, a melodic line emerges in the treble of the accompaniment, and it is repeated in measures 9–11. It, too, must be subservient to the vocal line, whose words at this point convey the real anguish of the poem.

A slight break in the vocal line before *quando moro* (when I die) will enhance the phrase and permit the designated *messa di voce* on the first syllable of *moro*. The bell-like octaves in the piano postlude should be crisp and *chiaro* (clear). The final arpeggios in the bass should not outweigh the higher treble octaves.

No. 8, *Vado di notte* (I go at night), brings a jarring, somber contrast to the gentler song that precedes it. The tempo is *largo quasi immobile* (slow, almost motionless), and the two-octave separation of the hands in the funereal opening measures establishes the contrast quickly. In this pattern, with its dotted rhythm, the sixteenth note should be played very short but not *staccato*. Marked *pp* and *senza colore* (without color), the opening bars must sound like an ominous distant death dirge. The voice enters *come di lontano* (as if in the distance), and the vocal quality should be hushed, also with little color. The shift of the accompaniment to the treble should minimize the need for vocal projection.

At the phrase *e ritrovai la morte* (and I find again death) a "lament" appears in contrary motion in the treble of the accompaniment; it is then imitated in an overlapping phrase one octave lower. Equal weight is required in the balance between voice and piano at this place for the effect to be realized. In the four-measure piano interlude before the final vocal phrase, the descending pattern of sixteenth notes in the bass clef should be articulated cleanly, for they anticipate the forthcoming section. The treble of the accompaniment returns here to the dotted pattern of the opening measures and should be similarly crisp.

The last poetic line, the devastating *mi disse—"Non cercar: l'ho sotterrato!"* (He [death] said to me—"Seek not: I have buried him!"), requires a slightly slower tempo and a very deliberate delivery, with a special emphasis on the final pattern of descending sixteenth notes (which was anticipated earlier in the interlude). The composer cleverly imitates this pattern immediately in the accompaniment and then varies it with a disjointed triplet pattern, creating a chilling effect, marked *stringendo* (compressed, quickening the tempo). In the final measures of the accompaniment the dirge returns *a tempo* and fades out as if passing into the distance.

The rugged humor of No. 9, *Oh! come fa la donna contadina* (Oh! What does the countrywoman do), should be established in the angular *staccato* chords and the irregular rhythm of the one-measure piano introduction. The next to the last chord should be clipped and the final chord strongly accented. This chord carries over under the entrance of the voice, whose high G clashes with the prevailing A-minor tonality. Short chords marked *secche* (dry) continue to propel the accompaniment. The vocal line begins as a shout and is followed by the crisp articulation of a series of eighth notes that set the title line. This line and the phrase to which it connects should be almost spoken. At the end of the line—at the word *passare* (passing by)—two slurred piano figurations point up the questioning aspect of the text. They act almost as an audible "shoulder shrug." A little break should occur before the *a tempo* begins in measure 6. The turning back of the lover (measure 10) requires a slightly slower tempo and a sweeter tone color. In measure 12 there is a return to *a tempo* and very *staccato* articulation.

The arpeggio in measure 13 can be stretched a bit as the voice swells on the word *Quando* (When). In measure 15 the chords should be very crisp, and the words *Sciò, sciò* (Shoo, shoo) should be spoken on the indicated pitches. A slight *ritardando* is required for the last vocal phrase, but the short piano postlude should return to the initial tempo *con spirito* (with spirit).

No. 10, *Sono stato all'inferno* (I was in hell), marks a distinct change of character in the *stelle cadenti*. The poem is much longer than the earlier poems, and the subject, while still expressed in folk-like images, is more philosophical and abstract. The musical language is also more Impressionistic than in the earlier songs.

The opening accompaniment pattern, with its atmospheric triplet figures in the treble and contrary motion below, sets the mood for the composition. The composer warns that the tempo, while not fast, must be *ben ritmato* (at a good pace). The rising inner-voice figure should not be buried in the texture; and when it appears in the treble (first notes of the piano part in measure 4), it should be accented as marked. This figure, which anticipates the word *Misericordia!* (Mercy!), then sets the word in the vocal line. It is obviously important to the composer and represents to some extent the awe that the protagonist feels at what he has seen. The figure is a clever contrast to the otherwise trancelike state induced by the ethereal triplet figures. Interestingly, every vocal phrase in the composition, with the exception of the last, begins with an upward pitch movement somewhat similar to that which sets *Misericordia*.

The poem is problematic; perhaps ascribing specific emotional states to the two contrasting thematic ideas is too speculative, but pointing up these contrasts, which appear so frequently in the work, creates an alternation of musical moods appropriate to the poem.

No. 11, *Ho visto la Sirena* (I saw the mermaid), is folk poetry at its best. Sincere human emotions are fantasized and expressed through the reactions of common, but nonhuman, creatures. To give a sense of place, the composer begins with widely spaced, rolled chords in a broad triple meter. His direction *col movimento largo di un'ondata tranquilla* (with the broad movement of a peaceful wave) sets the mood. The quintuplet pattern of eighth notes, which appears in measure 2 and thereafter, could, with some stretch of the imagination, represent the flick of white foam on that wave. The pattern is used later in the vocal line itself. Throughout the first section of the song the piano continues to develop the "sea sounds" of the first two measures, often with subtle interesting effects. In measures 4, 5, and 6 a pattern of descending *tenuto* quarter notes appears in the lower line of the treble clef; it modifies and appears again in the *staccato* eighth notes of measures 7, 8, and 9.

The second principal section of the song begins with the mermaid's speech in measure 12. The meter change to 2/2 is only part of the heightened emotional content of the section. Again the inner-voice line of the piano part is important; it adds immediately to the excitement and appears transposed to the treble with full chords by measure 19. The juxtaposition of these full, rolled chords with the quintuplet pattern from the first section creates an excellent support for the soaring vocal line, which reaches a climax in measure 23 at *fa cento morti il giorni* (dies a hundred times a day). The vocal line rides the "crest of the wave." The melodic motive that sets these words,

also sets *e vive sempre* (and lives still). It then appears transposed as an echo in the piano part in the interlude before the final phrases and in the accompaniment pattern beneath them.

There are balance problems in this song in that the piano often has widely spaced chords when the voice is in mid-range. The vocal line is quite melodic, and there are no breathing problems to require compensation in the extension of the phrases. If some of the subtle motivic relationships alluded to earlier can be clarified in performance, this song can be emotionally intense and musically satisfying.

No. 12, *Quando, bellino, al cielo salirai* (When, pretty one, you go up to heaven), while not without its own internal force, provides a fitting "celestial" conclusion to this set of songs, whose collective title relates to heaven. The song carries the initial direction *serenamente—non troppo mosso* (serenely, not too much motion), and the rocking 12/8 meter contributes to its gentle flow. The long piano introduction is marked *chiaro e dolce* (clear and sweet), and an impression of a clear, broad expanse of sky continues beneath the lyrical vocal line. Inner-voice movements in the piano part are again given *tenuto* indications, as they were in earlier songs in this set, but they are less important here and do not show up with any significant motivic importance later. The most important theme appears in the first three measures of the composition, and it remains, repeated in original form and with variation, the central organizing musical device of the song. The voice line builds to a mild climax at the final phrase *in Paradiso, in mezzo alli splendori* (in Paradise, in the midst of the splendor), but the piano continues to increase this climactic feeling in the long postlude. Carrying the implications of the word *splendori*, broad chords and a *largo* tempo make a final statement of the theme before the song ends with the *luminoso* (luminous) texture of the last two measures. In character, if not in thematic reference, the final page sums up much of the profundity and sincerity of the emotions expressed in the preceding songs.

stelle cadenti: A. Forlivesi, 1919.   10751

L'Infinito

(*Giàcomo Leopardi*)

1   Sempre caro mi fu quest'ermo colle,
2   e questa siepe, che da tanta parte
3   dell'ultimo orizzonte il guardo esclude.
4   Ma sedendo e mirando, interminati
5   spazi di là da quella, e sovrumani
6   silenzi, e profondissima quiete
7   io nel pensier mi fingo; ove per poco
8   il cor non si spaura. —E come il vento
9   odo stormir tra queste piante, io quello
10 infinito silenzio a questa voce
11 vo comparando: e mi sovvien l'eterno,
12 e le morte stagioni, e la presente
13 e viva, e il suon di lei. Così tra questa
14 immensità s'annega il pensier mio,
15 e il naufragar m'è dolce in questo mare.

Infinity

1   Always dear to me was this solitary hill,
2   and this hedge, which so many parts
3   of the farthest horizon excludes from view.
4   But sitting and gazing, endless
5   spaces over there by that hedge, and superhuman
6   silences, and profoundest quiet
7   I in thought imagine; where for a short time
8   the heart is not afraid. —And like the wind
9   (that) I hear rustling among these trees, I that
10 infinite silence to this voice
11 compare: and the eternal helps me,

12 and the dead seasons, and the one present
13 and alive, and the sound of it. Thus amid this
14 immensity my thought drowns,
15 and the shipwreck to me is sweet in this sea.

There is a solid, majestic quality to the opening bars of *L'infinito* (Infinity). The tempo is *lentissimo* (very slow) and *calmo e contemplativo* (calm and contemplative), and the tonality centers on C major. Even though the rhythm patterns are to be played *dolce e legato* (sweet and smooth), they propel the line with processional precision. The opening measures are the composer's basic theme, on which the rest of the composition is organized.

Some slight increase in tempo is called for at the entrance of the voice, but the atmosphere of calm and grandeur, established at the opening, should be maintained. The texture of the accompaniment thins as the singer describes the hill and the limitless horizon, but the opening theme (transposed to the dominant) appears immediately at the end of the poetic line.

The second section proceeds much as the first, the theme appearing under the last phrase of the text as well as in the measure of interlude preceding the third section of the song. Measure 13 requires a little more color from the singer. The accompaniment is a simple sustained chord that decreases dynamically as the singer creates the mood of "profound quiet." The second repetition of the central theme (measure 15) carries the direction *lontano* (distant).

The composer indulges in some tone-painting as the last section of the song begins, in measure 16. A trill starting at the word *vento* (wind) continues through the next seven measures with the warning *appena sensibile il trillo* (hardly noticeable, the trill). Thereafter, a general increase in activity—rhythmic, harmonic, and textural—leads to the conclusion of the song. There is some heightening of emotion in the final lines of poetry, but the composer is careful to keep the dynamic level subdued. The central theme of the composition—fragmented and in its entirety—weaves under and between the short vocal phrases. (The alternate C given for the last note of the voice part could be raised one octave to be more in keeping with the required *pp dolcissimo* dynamic marking.) The last statement of the central theme in the piano part carries the marking *estatico* (ecstatic, enraptured).

L'infinito: A. Forlivesi, 1921; Repr. 1933.   10906

La barba bianca

(*Luigi Bertelli*)

1   —"Babbino mio, vorrei saper perchè
2   tu hai la barba bianca . . ."—"Eh! figlio mio,

3   perchè ho parecchi annetti più di te"
4   —"Ma quando avrò parecchi annetti anch' io,
5   avrò pur io la barba bianca?"—"Sì,
6   ma allor la mia t'avrà già detto addio"
7   —"Perchè, babbo?" —"Perchè . . . perchè è così,
8   e il perchè sia così niun può sapere.
9   Le barbe bianche hanno brevi i lor dì."
10 "Forse verrà a tagliartela il barbiere?"
11 —"Sì, un che falcia barbe a tutte l'ore
12 e insapona le faccie ch'è un piacere . . ."
13 —"E te la spruzzerà l'acqua d'odore?"
14 —"No, ma sapendo che l'odor mi garba,
15 tu, figliuol mio, mi darai spesso un fiore . . .
16 Baciami intanto . . . e lascia star la barba."

The white beard

1   "My daddy, I would like to know why
2   you have a white beard . . ."—"Eh, my son,
3   because I am several years older than you"
4   —"But when I am several years older also,
5   will I too have a white beard?"—"Yes;
6   but by then my own will have already said goodbye to you."
7   —"Why, daddy?"—"Because . . . because it is so,
8   and why it is so no one can know.
9   White beards have their brief days."
10 —"Perhaps the barber will come to cut it?"
11 —"Yes, one who cuts off beards at all hours (of the day)
12 and lathers faces because it is a pleasure . . ."
13 —"And will he sprinkle you with perfumed water?"
14 —"No, but knowing that perfume pleases me,
15 you, my little son, will give me often a flower . . .
16 Kiss me meanwhile . . . and leave my beard alone."

La barba bianca (The white beard) is a perfect example of Castelnuovo-
Tedesco's natural facility for setting simple, unpretentious poetry. His eco-
nomical harmonic language and uncomplicated structure reduce the senti-
mentality of the poem and produce a warm, affecting song. The tempo marking *allegretto tranquillo* (cheerful, tranquil) and the direction *semplicemente*
(simply) indicate the style of interpretation. The principal structural device
of the song is the melody of the opening vocal line:

After its initial statement, this melody appears twice more in the vocal line (once in transposition) and several times thereafter in the accompaniment, fragmented and in transposition. It ties together the increasingly conversational style of vocal writing as the composition progresses. The song is basically a conversation between father and son, and some contrast is needed to differentiate their respective lines. However, changes of vocal color seem overly dramatic for the simple, touching sentiment of the text. Instead, the singer should realize that the child's statements are innocent, direct questions, while the father's are reflective responses, seen in the larger context of life. If the singer can project this understanding, sufficient contrast—and the essence of the song—will be realized.

The composer offers several clues to his intentions. For example, the father's response as to why beards die (measure 16) is marked *gravemente* (gravely) with the tempo *un poco più lento* (a little slower); the child's question about the barber is marked *giocoso* (playful) and again carries a change of tempo (measures 20–21). There are many such directions throughout the work.

Whenever the original melodic theme appears it should be brought out from the overall texture of the composition. This is particularly important beginning in measure 30, where the theme is stated in the upper voice of the bass-clef line of the accompaniment. The composer marks it *intenso* (intense). The canonic imitation between voice and piano in measure 34 also merits attention, as does the final statement, which begins in measure 37. Each appearance of the theme is given an expression marking and an indication for keyboard articulation; these must be followed.

La barba bianca is a charming song and would make an excellent encore.

La barba bianca: A. Forlivesi, 1924.   11018

Due preghiere per i bimbi d'Italia

No. 1, Preghiera del mattino

(*Luigi Bertelli*)

1 O Dio, che ti riveli
2 nel sole alto dei cieli
3 che annunzia il nuovo dì,
4 fa' che del sol la fiamma
5 scaldi il babbo e la mamma
6 per cent'anni così!
7 Fa' ch'io sia sempre buono

8   e dammi il tuo perdono
9   s'io cada in qualche error;
10 fa' che nel mondo ov'io
11 debbo vivere, o Dio,
12 sien tutti buoni ognor.

Two prayers for the children of Italy

No. 1, Morning prayer

1   O God, you reveal yourself
2   in the sun high in the heavens
3   that heralds the new day,
4   make the flame of the sun
5   warm my daddy and my mamma
6   for a hundred years thus!
7   Make me always be good
8   and give me your pardon
9   if I fall in some error;
10 make in the world where I
11 must live, O God,
12 everyone be good always.

No. 2, Preghiera della sera

(*Luigi Bertelli*)

1   Dio, nella tenebra
2   che il mondo oscura
3   non ha paura
4   chi in cuore ha fè'.
5   In Te quest'anima
6   s'affida e crede,
7   nel cuor che ha fede
8   timor non è;
9   e pria di chiudere
10 nel sonno gli occhi
11 piego i ginocchi
12 dinanzi a Te.

No. 2, Evening prayer

1   God, in the darkness
2   that obscures the world

3   he is not afraid
4   who has faith in his heart.
5   In Thee this soul
6   trusts and believes,
7   he who in his heart has faith
8   has no fear;
9   and before closing
10 my eyes in sleep
11 I bend my knees
12 before Thee.

Due preghiere per i bimbi d'Italia (Two prayers for the children of Italy), written at Easter 1923, should be performed as a set. The texts represent two aspects of a common petition: protection and guidance in day and night. The two songs are related in key, mood, and melodic motives.

Preghiera del mattino (Morning prayer) is marked *lento ed estatico* (slow and enraptured). Since the phrases are short, a tempo of approximately ♩ = 44 would create the appropriate mood while still permitting the forward flow of the text. The vocal line, although fairly narrow in range and speechlike in rhythm, carries most of the musical interest and is quite melodic. The accompaniment provides a harmonic underpinning, centering around A minor (or Aeolian modality) with excursions to F♯ minor and a final cadencing in A major. The composer directs that each chord change have a separate pedaling, except where marked differently. He also indicates that the tone quality of the piano be sweet and clear.

The singer's approach to the work should be simple and direct, stressing the most important words, such as *Dio* (God), which are usually marked *tenuto*. The falling sixteenth-note pattern, which appears in several phrases in the first half of the song, has a Sephardic, folk-like cast and a special exhilarating effect. Care should be taken to keep the vowel pure through this figure.

The second half of the prayer, beginning with *Fa' ch'io sia sempre buono* (Make me always be good), is a little more active than the first. The inner-voice line of the accompaniment beneath this phrase (derived from the chord pattern of the preceding measures) is marked *p ma in rilievo—quasi tromba* (quiet, but in relief—almost like a trumpet). The song builds to the final phrase, *fa' che nel mondo ov'io/debbo vivere, O Dio,/sien tutti buoni ognor* (make in the world where I/must live, O God,/everyone be good always). The direction here is *con intenso fervore* (with intense fervor). The descending octaves in the third from the last measure should be played simultaneously with the held chords, and the "trumpet figure" in the last measure should be heard but not forced. The shifting meters should prove no problem in the song since they simply expedite the flow of the speechlike rhythm.

Preghiera della sera (Evening prayer) has a slightly darker quality and could take a slightly slower tempo. The composer directs *dolce e grave—con raccoglimento* (sweet and grave, with recollection). The whole song is constructed over a ground bass A, for which the composer indicates *quasi timpani* (almost like kettledrums). The vocal line, as in the first song, is prominent, and the deceptively simple accompaniment is very interesting. The result is a very well integrated composition. The opening vocal line, chantlike and narrow in range, is supported by a series of parallel chords built on an ascending scale in Hypophrygian mode. While the voice holds its final note, there appears an accompaniment figure marked *dolce e in relievo quasi trombe lontane* (sweet, in relief, like distant trumpets), which is similar to the trumpet figure in *Preghiera del mattino*. The song builds to the final phrase of text, *e pria di chiudere/nel sonno gli occhi/piego i ginocchi/dinanzi a Te* (and before closing in sleep my eyes, I kneel before Thee), but the dynamic level, even though it is marked *più intenso* (more intense), should not go above *mezzo forte*. The last half of the phrase is repeated with a change of rhythm over a series of seventh chords that ultimately resolve to A major. The expression marking is *dolce devotamente* (sweet, devoutly). A vocalise, derived from the trumpet figure in the accompaniment, is sung in canonic imitation with the figure to complete the song. The singer's final note should be allowed to die away, and the final piano chord—a polytonal F$\sharp$ chord (minus the third) over an A-major chord (minus the third)—should *lascia vibrare* (be allowed to vibrate) until it vanishes.

The key to performing both songs is utmost simplicity and a complete lack of affectation.

Due preghiere per i bimbi d'Italia: A. Forlivesi, 1925.   11258 (Set)
   1. *Preghiera del mattino*
   2. *Preghiera della sera*

Sera

(*Dante,* Purgatorio, *Canto VIII°*)

1 Era già l'ora che volge il desìo
2 ai navigante e intenerisce il core
3 lo dì che han detto ai dolci amici addìo,
4 e che lo novo peregrin d'amore
5 punge, s'ode squilla di lontano
6 che paia il giorno pianger che si muore.

Evening

(*Dante,* Purgatory, *Canto VIII*)

1 It was now the hour that turns back the desire
2 of the sailors and softens the heart

3   the day they have said goodbye to their dear friends,
4   and the new pilgrim by love
5   is pricked when he has heard the bell in the distance
6   that seems to cry for the day that is dying.

An atmosphere of reflective quiet permeates the hollow, open chords that introduce *Sera* (Evening). The tempo is *largo, quasi immobile* (slow, almost motionless), and the dynamic level is *p dolce*. The chords should be totally connected through absolute *legato* in the attack and by the use of both sustaining and soft pedals. (Every pedal change in the work is specifically indicated by the composer.) Middle C, which enters after the principal beats of each measure and acts as a "ground," should be given light stress, as the *tenuto* indications show. The opening chord pattern (bells?) is the central organizing device for the song. The ascent first to A♭ and then to A♮ is repeated, interrupted briefly, and then appears on the second page of the song an octave higher. It returns yet a fourth time, as originally stated, to form a two-measure postlude.

The vocal line is totally integrated into the composition, usually doubling one of the chord tones of the underlying accompaniment. The speech rhythms are never distorted, but the composer does modify them to create a broader, arched phrase appropriate to the mood of the poem.

A very slight holding back of the tempo is required at the crucial phrase *s'ode squilla di lontano* (he has heard the bell in the distance), and the song should proceed from there to a quiet conclusion. There is an important *sf* on the very last note, which must not be missed. In thirteen measures the composer has totally captured the special qualities of the close of day. A recollection of that quality should provide both singer and pianist with the proper interpretive approach to the song.

Sera: Curci, 1927.   F. 434 C.

Cinque poesie romanesche

No. 1, Sogni

(*Mario Dell'Arco*)

1   Er salice piangente sogna la permanente.
2   Er girasole sogna de fa er paino
3   co l'occhiali da sole.
4   Er merlo sogna che se trova addosso
5   la spilla cor rubbino

6   che ha visto da lontano ar pettirosso.
7   E le ranocchie, ammollo ner pantano,
8   sogneno mosce mosce un paro de galosce.

Five Roman poems

No. 1, Dreams

1   The weeping willow dreams of a permanent wave.
2   The sunflower dreams of becoming a dandy
3   with sunglasses.
4   The blackbird dreams of finding himself wearing
5   the pin with the ruby
6   that he saw from a distance on the robin.
7   And the very flabby frogs, soaking in the swamp,
8   dream of a pair of galoshes.

Each of the *Cinque poesie romanesche* (Five Roman poems) has a degree of musical independence, but the keys, tempo changes, chord structures, and changing moods are related in such a way that the songs should be performed as a set. The settings take their musical character from the texts; the composer establishes an appropriate chord structure or accompaniment pattern and then finds a multitude of ways to use it. Vocal lines are often melodic, but the primary purpose of the line is to deliver text; most of the songs are within a moderate range to facilitate this purpose. The accompaniments are difficult, particularly at the *tempi* the composer indicates, and they do not fall easily under the fingers.

No. 1, *Sogni* (Dreams), begins with a dissonant chord structured on the intervals of a major seventh and an augmented fourth. (This chord appears throughout the five songs.) The quiet dynamics and slow tempo establish a dreamy atmosphere, and the two short phrases of the opening vocal line have a lazy character. The song actually "starts" with the arpeggiated accompaniment in measure 4, where the composer indicates increased movement in the tempo and the piano repeats the melodic configuration first introduced by the voice. The vocal line is in speech rhythm, and the important stresses are marked *tenuto*. By measure 8, the song has modulated to the tonal area of C♯ minor and the treble of the piano part has reintroduced the augmented fourth and major seventh that opened the work. After some variation, this figure becomes an *ostinato* that lasts until the end of the work. It may or may not represent the frogs, mentioned in the text, but it is a very insistent sound.

A slower, melancholy tempo is called for in measure 14 to set the last two lines of poetry. The movement of hollow fifths (swamp?) should be stressed in the bass clef of the piano part and should be played *legato*. The final "punch line" is quiet, *ma con spirito* (but with spirit). The short piano postlude repeats this melodic motive and should have exactly the same character—as if spoken. The insistent major seventh appears again at the very end, but very, very quietly.

No. 2, Palloncini

(*Mario Dell'Arco*)

1   Quanno scappa per aria un palloncino
2   a l'improviso,
3   e vola ner turchino,
4   lo sai dove finisce?
5   In Paradiso.
6   Figurete la gioia
7   de l'angioletto che lo rubba ar vento,
8   ma dieci, venti, cento
9   resteno co la voja.
10 Signore, er giorno
11 che te vedi intorno
12 angioli e cherubbini,
13 tutti a passeggio
14 co li palloncini,
15 perdona ar peccatore
16 che ha tajato lo spago ar venditore.

No. 2, Toy balloons

1   When a balloon escapes into the air
2   unexpectedly,
3   and flies into the deep blue,
4   do you know where it ends up?
5   In Paradise.
6   Imagine the joy
7   of the little angel who steals it from the wind,
8   but ten, twenty, a hundred
9   remain with the desire (for one).
10 Lord, the day
11 that you see around you
12 angels and cherubim,
13 all promenading
14 with the balloons,
15 forgive the sinner
16 who cut the string(s) from the vendor.

Palloncini (Toy balloons) is in a modified three-part form and uses two devices to capture the spirit of the poem. The piano introduction is made up of two measures of alternating fourths, followed by a downward progression of perfect fourths in quick sixteenth notes. This device, with modification, is repeated as a bridge to part B, then as a transition to the return of A, and again at the conclusion of the song. Alternating with the piano configuration is a simple vocal melody, built primarily on ascending sequential thirds and supported by a clear-textured chordal accompaniment. The singer tells the story while the piano provides appropriate color for the poetic imagery.

In part B, which begins in measure 13, the vocal melody has the same character as the beginning of the song, but the accompaniment changes to a series of tinkling, high-treble sixteenth notes, supported by *staccato* eighth-note arpeggios. The direction is *gaio e leggero* (gay and light), and there is a specific indication, *sempre mosso* (always moving), to keep the *presto* tempo established at the beginning.

The return of part A is preceded by two important measures of *ritardando* and a change of tempo in which the quarter note now equals the half note of the previous section. The second A (beginning in measure 43) is quieter, and the accompaniment, still built on ascending thirds, features a series of suspensions. The *quasi-religioso* atmosphere of this section is interrupted by some fast triplet figures (measures 50–52) leading back to the sweeping arpeggios and descending fourths that appeared at the opening of the composition. A short postlude, derived from this pattern, returns to the original *presto* tempo ($\quarternote = \eighthnote$) of the preceding section. Two interesting bits of imitation between voice and piano (measures 12–15 and 47–50) should be brought out in the texture.

This song requires dexterity from the pianist and a clear, uncomplicated word delivery from the singer.

No. 3, Piove

(*Mario Dell'Arco*)

1 Appena appena casca
2 la prima goccia d'acqua
3 su la frasca,
4 er pino apre l'ombrello
5 e sotto: er calabbrone, er grillo,
6 la lucertola, er fringuello.
7 Mentre er cipresso,
8 solo, in un cantone,
9 resta confuso
10 co l'ombrello chiuso.

No. 3, It is raining

1   Just as soon as falls
2   the first drop of water
3   on the bough,
4   the pine tree opens its umbrella
5   and underneath: the hornet, the cricket
6   the lizard, the chaffinch.
7   While the cypress,
8   alone, in a corner
9   remains confused
10 with its umbrella closed.

Piove (It is raining) begins with a very clear musical imitation of the subject. A series of tritones alternate with *staccato* octaves in the treble area of the piano to depict the steady fall of raindrops. This pattern, with variation, is the central device of the entire song. The composer calls for *mosso giocoso* (playful motion) with the accompaniment *chiaro e leggero* (clear and light). The singer-narrator has a flowing vocal line, which should be sung *legato* with careful attention to the text. An additional bit of tone-painting appears in measures 11–12, where an upward arpeggio supports the melodic line carrying the texts *er pino apre l'ombrello* (the pine tree opens its umbrella). A little less motion is called for at the phrase *er calabbrone, er grillo, la lucertola, er frinquello* (the hornet, the cricket, the lizard, the chaffinch), but there is no attempt to imitate them in sound.

A change of mood—*lento-maliconico* (slow, melancholy)—and a change of meter from 6/8 to 4/4 mark the setting of the last line of poetry. It should be interpreted lightly; the poetic image is poignant, not tragic. The musical texture remains open and lean, the dynamic level soft. The syncopated octave pattern (measure 25) that brings about this mood change should be stretched out, in observation of the *tenuto* markings; and it should be very *legato,* in contrast to the previous articulations.

A four-measure postlude concludes the song. The original falling octaves, tritones, staccato articulation, and Tempo I° return with the direction *mosso, ma un poco meno* (moving, but a little less). The meter change to 9/8, with a rest on the final beat, is very important since it creates a hesitation in the, until now, regular motion of the rain. The pattern should more or less vanish, as the direction *perdendosi* (dying away) indicates.

No. 4, Grandine

(*Mario Dell'Arco*)

1   Nuvole, nuvolette, nuvolone
2   correno come tanti regazzini

3   cor zinalone bianco, griggio, rosa.
4   E una nuvola in abbito da sposa
5   apre er sacchetto de li confettini.

No. 4, Hail

1   Clouds, little clouds, big clouds
2   they run like so many little boys
3   with big aprons, white, grey, red
4   and one cloud dressed like a bride
5   opens her little sack of confetti.

The quick, close chromatic figuration in the piano introduction establishes the mood for *Grandine* (Hail). It should be phrased over two measures, with the indicated rise and fall in dynamics, and played very *legato*. The speed must be determined by the pianist, but should fall within the parameters of the indicated *Presto* ($\downarrow$ = 168–200).

The vocal line, which enters in measure 9, is phrased over four measures and is almost folk-like in its simplicity. The words *bianco* (white), *griggio* (gray), and *rosa* (red), although separated by rests, should maintain a feeling of connection.

The song is not complicated, but attention to the varying phrase lengths and the differences in phrase lengths between voice and piano will maximize its cleverness. The cascade of dissonant sevenths and ninths aptly describes the hail of the title and the poet's poetic allusion to confetti in the final line. The *decrescendo* for the postlude is written out in individual dynamic marks. The final *pp* chord should be held until the sound completely disappears.

No. 5, Er treno

(*Mario Dell'Arco*)

1   Er treno è un coso buffo
2   cor cappello a cilindro e lo stantuffo:
3   pe mija e mija e mija
4   se porta appresso tutta la famija.
5   Tocca er mare.
6   e spalanca i pormoni;
7   s'arampica sur monte
8   e s'arza er bavero;
9   e fa sboccià un papavero
10   a tutte le stazzioni.

No. 5, The train

1   The train is a funny thing
2   with a top hat and a piston:
3   for miles and miles and miles
4   he brings close behind all the family.
5   He touches the sea
6   and opens wide his lungs;
7   he climbs up the mountain;
8   and he raises his collar;
9   and makes a poppy blossom out
10 at all the stations.

Er treno (The train) is a lighthearted, direct musical description of its subject. The composer states his intention with the tempo marking, *allegretto moderato e umoristico* (moderately quick and humorous). The "piston-descriptive" bass-clef piano part requires an accent on the principal chord with a tapering off on the second eighth note of the inner voice. This "drop-lift" motion should be maintained throughout the song. As with the earlier repeated-pattern accompaniments, the units are sometimes phrased over two measures, sometimes more. A realization of these differences can have a subtle effect on the overall interpretation of the song.

The middle section of the composition (beginning in measure 20) shows some changes in the basic pattern. The repeated chords have moved to the treble, and descending chromatic thirds underscore them, perhaps in an abstract imitation of the train whistle. The composer indicates the same tempo or motion, but with expression. The *staccato* articulation in the pattern is very important.

The final page of the song begins with increased motion and a subtle *crescendo*. A *stringendo molto* (very pressed) tempo is indicated in measure 51, at the beginning of an important ascending chromatic scale in the bass. Then both expressive devices increase to climax in measure 57, marked *presto* and *ff*. The composition ends with the "signature chord"—structured on an augmented fourth and a major seventh—high in the treble.

Throughout the song the vocal line rides above the colorful, very active accompaniment. The more important words are given special emphasis through *tenuto* indications, increased time value, or high pitch. There is some word-painting, as in the phrase *s'arampica sur monte* (he climbs up the mountain), which is set with a rising melodic line. In most songs the vocal line advances the text with heightened emotion, but in the songs of this set the composer tends to use the piano as the primary means of expressing the essential features of the text.

Cinque poesie romanesche: A. Forlivesi, 1948.   12031 (Set)
1. *Sogni*
2. *Palloncini*
3. *Piove*
4. *Grandine*
5. *Er treno*

Goffredo Petrassi

(1904–   )

•

GOFFREDO PETRASSI was born on July 16, 1904 into a family of humble origin in Zagarolo. This town is in the Roman countryside near Palestrina, the birthplace of the great Renaissance papal chapel composer; it is perhaps a significant coincidence that Petrassi had a lifelong interest in Gregorian chant.

In 1911 the family moved to Rome, where the young Goffredo, who had a fine voice, sang in several churches. In 1913 he was admitted to the Schola Cantorum of San Salvatore in Lauro, a choir school that also offered instruction in general subjects. There he was exposed to Renaissance and Baroque choral masterpieces in a setting of Baroque art, architecture, and interior decoration. He showed outstanding musicianship, and, as part of his theoretical training, he attempted some composing.

In 1919, when Petrassi was fifteen, his voice broke, and he went to work in a music shop in Rome. Using the situation to advantage, during slow periods and off hours, he studied a wide variety of musical scores, including contemporary compositions, and in general advanced his education. Alessandro Bustini, a patron of the store, took notice of his unusual musical talent and offered Petrassi free piano lessons.

In 1925 Petrassi started formal study of harmony with Vincenzo di Donato; and in 1928 he entered the Conservatorio di Santa Cecilia studying composition under Bustini and organ under Fernando Germani. He was awarded a diploma in composition in 1932 and one in organ in 1933.

In 1932 Alfredo Casella heard Petrassi's graduation composition, recognized the young composer's gifts, and began a friendship that lasted until the elder composer's death. As a result of Casella's influence Petrassi developed an enthusiasm for the neo-Classical movement and the music of Paul Hindemith. Also in 1932, Petrassi's *Partita* for orchestra won two competitions: one sponsored by the Sindacato Nazionale dei Musicisti and another by the Féderation Internationale des Concerts in Paris. On June 13, 1933 this work was performed, with Casella conducting, as the only Italian entry in the International Society for Contemporary Music festival in Amsterdam. The work is basically neo-Classical, contrapuntal, and dissonant, somewhat like Casella's third style, but based structurally on Baroque dance forms.

From 1934 to 1936 Petrassi taught harmony, counterpoint, and choral composition at the Accademia di Santa Cecilia and studied conducting with Bernardino Molinari. During this time he acted as secretary to a union of music societies that formed part of the Centro Lirico Italiano. In 1935 he was appointed by the Italian government to the Inspectorate of Theaters. This position led to his becoming director of La Fenice, the famous Venetian opera house, from 1937 until 1940.

In 1939 Petrassi was appointed professor of composition at the Conservatorio di Santa Cecilia, where he became very active in the cause of modern Italian music. He founded the society Musica Viva to promote new works and modern "classics," and in 1947 he became artistic director of the Accademia Filarmonica Romana, which had the same objectives. His presidency of the International Society for Contemporary Music (1955–56) led to wide travels. He visited the United States to attend the premiere of his *Fifth Orchestral Concerto* in 1955 and to conduct master classes in composition during the summer of 1956 at Tanglewood, where his *Sixth Orchestral Concerto* was performed by the Boston Symphony Orchestra conducted by Charles Münch.

In 1959 Petrassi left his position at the Conservatorio di Santa Cecilia to succeed the retiring Ildebrando Pizzetti as professor of advanced composition at the Accademia di Santa Cecilia. In this new post he was responsible for the training of a number of prominent composers from Italy and abroad, including Cornelius Cardew, Kenneth Leighton, Peter Maxwell Davies, Aldo Clementi, Domenico Guaccero, and Fausto Razzi.

From 1965 onward Petrassi had to curtail his conducting engagements and travels because of failing eyesight, but he did teach at the Accademia Chigiana in Siena during the academic year 1966–67. He retired formally from the Accademia di Santa Cecilia in 1974.

As an inheritor of the reforms of the tradition-breaking first generation of Italian composers, Petrassi's problems before 1940 were not so much with form and style as with finding a personal vocabulary congenial to current European trends. Although many analysts see marked influences of Hindemith, Stravinsky, and Casella in his early music, Petrassi still managed to project his own identity. Unlike Casella, Petrassi was oriented toward the Baroque rather than the neo-Classical, and, unlike Hindemith, he leaned toward a vocal conception rather than an instrumental one. While maintaining an interest in vocally conceived melody, Petrassi likes the Baroque-influenced dramatic opposition of extremes.

Salmo IX (1934–36) for mixed voices, strings, brass, two pianos, and percussion shows Petrassi's early interest in the problems and possibilities of the voice and relies heavily on Gregorian chant. Still, Baroque contrast, which is important for the instrumental writing, is highly developed while the vocal lines are consciously simplified.

The optimistic qualities of Petrassi's music changed with Italy's entrance into World War II. His "dramatic madrigal" *Coro di Morte* (1941), a setting of a poem by Leopardi, is a pessimistic composition that contrasts modal choral writing with less-diatonic, more-chromatic instrumental parts and bears some Schoenbergian elements.

The ballet score *La follia di Orlando* (1942–43) comes close to total chromaticism; the baritone solo in this work is pure declamation following the metrical articulation of speech. In the early 1950s Petrassi moved more and more toward twelve-tone technique. This style is exemplified especially by his masterwork *Noche Oscura,* a cantata for chorus and orchestra based on a text by the sixteenth-century Spanish Carmelite monk, San Giovanni Della Croce (Saint John of the Cross).

In his mature works Petrassi continued the use of twelve-tone technique, but never rigidly. Eventually he evolved a free atonal style that bears some affinity to the later works of Bartók. Petrassi continued to write declamatory vocal lines and to differentiate the style of the vocal line from the style of the accompaniment. His songs reflect the evolution of his musical language and the influences of his training and interests.

Benedizione

(*Dalla Genesi*)

1   Ecco, l'odore del figlio mio
2   È come l'odore d'un campo fiorito
3   benedetto dal Signore
4   Iddio ti dia della rugiada del cielo
5   e della grassezza della terra
6   Abbondanza di pane e vino
7   A te servano i popoli
8   A te s'inchinino le tribù
9   Sii il Signore de' tuoi fratelli
10   ed a te si prostrino i figli di tua madre
11   chi ti maledirà sia egli maledetto
12   e chi ti benedirà sia ricolmo di benedizioni

Benediction

1   Here, the smell of my son
2   is like the smell of a field of flowers
3   blessed by the Lord.
4   May God give you some dew from the sky
5   and some richness from the land.
6   An abundance of bread and wine

7   the people serve to you.
8   The tribes bow to you.
9   May you be the Lord of your brothers
10 and to you may the sons of your mother bow down.
11 Whoever curses you, may he be cursed
12 and whoever blesses you, may he be overloaded with blessings.

The text for Petrassi's *Benedizione* (Blessing) is drawn from Genesis 27, and an understanding of its context is essential to interpreting what outwardly might seem an inappropriate setting for such benevolent words. In the story, Isaac, now old and blind, calls for his firstborn son, Esau, that he might bestow upon him the blessing of his birthright. Overhearing the request, Rebecca, wife of Isaac and mother of the twins Esau and Jacob, prefers that the blessing be given to her favorite, Jacob, who was born second. Wearing Esau's clothes and a sheath of kidskin to disguise his smooth hands, Jacob presents himself to Isaac. Suspicious at first, Isaac feels the rough skin, catches the scent of Esau's garments, and bestows the unretractable blessing on Jacob—an act that later leads to conflict between the brothers and division among their descendents. It is this subterfuge and potential conflict that Petrassi's setting underscores.

The introduction begins *fortissimo,* with the direction *rude con forza* (rough, with force). The pattern of repeated sixteenth notes is quite rapid at the suggested tempo ($\downarrow$ = 60), and the accent marks are very important. Harmonic changes are brought about by the movement of the octaves in the bass; these, too, should be accented and punctuated by the indicated pedal changes. (Pedal indications are given only for the opening phrase; the rest of the pedaling is at the discretion of the performer but following the model of the first phrase.) The singer's opening phrase is Isaac's joyful exclamation at the recognition of what he believes to be his favorite son. After the climax at the end of the melismatic setting of *mio* (my) the accompaniment begins to *diminuendo* and become more consonant in preparation for the second phrase. Here, Isaac presents a lovely metaphor for the qualities of Esau, ending with the word *Signore* (Lord); the tempo slows, the accompaniment pattern becomes a long series of repeated octaves over a very slight harmonic movement in the base, and the section ends quietly with a *fermata* over the final notes.

The *andante* beginning in measure 17 marks a complete change from the preceding section of the song and provides a two-measure mood-setting introduction for the blessing proper. The time signature is now 3/4, but the accompaniment is phrased as if it were in 6/8. The contrast between a simple meter in the vocal line and a compound meter in the accompaniment in measures 19–24 gives even these gentle phrases a slightly offbeat character. The accompaniment is also marked *staccato,* especially in the bass, and the chords carry the indication *sempre lo stesso suono, uniforme* (always the same sound, uniform). The voice is marked *sempre la stessa intensità* (always the same intensity).

By measure 27 the agitated sixteenth notes have returned, and both the accompaniment and the vocal line begin a slow *crescendo* through the phrases in which the supremacy of the birthright is falsely bestowed. The dramatic climax occurs at the phrase *chi ti maledirà sia egli maledetto* (Whoever curses you, may he be cursed). The word *egli* (he) (referring to Esau, who will later plot revenge against Jacob) receives brilliant melismatic treatment against the doubling of the accompaniment figure to 32d notes marked *stesso tempo* (same tempo). A crashing cascade of octaves punctuates *maledetto* (cursed) and requires a slight *ritardando*. The section ends with a return to the initial tempo of the song and a repetition of the introductory measures.

The final eight measures of the song are *lento, sempre pp a uniforme* (always uniformly very soft) and *dolce* (sweet). The blessing now given, even though under deception, is Jacob's. Whoever blesses him, as the new head of the family, shall be blessed as well. The repeated sixteenth notes, however, continue to the end of the song; and the dissonant A♭, which has been introduced into the C-major chord, continues against the final G♮ of the vocal line and into the last chord of the composition. The sense of disquiet remains.

This song is a dramatic miniature *scena* that requires real virtuosity from both singer and pianist. It would make an excellent opening or closing number for a group or program of *liriche*.

Benedizione: A. and G. Carisch, and C., 1935.   17281

Lamento d'Arianna

(*Parole di Libero de Libero*)

1   Il mio rimpianto non è lode,
2   per inganno esule sposa:
3   ai paterni giardini me rapita
4   abbandoni alla sorte del mare
5   ancora d'anni bella.
6   Già promessa la mano mi togli
7   come al nemico la preda
8   ed in premio mi doni allo scoglio,
9   prigione delle vuote braccia:
10 e fosse l'eco almeno pietosa compagna
11 alla pena del grido.
12 Non tu vedrai me morta
13 tra lo stuolo di nebbia,
14 inutile ombra non compianta.

Ariadne's lament

1 My regret is not praise,
2 in order to deceive the exiled bride:
3 in the paternal gardens he abducted me:
4 abandoned to the fate of the sea
5 still beautiful with years.
6 As already promised you take me by the hand
7 as the enemy ravages it
8 and for a reward you give me difficulty,
9 imprisonment of empty arms:
10 and were the echo at least a compassionate companion
11 to the suffering of crying,
12 you will not see me dead
13 within the denseness of the fog
14 a useless unlamented shade.

Ariadne, Princess of Crete, has defied her father, King Minos, and her people and helped Theseus escape from the labyrinth with the aid of a ball of thread. Now married to the ungrateful Theseus, she has been abandoned on the island of Naxos, where she sings *Lamento d'Arianna* (Ariadne's lament). Petrassi's setting is rather free and organized around the subtle development of motivic fragments mostly in the piano part. The song opens calmly and sadly as Ariadne states her situation. Here singer and pianist should achieve a total *legato* line. One of Petrassi's trademark chants appears almost immediately, in measure 9, setting the word *lode* (praise); and a similar line appears above the word *mare* (sea) in measure 19. By the second vocal entrance, at *ai paterni giardini* (in the paternal gardens), in measure 15, Ariadne's emotional level has risen (the *poco più mosso* should be established by the pianist in the measure before this entrance). It reaches a true *agitato* with the entrance of the repeated sixteenth-note accompaniment beneath the word *bella* (beautiful) in measure 22. The direction *cedendo* in the measure preceding the *agitato* translates as "subsiding." The vocal line should build throughout the *agitato* section of the song, but remain relatively *legato* until the climax at *e fosse l'eco* (and were the echo), where a greater declaration is called for. In this climactic phrase it would be best for the singer to breathe immediately before *pietosa* (compassionate) in order to keep together the word–phrase, *pietosa compagna alla pena del grido* (compassionate companion to the suffering of crying). This phrase is "echoed" immediately in a musical sequence.

In the final lines of the song a calm similar to the opening has returned, but the section is stronger, in keeping with Ariadne's resolve not to go unremembered and unlamented. Throughout the song the pianist should be aware of the repetition and play on motives such as

at the phrase *per inganno esule sposa* (in order to deceive the exiled bride), and

at *premio mi doni allo scoglio* (and for a reward you give me difficulty), which appears in transposition in several instances. Most importantly, this motive reappears in augmentation in the final section of the song, contributing to the sense of resolve required by the poetry. Throughout the accompaniment there are many widely spaced chords. Whenever possible, with the help of the pedal if needed, they should be played together rather than rolled.

Lamento d'Arianna: G. Ricordi, 1936; Repr. 1947.   123793

Due liriche di Saffo

No. 1, Tramontata è la luna
(*Traduzione di Salvatore Quasimodo*)

1 Tramontata è la luna
2 e le Plejadi a mezzo della notte;
3 anche giovinezza già dilegua,
4 e ormai nel mio letto resto sola.
5 Scuote l'anima mia Eros
6 come vento sul monte che irrompe entro le querce;
7 e scioglie le membra e le agita,
8 dolce amaro indomabile serpente.
9 Ma a me non ape, non miele;
10 e soffro e desidero.

Two lyrics by Sappho

No. 1, The moon has set

(*[Italian] translation by Salvatore Quasimodo*)

1 The moon has set
2 and the Pleiades are halfway through the night;
3 even the young people have already dispersed
4 and by now in my bed I lie alone.
5 Eros shakes up my soul
6 like the wind on the mountain that rushes into the oak trees;
7 and loosens my limbs and agitates them,
8 sweet bitter indomitable serpent.
9 But for me there is no bee, no honey;
10 and I suffer and I desire.

The first song of *Due liriche di Saffo* (Two lyrics by Sappho), *Tramontata è la luna* (The moon has set), is about frustrated physical passion, and almost every musical element in the composition serves to emphasize it. The double-octave spacing and angular movement of the piano introduction, even allowing for the slow *moderato* tempo, immediately creates a mood of restlessness. The vocal line is more linear but weaves its references to the Pleiades and youth against the piano's angularity. (The Pleiades were the seven daughters of Atlas and Pleione. After having love affairs with the gods, they were changed into stars to escape Orion, the hunter.) At the end of the first section a breath should be taken as indicated after *letto* (bed) to get the full emphasis on *resto sola* (I lie alone). Note the *tenuto* and *staccato* markings that stress the latter word. The rapidly alternating thirds in the piano accompaniment at this point anticipate the next section of the song. The *poco agitato* should be sudden and forceful, and the entrance of the singer on the words *Scuote l'anima mia Eros* (Eros shakes up my soul) must be intense. (Eros was the most beautiful of the gods and represents physical passion.) A breath may be taken after *Eros* so that no intensity is lost on the word *querce* (oak trees) at the end of the phrase, and again after *amaro* (bitter) so that *serpente* (serpent) does not lose stress.

In the last section of the song the singer should make the most of the sinuous chromatic line on the word *miele* (honey) and maintain intensity on *soffro* (suffer) and the stretched-out triplet rhythm of the final word, *desidero* (I desire). Performers should be aware that throughout the song some eighth notes are grouped as duplets and some as triplets. The barring does not always indicate this clearly.

No. 2, Invito all'Eràno

(*Traduzione di Salvatore Quasimodo*)

1 Venite al tempio sacro delle vergini
2 dov'è più grato il bosco
3 e sulle are fuma l'incenso.
4 Qui fresca l'acqua mormora tra i rami dei meli:
5 il luogo è all'ombra dei roseti,
6 dallo stormire delle foglie nasce profonda quiete.
7 Qui il prato ove meriggiano i cavalli
8 è tutto fiori della primavera
9 e gli aneti vi odorano soavi.
10 E qui con impeto, dominatrice
11 versa Afrodite nelle tazze d'oro
12 chiaro vino celeste con la gioia.

No. 2, Invitation to Erano

([*Italian*] translation by Salvatore Quasimodo)

1 Come to the sacred temple of the virgins
2 where the woods are most pleasant
3 and on the altars incense smokes.
4 Here fresh water murmurs through the branches of the apple trees:
5 the place is in the shade of the rose gardens.
6 From the rustling of the leaves a deep quiet is born.
7 Here the meadow where the horses take their midday rest
8 is all flowers of spring
9 and the dill smells sweet.
10 And here with impetuosity, commanding,
11 Aphrodite pours into the golden cups
12 heavenly clear wine with joy.

Despite the visions of peaceful shade trees and rose gardens, the underlying mood of *Invito all'Eràno* (Invitation to Erano) is restless passion, culminating with Aphrodite, goddess of sensual love, pouring wine for the invited with heavenly joy.

The initial tempo should be a rather brisk *allegro* established by the opening dissonant *staccato* accompaniment chords and felt as one pulse to the measure. The voice rides above both the *staccato* chords and the *legato* octaves following the natural accent of the words. Catch breaths may be taken after *vergini* (virgins) in the first verse and *mormora* (murmurs) in the second, but they should in no way break the forward thrust of the line. The two measures marked *poco meno* between the verses should be an abrupt contrast, as marked. Another catch breath may be taken on the long *diminuendo* after the word *nasce* (is born) but there should be no break between *profonda* (deep) and *quiete* (quiet). At this point the pedal must be held underneath the bell-like arpeggio in the accompaniment. The *rallentando* does not start until after the release of this figure.

The third section of the song has the built-in contrast of a *moderato* tempo and decorative repeated sixteenth notes in the piano part. A breath may be taken after *fiori* (flowers), and the direction *calmo* (calm) should be observed. The passion toward which the composer has hinted from the beginning of the song is apparent in the *accelerando* leading to the final verse. The *forte*-level accents and the *tenuto* indications create a *marcato* effect in the vocal line that can be maintained until the end of the song. A breath after *celeste* (heavenly) will help the singer to observe the final *crescendo* on *gioia* (joy). Singer and pianist must release together quickly and with gesture.

Due liriche di Saffo: Suvini Zerboni, 1942.   S. 3945 Z.
   1. *Tramontata è la luna*
   2. *Invito all'Eràno*

Tre liriche

No. 1, Io qui vagando

(*Giàcomo Leopardi*)

1   Io qui vagando al limitare intorno,
2   invan la pioggia invoco e la tempesta,
3   acciò che la ritenga al mio soggiorno.
4   Pure il vento muggìa nella foresta,
5   e muggìa fra le nubi il tuono errante,
6   pria che l'aurora in ciel fosse ridesta.
7   O care nubi, o cielo, o terra, o piante,
8   parte, parte la donna mia: pietà, pietà se trova
9   pietà nel mondo un infelice amante.
10 O turbine, or ti sveglia, or fate prova
11 di sommergermi, o nembi, insino a tanto
12 che il sole ad altre terre il dì rinnova.
13 S'apre il ciel, cade il soffio, in ogni canto
14 posan l'erbe e le frondi, e m'abbarbaglia
15 le luci il crude Sol pregne di pianto.

Three lyrics

No. 1, I wandering here

1   I wandering here near the threshold,
2   in vain invoke the rain and the tempest,
3   so that you may consider it during my stay.
4   Yet the wind roars in the forest,
5   and the wandering thunder roars among the clouds
6   before dawn may awaken the sky.
7   O dear clouds, O sky, O earth, O plants
8   she is leaving, my lady is leaving: pity, pity,
9   if only an unhappy lover could find pity in the world.
10 O whirlwind, now it awakens you, now you try
11 to overwhelm me, O clouds, until
12 the sun renews the day in other lands.
13 The heavens open, a breath of air falls, everywhere
14 rest the grasses and leafy branches, and the harsh sun
15 dazzles my eyes full of tears.

Petrassi's *Tre liriche* (Three lyrics) of 1944 represent the composer at the height of his terse dissonant wartime style and occupy an important place in the repertory since they bear the infrequent designation "for baritone." They are difficult songs, high in *tessitura,* intense in delivery, and basically atonal, showing glimpses of the composer's growing interest in twelve-tone technique. However, the phrases are not overly long, and the word rhythms carefully follow the natural inflections of speech. Contrast—of the dense, dissonant piano part and a declarative, free, relatively simple vocal line—is Petrassi's primary consideration in the writing and the key to interpreting the work.

Io qui vagando (I wandering here) evokes a stark imagery at the very outset of the piano introduction. A long ascending line of rising and falling intervals in measure 4 reappears in various guises at later points in the composition, for example, in measure 14. This rising-falling line and a figure of repeated octaves and unisons (or a variation of it) serve throughout all three songs as organizing devices. Although they are sometimes hidden in inner voices or in disguised rhythms, these devices should be allowed to emerge from the total fabric whenever they appear. Since the vocal phrases are relatively short, the *adagio* tempo should be set primarily by the pianist, who has difficult widely spaced chords and rhythmic figures to play at faster *tempi* later in the work. The widely spaced chords—which should be played together, not rolled, whenever possible—demand creative fingering.

Throughout the song the vocal line is essentially declarative and relatively simple. Most of the emotional intensity lies in the first two-thirds of the poem and is reflected in the frequent dynamic climaxes in the musical setting. The direction *sordo* in the piano part at the first *agitato* translates as "mute." The repeated-octave pattern first appears here, and the dynamic outbursts punctuate key words in the text—*tuono errante* (wandering thunder) and *ciel* (sky). Both singer and pianist must observe the stunning *subito piano* at the phrase *fosse ridesta* (may awaken), and the pianist should be aware of the canonic imitation (in diminution) of the descending arpeggio marked *calmando* (calm). Again, contrast is the key ingredient as phrases alternate between *agitato* and *calmando,* and the contrasts should be of color and character more than of *tempi.* At the phrase *O turbine, or ti sveglia* (O whirlwind, now it awakens you) the direction *cupo* translates as "dark."

The final section of the song is marked *calmo* but it should not lose intensity. The pianist should be cognizant of the directions for articulation, particularly the marking *senza arpegg.* (without rolling).

No. 2, Alla sera

(*Ugo Foscolo*)

1   Forse perchè della fatal quiete
2   tu sei l'immago, a me sì cara
3   vieni, o sera!
4   E quando ti corteggian liete
5   le nubi estive e i zeffiri sereni,
6   e quando dal nevoso aere
7   inquiete tenebre e lunghe
8   all'universo meni,
9   sempre scendi invocata,
10 e le secrete vie del mio cor
11 soavemente tieni.
12 Vagar mi fai co' miei pensier
13 su l'orme che vanno al nulla eterno;
14 e intanto fugge questo reo tempo,
15 e van con lui le torme delle cure,
16 onde meco egli si strugge;
17 e mentre io guardo la tua pace,
18 dorme quello spirto guerrier
19 ch'entro mi rugge.

No. 2, To evening

1   Perhaps because of inevitable stillness
2   you are the image, to me so dear

3   come, O evening!
4   And when you are courted happily
5   (by) the summer clouds and tranquil zephyrs,
6   and when from the snowy air
7   restless, dark and distant
8   you bring to the universe,
9   always you descend invoked,
10   and the secret ways of my heart
11   you gently hold.
12   You make me wander with my thoughts
13   on the footprints that go to the eternal nothing;
14   and in the meantime this evil time flees,
15   and with it go the swarms of cares
16   so that with me it consumes itself;
17   and while I look at your peace,
18   that warlike spirit sleeps
19   that within me rages.

An angular ascending arpeggiation, similar to that found in *Io qui vagando,* appears immediately in *Alla sera* (To evening), in measures 2 and 3 and again in measures 4 and 5 of the piano introduction. The repeated chords, stretched over an octave, appear in measure 7. The tempo is slower than that of the first song of the set; and although *Alla sera* begins *pianissimo* it is also marked *sonoro* (sonorous or resonant). The vocal line is again declamatory and bears little relationship to the accompaniment. The song phrases are longer and require breaths at logical points within them; for example, after *quiete* (stillness) in the opening phrase. The first tempo change carries the direction *scorrevole* (flowing). The whole mood of this section should be lighter through and including the measures marked *morbido* (soft, delicate). When textual phrases must be broken they are generally well marked. A judicious use of pedal will help to carry the widely spaced chords and awkward bass-clef octaves at the section marked *molto calmo.*

A climax of sorts appears at the phrase *che vanno al nulla eterno* (that go to the eternal nothing). The increase in vocal intensity that accompanies the tempo change should taper off on the second syllable of *eterno,* as the pianist plays the octave figure. The following phrases present awkward breathing problems. Logically the breath should come after *cure,* even though it interrupts an eighth-note triplet: *e van con lui le torme del cure' onde meco egli si strugge* (and with it go the swarms of cares' so that with me it consumes itself). The true emotional climax of the poem and the song comes in the final phrase, *ch'entro mi rugge* (that within me rages), and the *messa di voce* in the vocal line is very important in expressing it.

No. 3, Keepsake

(*E. Montale*)

1   Fanfan ritorna vincitore;
2   Molly si vende all'asta:
3   frigge un riflettore.
4   Surcouf percorre a grandi passi il cassero,
5   Gaspard conta denari nel suo buco.
6   Nel pomeriggio limpido è discesa la neve,
7   la Cicala torna al nido.
8   Fatinitza agonizza
9   in una piega di memoria,
10 di Tonio resta un grido.
11 Falsi spagnoli giocano al convento i Briganti,
12 ma squilla in una tasca la sveglia spaventosa.
13 Il Marchese del Grillo è rispedito nella strada,
14 infelice Zeffirino torna commesso;
15 s'alza lo Speziale e i fulminanti sparano sull'impiantito.
16 I Moschettieri lasciano il Convento,
17 Van Schlisch corre in arcioni,
18 Takimini si sventola,
19 la Bambola è caricata.
20 (Imary torna nel suo appartamento).
21 La rivaudière magnetico, Pitou, giacciono di traverso.
22 Venerdì sogna l'isole verdi e non danza più.

No. 3, Keepsake

1   Fanfan (windbag) returns victorious;
2   Molly sells herself at auction:
3   A floodlight sizzles.
4   Surcouf runs across the quarterdeck with great strides.
5   Gaspard counts money in his cubbyhole.
6   In the clear afternoon snow has fallen,
7   the Cicada returns to her nest.
8   Fatinitza agonizes
9   in a turn of memory,
10 from Tonio a cry remains.
11 False Spaniards, the Brigands, play at the convent,
12 but in a pocket the alarm clock blares frightfully.
13 The Marquis del Grillo is sent again into the street,
14 unhappy Zeffirino returns moved

15 the Druggist rises and the electric cutters shoot at the installation
        (plant).
16 The Musketeers leave the convent,
17 Van Schlisch runs on horseback,
18 Takimini waves himself in the wind,
19 the Doll is charged
20 (Imary returns to his apartment).
21 The magnetic peasant, Pitou, lies askew.
22 Friday dreams of green islands and no longer dances.

World War I and the death of his voice teacher turned Eugenio Montale
from his musical studies to a full-fledged and successful literary career. But
the poet never lost his interest in music or the lyric theater, and he even
served from 1951 to 1967 as a music critic for Milan's *Corriere d'informa-
zione*. He was active as a translator of opera *libretti* for several composers,
and for Goffredo Petrassi he wrote the libretto for the opera *Cordovano* and
the song *Keepsake*.

The poem is a wild cascade of images—people and events occurring
simultaneously or in juxtaposition before a detached viewer, much as an
audience viewing a frantic, surrealist performance of *commedia dell'arte*.
There is no "sense" in conventional meaning.

The piano introduction sets up the artificiality of the scene. The *allegretto*
is qualified *non molto mosso, quasi danzante* (not much motion, hardly
dancing), and the opening notes are an angular arpeggio marked *staccato*
or *quasi staccato* and *brillante* (brilliant). The chords and detached patterns
of fifth and sixths that follow are in irregular metric patterns, further emphasizing the brittleness of the scene. The baritone voice enters without
accompaniment to the directions *con enfasi, non esagerata* (with emphasis,
not exaggerated), and the song takes off. Thereafter, the structure of each
vocal phrase and its accompaniment are generally related to the imagery in
the poetic phrase; for example, the ascending pattern that culminates on a
sustained high F on *vincitore* (victorious), the downward arpeggio with *staccato* accompaniment on *frigge un riflettore* (A floodlight sizzles), and the
repetitious *staccato* chords marked *più mosso* in the measures preceding and
accompanying *Surcouf percorre a grandi passi* (Surcouf runs across with
great strides). The descriptions continue: in measure 21, and the word *buco*
(cubbyhole) the pitch literally drops into a "hole" with the direction *nota
parlata, ma nel registro basso* (note spoken, but in the bass register).

In measure 32 a series of *staccato* eighth notes interrupted by a quick
angular arpeggio introduces the *Falsi spagnoli* (False Spaniards); the same
figures appear again in measure 68. The active bass line should emerge
slightly from the rest of the texture in both of these passages and in measures
51–56, where it is chromatic and imitative of earlier quasi-chromatic lines
in the vocal melody (measures 37–41).

Most of the vocal phrases are short enough to be sung on one breath. The long line *Imary torna nel suo appartamento* (Imary returns to his apartment) could break after *torna,* but the composer's direction for *falsetto* on the final sustained high note (requiring less breath) may make this unnecessary.

This song depends on both performers having absolute command of the text, the singer so that each textual image is reflected in the proper color and speech inflection and the pianist so that articulation of the supporting piano figurations match this. However, it is a very difficult song and requires real virtuosity, technically and musically. Otherwise, the composer's directions are clear and no interpretive "elaborations" are needed.

Tre liriche: Suvini Zerboni, 1947.   S. 4187 Z.
1. *Io qui vagando*
2. *Alla sera*
3. *Keepsake*

Part III

Additional Composers

Song, widely recognized as a natural part of Italian cultural life, interested many Italian composers. In addition to those representing the major achievements in *liriche* there were composers whose primary interests were operatic or instrumental, but who produced an exquisite song or two. By the same token, other composers, while almost exclusively devoted to song writing, were unable to produce more than one or two really fine songs.

To round out the work of the major *liriche* composers, this section is devoted to songs chosen for their first-rate quality within the *liriche* tradition and for their unique characteristics.

Alessandro Bustini

(1876–1970)

•

Tre liriche

No. 1, Esame di coscienza

(G. Edoardo Mottini)

1 Quanto ignoro, mio Signore!
2 Sono stolido perfetto
3 come un ebete novizio
4 che conosce solo un salmo
5 e coltiva solo un vizio!
6 O Signore, l'ignoranza
7 nel mio petto ha preso stanza!
8 Non so un'acca di cinese
9 e non so i giorni del mese!
10 Non so andar sopra un cavallo,
11 non so spinger la barchetta
12 Quanta carta non ho letta!
13 Quante cose non per me!
14 Guardo il mondo dipanare
15 senza mai nulla afferrare!
16 Il mio nome forse so,
17 ma non so perchè son nato
18 e non so perchè morrò.

Three lyrics

No. 1, Examination of conscience

1 How ignorant am I, my Lord!
2 I am thoroughly stupid
3 like a dull-witted novice
4 who can recite only one psalm
5 and cultivates only one vice!
6 O Lord, ignorance
7 resides in my heart!
8 I know nothing about Chinese
9 and I don't know the days of the month!
10 I don't know how to ride a horse,
11 or how to row a skiff.
12 How many books have I not read!
13 How many things are not for me!
14 I watch the world go round
15 without ever understanding anything!
16 I may know my name,
17 but I don't know why I was born
18 and I don't know why I will die.

Alessandro Bustini's musical language is refreshingly simple and totally appropriate for the unpretentious, affecting poetry he chose to set in *Tre liriche* (Three lyrics, 1934). The songs are independent of each other, but the shared emotional simplicity of the texts and the musical variety among the settings argue logically for programming them together.

The text for *Esame di coscienza* (Examination of conscience) is modeled on the practice of prayerful self-examination required by the Catholic church before participating in the sacrament of confession. There is a subtle ambiguity in the poem. The protagonist overtly professes his stupidity, his "one" vice; but indirectly stupidity may be professed to excuse whatever true vices he possesses.

The song is in simple ABA form. The introduction consists of a few organlike mood-setting chords and the singer's opening address to the Lord. Section A begins *allegro con brio* (lively with spirit) with a series of bell-like chords in the accompaniment. They are marked both *staccato* and *tenuto* to indicate a detached attack but full resonance. Throughout the song the specified piano articulations are essential to the interpretation. Contrasts of *staccato* and *legato* occur both between phrases and within phrases and must be observed scrupulously since the piano provides constant commentary on the utterances of the singer; for example, the motivic reiteration after *un vizio* (one vice) in measures 13–14. The rapid harmonic movement of the song comes to its first real cadence beneath *ha preso stanza* (resides) in measure 18, and then section B begins.

As the catalogue of "stupidities" progresses in section B, the piano continues to comment. The irregular, loping accompaniment pattern that begins in measure 22 anticipates the horse (*cavallo*) mentioned in measure 25; the *legato* barcarolle that begins in measure 26 anticipates the skiff (*barchetta*) mentioned in measure 27. The emotional climax of the song and the poet's deepest inward look comes in the phrase *ma non so perchè son nato e non so perchè morrò* (but I don't know why I was born and I don't know why I will die). Anticipated by a *rallentando* and a *diminuendo* under *afferrare* (understanding) in the previous phrase, the climactic phrase is set by a series of rising harmonic sequences moving toward *morrò*. The intensity of the phrase is contained entirely in this harmonic device, and the composer cautions specifically against any strong increase in dynamics at this point. The low pitch and slower harmonic movement in measures 44 and 45, marked *lentamente,* comment on the final word of the phrase. The *staccato* chord in measure 46 abruptly stops these solemn thoughts, and the *glissando* introduces the lighthearted return to section A. The chords are now quasi-arpeggiated, and with a repetition of the poem's opening words the song progresses to a bright, forceful finale in C major.

This light and cheerful musical setting bespeaks a somewhat "tongue in cheek" philosophy in this "examination of conscience," but there are true introspective moments, and the presentation adds up to a very human statement.

No. 2, Per una strada ripida

(*G. Edoardo Mottini*)

1   Il bambino che penzola in collo alla mamma
2   che l'ha ben coperto prima di darlo
3   fuori al freddo acuto,
4   mi guarda mentre il passo lo tentenna.
5   Su e giù, su e giù la strada irta è di breccia,
6   e la testina cionca su e giù.
7   Ma quegli occhietti, non senza malizia
8   guardano me che m'arrampico dietro;
9   dicon: "Tu soffi, ed io salgo portato.
10   Tu sei vestito poco ed io son caldo.
11   Tu sei brutto e sparuto, ed io grassotto.
12   Tu vedi storto, che porti gli occhiali,
13   ed io vedo come il passerotto.
14   Tu sei solo, e cammini come il vecchio,

15   con me è la mamma che mi regge e bacia.
16   La tua strada finisce in un burrone,
17   la mia diventa sempre bella più."
18   E la testina cionca su e giù.

No. 2, On a steep road

1   The child who hangs from the neck of its mamma
2   who has dressed him well before taking him
3   outside into the acute cold,
4   (he) looks at me while the walking shakes him,
5   up and down, up and down the rough road is of broken stones
6   and the little head bounces up and down.
7   But those little eyes, not without mischievousness
8   look at me clambering behind;
9   they say: "You huff and puff, and I am carried up.
10   You are clothed scantily and I am warm;
11   You are ugly and haggard, and I am plump.
12   You see crooked and wear glasses,
13   and I see like a little sparrow.
14   You are alone, and walk like an old man,
15   With me is my mamma who holds me and kisses me.
16   Your road ends in a deep ravine,
17   mine becomes ever more beautiful."
18   And the little head bounces up and down.

The gentle jog of the mother's steps along the steep road is depicted in the opening measures of the piano accompaniment of *Per una strada ripida* (On a steep road). This figure appears throughout the song as a reminder of the physical activity occurring concurrently with the thoughts being expressed in the poem. The song is through-composed, the vocal line telling the story in speech-inflected rhythms while the piano provides the accompanying color or illustrates a specific image. The changes within the song are subtle, in keeping with the overall calmness of the poem. While serious thoughts are expressed, there is a nondramatic inevitability about them. The baby cannot change his state of youth, nor can the poet alter his state of age. The song should be examined carefully for slight changes of *tempi* and articulation and for differences in phrase lengths as they relate to the text. At the word-painting in the vocal line at *Su e giù, su e giù* (up and down, up and down), the singer should carry through the energy from the previous phrase even though the rests are observed. The slight *rallentando* at *dicon* (they say) sets up the baby's "thoughts," and the change of accompaniment in the following phrase subtly underscores the new idea. Here and in the following measures articulations, such as the *staccato* markings on *grassotto* (plump) and the choppy accented phrasing at *Tu vedi storto* (You see crooked), point up the meaning or mood of the words. The measure of triplet figures and descending short *appoggiature* after *passerotto* (little sparrow) aptly describe the hopping little bird.

The climax of the song comes at *mi regge e bacia* (holds me and kisses me), indicating perhaps that the poet, in whose mind this dialogue takes place, is more envious of the baby's assured affection than of his youth. At any rate, the poet finds some difficulty in accepting these life contrasts, as indicated in the chords marked *stendando* (stretched out) under the phrase *la mia diventa sempre bella più* (mine becomes ever more beautiful). A final descriptive comment ends the singer's line. The piano, returning to the figure that opened the song, fades away in the postlude. The characters disappear up the steep road.

No. 3, Solo

(*Giovanni Bizzarri*)

1 La gioia s'è fermata stamani nella mia casa.
2 Prima di stringerla al cuore
3 ho girato tutte le stanze sempre gridando:
4 La gioia, è venuta la gioia a trovarmi!
5 Sono corso alla finestra,
6 sono uscito fuor della porta,
7 ho cominciato a chiamare:
8 Venite, venite tutti, correte, correte:
9 in casa mia c'è la gioia!
10 Nessuno io sentivo arrivare.
11 Ho detto allora alla gioia:
12 Non ho nessuno in casa mia,
13 non ho nessuno, ripassa un'altra volta.

No. 3, Alone

1 Joy stopped this morning at my house.
2 Before pressing her to my heart
3 I went around all the rooms always crying:
4 Joy, joy has come to find me!
5 I ran to the window,
6 I went outside the door,
7 I began to call out:
8 Come, come, everyone, run, run:

9 in my house there is joy!
10 I heard no one arrive.
11 I said therefore to joy:
12 I have no one in my house
13 I have no one, call again another time.

Some of the most affecting human emotions are those associated with disappointment. When coupled with loneliness the result can be devastating. Such is the poem *Solo* (Alone) by Giovanni Bizzarri. Technically, Bustini's setting is a through-composed song that divides into two major sections corresponding to the major contrasts in the poem.

The piano introduction expresses great optimism—with its *allegro* tempo, an ascending *arpeggio,* and upward-leaping intervals in dotted rhythms—all anticipating the opening words, *La gioia* (Joy), which are set with an upward leap of a fifth. The accompaniment's continued angular intervals in dotted rhythm and short repeated chords in the bass contribute to the singer's sense of urgency. (The pianist should look carefully at the articulations Bustini specifies. Although many notes are connected with phrase marks, he still indicates a *staccato* attack. The effect supports the emotional quality of the poem.) Subtle *rubati* in the phrasing are clearly marked by the composer. Particular attention should be paid to the *agitando* (agitated) and *affrettando* (quickening) that lead to the second occurrence of the word *gioia* (joy), in measure 10. As the first section of the song progresses, there is an irregular, but recognizable repetition of the accompaniment patterns from earlier phrases. They build broadly with increasing tempo and dynamics and thickening texture to the climactic *gioia* (joy) in measure 25.

The singer should be careful not to start the vocal *crescendo* too early and to build the excitement in tone quality as well as dynamically in these phrases. There should be a breathless quality to the section; it is perhaps one of the few places in vocal literature where an audible breath would not be inappropriate, for example, between *Venite* (Come) and *venite tutti* (come, everyone), and between *correte* (run) and *correte.* The climactic *gioia* should be prepared by a careful observance of the *rallentando* in measure 23 and the sustained, drawn-out chords from the piano in measure 24. The coordination of voice and piano at *gioia* is somewhat difficult. The chord on the fourth beat in the piano part both finishes the previous phrase and acts as a springboard for the next. The introduction suggests that it is more logical to place this chord with the preceding phrase and begin the Tempo I° with the three sixteenth notes leading to the next line. The piano interlude depicts the protagonist, who continues to run from room to room, finally slows down, hesitates, and—stops.

The final section of the song is a complete contrast to all that has gone before. The singer's entrance on *nessuno* (no one) need not be in strict metric relation to the piano figure in the measure, but it should establish the new, slow tempo. The word *nessuno* is the most important in the whole final section and should be expressed in vocal color as well as accent. The pianist's arpeggios should be very *legato* and take their color as much as possible from the singer. There should be a slight break before the Tempo I° returns in the final two measures with the heartbreaking echo of joy remembered—or the poet's determination that joy must return!

Tre liriche: G. Ricordi, 1934; Repr. 1955.
  1. *Esame di coscienza*   123234
  2. *Per una strada ripida*   123235
  3. *Solo*   123236

Arturo Buzzi-Peccia

(1856–1943)

•

Lolita: Serenata spagnola

1 Amor, amor che langue il cor
2 la sua canzon ti vuol cantar
3 E ti vo' dir i suio martir,
4 le pene che Lolita può sol calmar
5 Ah vien, che i baci che ti vo' dare,
6 le stelle in ciel non le potrian contare,
7 E le carezze ed i sospir
8 tu sola o bella li potrai ridir. Ah.
9 Amor se 'n vien, è l'ora gradita,
10 senza il tuo ben dimmi come fai Lolita?
11 Olezza il fior e dolce invita
12 O mia Lolita.
13 Vien all'amor, ah vien diletta,
14 più non tardare, che al seno stretta
15 ti vo' baciar, baciar
16 Ah vien diletta Lolita, vien
17 che morire mi farai se tu non vieni.

Lolita: Spanish serenade

1 Love, love that makes the heart languish
2 wants to sing you her song
3 and wants to tell you of her sufferings,
4 the pain that only Lolita can soothe.
5 Ah, come, because the kisses I wish to give you

6   the stars in the sky could not count them.
7   And the caresses and the sighs
8   you alone, o beautiful one, could ever repeat them. Ah.
9   Love, come here, it is the favored hour.
10 Without your beloved, tell me, what will you do Lolita?
11 The flower smells sweet and softly invites,
12 O my Lolita.
13 Come to love, ah, come, delightful one,
14 no longer tarry, because close to my breast
15 I wish to kiss you, kiss you.
16 Ah, come, delightful Lolita, come
17 because you will make me die if you don't come.

The songs of Arturo Buzzi-Peccia achieved considerable popularity as encores on the programs of Enrico Caruso and other Italian singers of Caruso's generation. Usually bright and rhythmic, they border on the more popular Neapolitan song genre, but the care lavished on their construction and the variety of texts and styles the composer chose place them within the art-song category. The harmonies are conventional, the voice carries virtually all the melodic interest, and the piano provides support and color, in most cases propelling the vocal line by means of a repetitive rhythmic motive.

Lolita, subtitled Spanish serenade, exemplifies all the above characteristics as well as the fascination with Spanish music common among many turn-of-the-century European composers. The brilliant piano introduction in Bb minor introduces the rhythmic pattern ♪♪♪ ♪♪ ♪♪ , which continues, with minor variations, throughout the song and creates its Spanish character. Taking a cue from the opening phrase, *Amor, amor che langue il cor* (Love, love that makes the heart languish), the composer gives the direction *con languore* (with languor) on the entrance of the vocal line. The poet complains of suffering and pain, but the many chromatic alterations in the melodic line and the bright, dancelike rhythms make his sincerity suspect. He may "protest too much" in order to press his suit upon the coy or reluctant girl. It is certainly not a sad song. *Rubato* is essential to the performance and is usually well indicated, for example, at *i suoi martir* (her sufferings). It is also appropriate elsewhere as the interpreter develops the message of the song. The many expression marks scattered throughout the composition—such as *più sentito* (more heartfelt, sincere), *con espressione* (with expression), *poco stendando* (a little stretched out), *lunga* (long, held), *dolcissimo* (very sweetly), and *con slancio* (with dash)—are indicative of the sentimental, rather free performance style required for the piece. At several points, particularly before the name *Lolita,* the direction *sospesa* appears. It translates as "suspended" or "interrupted" and indicates a break in the flow of the phrase to emphasize the "object of desire." The change to Bb major midway in the song makes a nice contrast to the first half of the composition and needs nothing further to enhance it; the protagonist seems to have gained a little more confidence by this time. However, the clever shift back to B♭ minor in the piano postlude indicates that a few doubts still linger about the success of this romantic pursuit. This song should not be oversentimentalized. The words are specific and the expression markings clear. The song should be sung for the entertainment of the audience.

Lolita: G. Ricordi, 1906; Repr. 1947.   112929

Colombetta: Serenata veneziana

1   La bella Colombetta
2   Al caldo si riposa
3   Ma vuol far un tantin la ritrosa
4   Al balcone mostrarsi non va
5   Rimane la furbetta.
6   Dietro al balcon ascosa,
7   Ascoltando la voce amorosa
8   D'Arlecchino l'amante fedel
9   Che di fuori all'acqua al vento
10 Chiede grazia e vuole entrar
11 E ripete dolcemente
12 La sua mite canzonetta,
13 Colombetta, Colombetta,
14 Apri l'uscio, non farmi penar
15 Del balcon solleva il velo
16 Apri amor se no qui gelo
17 Colombetta, Colombetta
18 Arlecchino gelando si sta.
19 Accorda il mandolin,
20 Il povero Arlecchin.
21 Ah! Ah! Ah! Ah! che fu?
22 Non canta più
23 Oh! povero Arlecchin!!!
24 Gelato
25 È forse là!!!
26 Arlecchin,
27 Rispondi.
28 Sei vivo?
29 Vieni qua
30 Deh, vieni poveretto
31 Amante mio fedele,
32 Colombetta fu troppo crudele

33 di lasciarti là fuori a gelar.
34 Ti vieni a riscaldare
35 dalla tua Colombetta
36 Nella piccola sua cameretta
37 E seduti vicino al Camin
38 Parleran del loro amore,
39 Colombetta ed Arlecchin
40 Già ti sento mormorare
41 E ripeter: Mia diletta
42 Colombetta, Colombetta
43 Arlecchino sol vive per tè
44 Ed allor a te vicino
45 Ti dirò caro Arlecchino:
46 Colombetta, Colombetta, è tutta per te
47 Vieni sorridimi caro Arlecchin
48 Bacciami pizzica stammi vicin.
49 Arlecchin!

Colombetta: Venetian serenade

1   The beautiful Colombetta
2   retires when it is warm.
3   But wants to be a little bit coy.
4   She does not show herself on the balcony
5   and continues her artful ways.
6   She hides behind the balcony
7   Listening to the beloved voice
8   of Arlecchino, the faithful lover,
9   who outdoors in the rain and the wind
10 asks for mercy as he wants to come in
11 and he repeats sweetly
12 his gentle little song,
13 Colombetta, Colombetta,
14 open the door, don't make me suffer.
15 She raises the curtain of the balcony.
16 Open, love, if not, I will freeze here.
17 Colombetta, Colombetta,
18 Arlecchino is here freezing.
19 He tunes his mandolin,
20 Poor Arlecchino,
21 Ah! Ah! Ah! Ah! What happened?
22 He sings no more
23 Oh! poor Arlecchino!!!
24 Frozen

25   He is perhaps (frozen) there!!!
26   Arlecchino,
27   Answer.
28   Are you alive?
29   Come here.
30   Pray come, poor little one,
31   My faithful lover,
32   Colombetta was too cruel
33   leaving you outside to freeze.
34   Come here to warm yourself
35   with your Colombetta.
36   In her little room
37   and seated near the fireplace
38   they talk of their love.
39   Colombetta and Arlecchino.
40   Already I hear you murmuring
41   and repeating: My delight
42   Colombetta, Colombetta
43   Arlecchino lives only for you.
44   And then beside you
45   I will tell you, dear Arlecchino:
46   Colombetta, Colombetta, is all yours.
47   Come, smile at me, dear Arlecchino,
48   Kiss me, bite me, stay near me.
49   Arlecchin!

The lighthearted gaity that pervades much of the music of Buzzi-Peccia (his songs were favorite encores of Italian opera singers of a generation ago) is very evident in *Colombetta*. This highly programmatic song is subtitled Venetian serenade. Although the time signature is given as 3/4, the eighth notes are grouped so that the meter throughout the song is duple, or 6/8, in the manner of a barcarolle. The piano imitates the simple accompaniment of a mandolin and often punctuates the descriptive actions of the song. The song is a complete miniature scene from the popular *comedia dell'arte* tradition, in which Colombetta, or Colombine, was a stock character. She was the mistress of Pulcinella and later of Arlecchino, and often acted as the *servetta* or soubrette character in the comedies of Goldoni. The song should be "acted" with the voice in accordance with the events of the story and the composer's specific directions.

The opening tempo is an *allegretto,* qualified by the term *giacoso* (playful, jesting). It should be relatively lively, but not so fast as to obscure the words or interfere with the acting. There are three characters: Colombetta, Arlecchino, and a narrator. The narrator's opening statements are made *con molto grazia* (with much charm). The accompaniment is *leggero* (light) and sometimes marked *staccato* and *elegante*. At the phrase *Che di fuori all'acqua al vento* (who outdoors in the rain and the wind) the tempo should increase a little and the accompaniment should be more *brillante*.

Arlecchino's entrance in measure 29 requires a slight change in vocal color which the pianist can support by observing the accent marks and the direction *capriccioso* (willful). A slight slackening of tempo and special stress should be given to the phrase *se no qui gelo* (if not, I will freeze here) in measures 36–37.

In measure 42 the singer is given the direction *ascoltando sorridente* (listening, smiling) and the pianist *come strappate di mandolino* (as though strumming the mandolin). The narrator enters in measure 46 *gaiamente* (gaily). In measure 52 the singer is given the direction *ascolta ancora* (she listens still) and the pianist is told *ridendo imitando colla mano l'accordare del mandolino* (laughing, imitating the hands tuning the mandolin). After a pause in measure 56 the question *che fu?* (What happened?) is asked *sorpresa* (surprised), and in measure 59 the singer's statement *Non canta più* (He sings no more) is given the direction *ascolta, inquieta* (listening, worried). After the phrase *Gelato/È forse la!!!* (He is perhaps frozen there!!!) the piano chords are *presto* and *fragoroso* (roaring). When Colombetta calls Arlecchino's name the pianist's figure bears the direction *risposta* di Arlecchino freddoloso* (reply of Arlecchino feeling the cold) and represents a shiver, with the entire section *tutto questa a piacere* (all this at the pleasure or discretion of the performers).

At the Tempo I° Colombetta's change of heart is underscored by light, delicate trills in the piano part. She invites Arlecchino into her little room *con civetteria* (with coquetry), and *amorosa* (amorously) they declare their love for each other. A coda to the modified ABA song form consists of repetitions of three descending notes with the words *Baciami pizzica stammi vicin* (kiss me, bite me, stay near me), and a final *brivido* (shiver) accompanies the last statement—*Arlecchino!*

The directions and colorful compositional devices are all contained in the score; it only remains for the performers to find suitable colors and gestures to bring this delightful story to life.

Colombetta: Ricordi Americana, 1924.   B.A. 7516

---

*This word is misspelled in the score as *riposta*. The corrected spelling *risposta* refers directly to the piano as Arlecchino's "reply."

Sebastiano Caltabiano

(1899–   )

•

Due liriche

No. 1, Profonda, solitaria, immensa notte

(Giosuè Carducci)

1 Profonda, solitaria, immensa notte;
2 visibil sonno del divin creato
3 su le montagne già dal fulmin rotte,
4 su le terre che l'uomo ha seminato;
5 alte dai casti lumi ombre interrotte;
6 cielo vasto, pacifico, stellato;
7 lucide forme belle, al vostro fato,
8 equabilmente, arcanamente addotte;
9 Luna, e tu che i sereni e freddi argenti
10 antica peregrina ai petti mesti
11 ed a' lieti dispensi indifferente:
12 che misteri, che orror, dite, son questi?
13 Che siam, povera razza dei viventi?
14 Ma tu, bruta quiete, immobil resti.

Two lyrics

No. 1, Deep, solitary, vast night

1 Deep, solitary, vast night;
2 visible sleep by the divine created

3   over the mountains already by lightning broken,
4   over the earth that man has sown;
5   tall shadows interrupted by pure lights;
6   sky spacious, peaceful, starry;
7   shiny beautiful forms, to your fate,
8   uniformly, mysteriously produced;
9   Moon, and you who the tranquil and cold silver,
10 old wanderer, to the sad hearts
11 and to the happy (you) dispense indifferently:
12 what mysteries, what horrors, say, are these?
13 What are we, poor living creatures?
14 But you, brutal calm, remain motionless.

The sophisticated poems by Giosuè Carducci to which *Due liriche* (Two lyrics, 1952) are set are in sonnet form. They each express one complete unified thought or idea. The rhyme scheme is grouped into a primary unit of eight lines (the octave) and a secondary one of six (the sestet). Caltabiano's musical settings are equally sophisticated, but uncomplicated; they enhance and elucidate the emotional qualities of the poetry while showing an awareness of the literary structure. If possible, the songs should be programmed together.

Profonda, solitaria, immensa notte (Deep, solitary, vast night) begins with quiet alternating seconds and thick chords low in the bass clef of the piano part that establish the awesome mystery of night. The entrance of the vocal line is unobtrusive. Its speech rhythms on single pitches are delivered above the sustained *legato* accompaniment. The increase in melodic and harmonic movement leading to *visibil sonno* (visible sleep) is marked *appena* (hardly, scarcely), indicating only the slightest dynamic increase. The pianist, however, must be aware of the chromatic countermelody in the left hand, which doubles the now more active vocal line. A carefully marked *rallentando* and *diminuendo*, slight at first, then increasing, leads to the second four lines of poetry. These are set very similarly to the first four lines, including a doubled melody beneath the words *lucide forme* (shiny forms).

The first real contrast in the song comes in measure 23, which introduces the secondary section, or final six lines of the poem—*Luna, e tu che i sereni e freddi* (Moon, and you who are the tranquil and cold). While the dynamic level remains *pp*, the change of texture and faster motion in the accompaniment create a feeling of anticipation. When the melodic doubling appears again in the bass clef of the piano part beneath *peregrina* (wanderer) it is one beat late, in canonic imitation to the vocal line, and enhances the feeling of urgency. The imitation follows the higher-pitched vocal melody to measure 31, which is marked *agitando subito* (suddenly agitated). From here, the broader harmony and short melodic phrases punctuated by incisive accompaniment figures build to great intensity at the agonizing, self-questioning central phrase of the poem, *Che siam, povera razza dei viventi?* (What are we, poor living creatures?). The required vocal intensity for this climaxing phrase must not let up until the release of *viventi* and the accented A♮ in the piano part, which completes the scale motion beneath it. In fact, both singer and pianist should feel the urgency and energy continuing beyond the release. There must be complete silence before the final phrase (which is almost identical to the opening of the song) reveals that night either has no answer to this question or refuses to reveal it.

No. 2, A questi dì, prima io la vidi

(*Giosuè Carducci*)

1   A questi dì, prima io la vidi. Uscia
2   a pena il fior di sua stagion novella:
3   e la persona pargoletta e bella
4   era tutta d'amore un'armonia:
5   vereconda su 'l labbro le fioria
6   l'ingenua grazia e la gentil favella:
7   come in chiare acque albor lontan di stella,
8   ridea l'alma negli occhi e trasparia.
9   Tal io la vidi. Or con disio supremo
10 lei per questo nefando aere smarrita
11 pur cerco e invoco; e sol mi sento, e tremo;
12 chè spento è al tutto ogni buon lume, e vita
13 già m'abbandona, e son quasi all'estremo.
14 Luce degli anni miei, dove se' gita?

No. 2, In such days as these first did I see her

1   In such days as these first did I see her. Just blossoming
2   was the flower of her new season (maturity):
3   and a young and beautiful woman
4   she was totally a harmony of love:
5   modest on her lips there bloomed
6   naive grace and kind speech:
7   like dawn in clear water far from the stars,
8   her soul laughed and shined through her eyes,
9   As such I saw her. Now with supreme desire
10 she, because of this nefarious atmosphere, lost,
11 I still search (for her) and cry out (to her); and I feel alone, and I
        tremble;
12 because every good source of light is entirely spent, and life

13 is already abandoning me, and I am nearly at the point of death,
14 Light of my years, where have you gone?

A questi dì, prima io la vida (In such days as these first did I see her) is written in a broad ABA form. The contrasts roughly follow the structure of the sonnet. The tempo of the introduction is essential to establishing the *nostalgico* (nostalgic) atmosphere the composer indicates. A marking of ♩. = 76, usually the slowest metronome indication for *andante,* might still be too fast for this flowing, gentle 9/8 meter. With a slow-moving harmony and an unobtrusive accompaniment, the lyrical vocal line allows the singer to luxuriate in the poet's description of the incredibly beautiful girl. The *rubati* and changes in dynamic levels are carefully indicated.

The contrasting B section occurs one-half line into the sestet (the last six lines) of the poem. Following the meaning of the words, the composer includes the phrase *Tal io la vida* (As such I saw her) with the music from part A that describes the girl. Part B, beginning with a meter change to 4/4 and the direction *un poco agitato,* is all passion and grief. Although still *legato,* the accompaniment pattern is more rapid, and both it and the vocal line ascend to a climax on the phrase *e sol mi sento, e tremo* (and I feel alone and I tremble). The *rallentando sensibilmente* (sensitively growing slower) is partly built into the rhythmic division in the accompaniment. The following, despairing lines of poetry are set with ever-descending pitch, and the *rallentando* and *diminuendo* must continue almost to the point of whispered speech at *e son quasi all'estremo* (and I am nearly at the point of death).

The return to 9/8 meter and the nostalgia motive:

mark the beginning of the final A section. The piano accompaniment continues the chord progressions and melodic motives associated with the loving description of the girl at the beginning of the song, but the singer's phrase builds to a climax almost equal in intensity to that which first described the poet's loss. Memory may be all he possesses, but the poet refuses to accept it willingly. The final phrase in the piano is a marked comment on this, and the final chord leaves an unresolved feeling in the air.

Due liriche: G. Ricordi, 1956.   129159 (Set)
   1. *Profonda, solitaria, immensa notte*
   2. *A questi dì, prima io la vidi*

Giorgio Cambissa

(1921–   )

•

Tre liriche

No. 1, Autunno

(Autore ignoto)

1 Ho respirato nell'aria la nuova stagione:
2 come un sorso d'acqua fredda di buonmattino
3 e tanta dolce tristezza di secche foglie cadenti.

Three lyrics

No. 1, Autumn

(Author unknown)

1 I breathed in the air the new season:
2 like a drop of cold water in early morning
3 and so much sweet sadness with dried leaves falling.

    Giorgio Cambissa's *Tre liriche* (Three lyrics, 1956) do not have a strong cyclical relationship, but the brevity of the first two songs argues for programming all three as a set. The harmonies are dissonant and the melodies roam rather freely, but the vocal line of each song ends on G♯ with implied tonalities of E major and C♯ minor.

    Autunno (Autumn) is a single-page recitative supported by chords in which the pitches G♮ and C♯ have the greatest prominence. The tempo suggestion, ♩ = 48, is approximate; the singer should follow the indicated speech rhythms, keeping the meter strict within each line of poetry but allowing slight breaks between the lines. Dynamics and pedal indications are carefully marked (note the breath marks in the piano score at the end of the first line) and must be just as carefully observed. There are important accents for the singer on two expressive words: *fredda* (cold) and *cadenti* (falling). The vague resolution of the last two measures seems to underscore the final word. The pianist is directed to hold the last chord for approximately fifteen seconds.

No. 2, Primavera

(*Autore ignoto*)

1 Vento leggero, di primavera,
2 odore del mare: mi ferite
3 nella profonda oscurità
4 di desideri inappagati.
5 Splende il sole.

No. 2, Spring

(*Author unknown*)

1 Light wind, of spring
2 smell of the sea: you wound me
3 in the deep darkness
4 of unsatisfied desires.
5 The sun is shining.

In *Primavera* (Spring) the pianist must establish the rapid, feathery accompaniment figure while still projecting an atmosphere of calm. The suggested tempo, ♩ = 58, should not be interpreted rigorously. The voice part is basically recitative on each pitch, but the ascending successive pitches and dynamic *crescendo* toward *mi ferite* (you wound me) create a broad melodic line. The sustaining pedal must be held through the entire first page until the chord change before *mi ferite*. The first statement of the phrase *Splende il sole* (The sun is shining) may start somewhat breathy and hushed, but the second statement must be exuberant. The final *fermata* is marked *corta* (short), implying that it not be held too long and that the cut off, after the *crescendo,* be abrupt. The cascading final E-major arpeggio in the accompaniment must be played without *ritard* and allowed to vibrate with the pedal until the piano part cuts off abruptly with the singer.

No. 3, Racconto

(*Autore ignoto*)

1   Dice il Re: "Vieni, bimbo sul prato fiorito:
2   vedrai farfalle dai mille colori
3   e insetti strani meravigliosi, misteriosi.
4   e berrai l'acqua fresca del ruscello
5   e miele mangerai e dolci frutta odorose, vieni!"
6   Corre il bimbo sul prato fiorito
7   e ansante rincorre le farfalle dai mille colori.
8   Sale dall'orizzonte rapido il fuoco del sole
9   e il bimbo avidamente si disseta
10 nell'acqua del ruscello.
11 "Dove vai, acqua bella e fresca?"
12 "Al mio mare."
13 Altri bimbi giocano sul prato
14 e inseguono farfalle bianche, rosse, rigate, a punti
15 o cerchiate di verde, azzurre, violette o nere
16 Ma chi le afferra
17 non stringe che polvere chiara e leggera
18 che il vento disperde.
19 "Dove sei, farfallina?"
20 "Nell'azzurro."
21 Sembra fermo il sole nell'ampia volta celeste.
22 L'ombre pian piano si fanno più lunghe,
23 sempre più lunghe.
24 Fa freddo.
25 A un tratto è sera.
26 "O mio Re, portami via di qui!"
27 "Io ti porto via di qui, se vuoi
28 Il Re, ora non c'è.
29 Vieni, vieni presto con me.
30 Nel mio rifugio c'è tanto posto anche per te:"
31 ghigna la Vecchia chiamando
32 col lungo dito adunco.
33 "Non vengo con te; chi c'è nel tuo rifugio?"
34 "Altri bimbi, buoni e cattivi, dormono là."
35 Si china e l'afferra tra le scarne braccia:
36 "Lasciami!"
37 Appare un istante tra nubi di fuoco,
38 sul bianco cavallo alato, il Re.
39 "Io verrò" dice.
40 S'aprono i cieli sfolgoranti
41 alla silenziosa notte

42 e il bimbo s'addormenta senza sogni
43 tra le scarne braccia della vecchia
44 dal lungo dito adunco.
45 Splendono aguzze le stelle
46 e la tagliente luna.

No. 3, Story

(*Author unknown*)

1   The King says: "Come, child, to the meadow full of flowers.
2   You will see butterflies of a thousand colors
3   and insects unusual, wonderful, mysterious
4   and you will drink fresh water from the stream
5   and you will eat honey and sweet fragrant fruit, come!"
6   The child runs into the meadow full of flowers
7   and panting runs after the butterflies of a thousand colors.
8   From the horizon rises rapidly the heat from the sun
9   and the child greedily quenches his thirst
10 with the water of the stream.
11 "Where are you going, beautiful and fresh water?"
12 "To my sea."
13 Other children play on the meadow
14 and chase the white butterflies, red, striped, with dots
15 or encircled with green, blue, violet, or black.
16 But whoever catches them
17 grasps only powder, clear and light,
18 that the wind scatters.
19 "Where are you, little butterfly?"
20 "In the blue."
21 The sun seems stopped in the spacious celestial vault.
22 The shadows slowly become longer
23 ever longer.
24 It is cold.
25 Suddenly it is evening.
26 "O my King, take me away from here!"
27 "I will take you away from here, if you wish.
28 The King, is no longer here.
29 Come, come quickly with me.
30 In my refuge there is lots of space also for you."
31 The old woman laughs derisively beckoning
32 with her long hooked finger.
33 "I'm not coming with you; who is in your refuge?"
34 "Other children, good and bad, are sleeping there."

35   She stoops down and catches (the child) between her thin arms.
36   "Let go of me!"
37   There appears for an instant among clouds of fire,
38   on a white winged horse, the King.
39   "I will come," he says.
40   The blazing heavens open
41   in the silent night
42   and the child goes to sleep without dreams
43   between the thin arms of the old woman
44   with the long hooked finger.
45   The bright stars shine
46   and the sharp moon.

Racconto (Story) falls into the long line of narrative songs that inevitably invoke comparison with Schubert's *Erlkönig*. As in all such songs it is essential that the singer find appropriate colors to differentiate the characters and that the pianist make appropriate comment on the action. Both tasks require a thorough understanding of the text. In the case of *Racconto* some musical devices anticipate an action or refer to aspects of the poem still to appear. The song opens with a series of repeated, majestic chords anticipating the narrator's announcement, *Dice il Re:* (The King says). The king's voice is *p ma ben scandito* (soft but well stressed), i.e., authoritative. Subtle color contrasts should be found for words such as *strani* (strange), *meraviglosi* (wonderful), and *misteriosi* (mysterious). The word *vieni* (come) can be commanding if the composer's indications for *crescendo-decrescendo* and a very slight *ritardando* are observed.

The tempo shift to *vivace* must be abrupt, describing in the *staccato* articulation of the piano the child plunging into the meadow and chasing butterflies. The *poco accelerando* must be observed, and the vocal color should be slightly breathless. At the phrase *Sale dall'orizzonte rapido il fuoco del sole* (literally, "rises from the horizon rapidly the fire of the sun") the ascending pattern in the bass clef of the piano part should be stressed.

Changes of vocal color must be found when the child asks, *Dove vai acqua bella e fresca?* (Where are you going, beautiful and fresh water?), and the water answers, *Al mio mare* (To my sea). When the narrator returns to describe other children at play, *Altri bimbi giocano sul prato* (Other children play on the meadow), the pianist should use the same *staccato* articulation that was used earlier to underscore this activity. In the second dialogue, between the child and the butterfly, beginning *Dove sei, farfallina?* (Where are you, little butterfly), the accompaniment requires the same shimmering chord alternation that provided background for the first.

A complete change of character precedes the phrase *Sembra fermo il sole* (The sun seems stopped), but the tempo should not decrease. The wider-spaced melodic rhythm slows down the words enough to set their meaning effectively. It is important to observe the dynamics as well as the accents on words such as *Fa freddo* (it is cold). The child's plea, *O mio Re, portami via di qui!* (O my King, take me away from here!), should show his fright. The accompaniment must punctuate it with a rapid dynamic increase on the three rumbling alternations in the bass.

Only by reading ahead in the poem does one discover that the next voice is that of the old woman, so color contrast is extremely important here. Her cackling laughter is not described in the piano until after her speech, as the narrator returns. When the child asks, *chi c'è nel tuo refugio?* (who is in your refuge?), an ominous figure in the accompaniment anticipates the *con voce cupa* (with dark voice) of the old woman's answer. The capture of the child, with attendant chromatic chords and piano *glissando,* needs nothing further for dramatic effect, but the measure immediately after this should be *vuota* (empty), as indicated.

The King's mysterious appearance, which follows the capture of the child, is supported by the calming effect of repeated triplets in the accompaniment, blurred by holding the pedal down throughout. His short comment is underlined by two rapid dynamic changes, also in the accompaniment. The opening of the heavens, *S'aprono i cieli sfolgonanti alla silenziosa notte* (The blazing heavens open in the silent night), is accompanied by harplike figurations widely separated from the bass pedal tone. However, the old woman retains the child, who goes to sleep to the accompaniment of a lovely lullaby in 6/8 meter and a clear C♯-minor tonality. In the poem the child goes to sleep *senza sogni* (without dreams), suggesting perhaps that he is dead. This would account for the sudden *fortissimo* dynamic in the short piano postlude of the lullaby. The two-against-three accompaniment rhythm in the final *allegretto* section sets the calm but unusual imagery of *aguzze le stelle* (bright stars) and *tagliente luna* (sharp moon). As the light atmospheric chords conclude the song, another sinister *fortissimo* appears in the bass, leaving considerable ambiguity as to the fate of the child.

Tre liriche: Boccaccini e Spada Editori, 1983.   B.S. 1112
   1. *Autunno*
   2. *Primavera*
   3. *Racconto*

Pietro Cimara

(1887–1967)

•

Fiocca la neve

(*Giovanni Pascoli*)

1 Lenta la neve fiocca, fiocca, fiocca.
2 Senti, una zana dondola pian piano.
3 Un bimbo piange, il picciol dito in bocca.
4 Canta una vecchia, il mento sulla mano.
5 La vecchia canta: Intorno al tuo lettino
6 c'è rose e gigli come un bel giardino.
7 Nel bel giardino il bimbo s'addormenta,
8 fiocca la neve lenta, lenta, lenta,
9 fiocca la neve, fiocca la neve.

The snow is falling

1 Slowly the snow is falling, falling, falling.
2 Listen, a cradle is rocking very slowly.
3 A child is crying, his little finger in his mouth.
4 An old woman is singing, her chin on her hand.
5 The old woman sings: "Around your little bed
6 there are roses and lilies like a beautiful garden."
7 In the beautiful garden the child falls asleep,
8 The snow is falling, slowly, slowly, slowly,
9 the snow is falling, the snow is falling.

Pietro Cimara's *Fiocca la neve* (The snow is falling) is one of the most popular of the *liriche da camera,* thanks, in part, to its appearance in a well-known anthology of modern repertory widely available in the United States.

The composer had a respectable career as a conductor, including a stint at the Metropolitan Opera. He wrote a number of songs, but their harmonic structures tend to be awkward, disturbing the melodic flow and resulting in largely unsatisfactory works. Fortunately, *Fiocca la neve* is a unique gem, worthy of its popularity. Previous published translations of the poem have often led to a somber interpretation of the song. There is nothing in the text to indicate that the child is more than restless, and the minor tonality that opens and closes the song merely sets the quiet gray mood of falling snow. Since a considerable portion of the accompaniment lies in the treble clef, the song works very well in lower transpositions and has been published in keys other than its original G minor.

The simple ABA structure follows the structure of the poem. The opening and closing sections each begin with repeated minor chords interspersed with falling major seconds, all in the treble clef. The description of falling snow is unmistakable. The vocal line describing the scene has a gentle rise and fall, following the implied melodic line in the supporting chord progressions that sit above it. The 6/8 meter, descriptive of both the falling snow and the rocking cradle, must be felt in an easy *moderato* tempo. It must not err on the side of becoming too slow. The dynamic level should be quiet with very little variation until measure 11, where the text describes the child crying. Even here, the upward leap of the melodic line should create a *crescendo* of its own without much additional attention on the part of the singer. It is not intended as a "wrenching" statement, and a *diminuendo* should begin as early as measure 15. A slight rise and fall in the accompaniment precedes the announcement *La vecchia canta:* (The old woman sings:). Since she is described in the previous phrase, *il mento sulla mano* (her chin on her hand), *La vecchia canta* requires little dynamic increase.

Part B is the "song within a song." The tempo should be slightly faster, and the piano tone should be brighter, perhaps as a result of the change from minor to major tonality. Although an old woman is singing, no change of vocal color is warranted. The melodic line should be sung as marked, *legato e dolce.* A little *ritardando* is called for at the final phrase of the section *come un bel giardino* (like a beautiful garden). The piano should follow the voice here and slow down even more as the accompaniment fades away before the return of the original G-minor tonality.

The final section should begin *a tempo* and at the same quiet dynamic level as the introductory measures. The *rallentando,* which begins at the words *lenta, lenta, lenta* (slowly, slowly, slowly), continues to the end of the composition, the final *fiocca la neve* (falls the snow) being stretched as marked with *tenuto* indications. The accompaniment should die away in the last three measures, and the penultimate chord, although marked *sf pesante* (suddenly loud, heavy), should be played within the mood of the song, not overaccented. The song has few technical demands and works well as an introduction to the *lirica da camera* repertory.

Fiocca la neve: Bongiovanni–G. Schirmer, 1939.   38818

Umberto Giordano

(1867–1948)

•

È l'april che torna a me

(Gavino Gabriel)

1 È l'april che torna a me
2 col tuo passo legger come un sospir.
3 E nel mio cor si specchia già la luce del ciel.
4 Ma tu non disparir
5 come nube nel sol primaveril,
6 o sorriso di mia vita,
7 che splendi al mio desir.
8 È l'amor che viene a me
9 col tuo passo legger come un sospir.
10 Ecco l'april.

It is April which returns to me

1 It is April which returns to me
2 with your step light as a sigh
3 And in my heart is already mirrored the light of the sky.
4 But you do not vanish
5 like clouds under the springtime sun,
6 O smile of my life,
7 who sparkles at my desire.
8 It is love which comes to me
9 with your step light as a sigh.
10 Here is April.

È l'april che torna a me (It is April which returns to me) was published in 1932, many years after Giordano's great success with *Andrea Chenier,* in 1896, but it is a good example of the interest shown even by established operatic composers in the emerging *liriche da camera.* The song, in a loose ABA form, has the qualities of a lyrical *arietta;* all interest is in the sweeping melodic vocal line, the piano merely providing harmonic support and color. It has a strong nineteenth-century character with a few forward-sounding harmonic excursions. The tempo, *Moderato mosso* ($\downarrow = 116$), should regulate the calm flow of the piano's introductory arpeggios. Pedal markings, including releases, are clearly marked and should help the performer achieve the indicated *legato.* Although the block chords between the arpeggiated passages are not usually marked with pedal, they should be played as *legato* as possible, observing the voice leading. The vocal line should be sung rather broadly; in two phrases the composer has added the direction *senza precipitare le semicrome* (without rushing the sixteenth notes). The climactic phrase of the B section is marked *con espansione* (with expansiveness), the finale *deciso* (decisive). The singer will need to breathe in several phrases without the advantage of punctuation in the text, but the composer has clearly indicated them with phrase markings and the logical melodic shape of the phrase. In the one exception to this, *E nel mio cor si specchia già la luce del ciel* (And in my heart is already mirrored the light of the sky), the breath may be taken after *gia,* providing the *crescendo* continues through to *luce.* At the finale of the song, the *rallentando* should begin in the arpeggiated accompaniment beneath *sospir* (sigh), a big breath should be taken before *Ecco l'april* (Here is April), and each note should be accented. The singer should release with the pianist on the final rolled chord.

È l'april che torna a me: G. Ricordi, 1932; Repr. 1950.   122573

Carlo Jachino

(1887–1971)

•

Santa orazione alla Vergine Maria

(*Dal 33° Canto del Paradiso di Dante Alighieri*)

1 Vergine Madre, figlia del tuo figlio,
2 umile e alta più che creatura,
3 termine fisso d'eterno consiglio,
4 Tu sei colei che l'umana natura
5 nobilitasti sì che il suo Fattore
6 non disdegnò di farsi sua fattura.
7 Nel ventre tuo si raccese l'amore
8 per lo cui caldo nell'eterna pace
9 così è germinato questo fiore.
10 Qui sei a noi meridiana face
11 di caritade, e giuso in fra i mortali,
12 sei di speranza fontana vivace.
13 Donna, sei tanto grande e tanto vali,
14 che qual vuol grazia ed a te non ricorre,
15 sua disianza vuol volar senz'ali.
16 La tua benignità non può soccorre
17 a chi domanda, ma molte fiate
18 liberamente al dimandar precorre.
19 In te misericordia, in te pietade,
20 in te magnificenza, in te s'aduna
21 quantunque in creatura è di bontade.

Sacred oration to the Virgin Mary

(From Canto 33 of Dante's Paradise)

1 Virgin and Mother, daughter of your son,
2 humble and elevated more than any creature,
3 fixed goal of the Eternal Council.
4 You are the one whom human nature
5 so ennobled that its Maker
6 did not disdain to become its creature.
7 In thy womb was rekindled the love
8 by whose warmth in eternal peace
9 thus has grown this flower.
10 Here thou art for us the noonday torch
11 of charity, and below among mortals,
12 you are the living source of hope.
13 Lady, you are so great and worthy
14 that he who wants grace and does not turn to you,
15 his aspirations want to fly without wings.
16 Your goodness not only assists
17 him who asks, but many times
18 freely anticipates the request.
19 In you is mercy, in you is pity,
20 in you is magnificence, in you gathers
21 whatever goodness that is in any creature.

Santa orazione alla Vergine Maria (Sacred oration to the Virgin Mary), Carlo Jachino's setting of Canto 33 of Dante's *Paradiso,* attempts to create an appropriately religious atmosphere while maintaining an equally appropriate atmosphere of human warmth. The music is reserved and avoids dramatic extreme, aptly conveying the prayerful respect of the speaker. Yet, undulating chromatic harmonies envelop the whole composition in a Romantic aura. The piano part is the composer's reduction of a string orchestra score, so it must be conceived in these terms. *Legato* is absolutely essential. The composer's phrase marks are extremely important, since the uneven units are a factor in the forward movement of the wandering harmony. Sequential relationships, such as those in measures 7–10 and 12–16, should be brought out. Throughout the song the rhythmic motive of a dotted quarter, an eighth, and a half note often serves as a unifying factor, relating the various phrase units of the work. Although it is difficult to identify all the structural elements in this song, its sinuous chromaticism acts as the principal binder that holds the song together, and it does so quite successfully.

In the second half of the work, beginning around measure 50, the rhythmic movement increases. A greater number of eighth notes act both as chord tones and as passing tones. (Short ascending units of these eighth notes recur in various voices and transpositions to the end of the song, and some are actually sequential, e.g., measures 65–66). At the same time, there is a subtle but noticeable increase in the emotion of the speaker. In general, the vocal part of the song is quite independent of the instrumental part, yet the two are mutually conceived and complimentary. The vocal part follows speech rhythms throughout. The composer is sensitive to the placement of important words and syllables in terms of accent and pitch; and despite the independence of the parts, he never starts a new instrumental phrase in conflict with the natural flow of the singer's speech. Most of the vocal phrases are short enough to be sung on one breath, even at the suggested *largo* tempo; those that are too long can easily be broken into subphrases. For a song full of harmonic dissonances, it has a strikingly lyrical quality. Obviously, the composer is in awe of the magnificent Dante text and has determined to set it with respect and without interference. The interpretation should be approached in exactly that spirit.

The piano postlude, which begins in measure 72, is an almost exact repetition of measures 33–38, and they, in turn, are a variation of the opening measures of the song.

Santa orazione alla Vergine Maria: G. Ricordi, 1967.   131282

Fernando Liuzzi

(1884–1940)

•

Tre canti popolari greci

No. 1, Di notte

(Versione di Niccolò Tommasèo)

1 Fanciulla quando noi ci baciammo era notte:
2 or chi ci ha visti?
3 Ci vide la notte e l'alba, la stella e la luna.
4 E la stella si chinò, lo disse al mare:
5 il mar lo disse al remo, il remo al marinaro,
6 e il marinaro lo cantò dalla sua gentile alla porta.

Three popular Greek songs

No. 1, In the night

([Italian] translation by Niccolò Tommasèo)

1 Young girl, when we kissed it was night:
2 Now who saw us?
3 The night saw us and the dawn, a star, and the moon.
4 The star bowed down and told it to the sea:
5 the sea told it to the oar, the oar to the sailor,
6 and the sailor sang it at the doorway of his beloved.

The poems Fernando Liuzzi chose for his *Tre canti popolare greci* (Three popular Greek songs) share a folk-like quality. Each one involves a young girl, by direct address in the first two poems and by implication in the third. Musically, the settings owe a debt to Impressionism, but they are less atmospheric—earth-toned rather than pastel, in keeping with the poetry. The melodic interest centers in the vocal line, while the piano provides harmonic support and appropriate color. The songs are effective when programmed as a set.

The only tempo indication for *Di notte* (In the night) is *poco mosso* (a little motion), but anything faster than ♩ = 56 seems rushed and destroys the delicacy of the setting. Since the entire accompaniment is conceived in sixteenth notes like flowing water, it is only essential to keep them moving to observe the composer's intention. The two indications for a slowing down of tempo are qualified by the adjective *appena* (scarcely). The *pp* and *dolce* markings in the first measure set the mood, which remains much the same throughout the song. There is a natural *crescendo* in the phrase *il mar lo disse al remo, il remo al marinaro* (the sea told it to the oar, the oar to the sailor), but the very next phrase returns to *pp*. The accompaniment is essentially *legato,* but the highest treble notes in the piano part are usually marked *staccato,* giving a little additional sparkle to the texture and perhaps representing the play of light on water. The song is direct and uncomplicated and should be interpreted in that fashion.

No. 2, Solitudine

(*Versione di P.E. Pavolini*)

1   Ieri al chiaro delle stelle, alla luna lucente,
2   una fanciulla sedeva e piangeva, al cielo domandava:
3   "Luna mia lucente, tutto intorno lucente,
4   lassù dove alta cammini ed in basso guardi,
5   non vedesti, non t'accorgesti del mio diletto,
6   che m'abbandonò come canna nel campo?
7   In quai palazzi siede? in quali capanne beve?
8   Quali occhi lo guardano? e i miei piangono,
9   Quali labbra lo baciano? e le mie si spezzano;
10   Quale mano gli mesce e la mia trema, trema,
11   come foglia di limone che la soffiano i venti."

No. 2, Solitude

([*Italian*] *translation by P.E. Pavolini*)

1   Yesterday under the brightness of the stars, and the shining moon,
2   a young girl was sitting and weeping, she asked of the sky:
3   "My shining moon, shining all around,

4   up there where you travel high above and look down below,
5   did you not see, did you not notice my beloved,
6   who abandoned me like reeds in the field?
7   In which palaces does he sit? In which huts does he drink?
8   Whose eyes are looking at him? While mine weep,
9   Whose lips are kissing him? While mine are breaking.
10 Whose hand pours for him while mine trembles, trembles,
11 like the leaf of the lemon tree which is blown by the winds.

The *quasi-lento* tempo of *Solitudine* (Solitude) need only be a little slower, ♩ = 54, than the tempo of *Di notte,* since the rhythmic movement is now in eighth notes. The character of this flowing accompaniment pattern could be derived from the final word of the poem, *venti* (wind), as if a gentle wind moved throughout the song. The indication *dolce e lontano* in the first measure is an important clue to the expression of much of the song. The piano should be subordinate to the vocal line and phrased independently of it until the short melodic fragment immediately after the word *domandava* (she asked). This fragment, marked *un poco espressivo e ritardando* (slightly expressive and slower), provides a break between the descriptions of the narrator and the direct speech of the young girl. The change in texture provides enough contrast so that a change in vocal color is not necessary, particularly since direct address by the young girl continues to the end of the song. The supportive harmonic accompaniment should be very *legato,* observing the *tenuto* markings and the long phrase lines. A little more motion in the accompaniment leads to the first climax of the song at *che m'abban-donò come canna nel campo* (who abandoned me like reeds in the field). Although it is not marked, the dynamic level here should come up to *mf.* After a short section of recitative, *In quai palazzi siede? in quali capane beve?* (In which palaces does he sit? In which huts does he drink?), the melodic motive

in the piano part leads to greater rhythmic activity, a thicker texture, and finally to the climactic phrase, *Quale mano gli mesce e la mia trema, trema* (Whose hand pours for him while mine trembles, trembles). This is the emotional high point of the poem and the song, and it requires a full *crescendo* and greater intensity from the singer. The pianist should observe the sustained bass notes through this section even though most of the interest lies in the treble. The final lines of the song should re-create the distant qualities of the opening measures. With so many phrases of equal eighth notes throughout this song, the singer should practice the words in speech rhythm before superimposing them on the vocal line, otherwise the flow of the language may be impeded. Also, in keeping with the "popular" origin of the poetry, the performers should avoid the temptation to overdramatize the song.

No. 3, Crepuscolo

(*Versione di Niccolò Tommasèo*)

1   Gli è notte e tarda:
2   anche questo giorno se 'n va;
3   e noi, e noi non ci siam baciati,
4   càndida mia colomba, colomba mia.

No. 3, Twilight

([*Italian*] *translation by Niccolò Tommasèo*)

1   It is night and late:
2   also this day is going by;
3   and we, and we have not kissed each other,
4   my pure-white dove, my dove.

The tango-like rhythm of *Crepuscolo* (Twilight) provides a clear contrast to *Solitudine*. While the composer indicates the style to be *armonioso, un po'languido* (harmonious and a little languid), he also wants the rhythm to be very distinct (*ben distinto il ritmo*). The tempo should be approximately $\int$ = 66 or even slower to satisfy the *molto moderato–quasi-adagio* indication. Since the piano introduction is long and the rhythm patterns are so distinct, care must be taken to subordinate the accompaniment when the singer enters. The *staccato* markings in the piano part beneath the *legato* voice line help to create this needed contrast. At the phrase *e noi, e noi non ci siam baciati* (and we, and we have not kissed each other), the voice imitates the melodic material introduced by the piano. This ornate line, repeated again at the word *colomba* (dove), may be derived from the "cooing" sounds associated with this bird. Despite the lack of a kiss, the song is a happy one and a fitting conclusion to the set.

Tre canti popolari greci: Forlivesi, 1920.   10853 (Set)
    1. *Di notte*   10850
    2. *Solitudine*   10851
    3. *Crepuscolo*   10852

Tre piccoli canti popolari

No. 1, Canto di pescatori

(*Poesia popolare di Grado*)

1   Me domandè indòla vago co' le arte?
2   vago potando su le restie del mar;
3   I rimi in barca e co' la vela in parte,
4   a pescà quela che me vol amar.
5   Xe* belo el mar e bela la marina,
6   bela la barca co' la va a velo,
7   ma tu se' una stela, o mia bambina
8   e Gravo xe per me el to gran cielo!†

Three little popular songs

No. 1, Song of the fishermen

(*Popular poetry from Grado*)

1   I am asked where I go with my skills?
2   I go trimming the transverse winds of the sea;
3   the oars in the boat and with the sail at half mast,
4   to fish for the one who wants to love me.
5   How beautiful is the sea and how beautiful is the sea shore,
6   How beautiful is the boat when it goes sailing,
7   but you are a star, o my child
8   and Grado is for me your great sky!

Following his penchant for folk poetry, Fernando Liuzzi sets *Tre piccoli canti popolari* (Three little popular songs) of 1922 in much the same style as his *Tre canti popolari greci* of 1920. This time, however, he shows even less Impressionist influence. The songs are uncomplicated in construction and language and successful because of their simplicity. Their brevity and common origin in folk poetry require that they be performed as a set, although one of them could be singled out as a short encore after a program group.

Canto di pescatori (Song of the fishermen) bears one of Liuzzi's trademarks—a repetitive, uneven rhythmic pattern, which here probably represents the rocking of the boat. Interest centers in the vocal line, with the piano

---

*X is pronounced the same as s [z].
†No syntactic doubling is used in these dialects of northern Italy.

supplying harmonic support. The *tenuto* markings over the descending bass line in measures 1 and 2 indicate that these notes should get some stress as well as their full time value; they constitute a sort of countermelody to the more important vocal line. The song is in two parts, each consisting of two identical phrases. Part two begins in measure 9 with the third phrase of the song, even though the meter change does not occur until measure 10. A tempo of approximately ♩. = 50 should create the proper *lento* atmosphere, but the performers should feel free to adjust it, providing that the quarter note takes an equivalent tempo after the meter change. The dynamic range of the song is very narrow, *pp* to *mf.* The town of Grado, from which the poetry originates, is a seaside resort near Trieste, and the verse is in the dialect of that area.

No. 2, Canto d'amore

(*Poesia popolare di Trento*)

1   Ho visto una colomba al ciel volare.
2   l'andava a riposarse su 'n giardino.
3   D'oro e d'argento la g'aveva l'ale,
4   e 'n bocca la portava un gelsomino;
5   e 'l gelsomino l'era il vostro cuore,
6   e l'ale d'oro l'era il nostro amore.

No. 2, Song of love

(*Popular poetry from Trento*)

1   I saw a dove flying in the sky,
2   It was going to rest in a garden.
3   It had wings of gold and of silver,
4   and in its mouth it was carrying a jasmine,
5   and the jasmine was your heart,
6   and the golden wing was our love.

Canto d'amore (Song of love) is the happiest of the three songs in this set. It consists basically of three phrases in ABA form. The accompaniment, again with Liuzzi's "off-beat" rhythm pattern, supports a floating melody with two especially decorative figures on the words *volare* (flying) and *cuore* (heart). Even though the melody has an expansive outline, this song should be intimate in character. The dynamic range is narrow, and the final piano tones should trail off to nothing. The *molto moderato* (approximately ♩ =

108), which the composer indicates, may be a bit fast and, if necessary, may be adjusted to achieve a proper feeling of intimacy. Trento is the capital of the province of the same name in the north of Italy, approaching the Dolomite Alps.

No. 3, Canto di falciatrici

(*Poesia popolare marchigiana*)

1 Oh! che serve ch'io canti, ch'io canti?
2 'l mio amore sta lontano e non me sente...
3 Ce sta parata 'na brancia de oliva,
4 la voce è piccolina 'e non ce arriva.
5 Ce sta parata 'na brancia d'argente [*sic*],
6 la voce è piccolina, e non se sente.

No. 3, Song of the female mowers

(*Popular poetry from Le Marche*)

1 Oh! Of what use is it for me to sing, for me to sing?
2 My love is far away and does not hear me.
3 There is an olive branch shielding it,
4 my voice is tiny and it will not reach him.
5 There is a silver branch shielding it,
6 my voice is tiny and will not be heard.

The third and most serious of the songs in this set, *Canto di falciatrici* (Song of the female mowers) is through-composed to follow the anguished lines of the poetry. The piano supports the vocal line with chromatic chords and rather little rhythmic movement until the second half of the song. While recognizably melodic, the voice part is more speechlike than in the first two songs. There are three changes of key, but they seem unrelated to the text, unless some obscure subtlety in the folklore and dialect of the region is responsible for it. Le Marche is the region of east central Italy beginning at the eastern slopes of the Appenine Mountains and running to the Adriatic Sea. Ancona is the regional capital. The song is a simple lament and should be interpreted as such; the final line makes the distinction most clear.

Tre piccoli canti popolari: Forlivesi, 1922.   10948 (Set)
    1. *Canto di pescatori*
    2. *Canto d'amore*
    3. *Canto di falciatrici*

Franco Mannino

(1924–   )

•

Ecco la notte

(Benedetto Gareth detto "Il Cariteo")

1 Ecco la notte; e il ciel scintilla e splende
2 di stelle ardenti, lucide e gioconde;
3 i vaghi augelli e fere il nido asconde
4 e voce umana al mondo or non s'intende.
5 La rugiada del ciel tacita scende;
6 non si move erba in prato o 'n selva fronde;
7 ogni corpo mortal riposo prende.
8 Ma non riposa nel mio petto amore,
9 amor d'ogni creato acerbo fine;
10 anzi la notte cresce il suo furore.
11 Ha sementato in mezzo del mio core
12 mille pungenti avvelenate spine,
13 e 'l frutto che mi rende è di dolore.

Night is here

1 Night is here; and the sky sparkles and glitters
2 with stars blazing, bright and cheerful;
3 the graceful birds and wild animals are hidden in their nests
4 and the human voice everywhere now is not heard.
5 The dew from the sky silently descends;
6 the grass does not move in the meadow nor the leaves in the woods;
7 every mortal body takes its rest.
8 But love is not at rest in my heart,
9 love of every creation (has) a bitter end;

10   indeed night increases its fury.
11   It has sown in the middle of my heart
12   a thousand pricking, poisonous thorns,
13   and the fruit that it yields me is pain.

The poem of *Ecco la notte* (Night is here) is divided into two sections. The first is essentially a description of night, silent and still, but filled with memories of sounds and movement. The second is a bitter outpouring of human emotion, intensified by the very silence of night. The musical contrasts are clever. Throughout the song the vocal line, while lyrical, follows the word flow of the language—the effect is that of expanded speech. The range is extremely wide, but high notes are never approached through disjunct intervals. There is little difference in the outline of the vocal line between the two sections of the poem. However, the shifting balances between piano and voice make the meaning of the poetry exceedingly clear. The slow, quiet, Impressionistic introduction in the piano part sets the mood one would expect for a description of night. The pedal sustains the chords, the dynamic levels are low, and the rhythmic activity is slow. After the climactic vocal line *di stelle ardenti, lucide e gioconde* (with stars blazing, bright and cheerful), the rhythmic activity of the accompaniment becomes rapid and busy, describing or commenting on the memory images of night. The vocal line is considerably diminished against this continuing virtuostic piano activity, and even the highest notes in the vocal phrase are marked *pianissimo*.

In the second half of the song, beginning with the phrase *Ma non ripose nel mio petto amore* (But love is not at rest in my heart), a sudden drop in the activity of the piano immediately focuses attention on the vocal line. Aided by the *fortissimo* dynamic level, the bitterness of the poet's experience with love is made excruciatingly clear. The final *pianissimo* sustained on high A♮ at the word *dolore* (pain, sorrow) is ingenious.

The song is dedicated to soprano Renata Scotto and would require a virtuoso singer of her caliber to accomplish the wide range and the very high *pianissimo* called for in the score. The pianist must be similarly skilled to negotiate the rapidly repeated articulations and wide arpeggio figures in the first half of the song.

Ecco la notte: G. Ricordi, 1968.   131382

Franco Margola

(1908–   )

•

Possa tu giungere

(Giuliano d'Egitto, versione italiana di Emilio Mariano)

1   Possa tu giungere, o naufrago,
2   sino alla riva dell'ombra,
3   possa tu giungere salvo:
4   e, credi, la colpa è dei venti
5   non è dell'acqua:
6   ma i venti nel corpo ti fecero a brani,
7   mentre a scivolo dolce
8   le acque ti hanno cullato.
9   Nel grembo della tua terra
10 le acque ti hanno cullato
11 fino alle tombe dei padri,
12 fino alle tombe.

May you reach your destination

(Giuliano d'Egitto, Italian translation by Emilio Mariano)

1   May you reach your destination, o shipwrecked one,
2   up to the shade of the shore,
3   may you reach it unhurt:
4   and, believe, it is the fault of the winds
5   and not of the water:
6   but the winds in the body made you into pieces,
7   while gliding gently
8   the waters have lulled you.

9   In the bosom of your land
10   the waters have lulled you
11   up to the tombs of your (fore)fathers,
12   up to the tombs.

   The strange ambiguity of the poetry of *Possa tu giungere* (May you reach
your destination) is given a conservative three-part structural setting, even
though the dissonant harmonies aptly reflect the 1957 copyright date. The
vocal line, following the rhythmic flow of the language, contains no distinguishable melody. However, an examination of the song *in toto* shows that
the phrases in the first and last sections are short and not very connected,
while the broad melodic arch in the middle section basically forms a single
phrase. The accompaniment clearly shows the ABA structure of the song.
Slow funereal chords in dirgelike motion provide a two-measure introduction
and continue as an *ostinato* through more than half of the first section. Section
B is introduced by a four-measure piano interlude of rapid sixteenth-note
arpeggios and scales that then continue under the vocal line. This may depict
the movement of the wind, which figures so prominently in the imagery of
the poem. During the last part of section B, *mentre a scivolo dolce le acque
ti hanno cullato* (while gliding gently the waters have lulled you), the harmonic movement slows and there is little motion in the keyboard part. A
slight holding back of tempo is called for before the return of the A section
dirges. The final line of the song is somewhat like a coda, repeating harmonic
material and motives from section A. It is difficult to project the text imagery
of this song, but the technical aspects are not particularly demanding on
either the singer or the pianist.

Possa tu giungere: G. Ricordi, 1957.   129538 (S-T); 129539 (Br-Ms)

Mario Persico

(1892–1977)

•

Una rota si fa in cielo

(*Anonimo del sec. XIV*)

1   Una rota si fa in cielo
2   de tutti i Santi in quel zardino,
3   là ove sta l'Amor divino
4   che s'infiamma del suo amore.
5   In quella rota vanno i Santi,
6   vanno li angioli tutti quanti,
7   a quello Sposo van davanti,
8   tutti danzan per amore.
9   In quella corte è un'allegranza,
10 un amor a smisuranza:
11 tutti vanno ad una danza
12 per amor del Salvatore.
13 Son vestiti de vergato,
14 bianco, rosso e frammezzato;
15 le ghirlande in mezzo el capo:
16 ben mi pareno amatori
17 Tutti quanti con ghirlande,
18 paren giovin' de trent'anni:
19 quella corte se rinfranche,
20 ogni cosa è pien d'amore.
21 Le ghirlande son fiorite,
22 più che l'oro son chiarite.

A wheel is made in the sky

(*Anonymous fourteenth-century verse*)

1 A wheel is made in the sky
2 of all the Saints in that garden,
3 there where divine Love resides
4 that becomes enflamed by your love.
5 In that wheel go the Saints,
6 all of the angels go,
7 to that Bridegroom they go before,
8 all are dancing for love.
9 In that court is a jubilation,
10 a love that is boundless:
11 all are going to a dance
12 for love of the Saviour.
13 They are clad in stripes
14 white, red, and a mixture;
15 with wreaths encircling their heads:
16 indeed to me they appear to be lovers.
17 All of them with garlands,
18 (they) appear to be youthful persons about thirty years old:
19 that court is reassuring,
20 everything is full of love.
21 The garlands are in bloom,
22 more than gold they are bright.

What an extraordinarily human view of heaven is contained in *Una rota si fa in cielo* (A wheel is made in the sky)! The exuberance of the words should be the primary consideration in interpreting the musical setting. The opening chords, even though marked *piano* and *dolce,* evoke the pealing of great church bells. The chord progression, while basically tonal, faintly suggests a Gregorian-intoned *alleluia.* The vocal line reflects more of the rollicking 6/8 meter and should be approached with an almost childlike wonder and excitement, scrupulously observing such directions as *con crescente fervore* (with growing fervor), at the phrase *vanno li angioli tutti quanti* (all of the angels go), and *con esaltazione* (with exaltation), at the phrase *In quella corte è un'allegranza* (In that court is a jubilation). The chantlike cadences on *amore* (love) and *Salvatore* (Saviour) bear a sequential relationship to each other. Each cadence is imitated immediately by the piano. The *tenuto* and accent markings should be observed to point up this imitation.

The middle section of the song should have a hushed quality. The pianist, observing the *subito piano,* merely provides a *legato* harmonic back-

ground for the singer's wide-eyed description of the colorful heavenly garments. When the underlying chord pattern repeats in sequence, it should be
one dynamic level higher. The singer's short melisma on the word *amatori*
(lovers) should be imitated with the same inflection when it appears in the
bass line of the accompaniment. The *rallentando* on this phrase should be
very slight, and the *a tempo* returns immediately at the beginning of the final
section of the song.

With the phrase *Tutti quanti con ghirlande* (All of them with garlands),
the chord progression that opened the song returns. This time the vocal line
follows the roots of the chords with one syllable to a note, further enhancing
the chantlike effect. This slowing down of melodic rhythm is counteracted
by the arpeggiation of the accompaniment chords, which builds through a
crescendo and an *allargando* to the coda, where sweeping septuplet scales
underscore the final exclamations with *luminoso esultante* (luminous rejoicing). Beneath the final vocal phrases a melodic motive appears three times
in the piano part.

It should be brought out each time it occurs, and the exuberance that permeates the song should continue to the final arpeggiated chord.

Una rota si fa in cielo: G. Ricordi, 1930; Repr. 1949.   121444

Carillon

(*Autore ignoto*)

1 I dardi d'amore m'han colto nel cor
2 e senza dolore ne han desto l'ardor.
3 Si scrive e si dice che Amore è dolor;
4 giammai più felice è stato il mio cor.

Carillon

(*Author unknown*)

1 The darts of love have struck me in my heart
2 and without pain (they) have awakened ardor.

3 One writes and says that love is pain;
4 never more happy has been my heart.

The word *carillon* in Italian, as in English, refers most commonly to the bells hung in a church steeple. However, the pitch and character of the piano introduction to this song are more descriptive of the tiny bell-like sounds of a music box. This effect is borne out by the composer's directions to the pianist, *automaticamente* (automatically), and to the singer, *quasi senza espressione* (almost without expression). The *rallentandi* and *a tempi* should be similarly mechanical. A constant dynamic level of *piano* should be maintained throughout the song, varied only by the gentle *crescendi* indicated at the climax of a phrase. Both singer and pianist must be aware of the canonic writing throughout the song; the inflections of the singer dictated by the words should be imitated as closely as possible by the accompaniment, and the *a tempo* at *I dardi d'amore* (The darts of love) in the return of part A should be very strict. The singer must observe the final *decrescendo* and also hold the final note until the release of the rolled chord in the accompaniment.

Carillon: Casa Editore Musicale F. Curci; Repr. G. Ricordi, 1938.   124329

Alberto Peyretti

(1936–   )

●

O Notte

(Giuseppe Ungaretti)

1   Dall'ampia ansia dell'alba svelata alberatura.
2   Dolorosi risvegli.
3   Foglie, sorelle foglie, v'ascolto nel lamento.
4   Autunni, moribonde dolcezze.
5   O gioventù, passata è appena l'ora del distacco.
6   Cieli alti della gioventù.
7   Libero slancio.
8   E già sono deserto.
9   Perso in questa curva malinconia.
10 Ma la notte sperde le lontananze.
11 Oceanici silenzi,
12 Astrali nidi d'illusione.
13 O notte.

O night

1   From the broad anxiety of daybreak reveal your grove of trees.
2   Painful awakenings.
3   Leaves, sister leaves, I listen to you in your lament.
4   Autumns, dying softness.
5   O youth, the hour of separation has hardly passed.
6   Celestial heights of youth.
7   Free impulse.
8   And already I am deserted.
9   Lost in this curved melancholy.

10 But night vanishes distances.
11 Oceanic silences,
12 Astral nests of illusion.
13 O night.

Alberto Peyretti's musical style, as seen in *O Notte* (O night), is strongly influenced by Impressionism filtered through the music of the Italian composers of the generation immediately preceding his. Italian lyricism is ever present, and the harmonic vocabulary is essentially conservative. Poet Giuseppe Ungaretti's extraordinary image-bearing language centers on the lines *E già sono deserto./Perso in questa curva malinconia* (And already I am deserted./Lost in this curved melancholy), which the composer selects as the focus for his moody musical setting.

The three-part song structure loosely follows the poem. The opening and closing sections describe the overall milieu and mood, while the contrasting B section is a more direct address to youth. The distinctive rhythmic motive of a sixteenth note and a dotted eighth on the first beat of the piano introduction is repeated in nearly every measure of section A, pointing up the impatient, nervous anxiety lurking beneath the surface of the poem. The motive does not require any special treatment by the pianist, for it is distinctive enough as written and should be made part of the overall phrase line. The piano carries almost all of the musical interest in the song. The vocal line follows speech rhythms and uses pitch area rather than distinctive interval relationships to express the meaning of the words. The integration of voice and piano is total. The short, choppy phrases in the vocal line of section A may seem to break the word flow, but actually they underscore the nervousness of the poetry. The vocal line should not, however, unduly influence the longer phrase units built into the piano part. A new motive appears with the direction *espressivo* in measure 15 and is repeated sequentially in measure 18. The *col canto* (with the voice) direction in the latter measure is intended to assist the expression of the singer on the words *v'ascolto* (I listen to you). The long piano interlude beginning in measure 20 builds to the first musical climax of the song, but it should not overshadow the peak dynamic phrase still to come in section B. The *staccato* bass notes and the *ppp* in measures 28–29 reflect the word *dolcezze* (softness).

The *più mosso* and the appearance of a new melodic idea mark the start of section B, which immediately launches into the song's most expansive musical phrase. The *decrescendo* from this climax should be interpreted liberally, as indicated in measure 37, and a projection of the return to the slower Tempo I° must also begin here since the composer forbids a *rallentando* in measure 39. Echoes of the B theme prepare the close of the section, but the final line, *E già sono deserto./Perso in questa curva malinconia* (And already I am deserted./Lost in this curved melancholy)—the phrase most revealing of the poet's desperation—should be sung freely and without accompaniment.

Section A returns with a piano introduction identical to the first measures of the song, but the vocal line does not repeat. The meter changes to 4/4 in the seventh measure of the section (measure 52). The piano repeats fragments of thematic material in harmonic sequence. The voice more or less "speaks" the final poetic *Oceanici silenzi,/Astrali nidi d'illusione./O notte* (Oceanic silences,/Astral nests of illusion./O night) above this, and the composer indicates a broadening and diminishing expression through to the end. Singer and pianist should release the final notes together.

O notte: G. Ricordi, 1968.   131315

Ora che sale il giorno

(*Salvatore Quasimodo*)

1 Finita è la notte
2 e la luna si scioglie lenta nel sereno,
3 tramonta nei canali.
4 È così vivo settembre
5 in questa terra di pianura,
6 i prati sono verdi
7 come nelle valli del Sud a primavera.
8 Ho lasciato i compagni,
9 ho nascosto il cuore dentro le vecchie mura
10 per restare solo a ricordarti.
11 Come sei più lontana della luna,
12 ora che sale il giorno
13 e sulle pietre batte
14 il piede dei cavalli!

Now that the day ascends

1 The night is ended
2 and the moon slowly releases itself, in the clear sky,
3 it sets in the canals.
4 September is so vivid
5 in this land of open plains,
6 the meadows are green
7 as in the valleys of the South in springtime.
8 I have left my companions,
9 I have hidden my heart within the old walls
10 in order to remain alone to remember you.
11 How much farther away are you than the moon,
12 now that the day ascends

13   and on the stones beats
14   the hoof of the horses!

With the same conservative language used in *O Notte* Peyretti again demonstrates his ability to create an appropriate musical mood, this time for the verses of Salvatore Quasimodo, *Ora che sale il giorno* (Now that the day ascends).

An undulating pattern of eighth-note triplets in the piano part provides a running background for most of the song. They are marked at the beginning *legato ed uguale* (smooth and steady) and must remain so to the very end of the composition. Above this murmuring background is a single-line melody of haunting expressiveness. The vocal line, entering after a long introduction, weaves in and around the piano melody, occasionally creating a casual sounding, but thoughtfully crafted, duet. The piano part could stand alone, much as it does in *O Notte,* but the greater prominence given the voice part in *Ora che sale* prevents attention from settling on only one part. Melodic ideas move freely from voice to piano and back, sometimes appear together (or in loose counterpoint), and many times overlap in independent musical phrases. A rich climax is reached at the phrase *a primavera* (in springtime), which should be stretched slightly at the composer's direction *ritenendo un po'* (slowing a little). The descending arpeggio in the piano, which extends this phrase, may also be stretched. A *diminuendo* and a *rallentando* bring the section to a close.

The introduction of the poet's direct action, *Ho lasciato i compagni* (I have left my companions), into what had been landscape description dictates a decided departure from earlier musical ideas as part B begins. The voice part is now prominent and much less melodic—*quasi*-declarative. These utterances should be sung liberally, but the short piano phrases that comment on them with nostalgic material from section A must be played *a tempo*. As the piano provides more harmonic support it is marked *sensibile* (sensitive, tangible) and finally *scuro* (dark) after the poet's longing takes full hold of him.

The third section of the song brings back the opening undulating triplet pattern and melodic line. The vocal line consists of different notes, but the construction is the same as in the earlier section. There is a short piano postlude of melodic fragments, but the voicing of the final chord leaves the tonality ambiguous.

Most of the vocal phrases can be sung on one breath. Two may need breaks: in section A, *È così vivo settembre in questa terra di pianura* (September is so vivid in this land of open plains), where the breath may be taken after *settembre;* and the final phrase of the song, *e sulle pietre batte il piede dei cavalli!* (and on the stones beats the hoof of the horses), where the breath may be taken after *batte.*

Ora che sale il giorno: G. Ricordi, 1968.   131316

Giacomo Puccini

(1858–1924)

•

E l'uccellino

(Renato Fucini)

1 E l'uccellino canta sulla fronda:
2 dormi tranquillo, boccuccia d'amore:
3 piegala giù quella testina bionda,
4 della tua mamma posala sul cuore.
5 E l'uccellino canta su quel ramo:
6 tante cosine belle imparerai,
7 ma se vorrai conoscer quant'io t'amo,
8 nessuno al mondo potrà dirlo mai!
9 E l'uccellino canta al ciel sereno:
10 dormi, tesoro mio, qui sul mio seno.

And the little bird

1 And the little bird sings on the leafy branch:
2 sleep calmly, little mouthful of love:
3 bend down that little blond head,
4 lay it on the heart of your mamma.
5 And the little bird sings on that branch:
6 so many beautiful little things you will learn,
7 but if you want to know how much I love you,
8 no one in the world will ever be able to tell you!
9 And the little bird sings in the serene sky:
10 sleep, my darling, here on my breast.

Puccini's song writing was confined primarily to his student days or to some specific commission. He was not a true composer of *liriche* in the integrated style of the major composers considered in this book. *E l'uccellino* (And the little bird), however, has a certain charm and, as a novelty, deserves to be included in a recital of *liriche*.

The style is folk-like, beginning with a simple accompaniment of repetitive figures in the bass and off-beat chords in the treble. It should be played very lightly, at a moderate tempo; and the contrast of *legato* and *staccato* indications should be highlighted. The vocal line is equally simple and should be sung without affectation, like a typical lullaby.

The operatic Puccini is never far distant, however; and the octave doubling (between voice and piano), sweeping melodic arch, and sudden modulation in the third phrase—*piegala giù quella testina bionda* (bend down that little blond head)—has all the earmarks of *Tosca* or *La Bohème*. The phrase is marked *dolce e carezzevole* (sweet and caressing). The song is strophic with an ABABA structure that follows the poem. *Rubato* is clearly indicated, and the song poses no problems of range or length of phrase. Suitable for all voice types without transposition, *E l'uccellino* provides a good introduction to Puccini for a young singer or a student.

E l'uccellino: G. Ricordi, 1899; Repr. 1946.   102625

Giulia Recli

(1890–   )

•

Bella bellina

(*Parole popolari senesi*)

1 Bella bellina, quando vai per acqua,
2 La via della fontana ti favella;
3 È 'l rusignuol che canta nella macchia,
4 E' va dicendo che sei la più bella. Ah!
5 Sei la più bella e la più graziosina,
6 sembri una rosa colta sulla spina;
7 Sei la più bella e la più graziosetta,
8 Sei la più bella, e la più graziosina,
9 sembri la rosa sulla fresca spina. Ah!

Pretty, pretty young girl

(*Popular Sienese poetry*)

1 Pretty, pretty young girl, when you go for water,
2 the way to the fountain talks to you;
3 It is the nightingale that sings in the bush,
4 And he goes about saying that you are the most beautiful. Ah!
5 You are the most beautiful and the most charming,
6 you seem like a rose picked above the thorns;
7 you are the most beautiful and the most gracious.
8 You are the most beautiful, and the most charming,
9 you seem like the rose above the fresh thorns. Ah!

Sienese folk poetry finds an appropriately simple musical setting in Giulia Recli'a song *Bella bellina* (Pretty, pretty young girl). The song is an ABA form with a change of key and tempo to mark the contrasting middle section. The melodic and rhythmic material are quite similar throughout the song. The *allegretto* tempo should be approximately ♩ = 120, with the composer's directions *con freschezza* (with freshness) and *grazioso* (graceful). The supporting piano accompaniment is marked *dolcissimo,* and the indication *due pedale* (two pedals) requires the use of both damper and soft pedals. The opening accompaniment is phrased in two-chord units, with a drop-release articulation. The vocal line, in longer units, rides above this, and the singer should be careful not to overaccent the weaker syllables in the long lines of equal eighth notes. This song has the rhythmic character of many popular folk songs that serve for both singing and dancing. The pianist should observe the change in the *staccato* style of accompaniment at the phrase *E' va dicendo che sei la più bella* (And he goes about saying that you are the most beautiful). When the phrase repeats, the composer asks for an echoing dynamic effect. The measure immediately preceding section B contains a *ritardando* and *fermati* and should be counted as if in four. The B section, beginning with *Sei la più bella, e la più graziosina* (You are the most beautiful, and the most charming), is slightly slower in tempo and is very cleverly constructed. The voice part introduces a new melody similar in character to section A, but clearly recognizable in its own right. The piano part is a transposed variation, again clearly recognizable, of the vocal melody from section A. The "duet" of countermelodies continues through the section until the voice sustains a single pitch "ah" and the piano beneath it repeats the earlier "echo" measure from section A. After six measures of transitional material the final division of this three-part form begins with a repetition of the first four lines of the poem and its corresponding original setting. A *ritardando* begins in the transitional material, and the *a tempo* should not return until the word *bellina* in the second measure of the last section of the song. The *pianissimo* and *rallentando* should be observed when the "echo" phrase appears in the penultimate line of the song. The final line should fade away gently. The high G at the end is preferable to the B alternative, but only if the singer can float this note lightly. Tenors should probably choose the lower note.

Bella bellina: G. Ricordi, 1926; Repr. 1949.   120014

Licinio Refice

(1883–1954)

•

Ombra di nube

(Emidio Mucci)

1 Era il ciel un arco azzurro di fulgor;
2 chiara luce si versava sul mio cuor.
3 Ombra di nube, non mi offuscare;
4 della vita non velarmi la beltà.
5 Vola, o nube, vola via da me lontan;
6 sia disperso questo mio tormento arcan.
7 Ancora luce, ancora azzurro!
8 Il sereno io vegga per l'eternità!

Shadow of a cloud

1 The sky was a blue archway of radiance;
2 bright light poured over my heart.
3 Shadow of a cloud, do not cover me;
4 do not conceal from me the beauty of life.
5 Move quickly, o cloud, move quickly far away from me;
6 let my secret torment be dispersed.
7 Still light, still blue!
8 May I see the clear sky forever!

Licinio Refice's setting of *Ombra di nube* (Shadow of a cloud) passes almost as quickly and simply as the passing cloud it describes. The song is divided into two sections corresponding to the two verses of the poem. The short piano introduction of descending thirds seems to lead in the direction of F minor, but after a short pause the song begins in A♭ major with an eight-measure period containing clear antecedent and consequent phrases. A second eight-measure period modulates to F minor, possibly in response to the poetic imagery of a dark cloud appearing in the otherwise clear blue sky. The overall dynamic level of the section is quiet and *molto intimo* (very intimate). When the shadow appears the song becomes more animated and moves toward its first climax, at the phrase *non mi offuscare; della vita non velarmi la beltà* (do not cover me; do not conceal from me the beauty of life). The composer is generous with breath indications; the first two can probably be overlooked in favor of a longer, shaped phrase, but the breath mark before the final *la beltà* may be needed for the louder sustained sound and the *ritardando* indicated in the score. At all times the very melodic vocal line carries the interest in the song, and the piano either supports it harmonically or doubles it.

The second half of the song, beginning with the Tempo I°, is an exact repetition of the first half of section one, this time at an even quieter dynamic level. The mood is abruptly broken with two short, somewhat louder phrases marked *implorando* (imploring)—a frightened reaction to the cutoff of light and sky from the exterior and interior worlds of the poet. The final consequent phrase duplicates the consequent phrase from the beginning of the verse and brings the song back to a clear A♭-major tonality. It is marked *estremamente piano e rall.* (extremely soft and slowed down).

With the exception of a few illogical chord progressions and the abrupt dynamic changes, there is little in the song to suggest its 1949 composition date. But the conservatism in itself is an apt statement for the simplicity of the poetry. It should be performed with no more drama than the composer indicates, and the final impression should be one of calm, not agitation. The composer has taken some poetic liberties in the final syllables of *fulgore—fulgor* (radiance), *cuore—cuor* (heart), *lontano—lontan* (away), and *arcano—arcan* (secret); the original poem by Emidio Mucci is printed correctly at the end of the song.

Ombra di nube: G. Ricordi, 1949.   128062

Francesco Santoliquido

(1883–1971)

•

Tre poesie persiane

I.

(*Negi de Kamare*)

1 Quando le domandai
2 la causa della nostra lontananza,
3 essa mi rispose: te lo dirò.
4 Io sono il tuo occhio, e sono la tua anima.
5 Perchè ti sorprendi se tu non mi vedi?
6 Dimmi: chi ha mai potuto vedere l'anima?
7 Dimmi? Dimmi?

Three Persian poems

I.

1 When I asked her
2 the cause of our distance,
3 she answered me: I will tell (it to) you.
4 I am your sight, and I am your soul.
5 Why are you surprised if you do not see me?
6 Tell me: who has ever been able to see the soul?
7 Tell me? Tell me?

II.

(*Omar Khayyam*)

1   Io mi levai dal centro della Terra.
2   A traverso la settima porta,
3   e m'assisi sul trono di Saturno.
4   E molti Enigmi divinai nel cammino.
5   Ma non l'Enigma della morte umana,
6   nè quello del destino.

II.

1   I rose up from the center of the Earth.
2   Through the seventh door,
3   and I sat on the throne of Saturn.
4   And I divined many Enigmas along the way.
5   But not the Enigma of human death,
6   nor that of destiny.

III.

(*Abu-Said*)

1   Le domandai:
2   A chi vuoi legare il tuo destino tu così bella?
3   Essa mi rispose:
4   a me stessa,
5   perchè sono l'unica!
6   Perchè sono l'amore,
7   son l'amante
8   e l'amata!
9   Perchè sono lo Specchio,
10   la Bellezza
11   e la visione!

III.

1   I asked her:
2   To whom do you want to tie your destiny, you so beautiful?
3   She answered me:
4   To myself,

5   because I am unique!
6   Because I am love,
7   I am the lover
8   and the loved one!
9   Because I am the Mirror
10 the Beauty
11 and the vision!

The exotic and somewhat mysterious *Tre poesie persiane* (Three Persian poems) provide Francesco Santoliquido with apt images for his neo-Romantic style. While not cyclical, in the sense of shared melodic material, they are key related (the keys ascend in major thirds), and they progress logically in *tempi* and dynamics to create a strong program group.

The first song is built around a distinctive melodic motive:

which appears again and again in the piano part, sometimes in the prominent upper voice and often in an inner voice line that resolves deep in the chord structure (see measure 7). Since it is the principal musical material of the song, the pianist must seek out all its appearances and endeavor to link them seamlessly throughout a section. Western minds often associate the languid quality of this motive with Middle Eastern art and style.

The song is in a free three-part form, and almost all the musical interest is in the piano part. The vocal line is little more than recitative at the beginning and end of the song and only picks up melodic interest in the middle, when it parallels a series of piano chord sequences. The composer asks for a slow tempo at the start of the song, but it should not be so slow that the forward motion is interrupted. The song could be conceived as one long, elastic phrase with fluctuations in tempo related to the emotion of the text. The response in the poem from the person the poet addresses should not be sung with a change of color. In all three songs the voices of the poet and the character who speaks to him are too mystically entwined to justify the change. A slight hesitation can be allowed after *mi rispose* (she answered me), and a mood change, *solenne* (solemn), rides over the whole measure. The last three measures of the song are marked *con grande lentezza* (with great slowness), but the rhythmic motion of the eighth and sixteenth notes still validates a forward movement of the phrase. The rather long vocal phrase in the middle section can be interrupted for breath after *occhio* (sight), *anima* (soul), and *sorprendi* (surprised) to provide stamina for the climax on *mi vedi* (see me).

The tempo for the second song, *allegretto bizzaro* (lively and bizarre), indicates the mood of the musical setting of this strange poem. The opening measure of the piano introduction, like that of the first song, provides distinctive material that links the sections of the song with its quasi-recitative vocal line. A motive buried in the bass line at measure 4 and marked *cupamente* (darkly) appears once again at the end of the song, underscoring the dramatic words *morte umana* (human death).

The opening statement of the singer, *Io mi levai* (I rose up), is enhanced by the ascending sixteenth notes in the accompaniment. It requires a *crescendo–decrescendo* dynamic scheme as it leads toward the sustained chords accompanying the next section. The alternation in the accompaniment between measures of great pianistic activity and measures of very little motion further contributes to the bizarre qualities called for at the beginning of the song.

There are two major climaxes: in measure 10, at the word *Saturno* (Saturn); and five measures from the end, when the piano builds toward the climactic words *Ma non l'Enigma della morte umana* (But not the Enigma of human death). The references to the seventh door and Saturn are obscure. In Roman mythology Saturn was the god of harvests and sat enthroned on Capitoline Hill.

The musical contrasts from section to section of the song can be enhanced by the pianist's articulation—the rapid sections somewhat marked and the sustained chords very *legato,* usually phrased over two measures. The vocal part should be close to speech, observing the composer's directions: *grave e mistico* (solemn and mystical), *cupo* (dark, gloomy), and *con solenne tristezza* (with solemn sadness). The final chords in the piano part must be played together, without arpeggiation.

The third song of the set is essentially through-composed, but there are clear-cut sections, and the opening accompaniment pattern returns in the final measures. This song has the most recognizably melodic vocal line of the three, in part because it is set off against an unobtrusive, arpeggiated accompaniment. For the first time in the set, the voice carries the musical interest. The tempo is *andante mistico, lentamente* (mystical andante, slowly). The eighth notes of the arpeggiated triplets are marked *eguale e tranquillo* (even and tranquil). The motion of the bass line, however, can be given slight stress to propel the vocal line. A slow *crescendo* and a slight increase in tempo build through all of page 3, climaxing at the second appearance of the word *l'unica* (unique).

In the contrasting middle section, interest shifts partially to the piano part, which first supports the vocal line and then provides a melodic link for the two variations on *l'amore* (love): *l'amante* (lover) and *l'amata* (loved one).

The final line of poetry is introduced over a sinuous line of eighth notes derived from the piano part of the preceding section. The vocal part, in a slowly rising melodic line, carries the direction *profondo e sonoro* (profound and resonant). A repetition of the final line of poetry builds to a *fortissimo* climax over an arpeggiated chordal accompaniment like that of the introductory measures of the song.

The poetic vision wrapped in this broad, intense setting provides an exciting finale for the song group.

Tre poesie persiane: Forlivesi, 1954.
       I.   10803
       II.   10804
       III.   10805

Achille Simonetti

(1857–1928)

●

Madrigale

(H. Ulrich, traduzione di Pietro Floridia)

1 Su la lontana e solitaria vetta,
2 che s'erge al cielo fra le nubi d'or,
3 io vo' abbracciarti, o bionda giovinetta,
4 bearmi in te d'un infinito amor!
5 Saperti mia, fra le mie braccia stretta
6 e darti tutto il cor!
7 Se separarci mai dovrà il destin,
8 la mia zampogna mesta echeggierà

9 per monti e valli, lungo il mio cammin,
10 querulo suon, che guida a te sarà,
11 finchè non torni ancora a me
12 il divino raggio di tua beltà!
13 Giù ne la valle, a la natìa chiesuola
14 non odi tu de l'Ave il tintinnar?
15 mentre il tramonto tinge di viola
16 il piano e fa le rocce folgorar.
17 A me ti stringi! È muta ogni parola
18 e tutto dice: "Amar!"
19 A me ti stringi, chè tutto dice: "Amar!"

Madrigal

(H. Ulrich, [Italian] translation by Pietro Floridia)

1 On the distant and solitary mountain peak,
2 that rises to the sky among the clouds of gold,

3   I want to embrace you, o blond young girl,
4   for me to delight in you of an infinite love!
5   To know you are mine, tight within my arms
6   and to give you all of my heart!
7   If destiny should ever separate us,
8   my bagpipe will sadly echo
9   through mountains and valleys, throughout my journey,
10 a mournful sound, that will be a guide to you,
11 until no longer comes back to me
12 the divine ray of your beauty!
13 Down in the valley, at the little native church
14 do you not hear the ringing of the Hail Mary?
15 While the sunset tinges with violet
16 the plain and makes the rocks shine.
17 I press you to me! Every word is silent
18 and everything says: "To love!"
19 I press you to me, because everything says: "To love!"

Achille Simonetti's *Madrigale* (Madrigal) is a simple three-part song form harking back to the folk-inspired settings crafted by the German composers of a generation or two earlier and sharing some elements with the even earlier form from which it takes its title. The piano provides a chordal accompaniment for most of the song while melodic interest centers in the vocal line. The melody has a very decided "Italian" flavor, rather like a tune one might hear wafting through a *piazza* on a sunny afternoon. The three parts of the song correspond loosely to the three divisions of the poem. In part A, initially and when it returns, the poet is in possession of his beloved, at least in his imagination. In part B the element of doubt and separation provides enough textual contrast to justify contrasting musical material.

The first vocal phrase, marked *con semplicità* (with simplicity), appears again in the piano part as a bridge to part B, where it is marked *marcata la melodia* (stress the melody). Part B is in the dominant key. After the third measure of the section, a countermelody in the piano part, *marcando dolcemente la melodia* (gently stressing the melody), introduces a nice textural variation. Just as the opening melodic material of part A acted as a bridge to part B, an exact repetition of the final four measures of part A cleverly leads into the final section, A¹ now in the tonic. A piano interlude using the opening theme leads to a short *codetta*.

The simplicity called for at the beginning of the song should be the prime interpretive consideration throughout. The pianist should stress the bits of melodic material that emerge in the transitional phrases and in the countermelody, and the singer should attempt a straightforward folk-like presentation of the words and melody. The song would make a good encore for a program of heavier *liriche*. The original German text is very freely translated into Italian by Pietro Floridia, who is well known for his modern arrangements of *arie antiche italiane*.

Madrigale: G. Ricordi, Repr. 1948.   100096

Ruggero Vené

(1897–   )

•

L'Att̲esa vana

(*Giovanni Improva*)

1 La s̲era è sc̲esa e tu n̲on sei venuta
2 e l'̲ombra ha pop̲olata
3 la pin̲eta di fanta̲sime strane.
4 Perchè n̲on sei venuta?
5 T'ho att̲esa tutto il gi̲orno al limite d̲el bosco,
6 sussultando ad ̲ogni batter d'ali,
7 ad ̲ogni fruscio d̲ei timidi ramarri,
8 e̲ mi fioriva in core un d̲olce madrigale,
9 e̲ rinverdiva una speme sopita,
10 e̲ un fuoco n̲el mio sangue ard̲ea più vivo.
11 Quanto tempo, c̲on l'anima prot̲esa
12 lontano lontano
13 sulla strada bianca, ho spiato il tuo arrivo?
14 Ora è già notte, e̲ invano l'occhio mio
15 tenta scrutare n̲ella tenebra f̲onda.
16 Perchè n̲on sei venuta?

The useless waiting

1 Evening has come and you have not come
2 and darkness has populated
3 the pine grove with strange phantoms.
4 Why have you not come?
5 I have waited for you all day by the edge of the woods,
6 startling at every beating wing,

7   at every rustle of the timid green lizards,
8   and within my heart was flowering a sweet madrigal,
9   and it revived a soothing hope.
10 and a fire in my blood burned more vividly.
11 How long, with my soul outstretched
12 far, far off
13 on the white road, have I watched for your arrival?
14 Now it is already night, and in vain my eyes
15 try to search in the deep darkness.
16 Why have you not come?

L'Attesa vana (The useless waiting) begins and ends with descriptions of the descent of night and a quiet questioning. The middle of the poem contains quicker, more vivid images and produces a mood of anxiety. The song, in modified ABA form, parallels the construction of the poem.

The pattern of the two-measure piano prelude, marked *melanconico e lento* (melancholy and slow), is conventional harmonically, and it continues without interruption beneath the entrance of the vocal line. Close examination of this part, especially of the tied notes and of the phrasing of the upper treble notes, reveals a subtle melodic motive. It begins on the third beat of each measure with a rising interval, in eighth notes, which then "lands" on the first beat of the next measure and tapers off to the second beat. This pattern may seem too subtle to be of any importance, but it appears too consistently to be ignored. It also accounts for the composer's dynamic indications, provides a sensible guideline for the pianist's phrasing of what could otherwise be a plodding accompaniment, and creates a forward-moving momentum beneath the longer phrases of the singer. The singer actually picks up this "motive" at the phrase that begins at *la pineta* (the pine grove). The composer's breath marking, placed before it, should be observed to point up the motive and to provide the energy for the broadened climax of the opening section. The final words before the key change, *Perchè non sei venuta?* (Why have you not come?), should be slightly separated from the preceding phrase and should be "spoken" in contrast to the earlier, more lyrical writing.

A key change marks the opening of the central section of the song, and the tempo more than doubles ($\quarternote$ = 132). The rippling sixteenth notes in the piano part cascade over a bass line that becomes audibly melodic in measure 15. The pianist should bring this out and give special attention to the *tenuto* markings in the treble at measure 18, where the pattern emerges again. It is interrupted in the next phrase by a change in the accompaniment that suggests the *batter d'ali* (literally, "beating of wings") and *fruscio dei timidi ramarri* (rustle of the timid green lizards). The writing in measures 19–23 is quite wonderful: over a ground bass E♮, the seventh chords move chromatically upward, then break into arpeggiations in the treble that move downward to the first beat of the next measure, at the same time paralleling the vocal line. The composer's direction *precipitare* (to rush ahead) is hardly needed since so much expression is built into the construction. In measures 24–26 the timidity of the green lizards is accounted for by the breaks in the vocal phrase, the slowing down of the accompaniment pattern, and the direction *molto ampio* (very broad).

At the tempo change in measure 28 a seemingly new accompaniment pattern emerges, but it bears some relationship to the inner voices of the introduction to the song. In measures 29–35 the upper treble notes refer to the melodic motive in the bass clef at measure 15. Anticipating the rise of emotion in the poem, Vené begins a new accompaniment pattern in measure 36, slows the tempo, and asks for *marcato* articulation. The piano chords are marked *pesante,* and the vocal line begins a long chromatic progression to the climax of the song in measure 45. The line is broken into two- and three-measure phrase units, but the singer should strive to connect them dynamically. A slow measure of stressed chords and two important *fermati* in measure 47 lead to the return of section A.

In measures 48–56 the piano patterns are an almost exact repetition of the opening of the song. While the vocal line is different, its relationship to the accompaniment is similar, and the original quiet, melancholy mood returns. A short, contrasting phrase interrupts (measures 57–60), carrying the direction *sommesso* (subdued), and soft pedal is required in the accompaniment. The final question of the poem is written above another repetition of the opening motive and partially parallels it. It should also be somewhat "spoken." The tempo is *lentamente,* and the quiet dynamic dies away to nothing as the final chord is held.

L'attesa vana: G. Ricordi, 1935.   123285

Stornello lunigiano

(*Autore ignoto*)

1 O rondinella che voli per l'aria
2 Ritorna indietro e fammelo un piacere.
3 Dammi una penna delle tue ali
4 Che scriver vo' allo mio amore!
5 Quando l'avrò scritta e fatta bella
6 Ti renderò la penna, o rondinella.
7 Quando l'avrò scritta e fatta pura,
8 Ti renderò la penna, o creatura.
9 E quando l'avrò scritta e fatta bene,
10 Ti renderò la penna che ti viene.

The swallow from Luni

(*Author unknown*)

1   O little swallow you who fly though the air
2   come back and do me a favor.
3   Give me a feather from your wings
4   because I want to write to my love!
5   When I will have written it and have made it beautiful
6   I will give back to you the feather, o little swallow.
7   When I will have written it and have made it pure,
8   I will give back to you the feather, o creature.
9   And when I will have written it and have made it good,
10 I will give back to you the feather that is yours.

Stornello lunigiano (The swallow from Luni) is a simple, affecting song. (Luni is the capital of the province of Etruria.) The song is rather conservative for the year in which it was published, 1935, but a close examination of the chords reveals a number of Impressionist tendencies. The prominent, very Italianate melodic line in the voice part carries the primary interest in the setting; it is more sophisticated, perhaps, but very similar to the lines of popular Neapolitan song.

In the opening measures of the piano part the sustained half notes in the treble should stand out a little from the texture and be phrased across four bar lines. A slight stretch of the accompaniment figures is called for in the measure just before the entrance of the voice. Following the upper treble line, as the piano part progresses, a faint but recognizable countermelody emerges in expressive opposition to the more important voice part.

The text is set with obvious attention to word rhythms and accents, but the song glories in the expressive capabilities of the human voice. This is definitely a song to be "sung," and the composer's directions bear this intention out. It is marked *semplice e libero* (simple and free) at the beginning, followed by *gaio e semplice* (gay and simple), *sostenendo un poco* (sustained a little), and *sostenendo molto* (very sustained). *Rubato* is the essence of its interpretation. Rather free measures—*quando l'avrò scritta e fatta bella* (When I will have written it and have made it beautiful)—are followed by very strict measures—*Ti renderò la penna* (I will give back to you the feather), which is marked *lento misurato* (slowly measured). At the climax of the song, which comes in the next to the last phrase, at the words *E quando l'avrò scritta e fatta bene,* the arpeggiated chords are marked *cadenzate* (rhythmic), that is, they should provide strict punctuation to complete the phrase. The final arpeggiated chords should be allowed to sound under the *fermata* being held by the singer. However, for a dramatic flair, the last bass octave should be struck and the pedal released as the singer releases.

Stornello lunigiano: G. Ricordi, 1935.   123286

Attesa del sogno

(*Giovanni Improva*)

1   Malinconia, mare senza confini
2   ove l'anima annega
3   ne la calma perenne,
4   desideri che languono,
5   ideali che non hanno più nome,
6   desideri che tornano,
7   ricordi che non hanno più volto.
8   Oltre il colle lontano
9   già scolora il tramonto
10 e la sera discende
11 in un continuo sovrapporsi
12 di flutti tenebrosi nel silenzio
13 in cui pare debba il mondo
14 sommergersi in eterno.
15 Chiuderò gli occhi stanchi
16 in attesa del sonno;
17 forse invano ho smarrito me stesso
18 in una viva nostalgia della luce;
19 ho smarrito il mio cuore sul cammino
20 d'un fantasma d'amore che m'ha detto:
21 stanotte tu veglierai sognando.

Waiting for sleep

1   Melancholy, sea without boundaries
2   where the soul drowns
3   in the perennial calm,
4   desires that recur,
5   ideals that no longer have names,
6   longings that return,
7   memories that no longer have faces.
8   Beyond the distant hill
9   the sunset is already fading
10 and the evening descends
11 in a continuous superimposing
12 of dark waves in the silence
13 in which it seems the world must
14 submerge itself into eternity.
15 I will close my tired eyes

16   while waiting for sleep;
17   perhaps in vain I have lost myself
18   in a vivid nostalgia by daylight;
19   I have lost my heart on the path
20   of a phantom of love that told me;
21   tonight you will stay awake dreaming.

The adjective *assopito* (drowsy), which qualifies the *lento* tempo marking at the outset of *Attesa del sogno* (Waiting for sleep), is the clue to establishing the correct mood for Vené's atmospheric setting of the poem. The piano carries the main melodic interest at the beginning of the song, with octaves in the upper treble set against a stepwise movement of altered chord tones in the left hand. This introduction should be quiet and very *legato,* with a sense of movement to the end of the phrase marking in measure 4, where it tapers off with the composer's direction *cedere* (to subside). When the new phrase enters, the piano part should be very clearly articulated because the same notes appear again later in the song to establish the modified ABA structure of the composition. The vocal line conveniently enters just as the introductory piano phrase tapers off. It needs no special stress other than an expressive rendering of the very word *malinconia* (melancholy). The vocal line here, and again at the end of the song, falls almost conversationally over the more recognizable melodic and harmonic elements in the accompaniment. The word phrases are short and fragmented with rests, very much as thoughts tend to be in the vague moments before sleep comes. Although the underlying piano chord progression must not lose its momentum, there should be considerable ebb and flow in the rhythm with which the singer expresses these thoughts; the composer helps by specifying tempo changes almost measure by measure.

In contrast to the fragmented opening lines, the center section of the poem is one long sentence: *Oltre il calle lontano . . . sommergersi in eterno* (Beyond the distant hill . . . submerge itself into eternity). Briefly, the poet has a complete vision of the descent of night, and the composer shifts attention to a broad, arched vocal line supported now by quarter-note chord progressions and sweeping sixteenth-note *fluido* (fluid) arpeggios. This section, marked *più mosso,* also carries the direction *aperto* (open) in the vocal line. At the phrase *e la sera discende* (and the evening descends) the accompaniment breaks into 32d-note arpeggiation in the treble clef over a pedal tone Eb in the bass. The shift of hand positions this change requires is assisted by the direction *rubare* (to steal or rob the tempo). It can be prepared by the singer with a slight hesitation on *e la* leading to *sera.* And, of course, the pianist must capture the bass note with the pedal. A progressive *diminuendo* of the accompaniment and a broadening of the tempo bring the section to a climax on the word *eterno.* As the tempo slows and the character of the accompaniment becomes calmer more breathing places are indicated in the score. The singer must take advantage of them to make the most of the words and to prepare for the high *forte* climax of the section. However, the section is still one long sentence, and a sense of that continuity must not be lost. As the voice tapers from the *fermata* to the second syllable of *eterno* (eternal), four eighth notes carrying *tenuto* markings lead into the final section of the song.

The chords that open the Tempo I° are similar in character to those that introduced the song, but it is not until the fourth measure of this section, where the 6/4 meter begins, that a phrase identical to the second phrase of part A begins. The vocal line above it, marked *sentito e triste* (sensitive and sad), has no melodic similarity to the first A section, but it does share the fragmentary phrasing as the poem again breaks into fragmentary visions. A second climax occurs on the phrase *ho smarrito il mio cuore sul cammino* (I have lost my heart on the path). As the dreamlike state takes over at the end, the singer's final note is marked *perdendosi* (dying away), and the pianist should allow a little more space between each note of the final arpeggio.

Many of the composer's favorite devices, heavily influenced by the Impressionist aesthetic admired by his generation, work to particular advantage in this setting—describing a state not quite asleep, not quite awake, but truly melancholy.

Attesa del sogno: G. Ricordi, 1937.   123863

Musica e luce

(*Adele Luzzatto*)

1   Musica e luce di mare adorato
2   e scorrere di vento fra gli ulivi
3   sogno in questo sepolcro senza pace.
4   Il coperchio non s'alza.
5   L'opprime il peso d'una vita cieca
6   e la vita ch'è mia intanto naufraga
7   come nell'acqua livida d'una palude
8   un moribondo sole.

Music and light

1   Music and light adored by the sea
2   and blowing of wind among the olive trees

3   I dream in this sepulchre without peace.
4   The cover does not raise itself.
5   It is held down by the weight of a blind life
6   and the life that is mine meanwhile is shipwrecked
7   as in the livid water of a swamp
8   a dying sun.

The falling fifths within the dissonant chords of the piano introduction of *Musica e luce* (Music and light) immediately establish the oppressive atmosphere of its poetry. However, the wide spacing of the chords and the octave doubling of fragmentary whole-tone and pentatonic scales lend a transparency to the setting that speaks of Vené's Impressionist influences and keeps the song from becoming ponderous. The composer's tempo marking is approximate and qualified by *comodamente sostenuto* (comfortably sustained). A fair degree of *rubato* is called for and is indicated by traditional musical terminology.

The first vocal entrance is constructed over a repetition of the opening falling chords and is marked *mf* and *colorito* (colored, vivid). The words, in loose speech rhythms, achieve a breathless quality in short phrases connected in a long ascending line marked *aumentando* (swelling). It culminates at *ulivi* (olive trees), while the piano, beneath, has rapid figurations representing *vento* (wind). This piano part could be blurred slightly with the pedal, but the pentatonic scale in octaves, which completes the figuration, should be articulated clearly.

The augmented chords in measures 12–14, at the opening of the next section, should resolve as indicated by the dynamics. The vocal phrase *sogno in questo sepolcro senza pace* (I dream in this sepulchre without peace) should be broken into two two-measure units with breath, as indicated, between them. This effect of weary sighing is enhanced by the separate dynamic rise and fall of each phrase. Measure 17, piano alone, interrupts before *senza pace* (without peace) is repeated at a lower pitch level. The next words, *Il coperchio non s'alza* (The cover does not raise itself) should be spoken quite clearly and freely using the written rhythm only as an indication. The information it imparts is crucial to the bitter frustration underlying the increased musical activity of the following phrases. At the *poco più mosso* (measure 23), a motive in octaves derived from the piano introduction sets the mood for the entrance of a long, *esteso* (wide) vocal line. The song climaxes at *la vita* (the life) and immediately begins to recede, *cedendo* (subsiding), toward the expressive word *naufraga* (is shipwrecked). The singer must observe the indicated breath marking and the *ritardando* that precede this word. Thereafter, the accompaniment and the vocal line begin a drop in pitch level to the *lento* section of the penultimate phrase *come nell'acqua livida d'una palude* (as in the livid water of a swamp). The despair of one who can make such an allusion to his own life is borne out in the final four measures of the composition. The tempo is *lentissimo,* the initial falling chords appear again in the treble stretched into a triplet figure, and the marking is *diminuendo e allargando poco a poco* (diminishing and broadening, little by little). Each syllable of the final words—*un moribondo sole* (a dying sun)—should feel as if it is being dragged out of the singer. The final piano chord can linger after the singer's last tone has died away.

Musica e luce: G. Ricordi, 1937.   124157

Ermanno Wolf-Ferrari

(1876–1948)

•

Quattro rispetti, Op. 11
No. 1, Un verde praticello senza piante

1 Un verde praticello senza piante
2 è l'immagine* vera del mio amante.
3 Un mandorlo fiorito all'acqua in riva
4 è dell'amante mio l'immagin* viva.
5 Tutti i raggi del sole e delle stelle
6 sono l'immagin* di sue luci belle.
7 Il dolce olezzo di giovane fiore
8 è l'immagine* vera del mio amore.
9 Amante, amante,
10 Amore, amore, amore,!
11 O vieni avaccio a ristorarmi il core!

Four rispetti, Op. 11
No. 1, A green lawn without trees

1 A green lawn without trees
2 is the true image of my lover.
3 An almond tree in bloom in the water at the shore
4 is of my lover the living image.
5 All the rays of the sun and of the stars
6 are the image of his beautiful eyes.
7 The sweet fragrance of a fresh flower
8 is the true image of my love.

*The word "immagin(e)" in lines 2, 4, 6, and 8 is printed incorrectly in the song text as "imagin(e)."

9   Lover, lover,
10   Love, love, love!
11   O come swiftly to restore to me my heart!

No. 2, Jo* dei saluti ve ne mando mille

1   Jo dei saluti ve ne mando mille
2   quante sono nel ciel minute stelle,
3   quante d'acqua nei fiumi sono stille,
4   quante dentro all'inferno son faville
5   e di grano nel mondo son granelle
6   e quante primavera foglie adorna
7   che sì bella e gentile a noi ritorna!

No. 2, I send you a thousand greetings

1   I send you a thousand greetings
2   as many as there are tiny stars in the sky,
3   as many as there are drops of water in the rivers,
4   as many as there are sparks in hell,
5   and as many as there are seeds in the grain of the world
6   and as many leaves as spring adorns
7   which returns to us so beautiful and pleasing!

No. 3, E tanto c'è pericol ch'io ti lasci

1   E tanto c'è pericol ch'io ti lasci
2   quanto in mezzo del mar fare un giardino
3   a torno a torno un muricciuol di sassi
4   ed in quel mezzo porvi un gelsomino.
5   E quando il gelsomin sarà fiorito
6   allora il nostro amor
7   il nostro amor sarà finito!

No. 3, And there is as much danger of my leaving you

1   And there is as much danger of my leaving you
2   as of planting a garden in the middle of the sea
3   surrounded by a low stone wall
4   and in the middle placing a jasmine.
5   And when the jasmine will have blossomed
6   then our love
7   our love will have ended!

*Jo is pronounced as if written io.

No. 4, O sì che non sapevo sospirare

1 O sì che non sapevo sospirare:
2 del sospirar me son fatta maestra!
3 Sospir se sono a tavola a mangiare,
4 sospir se sono in camera soletta,
5 sospir se sono a ridere e a burlare,
6 sospir se sono con quella e con questa,
7 sospiro prima sospirando poi:
8 Sospirare mi fanno gli occhi tuoi.
9 Sospiro prima e sospiro fra un anno
10 e gli occhi tuoi sospirare mi fanno.

No. 4, O yes, I didn't used to know how to sigh

1 O yes, I didn't used to know how to sigh:
2 of sighing I am now a master!
3 I sigh if I am at the table eating,
4 I sigh if I am in my room alone,
5 I sigh if I am laughing and joking,
6 I sigh if I am with this one and with that one,
7 I sigh once and continue sighing:
8 Your eyes make me sigh.
9 I sigh once and sigh for a year
10 and your eyes make me sigh.

A *rispetto* is an Italian verse form of eight lines, the first four rhyming alternately, the last four rhyming in pairs. In Ermanno Wolf-Ferrari's *Quattro rispetti,* Op. 11, no source is given for the four simple poems. The settings date from 1902 and are early in the Italian *liriche* tradition. They show strong nineteenth-century musical influence as well as the Germanic style deriving from the composer's training and his part-German parentage. They are mainly lyrical and traditional in form and harmony, except for certain jarring modulations and chord resolutions that show Wolf-Ferrari's awareness of the modern style. Although any of the songs could be performed singly, they are not titled separately and should be performed as a set.

The first song begins in A minor very much in the style of a German folk song. All melodic interest is in the vocal line, with the piano providing rhythmic and harmonic support. The only direction given is *tranquillo,* but the character of the song calls for *andante moderato* (approximately ♩ = 84). The poetry uses images from nature to describe the lover, and the music decorates the more colorful words with slightly florid extensions. The phrases are short enough to be sung on one breath except where *rubato* stretches the phrase; for example, in *Tutti i raggi del sole e delle stelle* (All the rays of the sun and of the stars) the composer adds a breath indication after *sole* and the implication is one of *ritardando* on *stelle*. The climax of the song comes with the repetition of *amante* (lover) and *amore* (love). The second *amante* should be an echo of the first, and the three renditions of *amore* should be progressively slower and softer. The final phrase should stretch through the word *ristorarmi* (restore to me), ignoring the breath mark after *avaccio* (swiftly). After *ristorarmi* a quick breath should be taken, and the final word *core* (heart) and the short finishing phrase of the accompaniment should be sung and played *a tempo*. The song ends in A major.

The second song is in a modified ABA form. The key is Db major, the enharmonic third of the A major of the first song. However, the opening chord, built on the second degree of the scale, is somewhat jarring. In general, a little time should be allowed between the songs of this set to soften the effect of the chord juxtapositions.

The poem *Jo dei saluti* can be described as "expansive"; everything is spoken of in extraordinary multiples, and the music must express that mood. The marking *con anima* (with soul, feeling) again only indicates character; a tempo close to that of the first song (approximately ♩ = 84) works equally well here since the triplet pulsations tend to propel the line. The singer should attempt to carry through the long phrases on one breath except for the places specifically marked in the score. Whatever *rubato* is required to make the most of such expressive phrases as *quante dentro all'inferno son faville* (as many as there are sparks in hell) should be judiciously allowed; rigid rhythm is not necessary. Shortly after the return of the A theme, an *accelerando* leads to an *allargando* over *bella e gentile* (beautiful and pleasing). The line continues with *tenuto* markings over *a noi* (to us) and *ri,* the first syllable of *ritorna* (returns). The piano must follow the inflections of the voice through this measure. The repetitive triplets in the next to the last measure should be *a tempo,* but a slight *ritardando* is called for in the final arpeggio. The singer may hold the final note through this arpeggio and release with the pianist.

The slower tempo of the final triplet arpeggio of the second song can set the tempo (approximately ♩ = 72) for the broad lines and triplet accompaniment of the third one. Since the image is of an undersea garden, the accompaniment pattern may follow the traditional "watery" effects of program music, but in all probability the composer simply uses the style to support the broad arching melodic lines. Again, most of the vocal phrases can be sung on one breath, but some are broken by an expressive breath suggested by the composer. *Rubato* is also essential in this song, in such places as the first mention of *un gelsomino* (a jasmine) and at the climax, *allora il nostro amor* (then our love). A slight quickening should precede this climax, beginning with the first statement of the sequential phrase *E quando il gelsomin* (And when the jasmine) rather than the second, as marked. If the *crescendo largamente e con passione* (increase broadly and with pas-

sion) takes too much breath from the singer, a break may be made immediately before *sarà finito* (will have ended) to replenish the energy.

The minimum metronome marking for *presto*, ♩ = 168, may be too fast
for the fourth song, even though that tempo appears to be the composer's
choice. The *scherzo* quality of the song depends on utmost clarity in the
words and clear phrasing and *staccato* articulation in the accompaniment.
If necessary the indicated tempo should be sacrificed to achieve the proper
character for the music. Although the rhythmic patterns are choppy, all the
phrases are at least three measures long. Both singer and pianist should be
aware of phrase direction and the way phrases are linked. An eight-measure
phrase leads to the first climax of the song at *sospiro prima sospirando poi*
(I sigh once and continue sighing), which broadens through the indicated
ritardando. Again, *rubato* is essential to the expression of the style. After
the long sustained *Sospirare* (sigh) in the final phrase, a breath may be taken
before *mi fanno* (make me). The quick *scherzo*-like piano figures that complete the song should be articulated briskly and without *ritard*.

Quattro rispetti, Op. 11: D. Kahter, 1902.   1911.3140 (Set)
    1. *Un verde praticello senza piante*
    2. *Jo dei saluti ve ne mando mille*
    3. *E tanto c'è pericol ch'io ti lasci*
    4. *O sì che non sapevo sospirare*

Quattro rispetti, Op. 12

No. 1, Quando ti vidi a quel canto apparire

1   Quando ti vidi a quel canto apparire
2   ti assomigliai alla spera del sole.
3   Abbassai gli occhi e non seppi che dire:
4   allora incominciava il nostro amore.
5   Ora che il nostro amor è cominciato
6   vogliami un po' di ben giovin garbato.

No. 1, When I saw you appear at that (street) corner

1   When I saw you appear at that (street) corner
2   I made you resemble the sunbeam
3   I lowered my eyes and I did not know what to say:
4   then our love began.
5   Now that our love has begun
6   wish me some love, gentle youth.

No. 2, Q guarda, guarda quel nobile augello

1 O guarda, guarda quel nobile augello
2 che va per l'aria e lo ricopre il sole!
3 E così fate voi giovane bello
4 quando di casa vostra escite fuore,
5 quando di casa vostra fuori andate
6 l'aria e la terra di fior seminate.
7 Quando di casa vostra fuora uscite
8 l'aria e la terra di bei fior coprite!

No. 2, O look, look at that noble bird

1 O look, look at that noble bird
2 that flies through the air and the sun conceals it!
3 And thus do you, handsome youth,
4 when you go outside of your house,
5 when you go out from your house
6 you sow the air and the earth with flowers.
7 When from your house you go out,
8 you cover the air and the earth with beautiful flowers!

No. 3, Angiolo delicato fresco e bello

1   Angiolo delicato fresco e bello
2   quanto vi seppe vostra mamma fare!
3   Nascesse mille voi siete il più bello,
4   fiorisce l'erba do' avete a passare.
5   Dove avete a passar fiorisce il grano.
6   Bello, nasceste colle rose in mano.
7   Dove avete a passar fiorisce il giglio.
8   Bello, nasceste colle rose in collo.
9   Dove avete a passar fiorisce il lino.
10 Bello, nasceste con un gelsomino.

No. 3, Delicate angel, fresh and beautiful

1 Delicate angel, fresh and beautiful
2 how much your mother knew in making you!
3 If a thousand were born you are the most beautiful,
4 the grass grows wherever you walk.

5 Wherever you pass the grain flourishes.
6 Beautiful one, you were born with roses in your hands.
7 Wherever you go the lily blooms.
8 Beautiful one, you were born with roses around your neck.
9 Wherever you go the flax flowers.
10 Beautiful one, you were born with a jasmine.

No. 4, Sia benedetto chi fece lo mondo!

1 Sia benedetto chi fece lo mondo!
2 Lo seppe tanto bene accomodare!
3 Fece lo mare e non vi fece fondo,
4 fece le navi per poter passare.
5 Fece le navi e fece il paradiso
6 e fece le bellezze al vostro viso.

No. 4, Blessed is he who made the world!

1 Blessed is he who made the world!
2 He knew so well how to arrange things!
3 He made the sea but didn't give it a bottom,
4 he made the ships in order to be able to cross it.
5 he made the ships and he made paradise
6 and made the beauties of your face.

Quattro rispetti, Op. 12, of 1904, are similar in style and structure to the settings of Op. 11, but at least the first two songs of the second cycle have a more Italian flavor—the phrases tend to be longer and more "vocal" in concept. The poems of the second set (which are also anonymous) are each a tribute to beauty. The composer attempts to capture their essence and to provide contrast among them. They are not titled separately, and whenever possible they should be programmed as a set.

The descending arpeggiation that opens the first song is marked *staccato,* but the pedal is held throughout. Although the *staccato* articulation continues with the alternating triplets that accompany most of the song, the overall phrasing should still be *legato.* The vocal line enters with equal eighth notes, often one to a syllable, but the singer must not allow the words to have equal weight; a semblance of speech inflection must be achieved. Observing the breath mark after *apparire* (appear) will allow the singer to stretch the melismatic decoration on the key word *sole* (sun); a tempo of approximately ♩. = 66 should enable all the vocal phrases to be sung as indicated. The phrase *allora incominciava il nostro amore* (then our love began) is one example of Wolf-Ferrari's frequent use of *rubato;* the piano figuration immediately after *amore* should act as an extension of the phrase. *Rubato* is again called for in the final, climactic phrase; and the breath indication should be observed after *ben.* When the *a tempo* returns, marked *raddolcendo* (sweetly, soothingly), the pianist must observe the *subito piano* at this point. Except for one chord marked *fp*$\smile$, the song should end quietly.

The second song begins with a soaring feeling and a broad vocal phrase. A breath may be needed after *augello* (bird) to carry the phrase through to *sole* (sun). A slight break is needed before the second phrase, beginning *E così* (And thus); the pianist must space the triplet figure in the accompaniment to accommodate the singer. The B section of the song, beginning here, should be very sustained. The frequent breath indications on the phrase *l'aria e la terra di fior seminate* (you sow the air and the earth with flowers) seem excessive. The breath after *fior* may be eliminated, but the *tenuto* markings above *seminate* do point up a little word-painting on this verb. Tempo I° marks the return of the opening melody, with slight modification. The stretching out of the final phrase is clearly indicated dynamically and by tempo fluctuation. The short piano postlude should continue the soaring feeling that underlies the whole song.

The third song takes its character from the three adjectives of the opening line: *delicato fresco e bello* (delicate, fresh and beautiful). The phrases are short, and the style is reminiscent of Wolf-Ferrari's German background. Crisp articulation is required to convey the pastoral scene. The piano supports the vocal line unobtrusively for the most part, but makes short imitative comments after *grano* (grain) and *giglio* (lily). The final phrase should be slightly more sustained than the rest of the song and performed *molto espressivo* by both singer and pianist.

A marchlike theme opens the fourth song with the forceful statement *Sia benedetto chi fece lo mondo* (Blessed is he who made the world). The accompaniment changes in the second phrase in reference to the sea. The word *paradiso* (paradise) is set with an expansive vocal line and a broad piano arpeggio. Each of these phrase expressions leads to the final phrase, where haltingly, almost coyly, the protagonist states, *e fece le bellezze—al vostro viso* (and made—the beauties—of your face). There should be a slight delay before the words *al vostro viso* to create an element of surprise in the final utterance. The piano, returning to the march rhythms that began the piece, brings it to a satisfying conclusion.

Quattro rispetti, Op. 12: D. Rahter, no date.   2620.3151 (Set)
   1. *Quando ti vidi a quel canto apparire*
   2. *O guarda, guarda quel nobile augello*
   3. *Angiolo delicato fresco e bello*
   4. *Sia benedetto chi fece lo mondo!*

APPENDIX

Other Recommended Composers and Songs

FRANCO ALFANO
Tre liriche: G. Ricordi, 1936; Repr. 1953.
   2. *Messaggio*   123622

Tre nuovi poemi: G. Ricordi, 1943; Repr. 1953. © renewed, 1971
   1. *Ninna nanna di mezzanotte*   125747

LUCIANO BERIO
Quattro canzoni popolari: Universal-Ed., 1975.   UE 15947 Mi (Set)
   1. *Dolce cominciamento*
   2. *La donna ideale*
   3. *Avendo gran disio*
   4. *Ballo*

LUCIANO BETTARINI
   Fanciullo Mendico: G. Ricordi, 1955.   128906.
   Stoppia: G. Ricordi, 1955.   128907.

BRUNO BETTINELLI
Tre liriche: G. Ricordi, 1955.   128775 (Set)
   1. *Nella sera*
   2. *La natura mi parla*
   3. *Dalla forza nasce la forma*

CESARE GIULIO BRERO
Tre liriche: G. Ricordi, 1936; Repr. 1956.   129200 (Set)
   1. *Alla luna*
   2. *Il piccolo fornaio*
   3. *Piero il malcontento*

RENATO BROGI
   Gotine gialle: Carish & Jänichen, 1907; Repr. Charles W. Homeyer, 1915.
                                                C.W.H. 124–3

   Le lucciole: Edizioni C. Bratti & C., di proprietà Ditta R. Maurri (no date).
                                                R. 6047 M.

   Mattinata: A. Forlivesi, 1914.   10451 (S-T); 10452 (Ms-Br)
   Un ricordo: A. Forlivesi, 1916.   10608

ALESSANDRO BUSTINI
   Le notti senza luna: G. Ricordi, 1931; Repr. 1954.   122203
   La tua villa: G. Ricordi, 1931; Repr. 1955.   122204

MARIO CASTELNUOVO-TEDESCO

Quattro sonetti da "La Vita Nova": A. Forlivesi, 1927.   11395 (Set)
   1. *Cavalcando l'altr'ier per un cammino*   11391
   2. *Negli occhi porta la mia donna Amore*   11392
   3. *Tanto gentile e tanto onesta pare*   11393
   4. *Deh, peregrini, che pensosi andate*   11394

briciole: A. Forlivesi, 1921.   10907 (Set)
   1. *Rio Bo*
   2. *Mezzogiorno*
   3. *Il passo delle Nazarene*
   piccino picciò: A. Forlivesi, 1922.   10968 (Ms-Br)

LUCIANO CHAILLY

   Lamento di Danae: G. Ricordi, 1957:   129247

PIETRO CIMARA

   Stornello: F. Bongiovanni, 1911.   F. 408 B.(S-T); F. 409 B.(Ms-Br)

Cinque liriche: F. Bongiovanni, no date.
   1. *Paranzelle*   F. 724 B.
   2. *Notte d'estate*   F. 725 B.
   3. *Presso una fontana*   F. 726 B.
   4. *Paesaggio*   F. 727 B.
   5. *A una rosa*   F. 728 B.

   Stornellata Marinara: G. Ricordi, 1931; Repr. 1954.
                                              119260 (S-T); 122295 (Ms-Br)
   Primaverina: A. Forlivesi, 1932.   11740

SANDRO FUGA

Canti d'amore: G. Ricordi, 1957.   129408 (Set)
   4. *Canto d'amore*   129408

GIORGIO GHEDINI

Quattro canti: Edizioni Suvini Zerboni, 1947.   S. 4192 Z. (Set)
   1. *Auciello che ne viene da caserta*
   2. *Arbero peccerillo*
   3. *La tortora ch'à perza la cumpagna*
   4. *Ci aggiu tutta 'sta notte cammenato*

BARBARA GIURANNA

   Canto arabo: G. Ricordi, 1934.   123139
   La Guerriera: G. Ricordi, 1928; Repr. 1955.   120926
   Ninna-nanna: G. Ricordi, 1934.   123191
   Stornello: G. Ricordi, 1928; Repr. 1950.   120925

GUIDO GUERRINI

Due canzoni abruzzesi: F. Bongiovanni, no date   1464 (Set)
   1. *St' Amore*   1465
   2. *Famme murì*   1466

   È l'ora dell'anima: Umberto Pizzi, 1928 (Property of Carish).   R. 2198 U.

Tre canti armeni: Edizioni Curci S.A., 1940.   E. 2382 C. (Set)
   1. *Maria, Madre Nostra*
   2. *Canto dell'emigrante*
   3. *Se la sciagura*

Canti della mia prigionia: F. Bongiovanni, 1948.   F. 2279 B. (Set)
    1. *Malinconia*
    2. *Aurora*
    3. *Se stanotte io morissi*
    4. *Tempo*
    5. *Lines*
    6. *Invocazione*
    7. *Ballata*

GIAN FRANCESCO MALIPIERO

Quattro sonetti del Burchiello; Edizioni Bongiovanni, 1921 (Pizzi & Co.).
    P. 1426 & C. (Set)
    1. *Cacio stillato*
    2. *Va in mercato, Giorgin*
    3. *Andando a uccellare*
    4. *Rose spinose*

Due sonetti del Berni: G. Ricordi, 1922.   119002 (Set)
    1. *Chiome d'argento fine*
    2. *Canchieri e beccafichi*

RICCARDO MALIPIERO

Motivi: Edizioni Suvini Zerboni, 1964. S. 6231 Z.
    1. *Ah, vù dii*
    2. *El poeta*
    3. *Na rosa ne sbrissada*
    4. *No'angossarte, putèl, spera*
    5. *Più de mi*
    6. *Schéi ne la man*

GIAN CARLO MENOTTI

Canti della lontananza: G. Schirmer, 1967.   46269C (Set)
    1. *Gli amanti impossibili*
    2. *Mattinata di neve*
    3. *Il settimo bicchiere di vino*
    4. *Lo spettro*
    5. *Dorme pegaso*
    6. *La lettera*
    7. *Rassegnazione*

VIRGILIO MORTARI

    chicco birillo: A. Forlivesi, 1935.   11760

giro giro tondo: A. Forlivesi, 1936.   11329 (Set)
    1. *il mago Pistagna*   11323
    2. *la storiella di Picicci*   11324
    3. *il ghiottone*   11325
    4. *la piccola strega*   11326
    5. *il porcellino di Pino*   11327
    6. *forno fornello*   11328

MARIO PERSICO

Sette piccole liriche: Edizioni Curci S.A., 1922.
    Fasciocolo 1-Quattro liriche   F. 163–166 C. (Set)
    1. *Paranzelle*
    2. *Assenza*

3. *Orfano*
4. *Notte dolorosa*
Fasciocolo 2-Tre liriche   F. 167–169 C. (Set)
   1. *Ultimo canto*
   2. *Notte di neve*
   3. *Con gli angioli*

ILDEBRANDO PIZZETTI
Tre liriche: A. Forlivesi, 1954.
   1. *Bebro e il suo cavallo*   11962
   2. *Vorei voler, signor, qual ch'io non voglio*   11963
   3. *In questa notte carica di stelle*   11964

VITTORIO RIETI
Quattro liriche italiane: General Music Publishing, 1966.   Quattro=22
   1. *E per un bel cantar*
   2. *La non vuol esser più mia*
   3. *E lo mio cor s'inchina*
   4. *Canti ognun*

GENI SADERO
Barcarola de la Marangona: Edizione Suvini Zerboni, 1940.   S. 3751 Z.

ANTONIO VERETTI
L'Allegria: G. Ricordi, 1958.   129786 (Set)
   1. *Fase*
   2. *Sereno*
   3. *Sonnolenza*
   4. *Rose in fiamme*
   5. *In memoria*
   6. *Solitudine*
   7. *Preghiera*

Sei Stornelli:G. Ricordi, 1958; Repr. 1950.   120878 (Set).

MARIO ZAFRED
All'Isonzo: G. Ricordi, 1956.   129073
Canti di Novembre: G. Ricordi, 1955.   128987

RICCARDO ZANDONAI
Sei melodie: G. Ricordi, 1913.   114837 (Set)
   3. *I due tarli*   114833, Repr. 1981
   4. *Serenata*   114834, Repr. 1950, 1982
   5. *Lontana*   114835, Repr. 1950, 1980
   6. *L'assiuolo*   114836, Repr. 1979

Sei liriche: Edizione Pizzi-F. Bongiovanni, no date.
   1. *Mistero*   F. 1174 B.
   2. *Notte de neve*   F. 1175 B.
   3. *Mistica*   F. 1176 B.

BIBLIOGRAPHY

Dictionaries and Books on Italian Diction

Castiglione, Pierina Borrani. *Italian Phonetics, Diction and Intonation*. New York: S. F. Vanni, 1957.

Colorni, Evelina. *Singers' Italian: A Manual of Diction and Phonetics*. New York: Schirmer Books, 1970.

Dizionario Garzanti: Italiano-Inglese, Inglese-Italiano. Milan: Garzanti Editore, 1967.

Gabrielli, Aldo. *Dizionario linguistico moderno*. 3d ed. Milan: Edizioni Scolastiche Mondadori, 1961.

Hoare, Alfred A. *A Short Italian Dictionary*. Cambridge: Cambridge University Press, 1954.

Palazzi, Fernando. *Novissimo Dizionario della lingua italiana*. 2d ed. Milan: Casa Editrice Ceschina, 1939.

Reynolds, Barbara. *The Cambridge Italian Dictionary*. Cambridge: Cambridge University Press, 1962.

Zingarelli, Nicola. *Vocabolario della lingua italiana*. Bologna: Nicola Zanichelli Editore, 1951.

Books and Articles on Contemporary Italian Vocal Music

Abbiati, Franco. *Storia della musica*. Vol. IV, *Il Novecento*. Milan: Garzanti, 1968. 879pp.

Allorto, Riccardo. *Piccola storia della musica*. Milan: G. Riccordi, 1959. 157pp.

————, ed. *Nuovo dizionario Riccordi della Musica e dei Musicisti*. Milan, 1976. 1155pp.

Approdo musicale, No. 1, January–March 1958. Dedicated to Alfredo Casella. No. 9, January–March 1960. Dedicated to Gian Francesco Malipiero.

Austin, William W. *Music in the 20th Century from Debussy through Stravinsky*. New York: W. W. Norton and Co., 1966.

Basso, Alberto. *Dizionario enciclopedico universale della musica e dei musicisti*. 4 vols. Turin: Unione Tipografico-Editrice Torinese, 1983.

Bastianelli, Giannoto. *La crisi musicale europea*. Florence: Vallecchi, 1976. 202pp.

————. "Ildebrando Pizzetti," *Il Convegno,* March–April 1921.

Berio, Luciano. "Poesie e musica—un'esperienza," *Incontri musicali,* August 1959, pp.98–111.

Boccia, Bruno. "Alcuni compositori romani del dopoguerra," *La Rassegna Musicale,* June 1958, pp.122–132.

Bohle, Bruce, ed. *The International Cyclopedia of Music and Musicians.* 10th ed. New York and Toronto: Dodd, Mead; London: J. M. Dent, 1975. 2511pp.

Bolletino Bibliografico Musicale. (Booklet published eight times a year for eight years; contains biographical material and lists of songs published by various composers.) Milan: Ettore Desderi, 1926–1933.

Bonisconti, Angiola Maria. "Giorgio Federico Ghedini e le sue ultime opere," *La Rassegna Musicale,* April 1949, pp.98–109.

Bontempelli, Massimo. *Gian Francesco Malipiero.* Milan: Bompiani, 1942.

Bortolotto, Mario. "Il Cammino di Goffredo Petrassi," *Quaderni della Rassegna Musicale* I (1964):11–79.

———. *Fase seconda: Studi sulla Nuova Musica.* Turin: G. Einaudi, 1969. 265pp.

———. *Le opere di Goffredo Petrassi 1957–1960.* Milan: Edizioni Suvini Zerboni, 1960.

Carratoni, Velio. *Da Gluck alla nuova musica.* Rome: Gesualdi, 1972. 123pp.

Casella, Alfredo. "Modern Music in Modern Italy," *Modern Music* 12 (1934):19–22.

———. *Music in My Time: The Memoirs of Alfredo Casella.* Trans. and ed. Spencer Norton. Norman: University of Oklahoma Press, 1955. (Contains list of works.)

Castelnuovo-Tedesco, Mario. "Alfredo Casella," *La Rassegna Musicale,* September 1957, pp.201–204.

———. "Liriche di Virgilio Mortari," *La Rassegna Musicale,* 1927.

———. *La Rassegna Musicale,* January 1953, pp.42–53. (List of works.)

Chailly, Luciano. *Cronache di vita musicale.* Rome: De Santis, 1973. 155pp.

Cobbett's Cyclopedic Survey of Chamber Music. 2d ed. Compiled and edited by Walter Willson Cobbett. With supplementary material edited by Colin Mason. London: Oxford University Press, 1963. (See "European Chamber Music since 1929," vol. III, pp.51–61.)

Cohn, Arthur. *Twentieth Century Music in Western Europe: The Compositions and the Recordings.* New York: J. B. Lippincott, 1965.

Confalonieri, G. *L'Opera di Adriano Lualdi.* Milan, 1932.

Cortese, Luigi. *Alfredo Casella.* Genoa: E. degli Orfini, 1935. (List of works, pp.107–129.)

Dallapiccola, Luigi. "Musicisti del nostro tempo: Vito Frazzi," *La Rassegna Musicale,* June 1937.

Damerini, A. *Profilo critico di Guido Guerrini: biografia e bibliografia.* Milan, 1928.

D'Amico, Fedele. *Goffredo Petrassi.* Rome, 1942.

———. "Goffredo Petrassi," *Il Diapason* 2, Nos. 5–6 (May–June 1951):17–20.

———. "Petrassi e il biografo imprudente," in *I casi della musica.* Milan. 1962.

———, and Guido M. Gatti, eds. *Alfredo Casella.* Milan, 1958.

D'Amico, Lele. "I lavori giovanili di Petrassi," *La Rassegna Musicale,* January 1942, pp.1–10.

Della Corte, Andrea. *Ritratto di Franco Alfano.* Turin: G. B. Paravia and Co., 1935.

———, and Guido Pannain. *Storia della Musica.* 3d ed. 3 vols. Turin: Unione Tipografico-Editrice Torinese, 1952. 4th ed. rev. Turin: Unione Tipografico-Editrice Torinese, 1964.

De' Paoli, Domenico. *La Musica Contemporanea.* Rome, 1952.

Desderi, Ettore. *La Musica Contemporanea.* Turin: Bocca, 1930. 193pp.

———. "Musicisti Piemontesi," *Musicalbrandé* (Turin), December 1959. (Autobiographical article.)

Eaglefield-Hull, A. *A Dictionary of Modern Music and Musicians.* London, 1924.

Enciclopedia dello spettacolo. 11 vols. Rome: Casa Editrice Le Maschere, 1954–1967.

Ewen, David. *American Composers: A Biographical Dictionary.* New York: G.P. Putnam's Sons, 1982. 793pp.

———. *The Book of Modern Composers.* 2d ed. rev. New York: Knopf, 1950. 586pp.

————. *The Complete Book of 20th Century Music.* Rev. ed. Englewood Cliffs, N.J.: Prentice Hall, 1959. 527pp.

————. *European Composers Today: A Biographical and Critical Guide.* New York: The H. W. Wilson Co., 1969. 639pp.

————. *Twentieth Century Composers.* New York: Thomas Y. Crowell, 1937.

————. *The World of Twentieth Century Music.* Englewood Cliffs, N.J.: Prentice-Hall, Inc., 1968. 989pp.

————, ed. *Composers of Today.* New York: H. W. Wilson Co., 1934. 314pp.

————, ed. *Composers Since Nineteen Hundred: A Biographical and Critical Guide.* New York: The H. W. Wilson Company, 1969. 639pp.

————, ed. *Living Musicians.* New York: The H. W. Wilson Co., 1940. 390pp.

Fellerer, Karl Gustav. *Der Futurismus in der Italienischen Musik.* Brussels: Paleis der Academiën, 1977. 68pp.

Fleischer, H. *La musica contemporanea.* Milan, 1937.

Fragapane, Paolo. *Guido Guerrini e i suoi poemi sinfonici.* Florence: F. Le Monnier, 1932. 29pp.

Gaburo, Kenneth. "Current Chronicle: Italy," *The Musical Quarterly* 42 (October 1956).

————. "Goffredo Petrassi . . . The Man and His Music," *The Musical Courier* 134 (September 1956):6.

Gaslini, Giorgio. *Musica totale.* Milan: Feltrinelli, 1975. 108pp.

Gatti, Guido M. "Franco Alfano," *The Musical Quarterly* IX, No. 1 (January 1923):556–577.

————. "Franco Alfano" (English translation by M. E. Marsh), *The Sackbut* VII, No. 6 (January 1927):157–163.

————. "Gian Francesco Malipiero," *L'Esame* (Milan), October 1923.

————. "Ildebrando Pizzetti," *The Musical Quarterly* IX, No. 1 (January 1923):96–121 and 271–286.

————. *Ildebrando Pizzetti.* Trans. David Moore. London: Dennis Dobson Limited, 1951; new edition, 1955.

————. "In Memory of Alfredo Casella, 1883–1947," *The Musical Quarterly* 33 (July 1947):504–508.

————. "Italy's Newest Recruits," *Modern Music* XI, No. 2 (January–February 1934):95–99.

————. "Malipiero: Romantic and Classic," *Monthly Musical Record,* February 1935.

————. "Modern Italian Composers: Goffredo Petrassi," *Monthly Musical Record,* January 1937.

————. *Musicisti moderni d'Italia e di fuori.* Bologna, 1920; 2d ed., 1925.

————. "I settanta anni di Pizzetti," *La Rassegna Musicale,* October 1950, pp.289–290.

————. "Some Italian Composers of Today," *Musical Times* 62 (1921):93.

————. "Vincenzo Tommasini," *La Rassegna Musicale,* January 1951, pp.48–49.

————. "Voci aggiunte a un Dizionario dei musicisti italiani contemporanei," *La Rassegna Musicale,* 1936–.

————. "Voci aggiunte e rivedute per un dizionario di compositori viventi," *La Rassegna Musicale,* 1960–.

————, ed. *La Musica-Dizionario.* 2 vols. Turin: Unione Tipografico-Editrice Torinese, 1968.

————, ed. *La Musica-Enciclopedia Storica.* 4 vols. Turin: Unione Tipografico-Editrice Torinese, 1966.

————, ed. *L'Opera di Gian Francesco Malipiero.* Treviso: Edizione di Treviso-Libreria Canova, 1952.

Gavazzeni, Giandrea. "Disegno di Mario Pilati," *La Rassegna Musicale,* February 1939, pp.57–60.

———. "La Musica di Ghedini," in *Musicisti D'Europa.* Milan, 1954.

———. *Tre studi su Pizzetti.* Como: Cavalieri, 1937.

———. *Trent'anni di musica.* Milan: Ricordi, 1958.

Gedda, Giulio Cesare. "Vincenzo Davico ed il suo impressionism," *Rivista Musicale Italiana* 38 (1931):638–643.

Ghigi, Alba. *Francesco Balillo Pratella.* Ravenna: Arti grafiche, 1930.

Ghiotti, Biano M. "Le liriche di Vincenzo Davico," *Musica d'oggi,* 1924.

Gould, Glen Hibbard. "A Stylistic Analysis of Selected Twelve-tone Works by Luigi Dallapiccola." Ph. D. diss., Indiana University, 1964.

Griffiths, Paul. *A Concise History of Modern Music from Debussy to Boulez.* London: Thames and Hudson, 1978. 216pp.

Helm, Everett Burton. "Malipiero in Retrospect," *The Music Review* 36 (1975):70–71.

La broca, Mario. *Malipiero, musicista veneziano; con il catalogo analitico compete della opere compilato da Biancamaria Borri.* Venice and Rome: Istituto per la collaborazione culturale, 1957.

———. L'Usignolo di Boboli (Cinquant'anni di vita musicale, 1908–1958). Venice: Neri Pozza Editore, 1959.

Lang, Paul Henry, and Nathan Broder, eds. *Contemporary Music in Europe: A Comprehensive Survey.* New York: G. Schirmer, Inc., 1965. (See Mario Bortolotto, "The New Music in Italy," pp.61–77.)

Lualdi, Adriano. *Il rinnovamento musicale italiano.* Milan: Treves-Treccani-Tumminelli, 1931.

Machlis, Joseph. *Introduction to Contemporary Music.* 2d ed. New York: W. W. Norton, 1979. 694pp.

Maglia, Michele. "Le dernier Petrassi," *Il Diapason* 1 (March 1950):19–23.

———. "Un musicien difficile," *Il Diapason* 1 (January 1950):16–17. (Article on Ghedini.)

Malipiero, Gian Francesco. "Alfredo Casella," *Ricordiana,* No. 4, 1956.

———. "Contemporary Music in Italy," *The Score and I. M. A. Magazine* 15 (March 1956):7–9.

———. *Così va lo mondo.* Milan, 1946. (Autobiography 1922–1945.)

Malipiero, Riccardo. *Introduzione alla musica contemporanea.* Milan: Ente autonomo Teatro alla Scala, 1971. 43pp.

Mariani, R. *Adriano Lualdi.* Rome, 1934.

———. "Musicisti del nostro tempo: Lodovico Rocca," *La Rassegna Musicale,* April 1938, pp.163–174.

———. "Musicisti del nostro tempo: Vergilio Mortari," *La Rassegna Musicale,* July-August 1937, pp.255–263.

Marinelli, Carlo. *Cronache di Musica Contemporanea.* Caltanissetta and Rome: S. Sciascia, 1974. 230pp.

Marinetti, F. T., and Maestro Giuntini. "Futurist Manifesto of Aeromusic," in Nicolas Slonimsky, *Music Since 1900.* Pp.556–557.

Martini, Gianmario. "Le liriche di Casella," *Il Diapason* 3, Nos. 3–4 (March–April 1952):9–13.

Mila, Massimo. *Cent'anni di musica moderna.* Turin: Edizione di Torino, 1981. 212pp.

———. "Ottorino Respighi," *Rivista Musicale Italiana* 40 (April 1933).

———. "Ultime tendenze della musica italiana: Goffredo Petrassi," *Domus,* February 1934.

Mioli, Pietro. "Carpi: Festivale internazionale di musica vocale de camera," *Nuova Rivista Musicale Italiana* 18 (1984):690–691.

Mura, Ettore de. *Enciclopedia della canzone napoletana.* Naples: Il torchio, 1969.

Musica d'oggi, ed. Guido Gatti (Milan), 1919–. New Series, 1958–.

Nardi, Piero. "I Settant'anni di Malipiero," *La Rassegna Musicale,* April 1952, pp.137–141.

Nathan, Hans. "The Twelve-Tone Compositions of Luigi Dallapiccola," *The Musical Quarterly* XLIV, No. 3 (July 1958):289–310.

Oliphant, E. H. C. "The Songs of Young Italy," *The Musical Quarterly* IX, No. 2 (April 1923):191–210.

Osborne, Charles. *The Concert Song Companion.* London: Gollancz, 1974. 285pp.

Palaczek, Dietmer. "Musik des Faschismus—Faschismus der Musik (Die Frage des Musikalischen Fortschritts in Mussolinis Italien)," *Neue Zeitschrift für Musik* (June 1983):9–13.

Panatero, M. "Le liriche di Ettore Desderi," *Revista Musicale Italiana* 1941, pp.281–295.

Pannain, Guido. *Modern Composers.* London, 1942 (1st ed., 1932). (English translation of *Musicisti di Tempi Nuovi,* published in *La Rassegna Musicale* from 1928.)

Parigi, L. "Pizzetti," in *Il Momento musicale italiano.* Florence, 1921.

Pestalozza, Luigi. "I compositori milanesi del dopoguerra," *La Rassegna Musicale,* March 1957, pp.27–43.

———. "I dialoghi di Gian Francesco Malipiero," *Ricordiana,* July 1957.

———. "Il sentimento dell' assoluto in Goffredo Petrassi," *La Ressegna Musicale,* October–December 1954, pp.318–327.

Petit, Raymond. *Les mélodies de Vincenzo Davico.* Nice: Delrieu frères, 1924.

Il Pianoforte, November 1921. (Pizzetti issue, containing articles by M. Castelnuovo-Tedesco, A. Della Corte, G. M. Gatti, and F. Luizzi.)

Pinzauti, Leonardo. "Vittorio Gui e Firenze," *Nuova Rivista Musicale Italiana* 10 (1976):204–210.

Piovesan, Alessandro. "Estetica di Malipiero," *La Rassegna Musicale,* February 1940, pp.109–114.

Pizzetti, Bruno, ed. *Ildebrando Pizzetti: Cronologia e bibliografia.* Parma: La Pilotta, 1980. 531pp.

Pizzetti, Ildebrando. "La Musica e il Dramma," *La Rassegna Musicale,* January 1932.

———. "A proposito di nuovi orientamenti dell'arte musicale, *La Rassegna Musicale,* April 1949, pp.85–91.

———. "Il settantacinquesimo compleanno di Pizzetti," *Ricordiana,* November 1955.

Prieberg, Fred K. *Lexicon der neuen Musik.* Freiburg im Breisgau: Karl Alber, 1958. (Entries include Berio, Dallapiccola, Maderna, Malipiero, Nielsen, Nono, Peragallo, Scelsi, Togni, and Vlad).

Prunières, Henri. "Gian Francesco Malipiero," *Mercure de France,* May 16, 1919; and *Revue Musicale,* January 1927.

———. "Ildebrando Pizzetti," *Nouvelle Revue d'Italie,* July 1920.

Quaderni della Rassegna Musicale (ed. Guido M. Gatti) I (1964). (Entire volume dedicated to Petrassi.)

La Rassegna Musicale (ed. Guido M. Gatti) 1920–1943 and 1947–1960. See especially September—October 1940, dedicated to Ildebrando Pizzetti, with contributions by U. Ojetti, G. Gavazzeni, V. Frazzi, R. Paoli, A. della Corte, A. Hermet, L. d'Amico, N. Costarelli, and G. M. Gatti; February–March 1942, dedicated to Gian Francesco Malipiero, with contributions by M. Bontempelli, M. Labroca, G. Rossi-Doria, L. d'Amico, A. della Corte, and others; and May–June 1943, dedicated to Alfredo Casella, with contributions by G. de Chirico, M. Mila, G. Gavazzeni, A. Mantelli, G. Rossi-Doria, F. d'Amico, D. Alderighi, and M. Labroca and a biography and bibliography.

Rensis, R. de. *Ottorino Respighi.* Turin, 1935.

Respighi, Elsa. "Appunti per un ritratto di Ottorino Respighi," *Musica* V, No. 2 (1946).

———. *Ottorino Respighi; His Life Story.* Milan: Ricordi, 1954. Trans. Gwen Morris. London: Ricordi, 1962. 342pp.

Rinaldo, M. "Giovani musicisti romani: Goffredo Petrassi," *Musica d'oggi,* May 1934.

Rocca, L. "Vincenzo Davico," *Bolettino bibliografico musicale* (Milan), 1932.

Rognoni, L. "Il linguaggio di Malipiero," *Ricordiana,* July 1956.

Rossi, Nick, ed. and compiler. *Catalogue of Works by Mario Castelnuovo-Tedesco.* New York: International Castelnuovo-Tedesco Society, 1977. 147pp.

Rostant, Claude. "L'Italie musicale actuelli," *Table ronde,* September 1957.

Sadie, Stanley, ed. *The New Grove Dictionary of Music and Musicians.* 20 vols. London and Washington: Macmillan, 1980.

Saint-Cyr, M. *Musicisti contemporanei.* Rome, 1936.

Saleski, Gdal. *Famous Musicians of Jewish Origin.* New York: Block Publishing Companies, 1949. 716pp.

Salvetti, G. "La lirica da camera di Giorgio Federico Ghedini," in *Collectanea historiae musicae,* vol. IV. Florence, 1966. 271pp.

Salzman, Eric. *Twentieth-Century Music.* Englewood Cliffs, N.J.: Prentice-Hall, 1974. 242pp.

Santi, Piero. "Musicisti italiani: Lucian Berio," *Il Diapason* 5, No. 1 (January 1955):26–29.

———. "Musicisti italiani: Luciano Chailly," *Il Diapason* 2, Nos. 7–8 (July–August 1951):14–16.

———. "Musicisti italiani: Riccardo Malipiero," *Il Diapason* 4, No. 2 (March 1953):22–26.

Sartori, Claudio. *Riccardo Malipiero.* Milan: Edizioni Suvini Zerboni, 1957. English translation by Reginald Smith-Brindle. Milan: Edizioni Suvini Zerboni, 1957.

———, ed. *Enciclopedia della Musica.* 4 vols. Milan: Riccordi, 1963.

Schweike, Irving. *Kings Jazz and David. 27 studies privately printed by the author.* Paris: Les Presses Moderns, 1927. 217pp. (Contains article on Davico reprinted from *The Musical Digest,* July 22, 1924.)

Slonimsky, Nicolas. "Modern Italian Music," *The Christian Science Monitor,* October 5, 1937.

———. *Music Since 1900: An Encyclopedic Survey of Modern Music 1900–1948.* 4th ed. New York: Scribner's, 1971. 1595pp.

———, ed. *Baker's Biographical Dictionary of Music and Musicians.* 7th ed. New York: Schirmer Books, 1984. 2577pp.

Smith-Brindle, Reginald. "Italian Contemporary Music," in *European Music in the Twentieth Century,* ed. Howard Hartog. London: Routledge and Kegan Paul, 1957.

Solmi, Angelo, ed. *Enciclopedia della musica.* 6 vols. Milan: Rizzoli-Riccordi, 1972.

Stevens, Denis, ed. *A History of Song.* New York: W. W. Norton and Co., 1960. (See chapter on Italy by Anthony Milner, pp. 293–303.)

Terenzio, Vincenzo. "Appunti su Respighi," *La Rassegna Musicale,* January 1956, pp.27–32.

Testa, Susan Eileen. "Atonality and dodecafonia in Italy to 1935," *Dissertation Abstracts* 43 (May 1983):3453A.

Thompson, Oscar. *Great Modern Composers.* New York: Dodd, Mead, 1941.

Valabrega, Cesare. *La musica da camera di Vincenzo Davico.* Rome: Edizioni de Santis, 1953.

Veretti, A. "Adriano Lualdi," *Rivista musicale italiana,* 1928, pp. 105–123.

Vlad, Roman. "Luigi Dallapiccola: 1948–1955," *The Score* 15 (March 1956):39.

———. *Luigi Dallapiccola.* Milan: Edizioni Suvini Zerboni, 1957. English translation by Cynthia Jolly. Milan: Edizioni Suvini Zerboni, 1957.

———. *Modernità e tradizione nella musica contemporanea.* Turin: Einaudi, 1955.

———. "Reflessi della dodecafonia in Casella, Malipiero, e Ghedini," *La Rassegna Musicale,* March 1957, pp.44–53.

Waterhouse, J. G. C. "The Emergence of Modern Italian Music." Ph. D. diss., Oxford University, 1968. 710pp.

Weber, Horst. "Südtirol: Musik des 20. Jahrhunderts," *Schweizerische Musikzeitung* 116 (1976):35.

Weissman, J. S. "Alfredo Casella, An Introduction," *The Listener* (London), November 2, 1950.

————. "Current Chronicle: Italy," *The Musical Quarterly* 39 (April 1953).

————. "Gian Francesco Malipiero, musicista veneziano," *The Listener* (London), January 10, 1963.

————. *Goffredo Petrassi.* Milan: Edizioni Suvini Zerboni, 1957. (Rev. ed., 1960, contains an appendix by M. Bortolotto, "Le opere di Petrassi dal 1957 al 1960.")

————. "Goffredo Petrassi and His Music," *The Music Review* XXII (August 1961).

————. "Goffredo Petrassi's Recent Music," *The Score* 3 (June 1950):49–62.

————. "La musica di Ghedini e il suo significato europeo," *Musica d'oggi,* 1961, pp.201–205.

————. "Petrassi and the Italian Tradition," *The Listener* (London), August 28, 1952.

————. "Petrassi," *The Chesterian,* April 1951, pp. 98–104.

————. "Le ultime opere di Goffredo Petrassi," *La Rassegna Musicale,* April 1952, pp.113–122.

Whittall, Arnold. *Music Since the First World War.* London: Dent, 1977. 277pp.

Yates, Peter. *Twentieth-Century Music: Its Evolution from the End of the Harmonic Era into the Present Era of Sound.* New York: Pantheon, Random House, 1967.

INDEX OF SETS, SONGS, OR FIRST LINES